FX

CREATED BY WAYNE OSBORNE

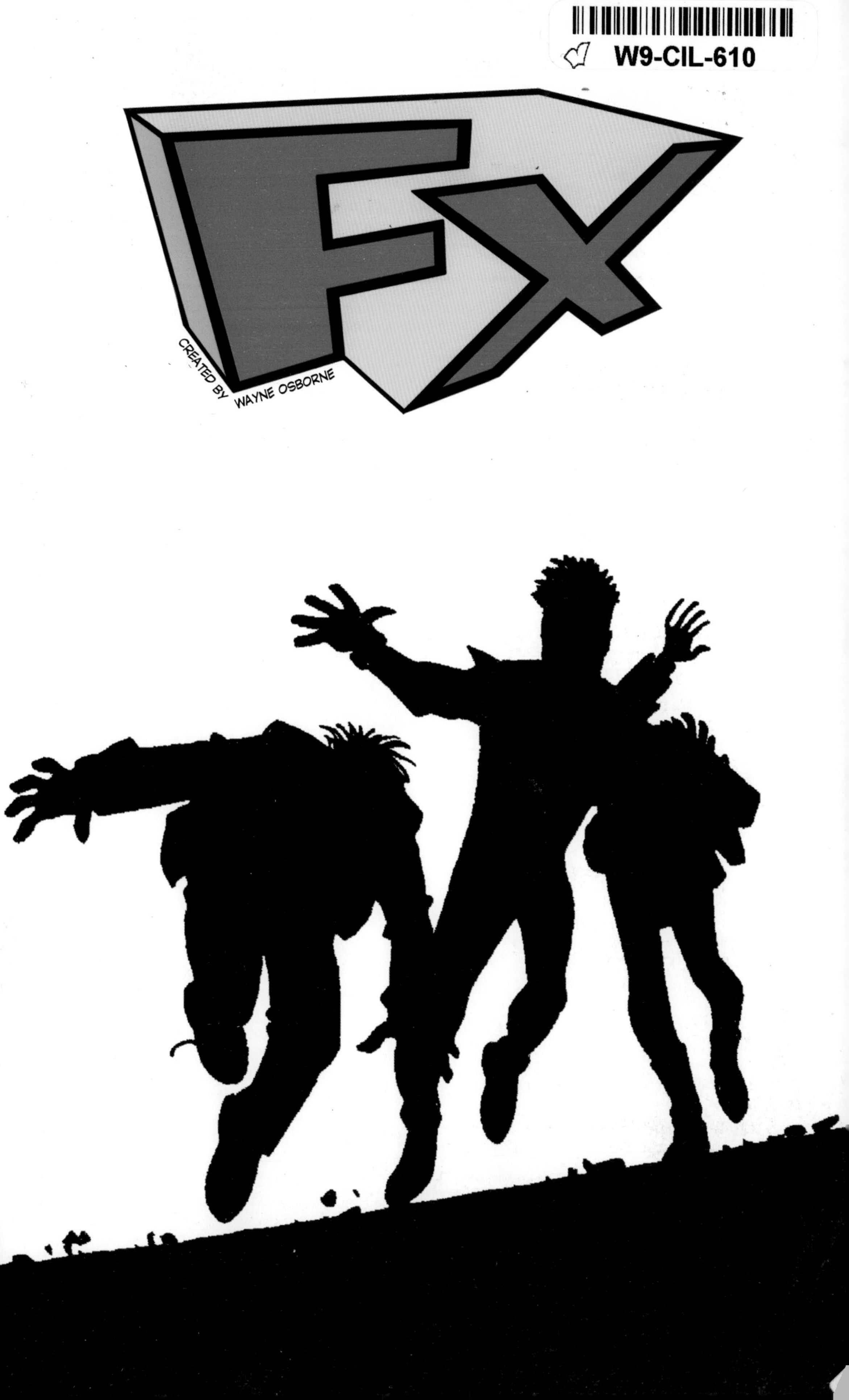

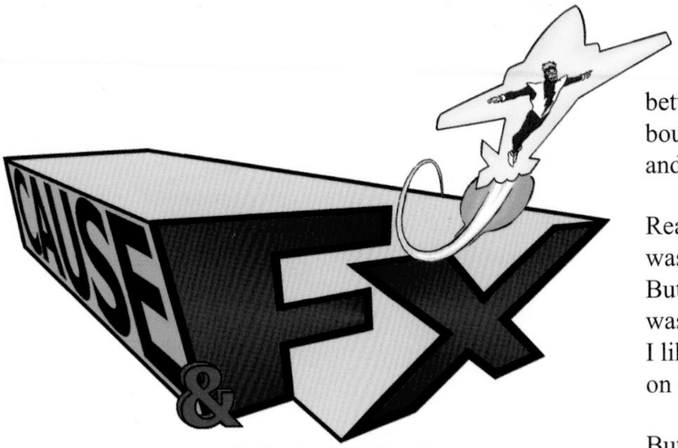
CAUSE
&
FX

by WAYNE OSBORNE

Growing up, my Grandmother didn't have running water, indoor plumbing, or air conditioning in her house. Sounds like a nice enough place to visit but you wouldn't want to stay there, right? Wrong, dead wrong. I wanted to spend every minute there that I could because what she had was books... lots and lots of books. Some of them were hers, the romance and mystery ones. And some of them were my Uncle Jack's. He had the really good stuff: Burroughs, Asimov, Zelazny, Tolkien, Heinlein, Bradbury… you get the idea. He had a whole paperback library full of grade-A science fiction and fantasy. And he had comics, a whole duffle bag full of Marvel and DC from the '60s. I would have stayed there forever (or until I'd read everything, whichever came first). It was perfect. And it was the foundation of the book you hold in your hands right now.

I was buying comics off the racks, mostly from the local Piggly Wiggly. This was in the age before Masterworks and Essentials. It was even before most reprints. But thanks to that duffle bag, I was able to read the past adventures of *The Avengers*, *Fantastic Four*, *Hulk*, *Thor*, and *Spider-man* alongside their current ones. I discovered Stan Lee, Jack Kirby, and Steve Ditko about the same time as I discovered Roy Thomas, John Buscema, Neal Adams, Tom Palmer, Gerry Conway, Gil Kane, and John Romita. Did I mention how perfect this was?

But life wasn't all paperbacks and comic books. Saturday nights were huge for me. *Chiller Theater* came on at 11:30 PM. In those double features, I watched all the greats: *Frankenstein*, *Dracula*, *The Wolfman*, *The Mummy*, and *The Creature*. I also got a good dose of *King Kong* and *Godzilla* and all his various buddies. I watched them all and loved every minute of it. TV wasn't just about reruns either. There was the *Six Million Dollar Man*, *Kolchak, The Night Stalker*, *The Planet of the Apes*, *Land of the Lost*, *Superfriends*, and of course, *The Hulk*. And at the movies, there was *Sinbad* and a little flick called *Star Wars*. Indeed, the '70s were good times. But as much as I enjoyed the movies and TV of the day, comics were my first and best love.

And then I discovered John Byrne. John Byrne had no link to the duffle bag. His art was like nothing I'd ever seen before and I had found an artist I could call my own. He became the focus of my love of comics. From *Star Lord* to *Iron Fist* to *Team-up* to *X-men* and all the stops in between; if John drew the cover or the interior art, I bought that comic book. He was my favorite artist then and he's my favorite artist now.

Reading this, you might have gotten the impression that I was a bit of a geeky kid. And, perhaps, you might be right. But I'm not going to hit you with my tale of woe here. I was a chubby kid and not very athletic. I was smart. And I liked comic books and science fiction. Yeah, I got picked on some but I don't think it was any more than most.

But then I grew up and lost the baby fat (although, today, I find that I've somehow stumbled into some grown-up fat —how'd that happen?) and gained some measure of hand-eye coordination. I adjusted, made some friends, went to college, and married my very own version of Raye. But I never left comics behind. I never stopped buying them, even if I did stop acting them out in my backyard. Leia (my wife) didn't have a problem with my hobby, but she might have had a problem with that.

She also didn't mind it when I started buying original comic art. It probably won't surprise you to learn that the first art I wanted to buy was John Byrne's art. This led me to Jim Warden, John's art dealer and one of my very best friends, who in turn introduced me to John. And roughly 17 years later, I took John up on his offer of a complete issue commission and used some ideas I'd had rumbling around in my head for about 10 years. The result was *FX* #1.

I took that with me to San Diego and showed it around to some publishers there. All of them were interested when I told them I had a comic drawn by John Byrne. And on the strength of the art, IDW offered to publish it if I could get John to do five or six more issues. I could and he did and you're holding the results in your hands. I poured everything I could into it in case I didn't get another chance at this. All the stuff I talked about above, most of my favorite things from childhood. Marvel comics, monsters, mythology, and a lot of the 12-year-old that I was... and still am in many ways, are in here. I hope you like it.

Shout out time:
Thanks to Joe Hollon for naming the letter column and to Thanos Kollias for helping with a real Greek bad-guy name. Also, thanks to Greg Cordier, Gerry Turnbull, John Workman, and Ian Sokoliwski for all their help with the comic. Obviously, thanks to my Mom and Dad for raising me right and paying for all the comics and books. Thanks to my sister, Robyn, and brother, Josh, for putting up with me. And once I left home, all this craziness got dumped on my wife Leia (Raye is her middle name), so I thank her for her love and support. And my daughter Torie (short for Victoria, as is Vicki) my proofreader and sounding board —I love you, kid.

And to John Byrne—for everything else. None of this would be here without your inspiration and help. Thank you.

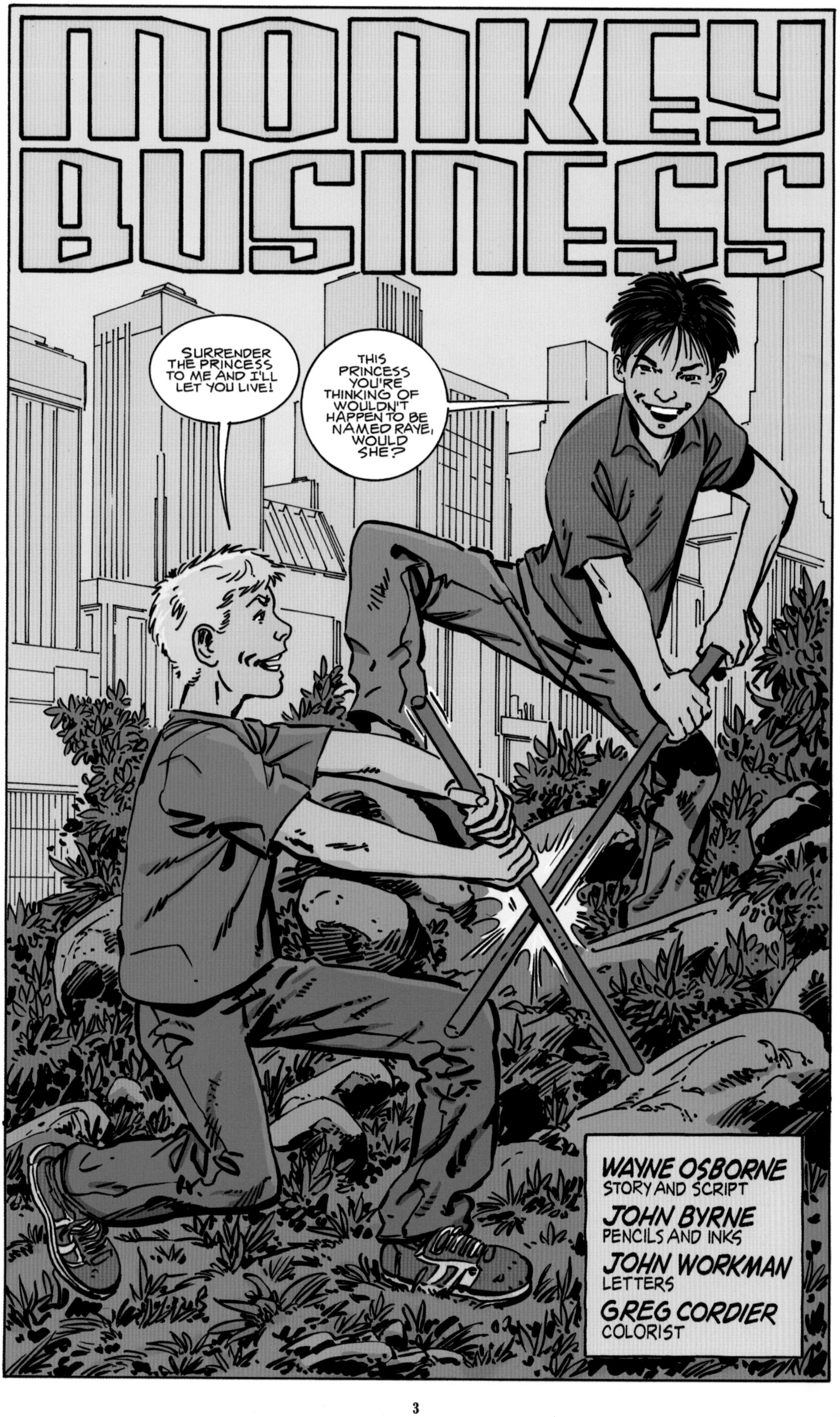
MONKEY BUSINESS
SURRENDER THE PRINCESS TO ME AND I'LL LET YOU LIVE!
THIS PRINCESS YOU'RE THINKING OF WOULDN'T HAPPEN TO BE NAMED RAYE, WOULD SHE?
WAYNE OSBORNE STORY AND SCRIPT
JOHN BYRNE PENCILS AND INKS
JOHN WORKMAN LETTERS
GREG CORDIER COLORIST

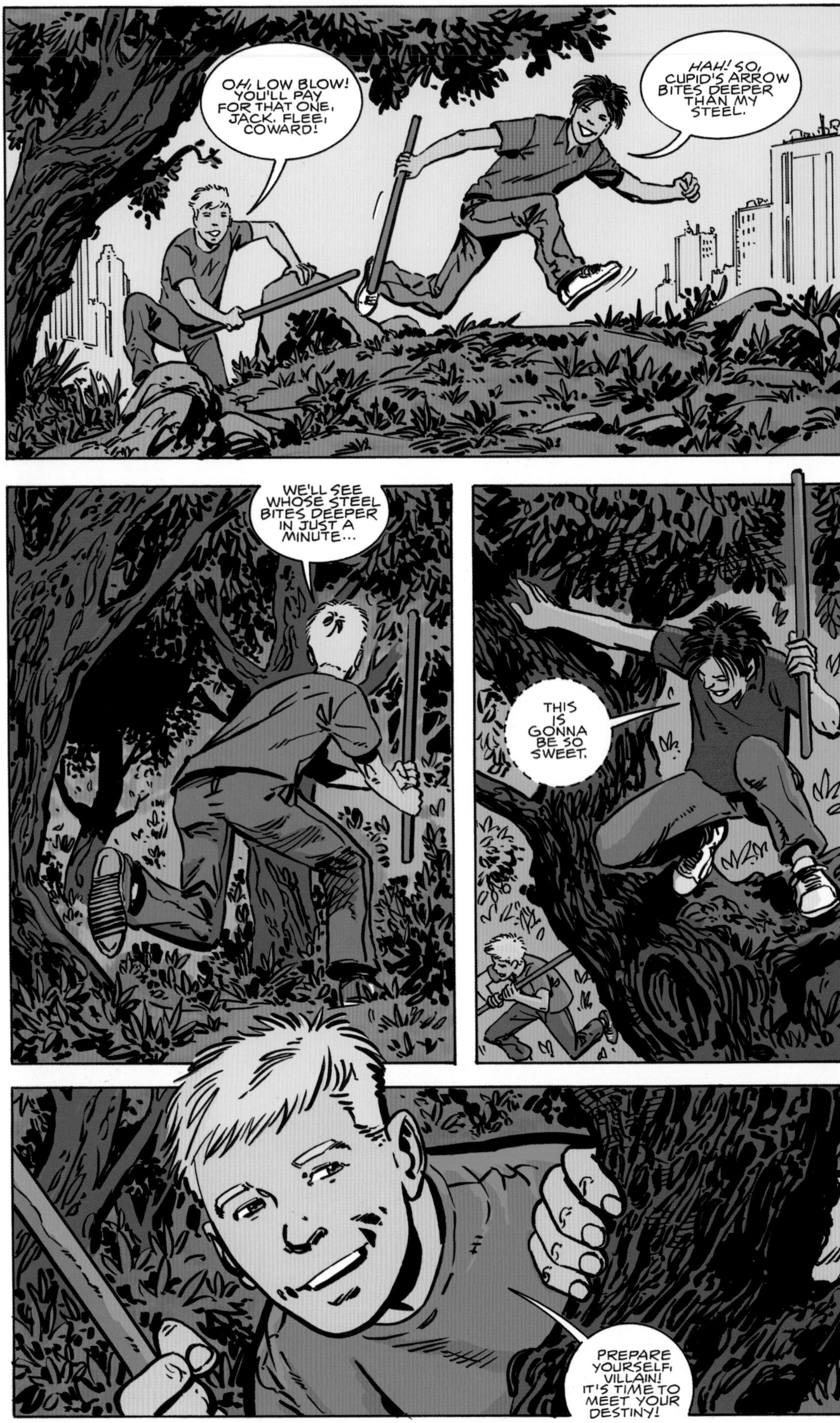
OH, LOW BLOW! YOU'LL PAY FOR THAT ONE, JACK. FLEE, COWARD!
HAH! SO, CUPID'S ARROW BITES DEEPER THAN MY STEEL.
WE'LL SEE WHOSE STEEL BITES DEEPER IN JUST A MINUTE...
THIS IS GONNA BE SO SWEET.
PREPARE YOURSELF, VILLAIN! IT'S TIME TO MEET YOUR DESTINY!

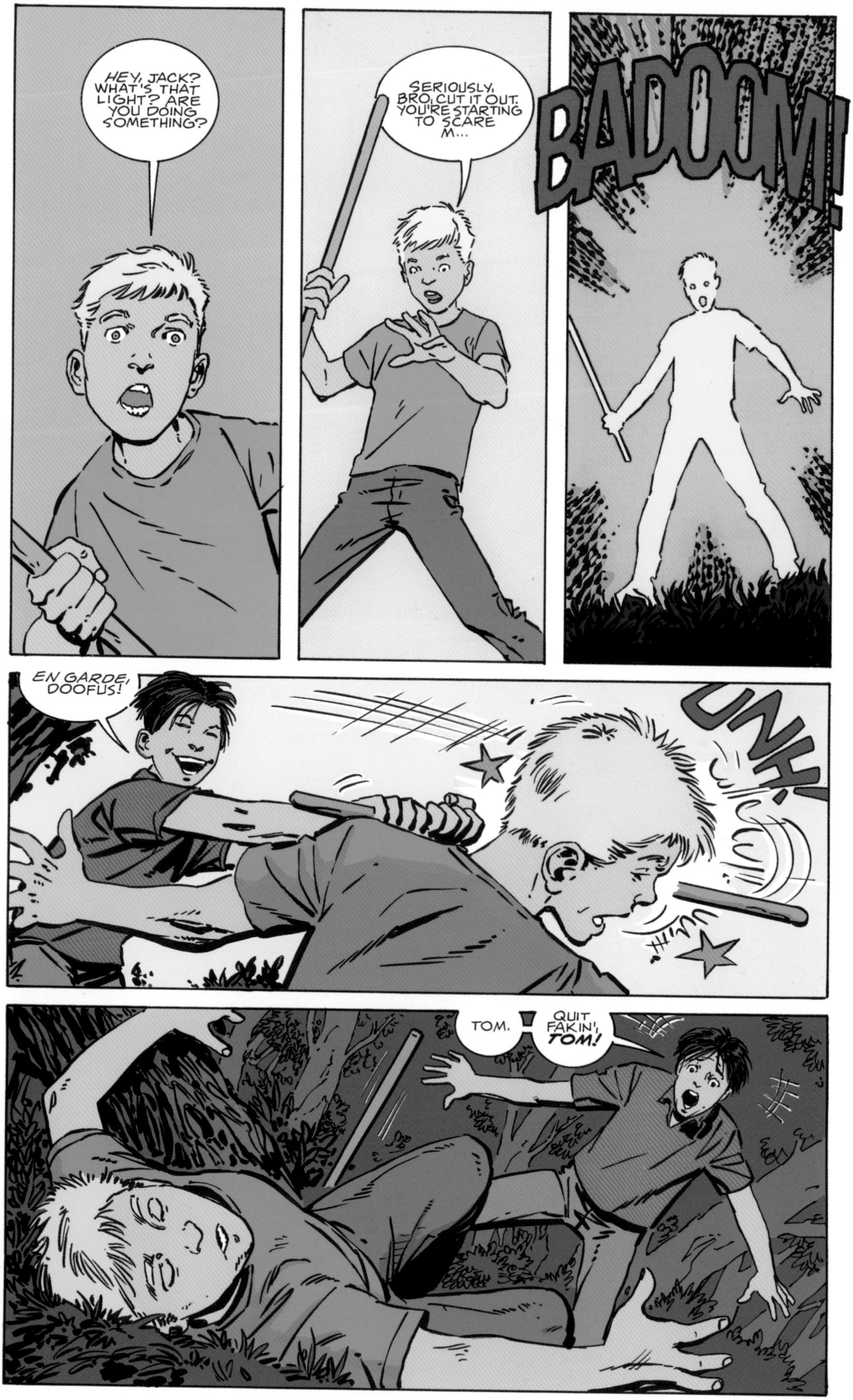
HEY, JACK? WHAT'S THAT LIGHT? ARE YOU DOING SOMETHING?
SERIOUSLY, BRO, CUT IT OUT. YOU'RE STARTING TO SCARE M...
BADOOM!
EN GARDE, DOOFUS!
UNH!
TOM.
QUIT FAKIN', TOM!

THE NEXT DAY...

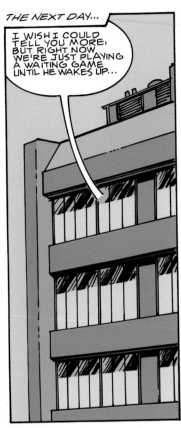

I WISH I COULD TELL YOU MORE, BUT RIGHT NOW, WE'RE JUST PLAYING A WAITING GAME UNTIL HE WAKES UP...

BUT THERE'S NO HEAD TRAUMA, NO SWELLING, RIGHT?

THAT'S RIGHT, MR. TALBOT. THERE ARE NO SIGNS OF PERMANENT INJURY. IN FACT, YOUR SON SHOULD BE AWAKE RIGHT NOW. HIS BRAIN ACTIVITY IS MOST UNUSUAL...

"MOST UNUSUAL!" WHAT'S THAT MEAN? IS THAT "DOCTOR" FOR... WE DON'T HAVE A CLUE?

RICHARD, PLEASE. THIS ISN'T HELPING. WHAT IF TOMMY CAN HEAR YOU SHOUTING?

I UNDERSTAND YOUR FRUSTRATIONS, AND I'M SORRY... BUT I HAVE OTHER PATIENTS TO SEE. I'LL CHECK IN WITH YOU LATER.

A FEW MINUTES LATER...

I FAIL TO SEE HOW EATING THAT CAFETERIA CRAP IS GOING TO MAKE ME FEEL BETTER...

OH, HELLO, JACK. ARE YOU OKAY?

I'M FINE, MA'AM.

CAN I SEE 'IM?

6

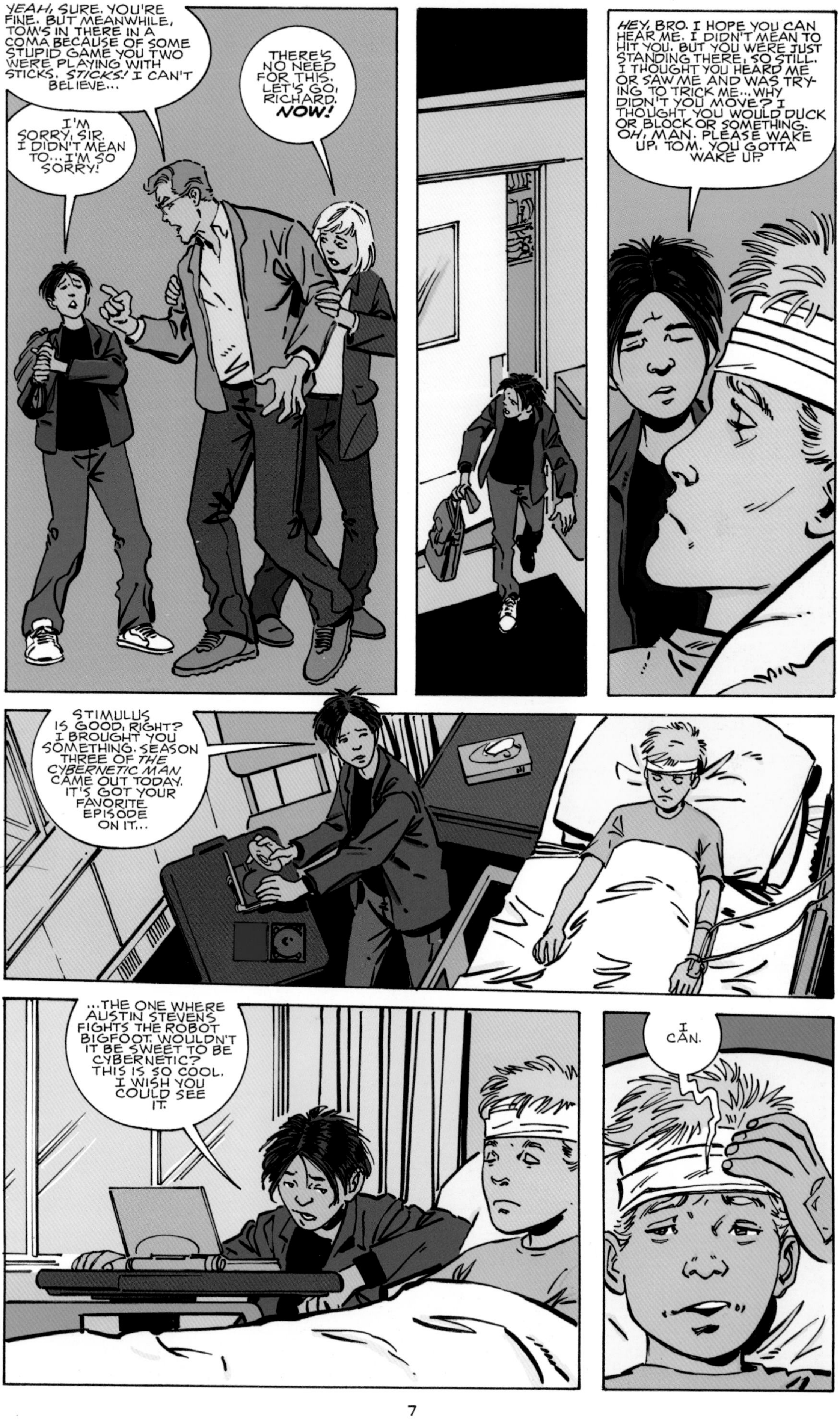
YEAH, SURE. YOU'RE FINE. BUT MEANWHILE, TOM'S IN THERE IN A COMA BECAUSE OF SOME STUPID GAME YOU TWO WERE PLAYING WITH STICKS. STICKS! I CAN'T BELIEVE...
I'M SORRY, SIR. I DIDN'T MEAN TO... I'M SO SORRY!
THERE'S NO NEED FOR THIS. LET'S GO, RICHARD. NOW!
HEY, BRO. I HOPE YOU CAN HEAR ME. I DIDN'T MEAN TO HIT YOU. BUT YOU WERE JUST STANDING THERE, SO STILL. I THOUGHT YOU HEARD ME OR SAW ME AND WAS TRYING TO TRICK ME... WHY DIDN'T YOU MOVE? I THOUGHT YOU WOULD DUCK OR BLOCK OR SOMETHING. OH, MAN. PLEASE WAKE UP, TOM. YOU GOTTA WAKE UP.
STIMULUS IS GOOD, RIGHT? I BROUGHT YOU SOMETHING. SEASON THREE OF THE CYBERNETIC MAN CAME OUT TODAY. IT'S GOT YOUR FAVORITE EPISODE ON IT...
...THE ONE WHERE AUSTIN STEVENS FIGHTS THE ROBOT BIGFOOT. WOULDN'T IT BE SWEET TO BE CYBERNETIC? THIS IS SO COOL. I WISH YOU COULD SEE IT.
I CAN.

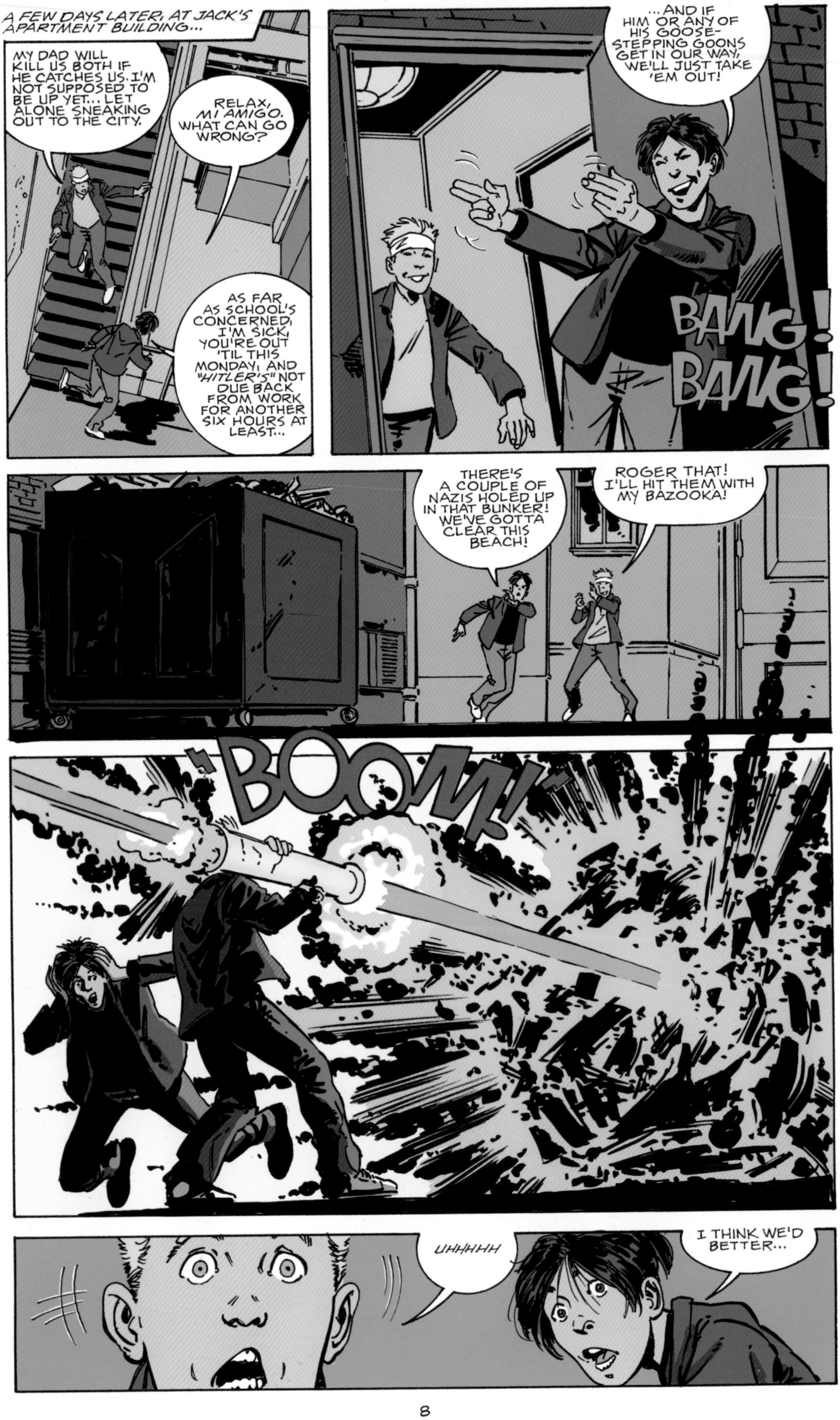
A FEW DAYS LATER, AT JACK'S APARTMENT BUILDING...
MY DAD WILL KILL US BOTH IF HE CATCHES US. I'M NOT SUPPOSED TO BE UP YET... LET ALONE SNEAKING OUT TO THE CITY.
RELAX, MI AMIGO. WHAT CAN GO WRONG?
AS FAR AS SCHOOL'S CONCERNED, I'M SICK, YOU'RE OUT 'TIL THIS MONDAY, AND "HITLER'S" NOT DUE BACK FROM WORK FOR ANOTHER SIX HOURS AT LEAST...
...AND IF HIM OR ANY OF HIS GOOSE-STEPPING GOONS GET IN OUR WAY, WE'LL JUST TAKE 'EM OUT!
BANG! BANG!
THERE'S A COUPLE OF NAZIS HOLED UP IN THAT BUNKER! WE'VE GOTTA CLEAR THIS BEACH!
ROGER THAT! I'LL HIT THEM WITH MY BAZOOKA!
"BOOM!"
UHHHHH
I THINK WE'D BETTER...

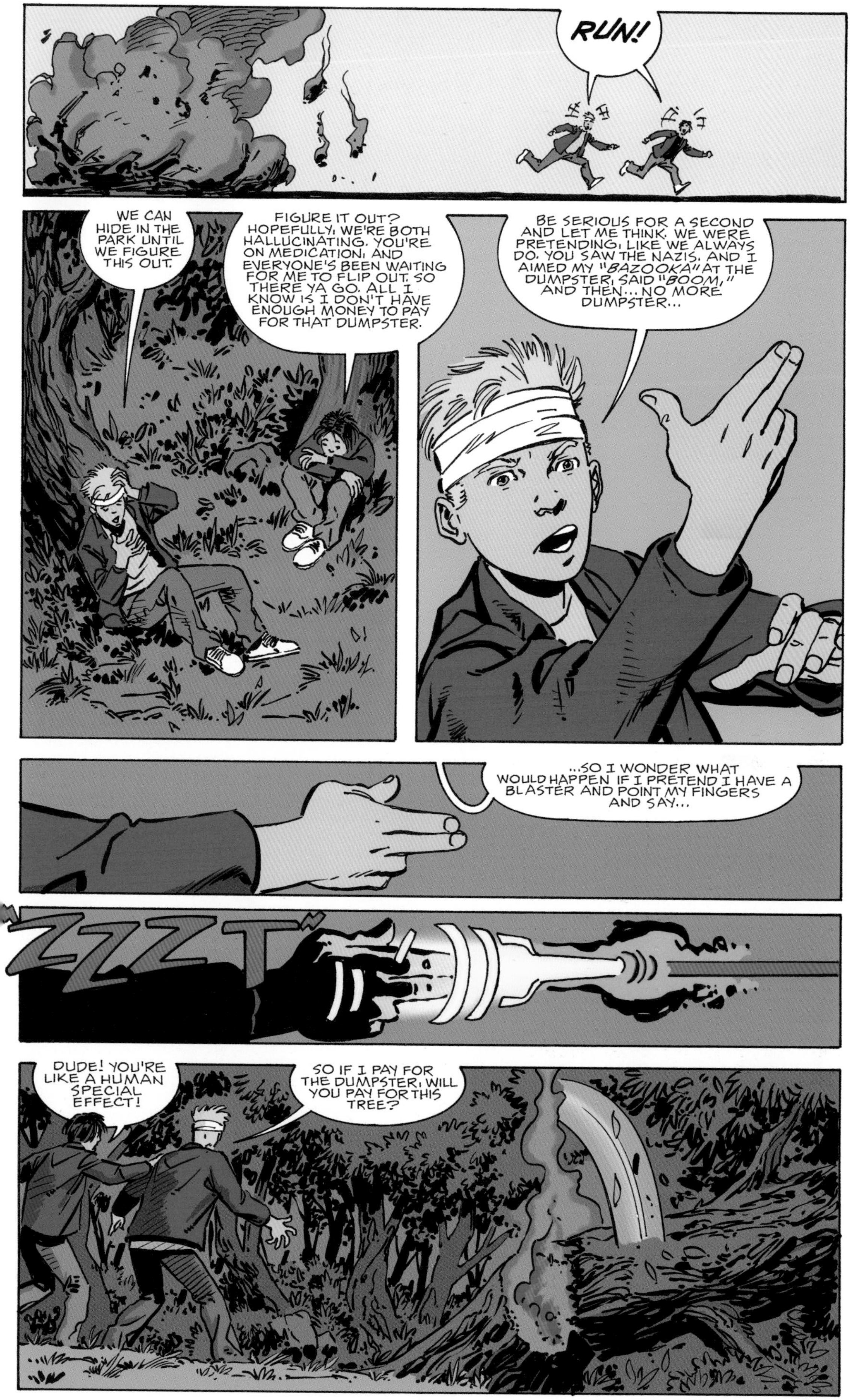
RUN!
WE CAN HIDE IN THE PARK UNTIL WE FIGURE THIS OUT.
FIGURE IT OUT? HOPEFULLY, WE'RE BOTH HALLUCINATING. YOU'RE ON MEDICATION, AND EVERYONE'S BEEN WAITING FOR ME TO FLIP OUT. SO THERE YA GO. ALL I KNOW IS I DON'T HAVE ENOUGH MONEY TO PAY FOR THAT DUMPSTER.
BE SERIOUS FOR A SECOND AND LET ME THINK. WE WERE PRETENDING, LIKE WE ALWAYS DO. YOU SAW THE NAZIS, AND I AIMED MY "BAZOOKA" AT THE DUMPSTER, SAID "BOOM," AND THEN... NO MORE DUMPSTER...
...SO I WONDER WHAT WOULD HAPPEN IF I PRETEND I HAVE A BLASTER AND POINT MY FINGERS AND SAY...
ZZZT
DUDE! YOU'RE LIKE A HUMAN SPECIAL EFFECT!
SO IF I PAY FOR THE DUMPSTER, WILL YOU PAY FOR THIS TREE?

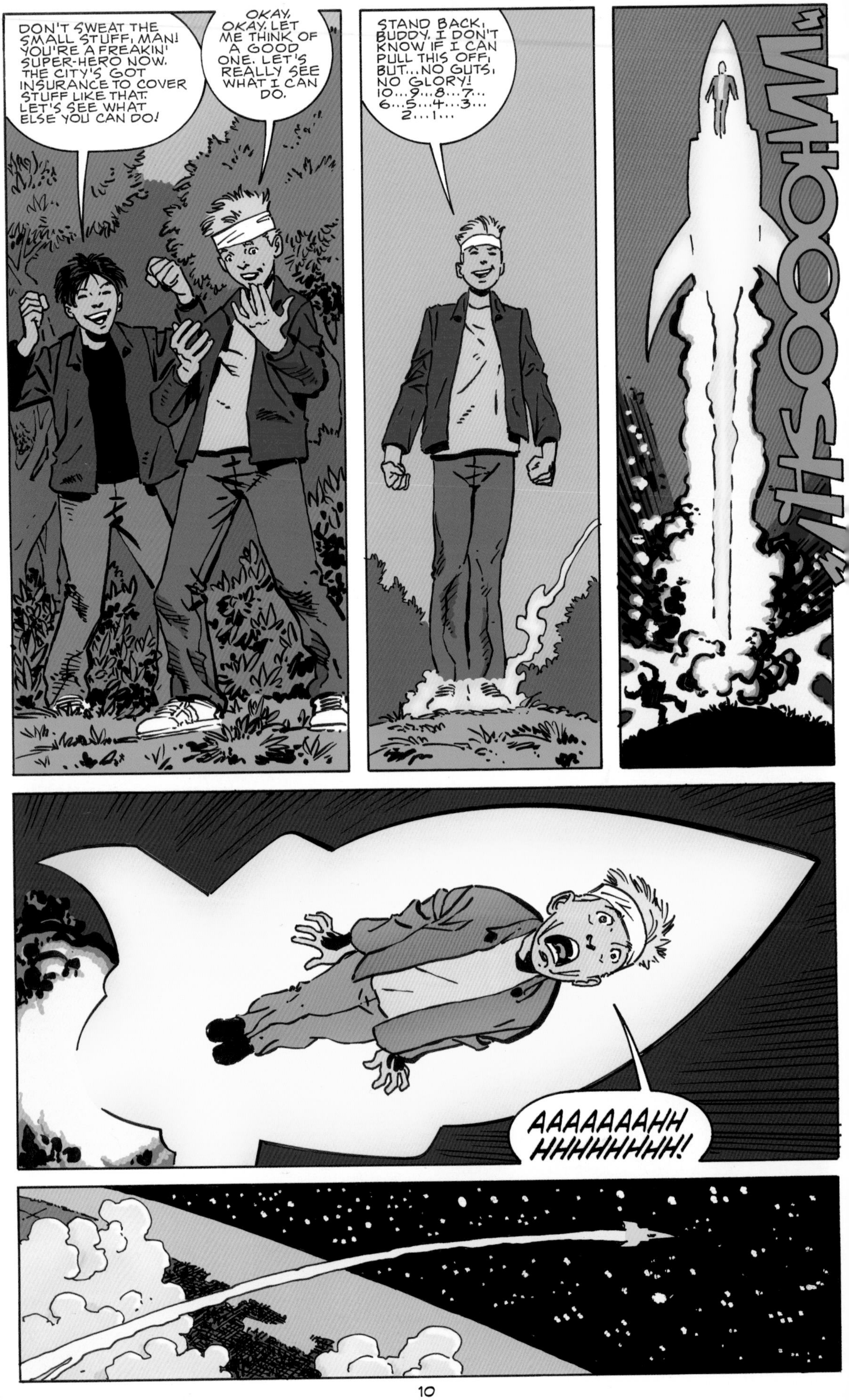
DON'T SWEAT THE SMALL STUFF, MAN! YOU'RE A FREAKIN' SUPER-HERO NOW. THE CITY'S GOT INSURANCE TO COVER STUFF LIKE THAT. LET'S SEE WHAT ELSE YOU CAN DO!
OKAY, OKAY. LET ME THINK OF A GOOD ONE. LET'S REALLY SEE WHAT I CAN DO.
STAND BACK, BUDDY. I DON'T KNOW IF I CAN PULL THIS OFF, BUT...NO GUTS, NO GLORY! 10...9...8...7... 6...5...4...3... 2...1...
WHOOOSH!
AAAAAAAHH HHHHHHHH!

THIS IS SO NOT GOOD...
C'MON, THINK, THINK...
THRRROOOOSH!
AWWWR RIIIGHT!
HOME SWEET EARTH!
NOTE TO SELF... ROCKET SHIP, NOT SUCH A GOOD IDEA.
THAT WAS TOTALLY INTENSE!

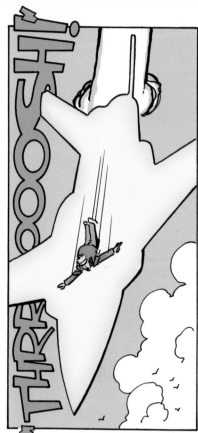

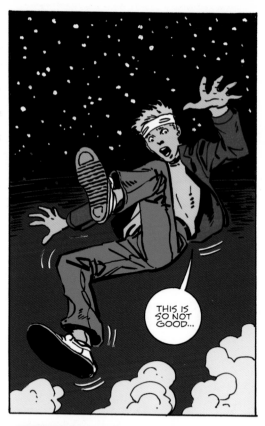

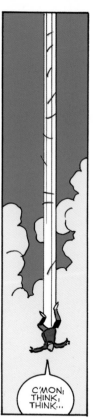

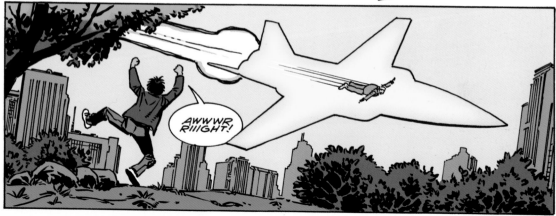

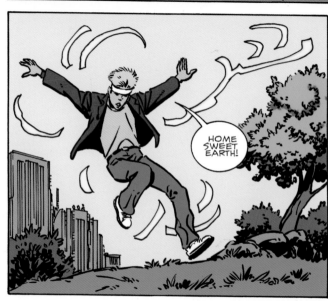

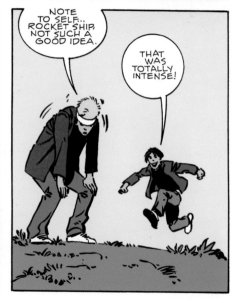

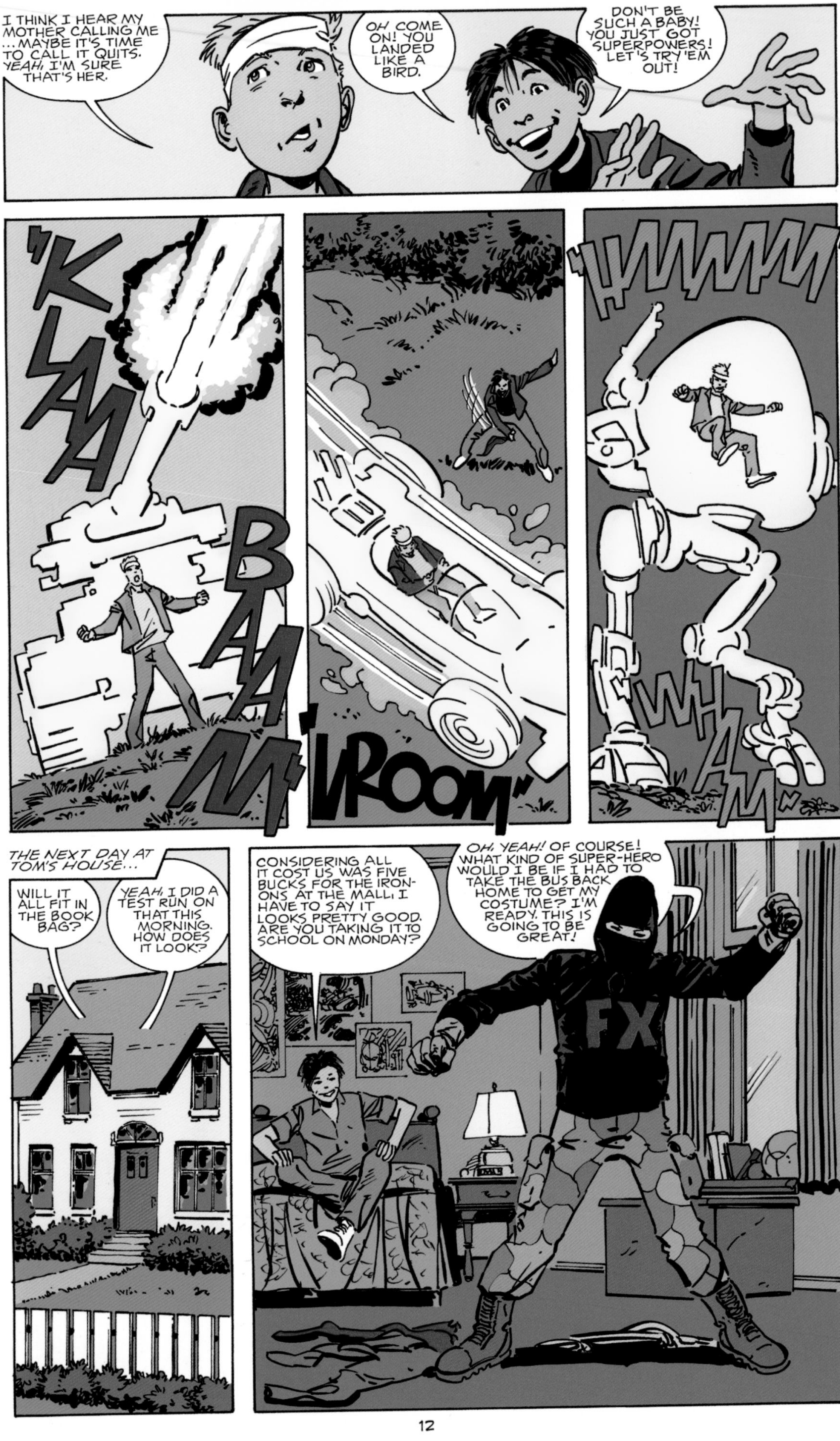
I THINK I HEAR MY MOTHER CALLING ME ... MAYBE IT'S TIME TO CALL IT QUITS. YEAH, I'M SURE THAT'S HER.
OH COME ON! YOU LANDED LIKE A BIRD.
DON'T BE SUCH A BABY! YOU JUST GOT SUPERPOWERS! LET'S TRY 'EM OUT!
"KLAAA BAAAM"
"VROOM"
"HMMMMM"
WHAM
THE NEXT DAY AT TOM'S HOUSE...
WILL IT ALL FIT IN THE BOOK BAG?
YEAH, I DID A TEST RUN ON THAT THIS MORNING. HOW DOES IT LOOK?
CONSIDERING ALL IT COST US WAS FIVE BUCKS FOR THE IRON-ONS AT THE MALL, I HAVE TO SAY IT LOOKS PRETTY GOOD. ARE YOU TAKING IT TO SCHOOL ON MONDAY?
OH, YEAH! OF COURSE! WHAT KIND OF SUPER-HERO WOULD I BE IF I HAD TO TAKE THE BUS BACK HOME TO GET MY COSTUME? I'M READY. THIS IS GOING TO BE GREAT!
FX

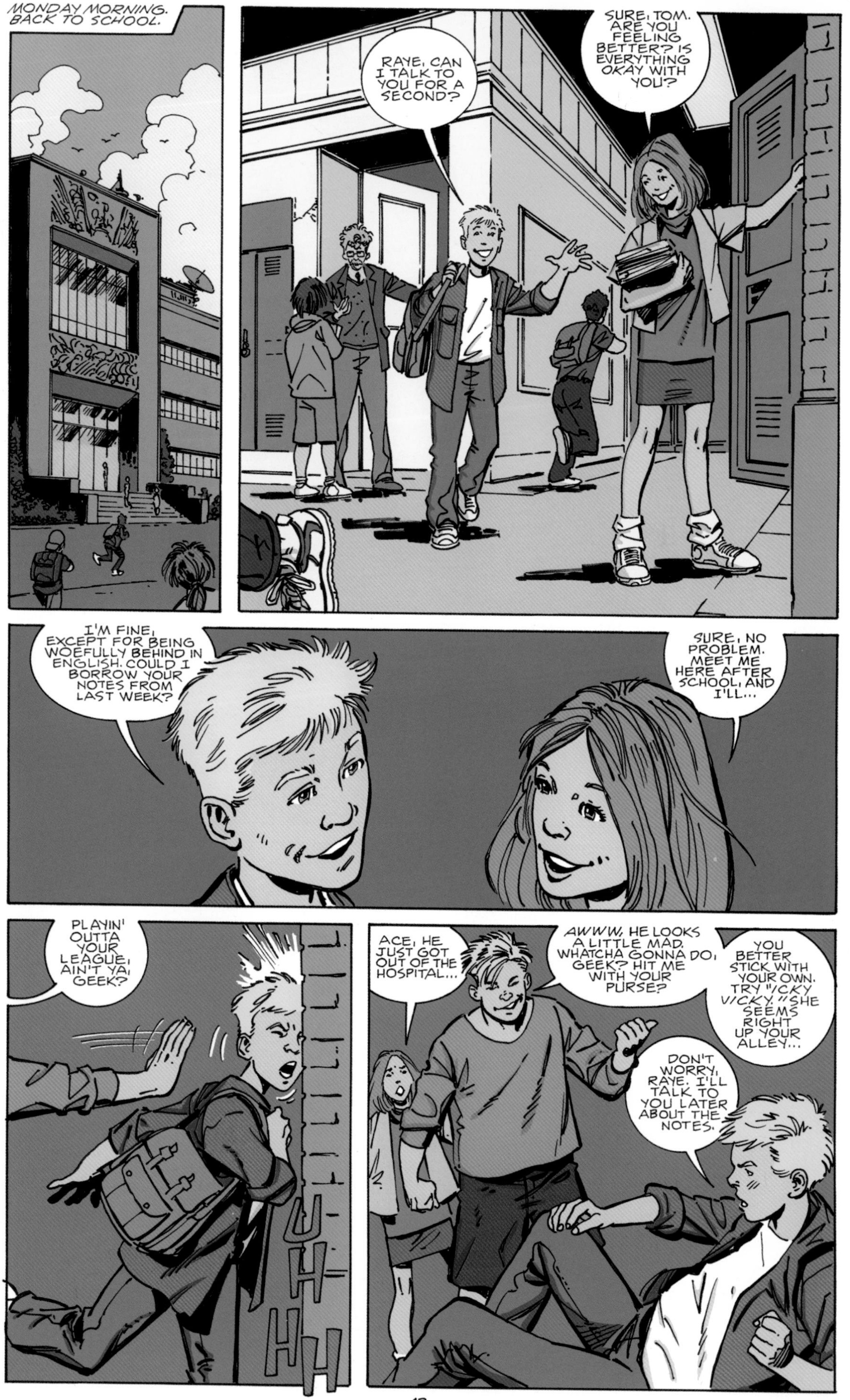
MONDAY MORNING. BACK TO SCHOOL.
RAYE, CAN I TALK TO YOU FOR A SECOND?
SURE, TOM. ARE YOU FEELING BETTER? IS EVERYTHING OKAY WITH YOU?
I'M FINE, EXCEPT FOR BEING WOEFULLY BEHIND IN ENGLISH. COULD I BORROW YOUR NOTES FROM LAST WEEK?
SURE, NO PROBLEM. MEET ME HERE AFTER SCHOOL, AND I'LL...
PLAYIN' OUTTA YOUR LEAGUE, AIN'T YA, GEEK?
UHHH
ACE, HE JUST GOT OUT OF THE HOSPITAL...
AWWW, HE LOOKS A LITTLE MAD. WHATCHA GONNA DO, GEEK? HIT ME WITH YOUR PURSE?
YOU BETTER STICK WITH YOUR OWN. TRY "ICKY VICKY." SHE SEEMS RIGHT UP YOUR ALLEY...
DON'T WORRY, RAYE. I'LL TALK TO YOU LATER ABOUT THE NOTES.

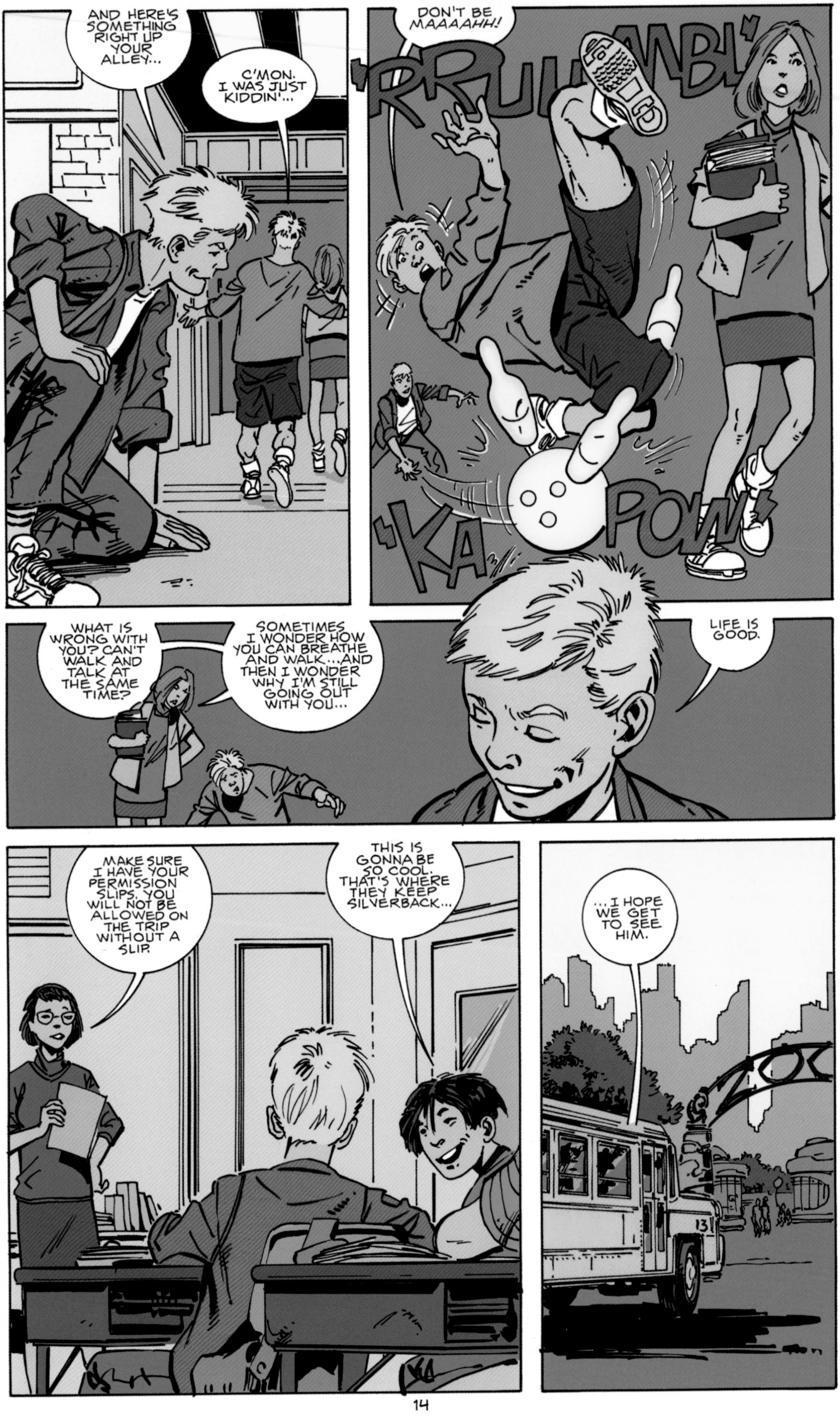
AND HERE'S SOMETHING RIGHT UP YOUR ALLEY...
C'MON. I WAS JUST KIDDIN'...
DON'T BE MAAAAAHH!
'RRUMMBL'
'KA POW'
WHAT IS WRONG WITH YOU? CAN'T WALK AND TALK AT THE SAME TIME?
SOMETIMES I WONDER HOW YOU CAN BREATHE AND WALK...AND THEN I WONDER WHY I'M STILL GOING OUT WITH YOU...
LIFE IS GOOD.
MAKE SURE I HAVE YOUR PERMISSION SLIPS. YOU WILL NOT BE ALLOWED ON THE TRIP WITHOUT A SLIP.
THIS IS GONNA BE SO COOL. THAT'S WHERE THEY KEEP SILVERBACK...
...I HOPE WE GET TO SEE HIM.

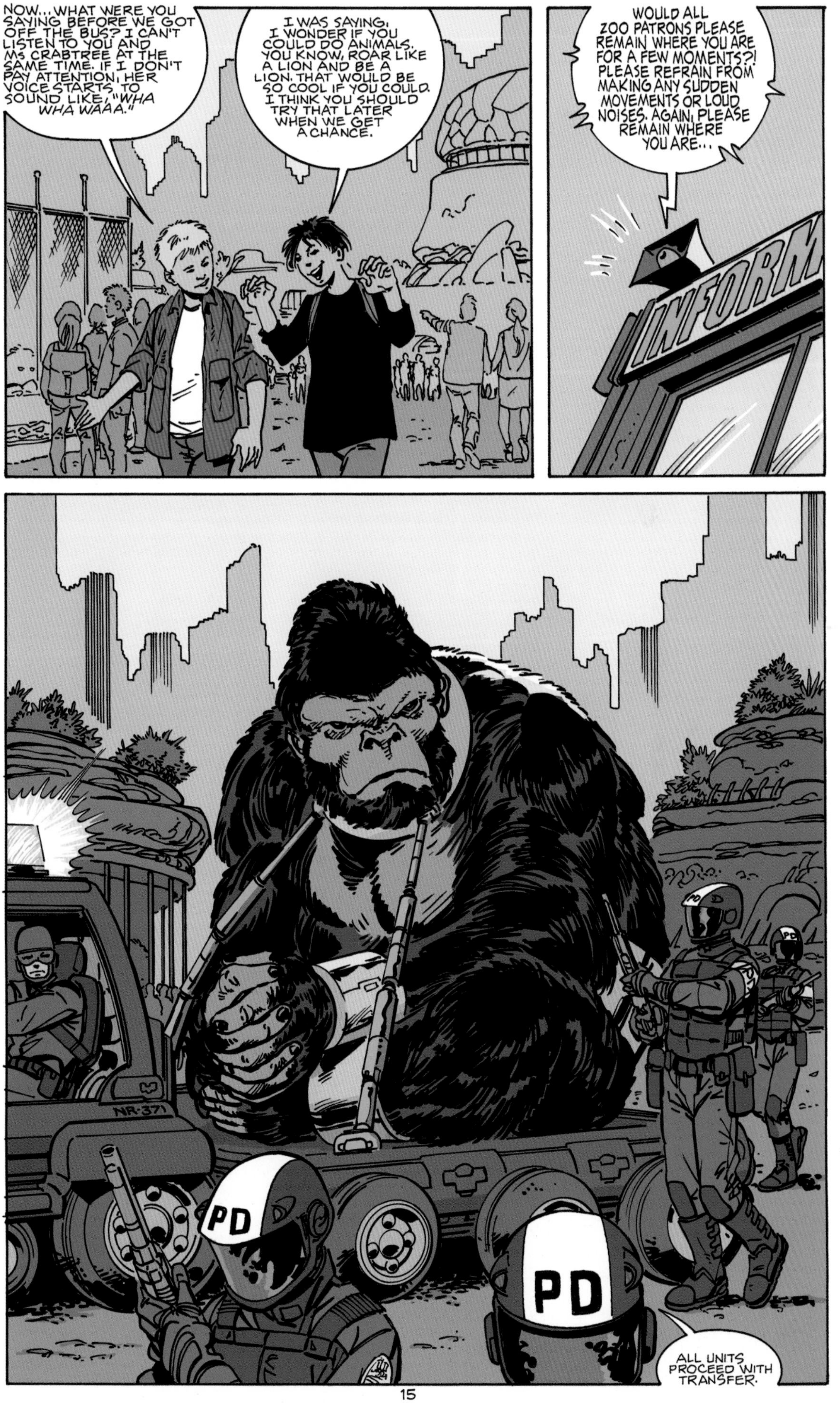
NOW... WHAT WERE YOU SAYING BEFORE WE GOT OFF THE BUS? I CAN'T LISTEN TO YOU AND Ms CRABTREE AT THE SAME TIME. IF I DON'T PAY ATTENTION, HER VOICE STARTS TO SOUND LIKE, "WHA WHA WAAA."
I WAS SAYING, I WONDER IF YOU COULD DO ANIMALS. YOU KNOW, ROAR LIKE A LION AND BE A LION. THAT WOULD BE SO COOL IF YOU COULD. I THINK YOU SHOULD TRY THAT LATER WHEN WE GET A CHANCE.
WOULD ALL ZOO PATRONS PLEASE REMAIN WHERE YOU ARE FOR A FEW MOMENTS?! PLEASE REFRAIN FROM MAKING ANY SUDDEN MOVEMENTS OR LOUD NOISES. AGAIN, PLEASE REMAIN WHERE YOU ARE...
INFORM
NR-371
PD
PD
ALL UNITS PROCEED WITH TRANSFER.

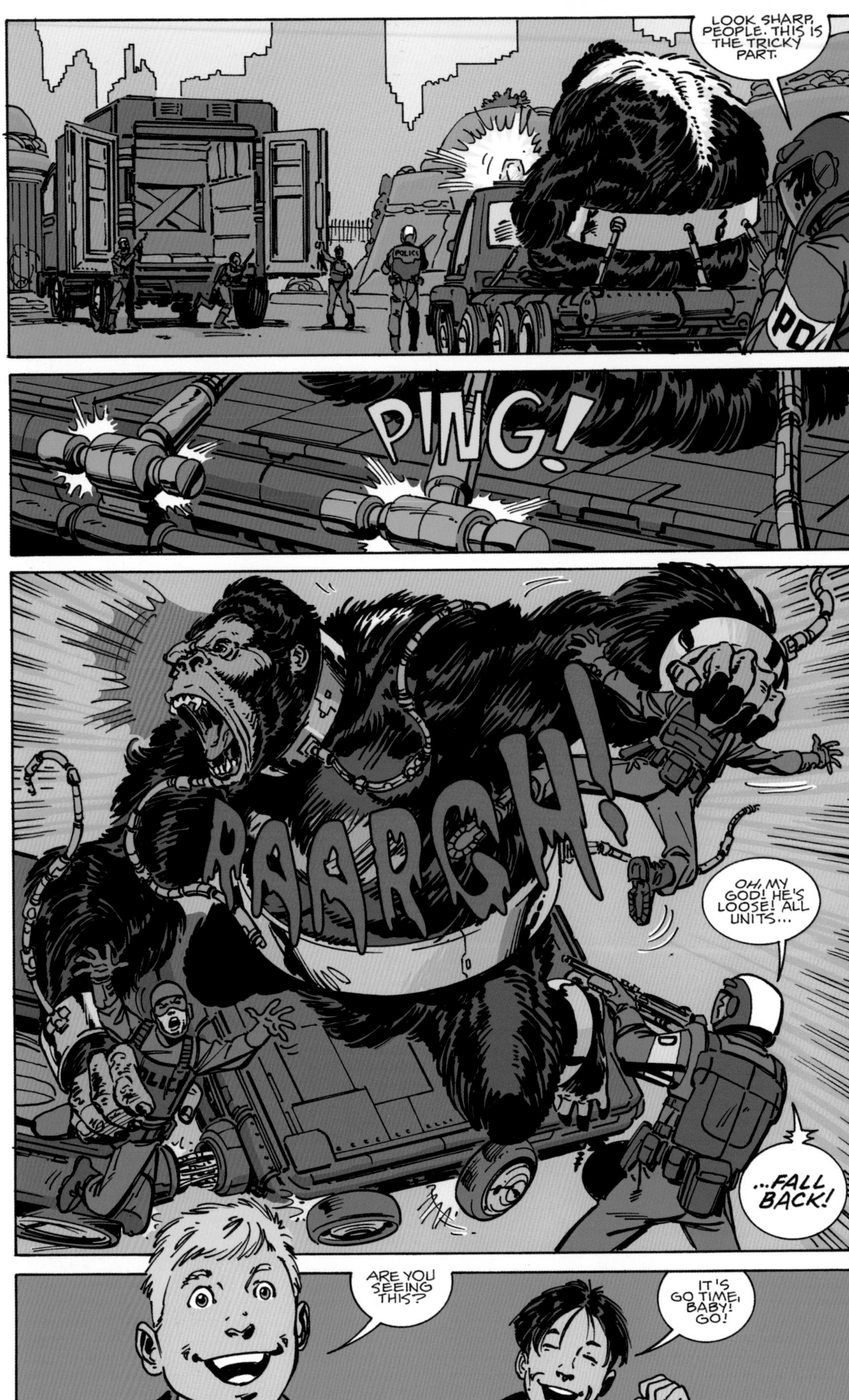
LOOK SHARP, PEOPLE. THIS IS THE TRICKY PART.
POLICE
PD
PING!
RAARGH!
OH, MY GOD! HE'S LOOSE! ALL UNITS...
...FALL BACK!
ARE YOU SEEING THIS?
IT'S GO TIME, BABY! GO!

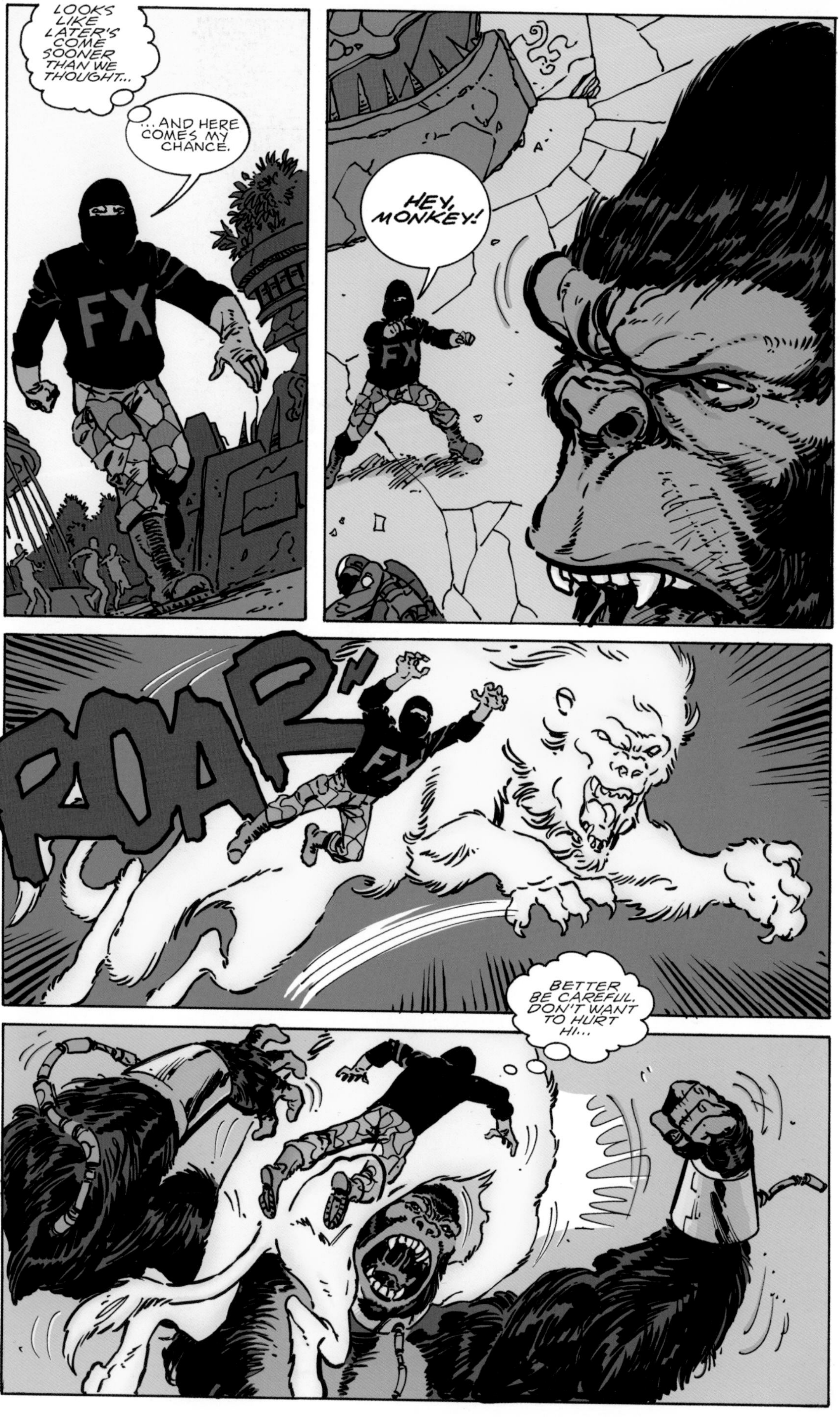
LOOKS LIKE LATER'S COME SOONER THAN WE THOUGHT...
...AND HERE COMES MY CHANCE.
HEY, MONKEY!
ROAR
BETTER BE CAREFUL. DON'T WANT TO HURT HI...

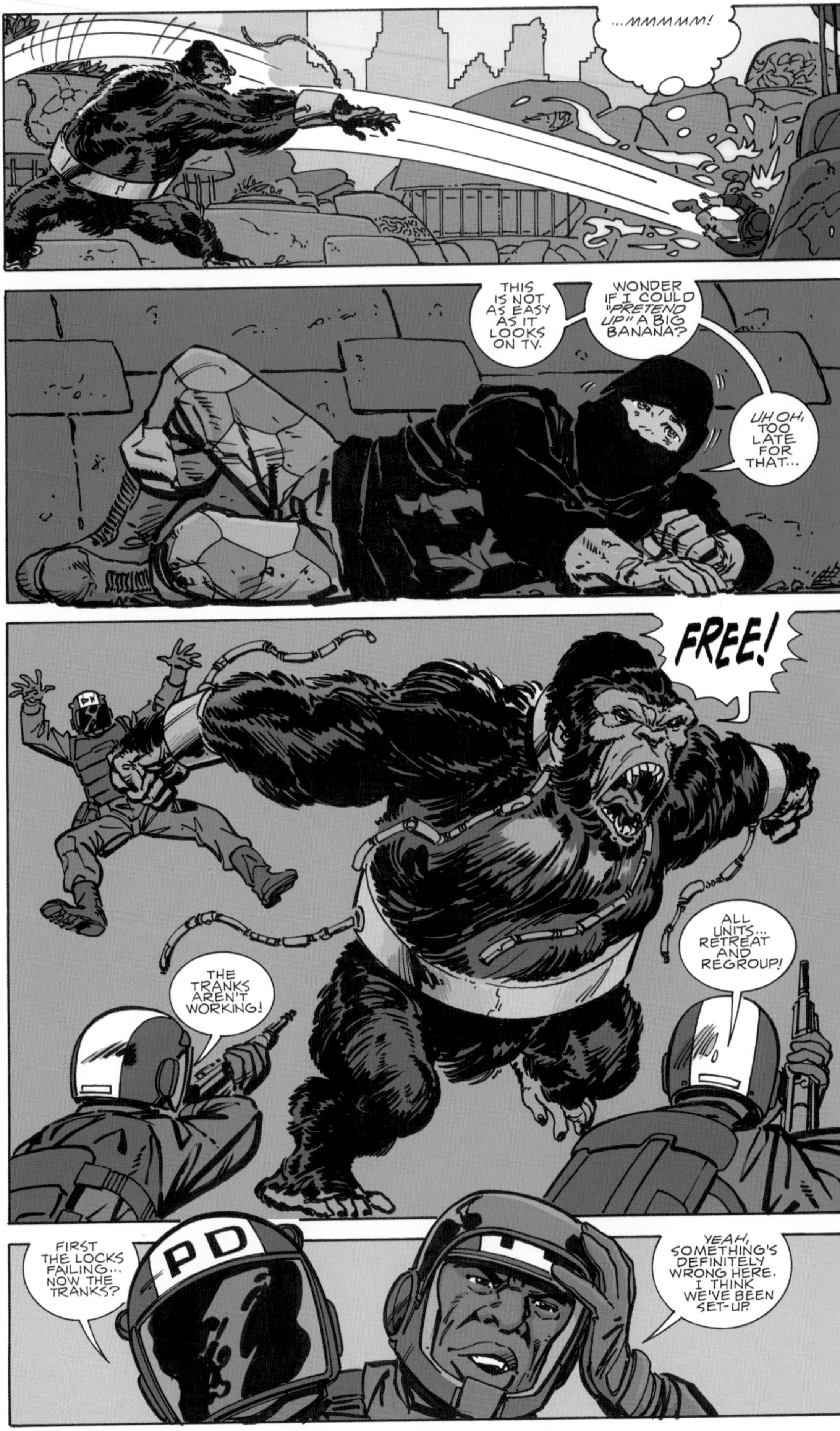
...MMMMMM!
THIS IS NOT AS EASY AS IT LOOKS ON TV.
WONDER IF I COULD "PRETEND UP" A BIG BANANA?
UH OH, TOO LATE FOR THAT...
FREE!
THE TRANKS AREN'T WORKING!
ALL UNITS... RETREAT AND REGROUP!
PD
FIRST THE LOCKS FAILING... NOW THE TRANKS?
YEAH, SOMETHING'S DEFINITELY WRONG HERE. I THINK WE'VE BEEN SET-UP.

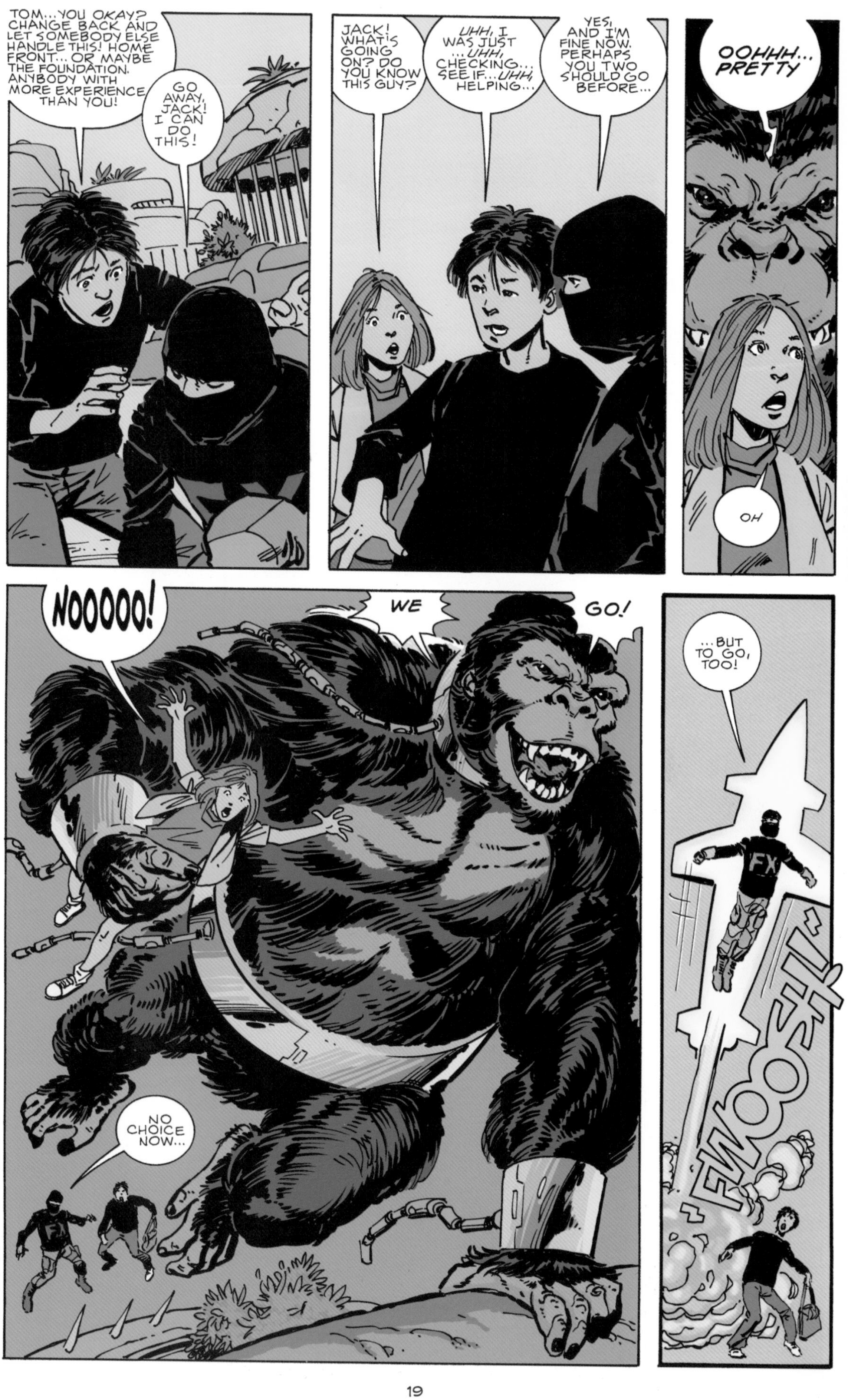
TOM... YOU OKAY? CHANGE BACK AND LET SOMEBODY ELSE HANDLE THIS! HOME FRONT... OR MAYBE THE FOUNDATION. ANYBODY WITH MORE EXPERIENCE THAN YOU!
GO AWAY, JACK! I CAN DO THIS!
JACK! WHAT'S GOING ON? DO YOU KNOW THIS GUY?
UHH, I WAS JUST ...UHH, CHECKING... SEE IF...UHH, HELPING...
YES, AND I'M FINE NOW. PERHAPS YOU TWO SHOULD GO BEFORE...
OOHHH... PRETTY
OH
NOOOOO!
WE
GO!
NO CHOICE NOW...
...BUT TO GO, TOO!
FWOOSH!

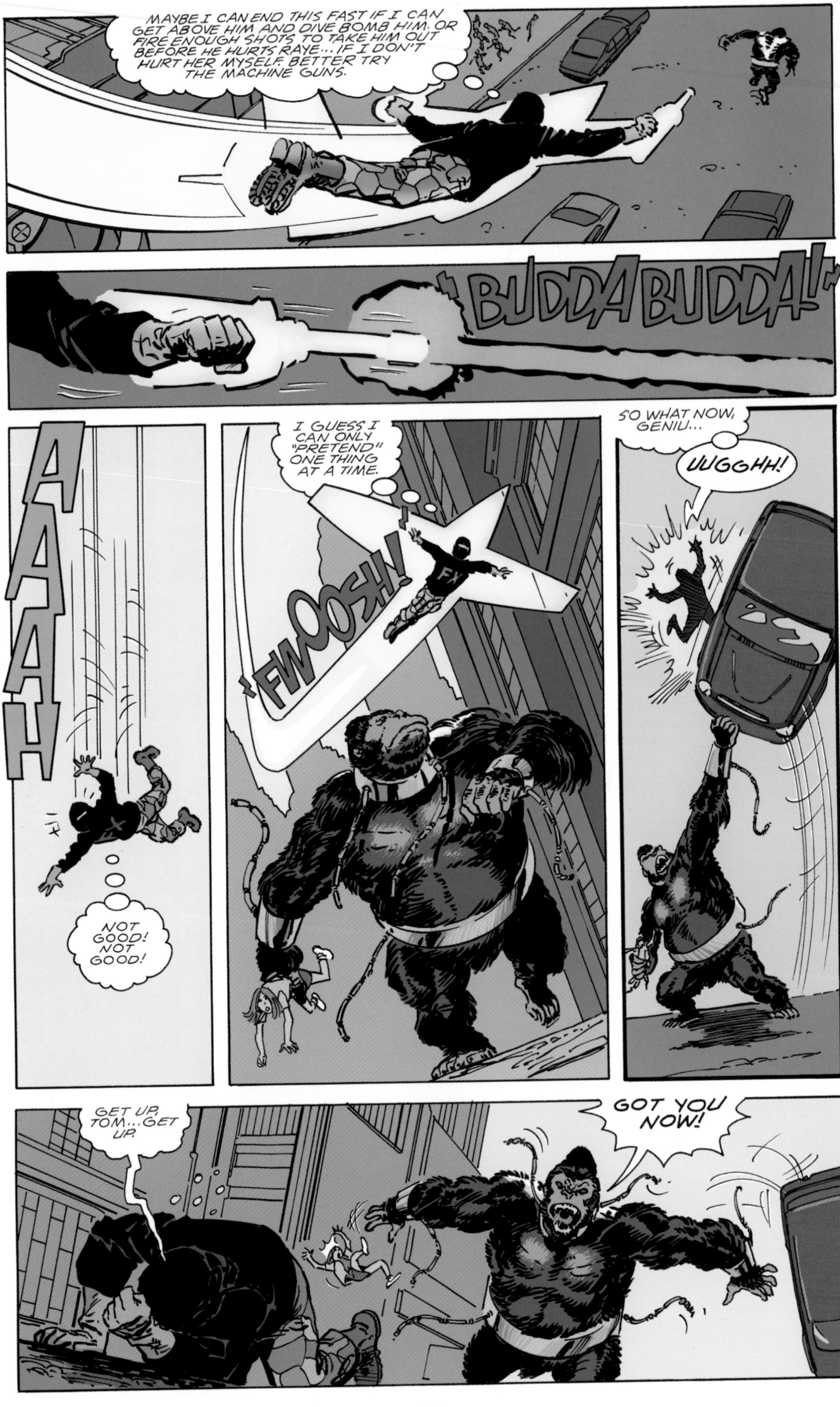
MAYBE I CAN END THIS FAST IF I CAN GET ABOVE HIM AND DIVE BOMB HIM. OR FIRE ENOUGH SHOTS TO TAKE HIM OUT BEFORE HE HURTS RAYE... IF I DON'T HURT HER MYSELF. BETTER TRY THE MACHINE GUNS.
BUDDA BUDDA!!
AAAAH
NOT GOOD! NOT GOOD!
I GUESS I CAN ONLY "PRETEND" ONE THING AT A TIME.
FWOOSH!
SO WHAT NOW, GENIU...
UUGGHH!
GET UP, TOM... GET UP.
GOT YOU NOW!

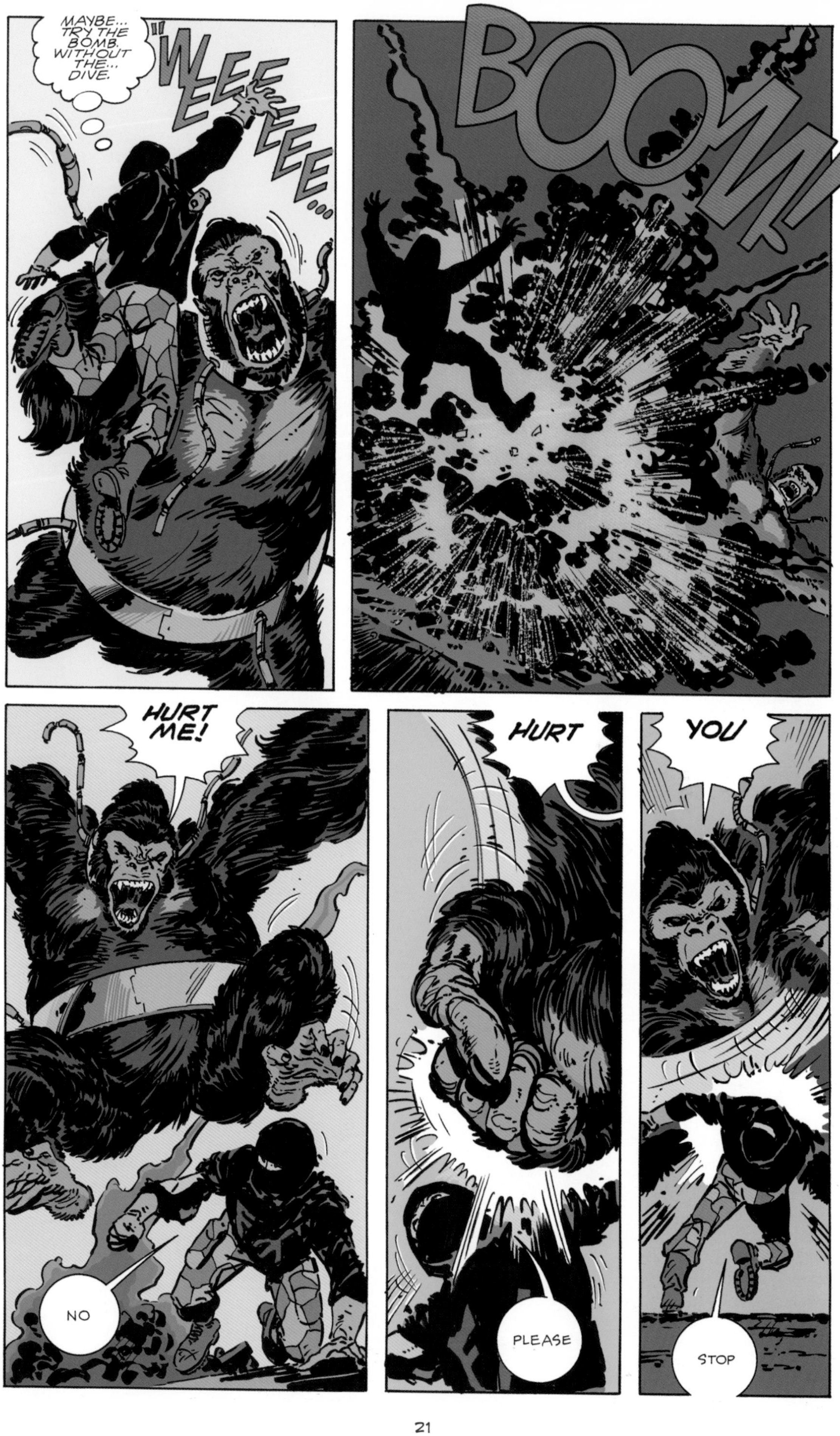
MAYBE... TRY THE BOMB. WITHOUT THE... DIVE.
"WEEEEEEEE...
BOOM!
HURT ME!
NO
HURT
PLEASE
YOU
STOP

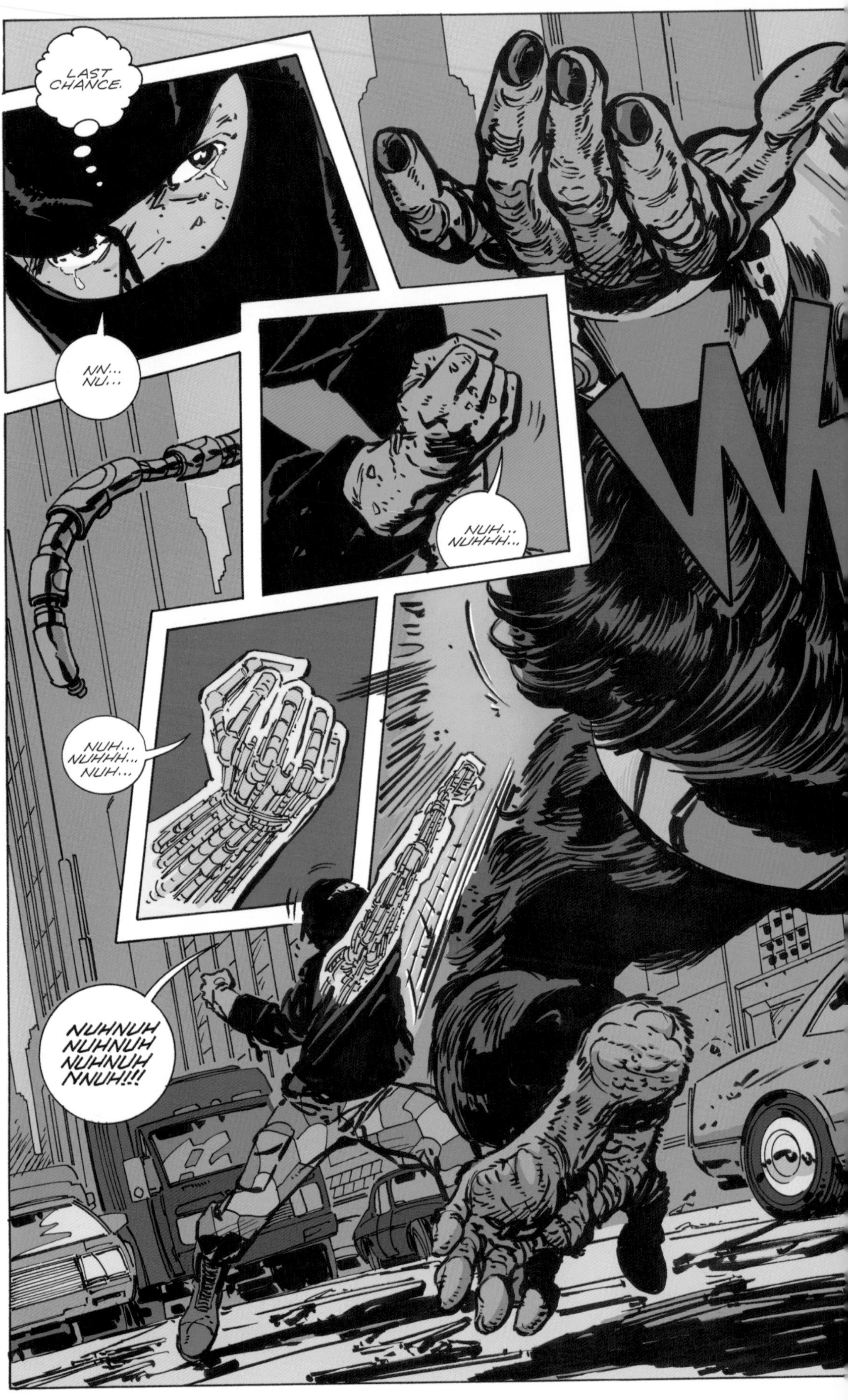
LAST CHANCE.
NN... NU...
NUH... NUHHH...
NUH... NUHHH... NUH...
NUHNUH NUHNUH NUHNUH NNUH!!!

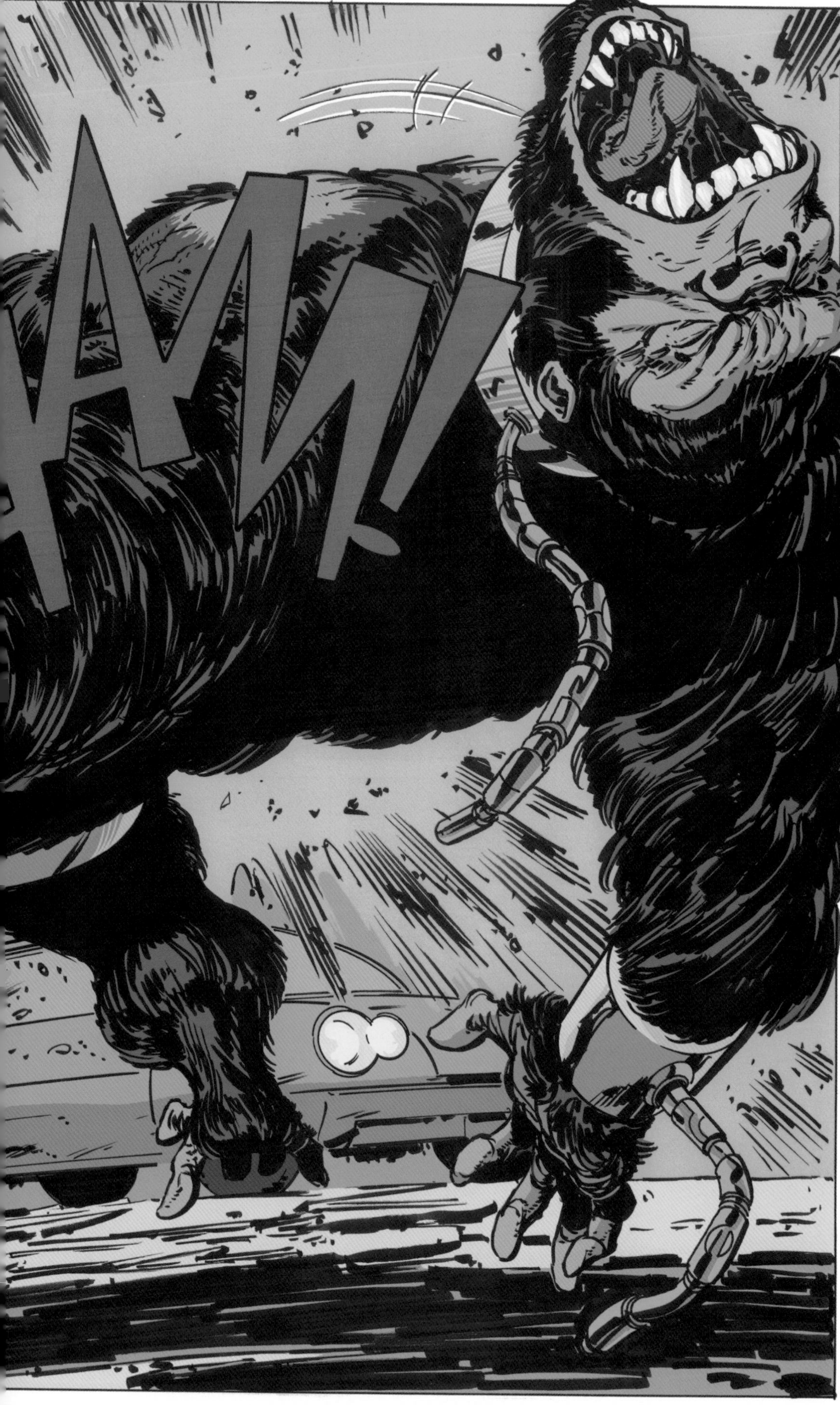

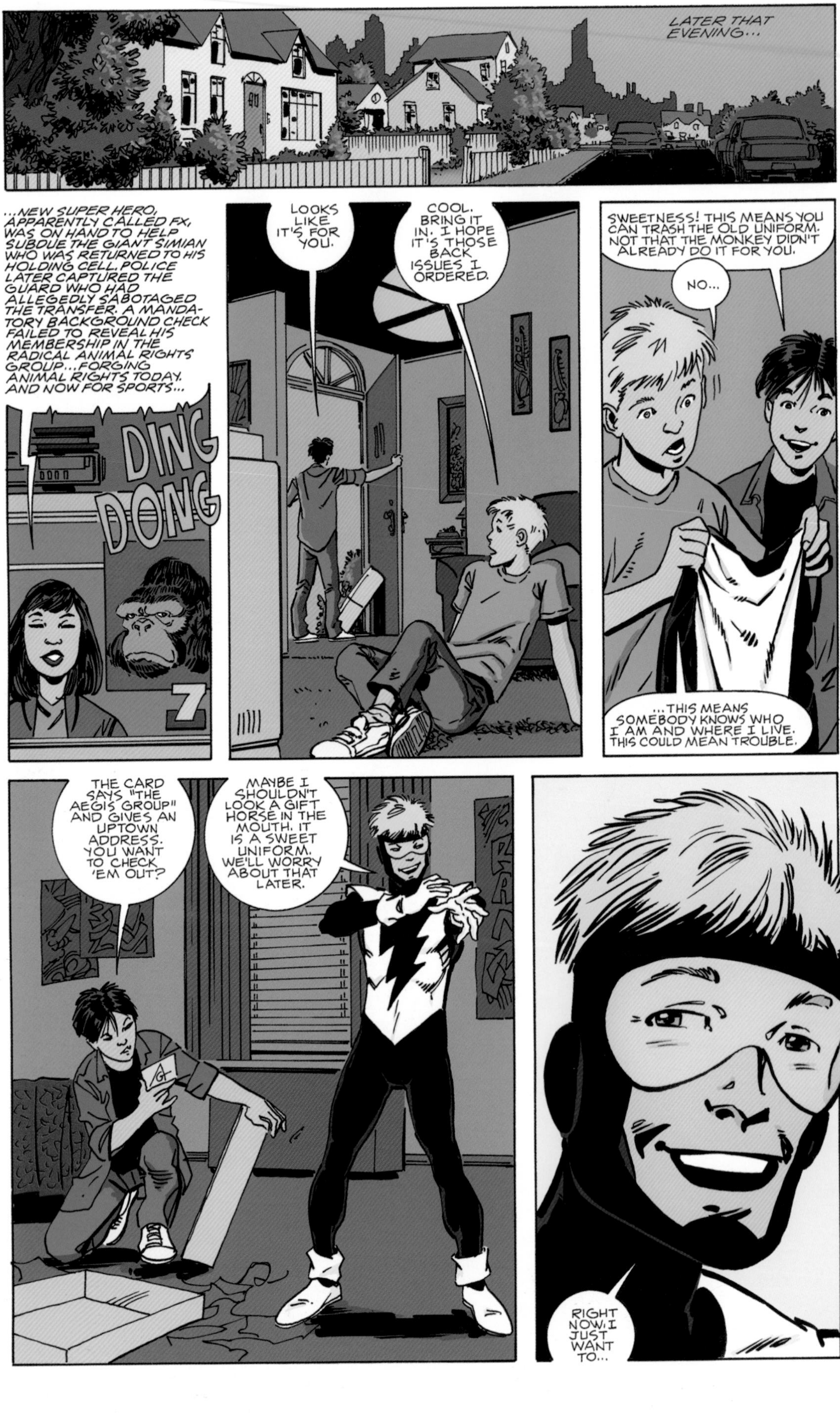
LATER THAT EVENING...
...NEW SUPER HERO, APPARENTLY CALLED FX, WAS ON HAND TO HELP SUBDUE THE GIANT SIMIAN WHO WAS RETURNED TO HIS HOLDING CELL. POLICE LATER CAPTURED THE GUARD WHO HAD ALLEGEDLY SABOTAGED THE TRANSFER. A MANDATORY BACKGROUND CHECK FAILED TO REVEAL HIS MEMBERSHIP IN THE RADICAL ANIMAL RIGHTS GROUP...FORGING ANIMAL RIGHTS TODAY. AND NOW FOR SPORTS...
DING DONG
7
LOOKS LIKE IT'S FOR YOU.
COOL. BRING IT IN. I HOPE IT'S THOSE BACK ISSUES I ORDERED.
SWEETNESS! THIS MEANS YOU CAN TRASH THE OLD UNIFORM. NOT THAT THE MONKEY DIDN'T ALREADY DO IT FOR YOU.
NO...
...THIS MEANS SOMEBODY KNOWS WHO I AM AND WHERE I LIVE. THIS COULD MEAN TROUBLE.
THE CARD SAYS "THE AEGIS GROUP" AND GIVES AN UPTOWN ADDRESS. YOU WANT TO CHECK 'EM OUT?
MAYBE I SHOULDN'T LOOK A GIFT HORSE IN THE MOUTH. IT IS A SWEET UNIFORM. WE'LL WORRY ABOUT THAT LATER.
RIGHT NOW, I JUST WANT TO...

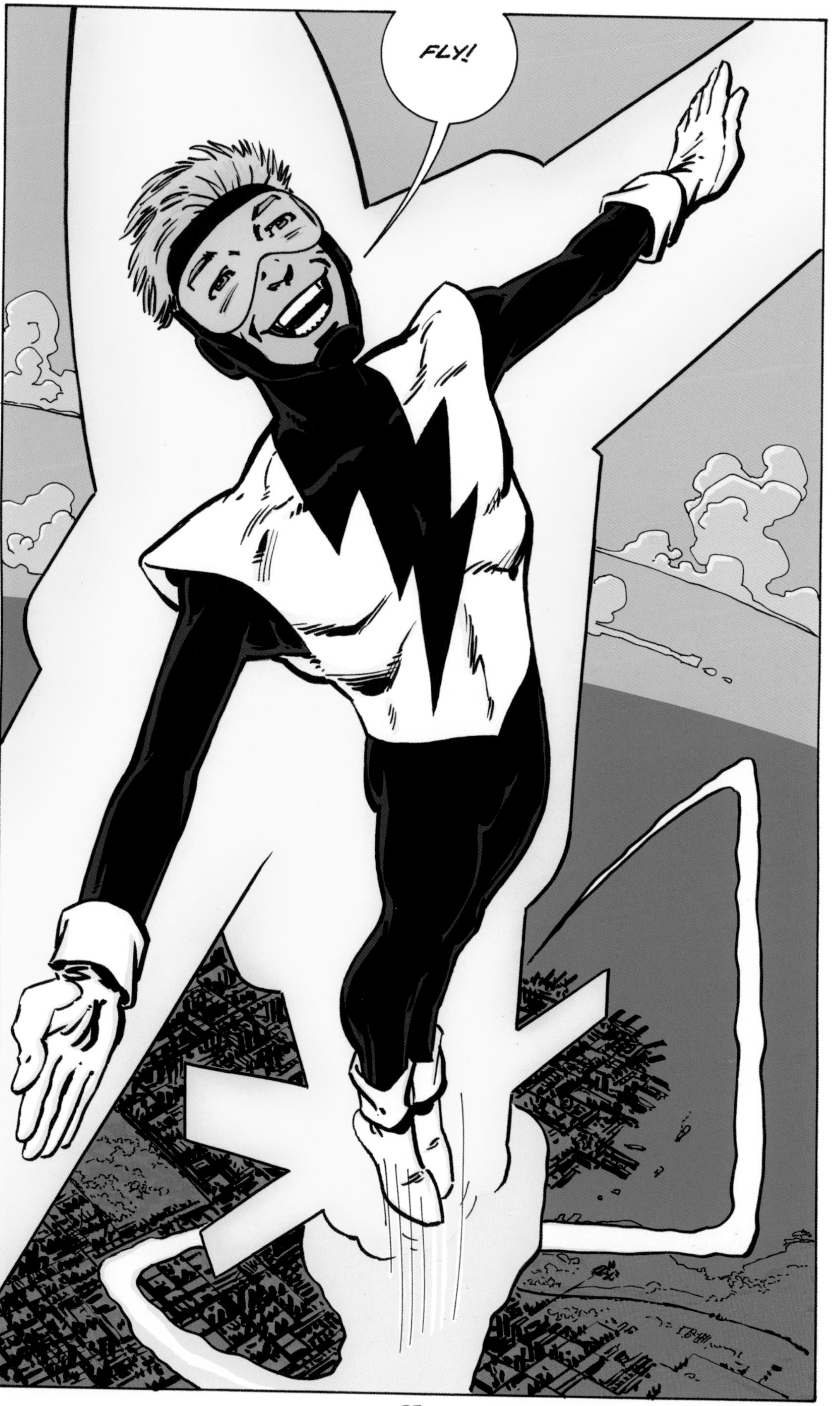
FLY!

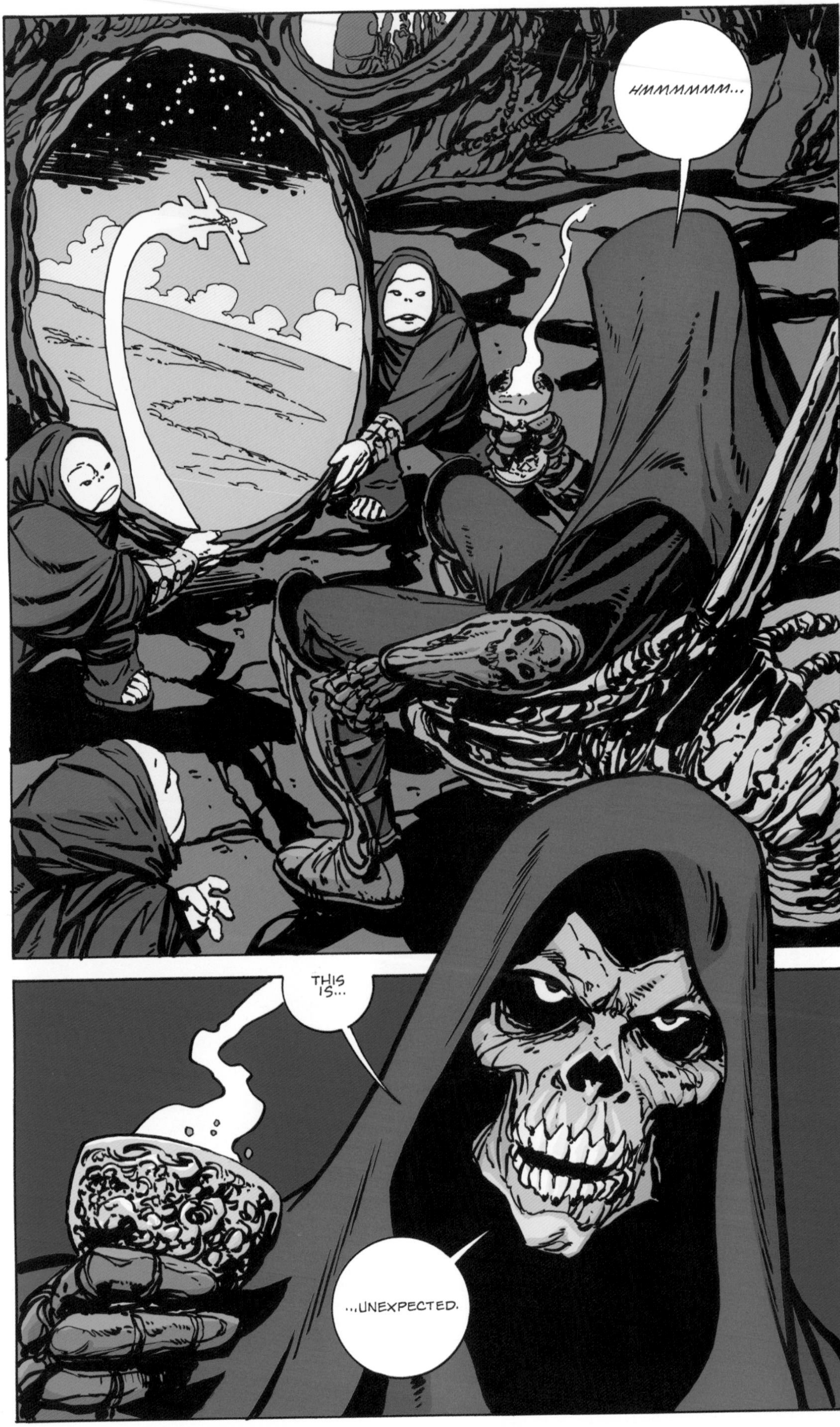
HMMMMMM...
THIS IS...
...UNEXPECTED.

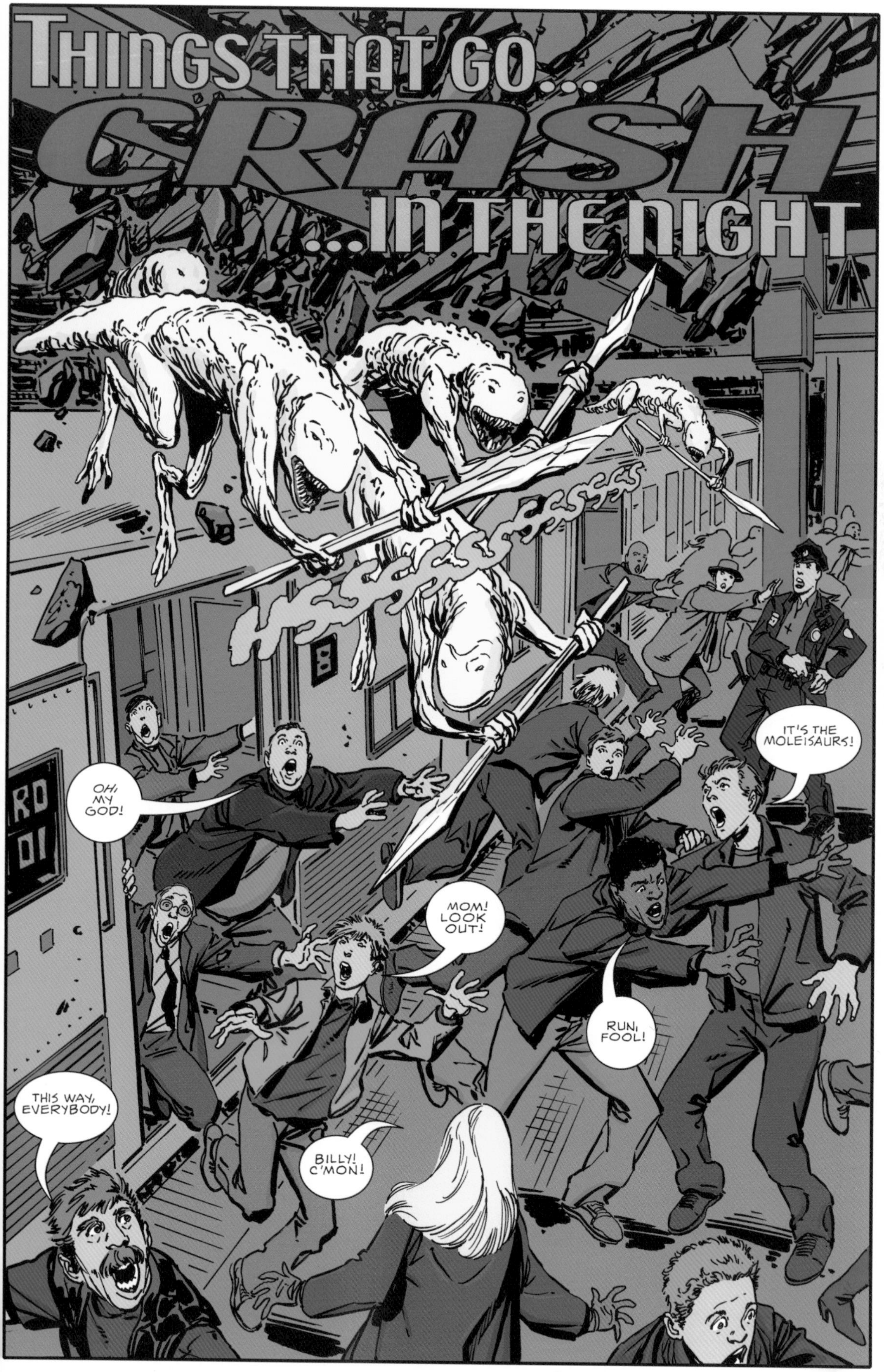
THINGS THAT GO...
CRASH
...IN THE NIGHT
HSSSSSSSSSSS
IT'S THE MOLEISAURS!
OH, MY GOD!
MOM! LOOK OUT!
RUN, FOOL!
THIS WAY, EVERYBODY!
BILLY! C'MON!

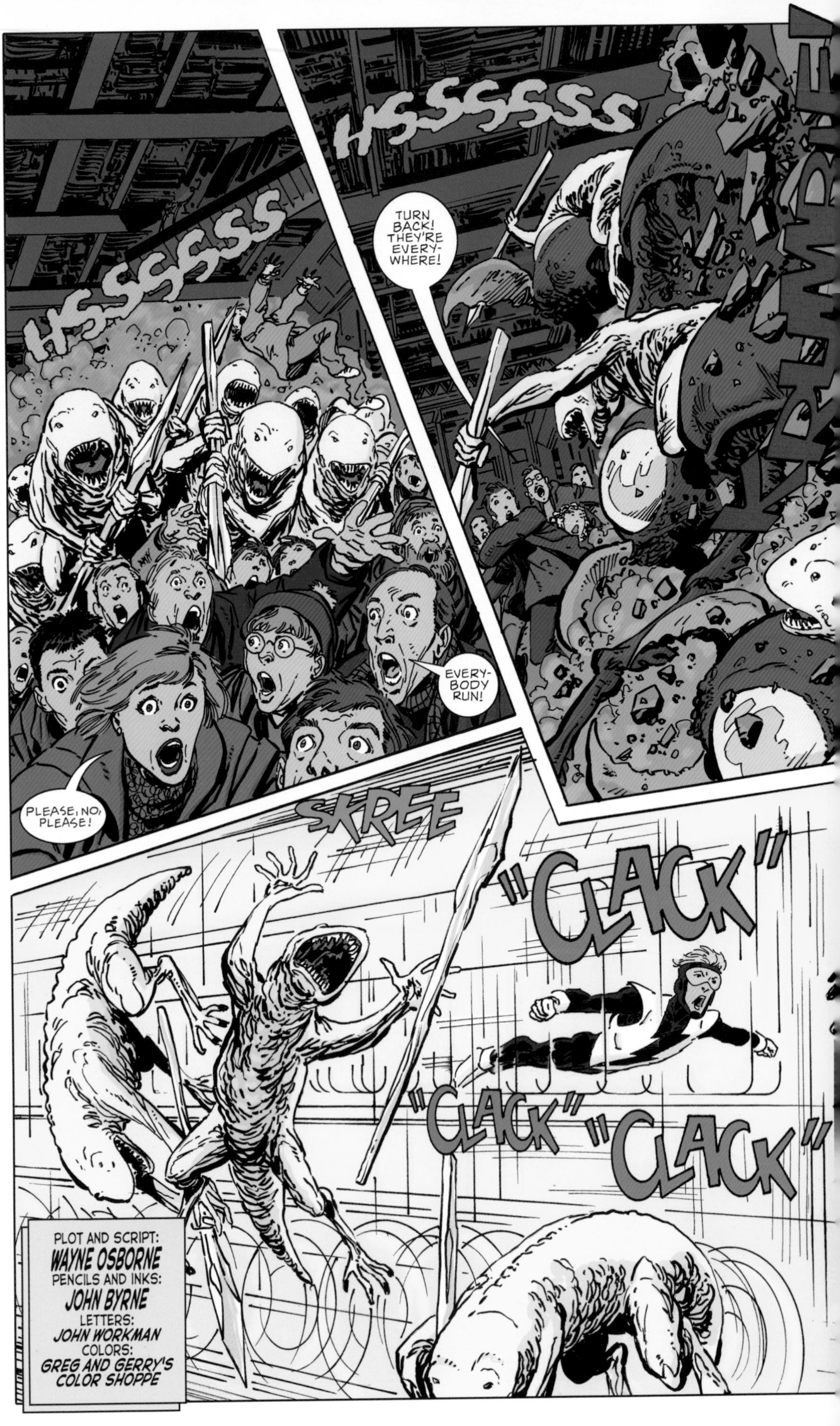

HSSSSSS
EVERY-BODY RUN!
PLEASE, NO, PLEASE!
HSSSSSS
TURN BACK! THEY'RE EVERY-WHERE!
SKREE
"CLACK"
"CLACK" "CLACK"
PLOT AND SCRIPT: WAYNE OSBORNE
PENCILS AND INKS: JOHN BYRNE
LETTERS: JOHN WORKMAN
COLORS: GREG AND GERRY'S COLOR SHOPPE

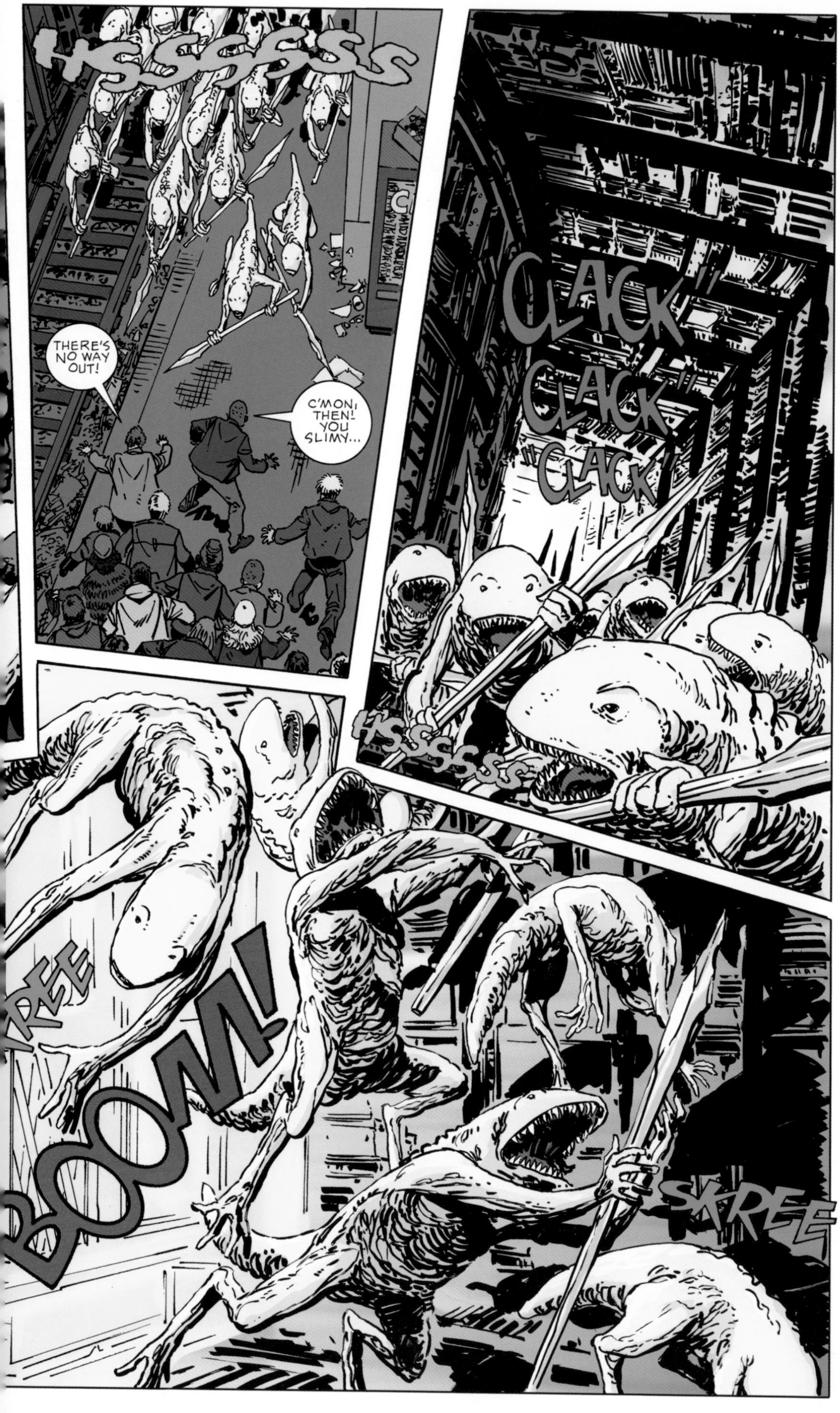
HSSSSSS
THERE'S NO WAY OUT!
C'MON, THEN! YOU SLIMY...
CLACK
CLACK
CLACK
HSSSSSS
KREE
BOOM!
SKREE

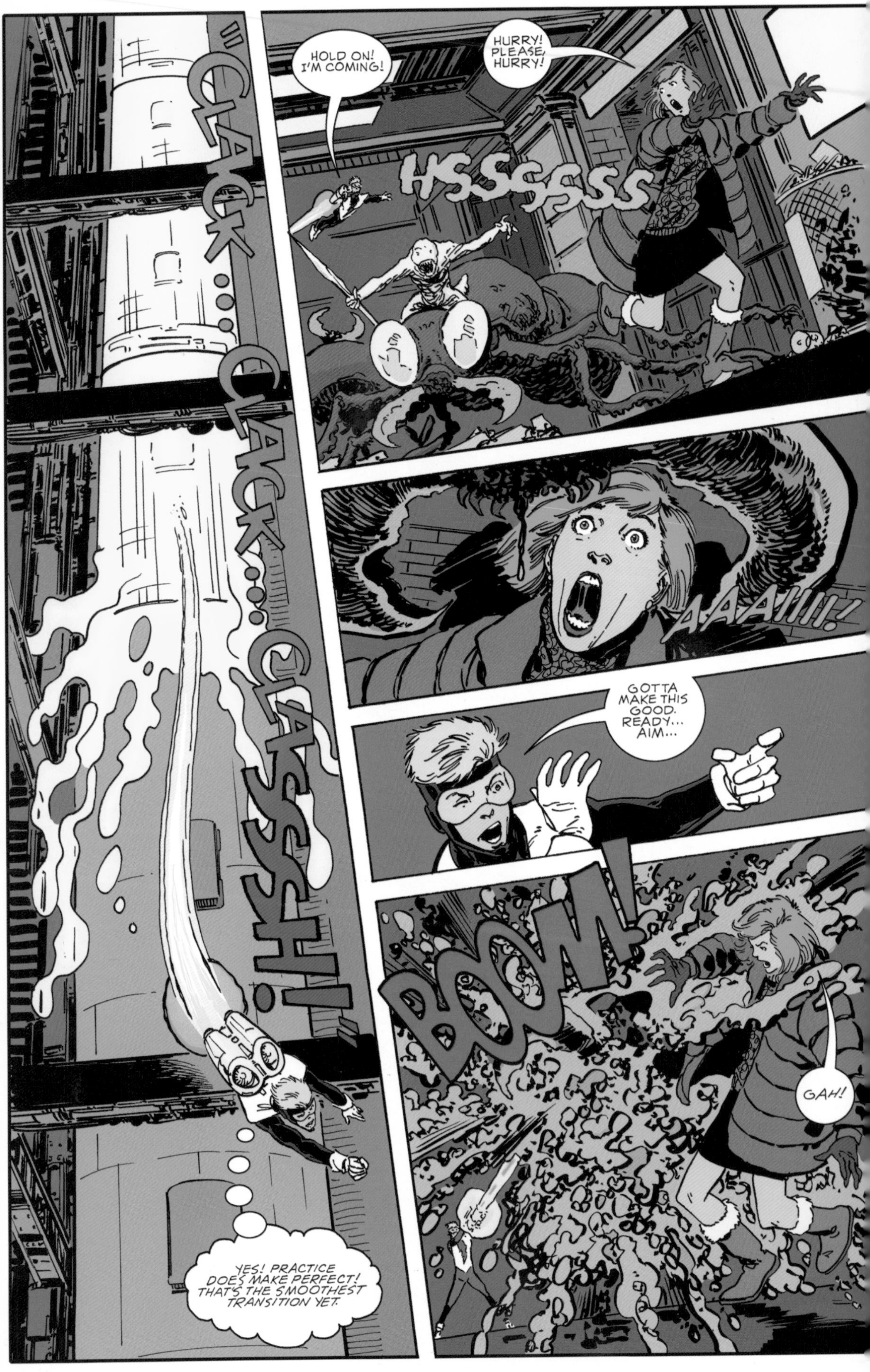

CLACK... CLACK... CLACK... CLASSH!!
HOLD ON! I'M COMING!
HURRY! PLEASE, HURRY!
HSSSSSS
AAAIIII!
GOTTA MAKE THIS GOOD. READY... AIM...
BOOM!
GAH!
YES! PRACTICE DOES MAKE PERFECT! THAT'S THE SMOOTHEST TRANSITION YET.

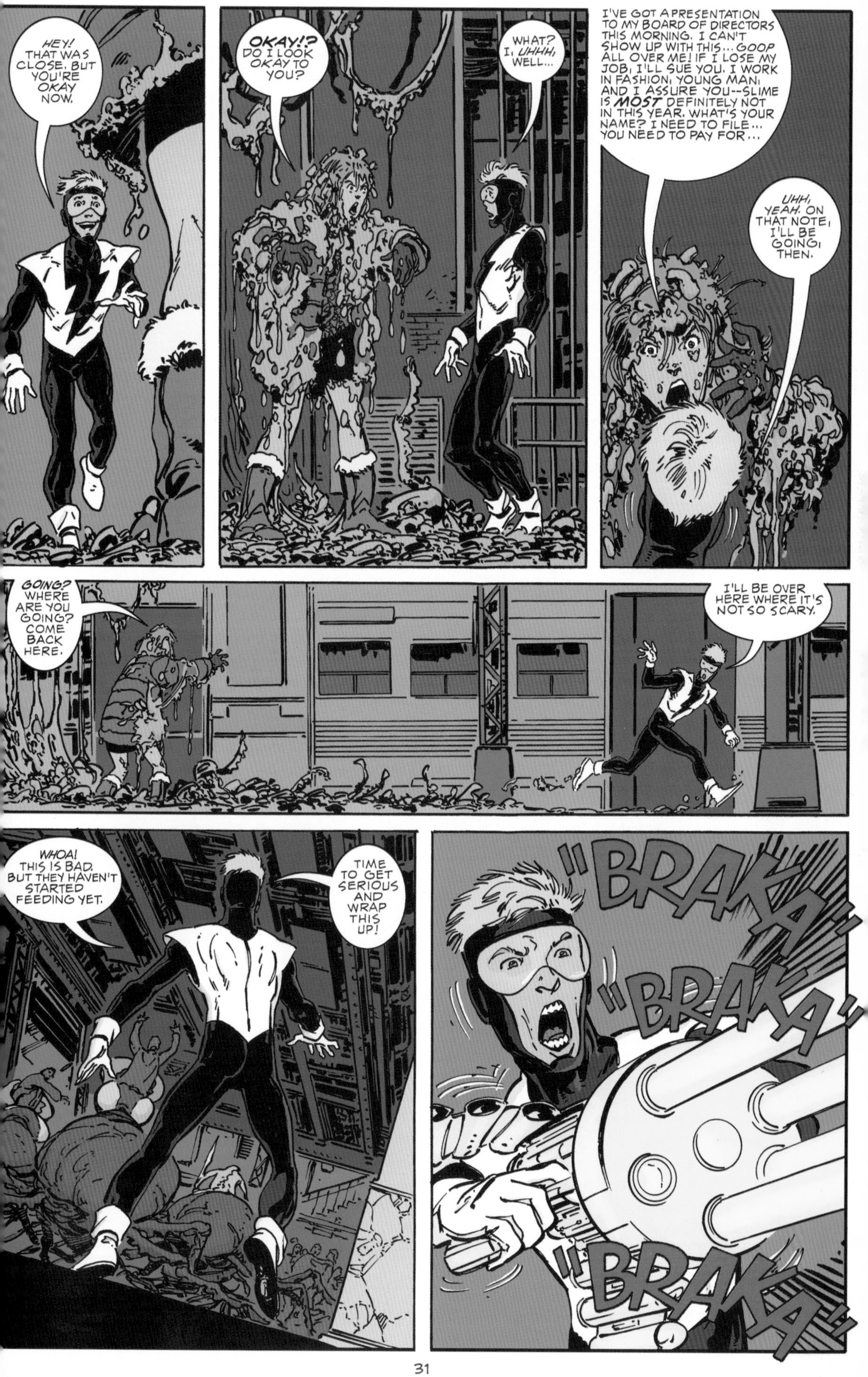
HEY! THAT WAS CLOSE. BUT YOU'RE OKAY NOW.
OKAY!? DO I LOOK OKAY TO YOU?
WHAT? I, UHHH, WELL...
I'VE GOT A PRESENTATION TO MY BOARD OF DIRECTORS THIS MORNING. I CAN'T SHOW UP WITH THIS... GOOP ALL OVER ME! IF I LOSE MY JOB, I'LL SUE YOU. I WORK IN FASHION, YOUNG MAN, AND I ASSURE YOU--SLIME IS MOST DEFINITELY NOT IN THIS YEAR. WHAT'S YOUR NAME? I NEED TO FILE... YOU NEED TO PAY FOR...
UHH, YEAH. ON THAT NOTE, I'LL BE GOING, THEN.
GOING? WHERE ARE YOU GOING? COME BACK HERE.
I'LL BE OVER HERE WHERE IT'S NOT SO SCARY.
WHOA! THIS IS BAD. BUT THEY HAVEN'T STARTED FEEDING YET.
TIME TO GET SERIOUS AND WRAP THIS UP!
"BRAKA"
"BRAKA"
"BRAKA"

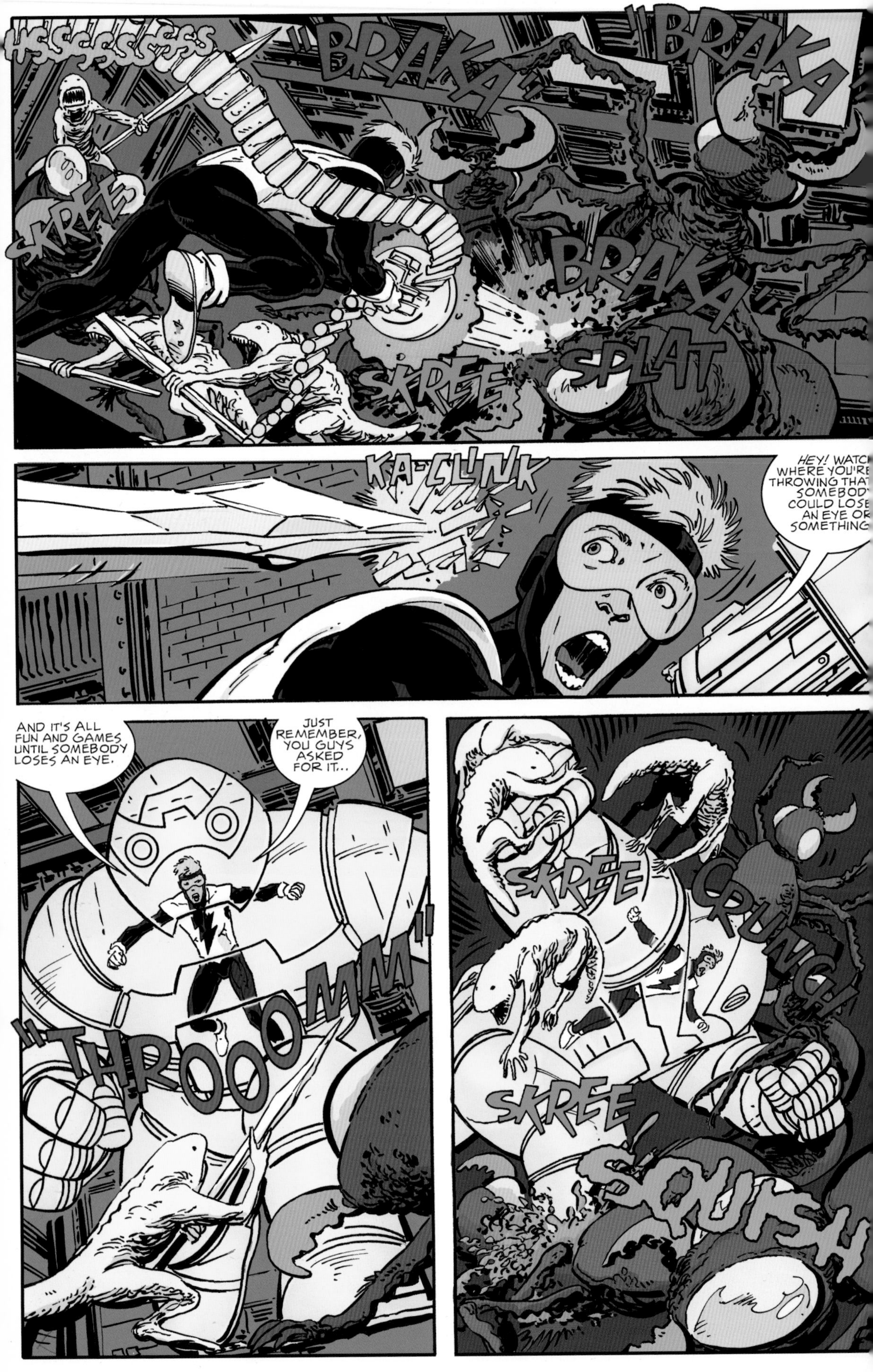
HSSSSSSSSSSS
"BRAKA"
"BRAKA"
SKREE
"BRAKA"
SKREE
SPLAT
KA-CLINK
HEY! WATCH WHERE YOU'RE THROWING THAT! SOMEBODY COULD LOSE AN EYE OR SOMETHING!
AND IT'S ALL FUN AND GAMES UNTIL SOMEBODY LOSES AN EYE.
JUST REMEMBER, YOU GUYS ASKED FOR IT...
"THROOOOMM"
SKREE
CRUNCH
SKREE
SQUISH

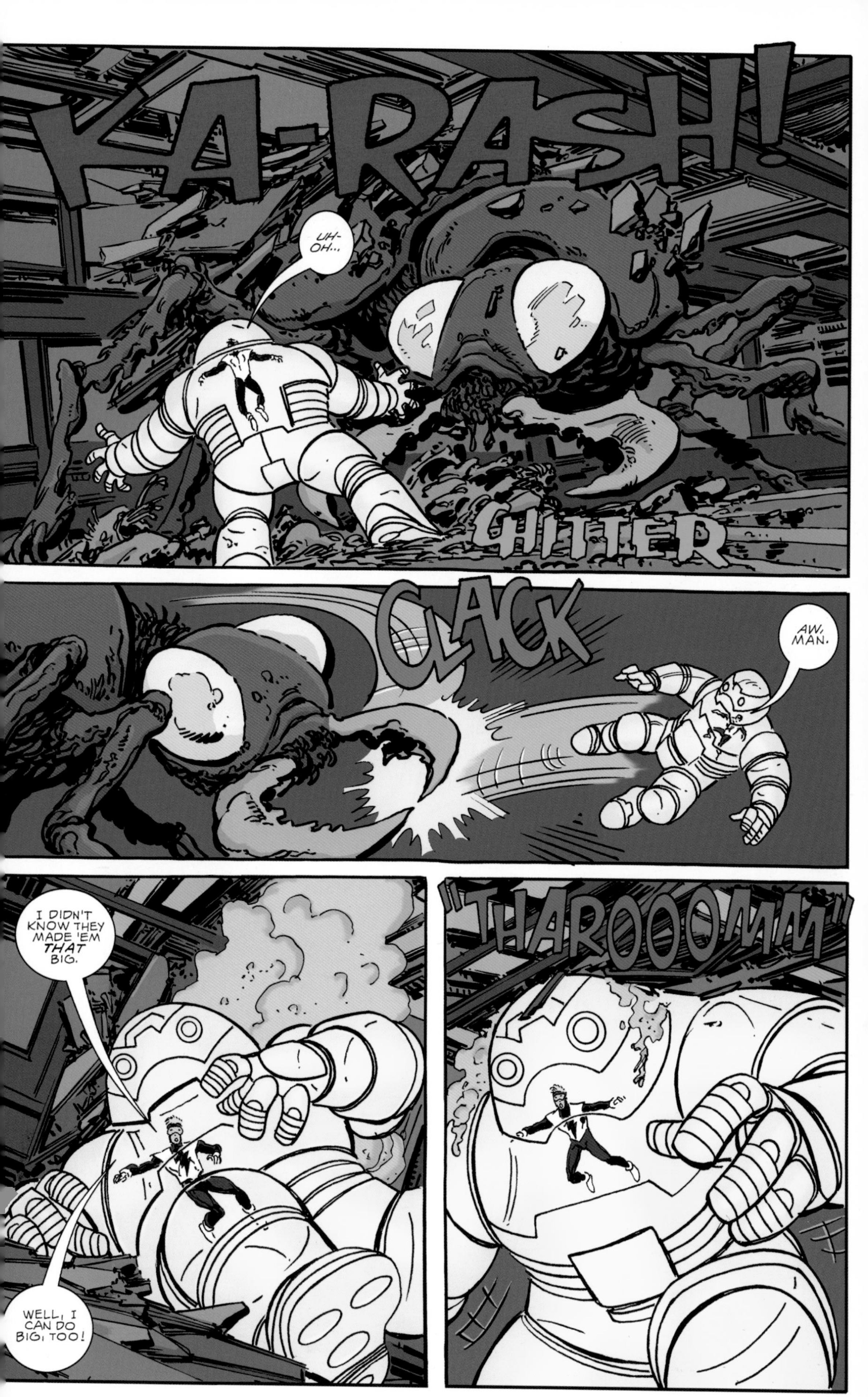
KA-RASH!
UH-OH...
CHITTER
CLACK
AW, MAN.
I DIDN'T KNOW THEY MADE 'EM *THAT* BIG.
WELL, I CAN DO BIG, TOO!
"THAROOOMM"

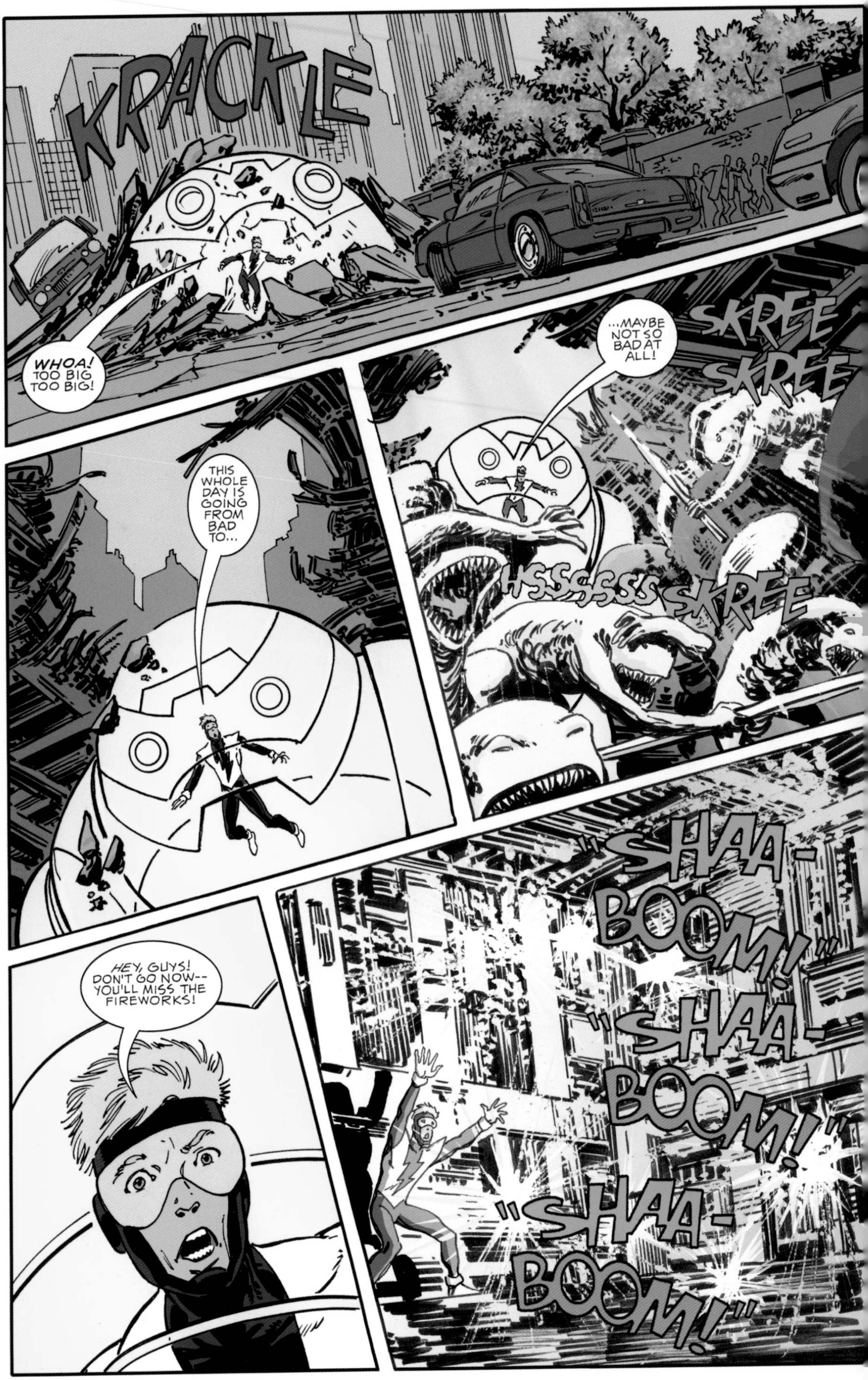
KRACKLE
WHOA! TOO BIG TOO BIG!
THIS WHOLE DAY IS GOING FROM BAD TO...
...MAYBE NOT SO BAD AT ALL!
SKREE
SKREE
HSSSSSS
SKREE
HEY, GUYS! DON'T GO NOW-- YOU'LL MISS THE FIREWORKS!
"SHAA-BOOM!"
"SHAA-BOOM!"
"SHAA-BOOM!"

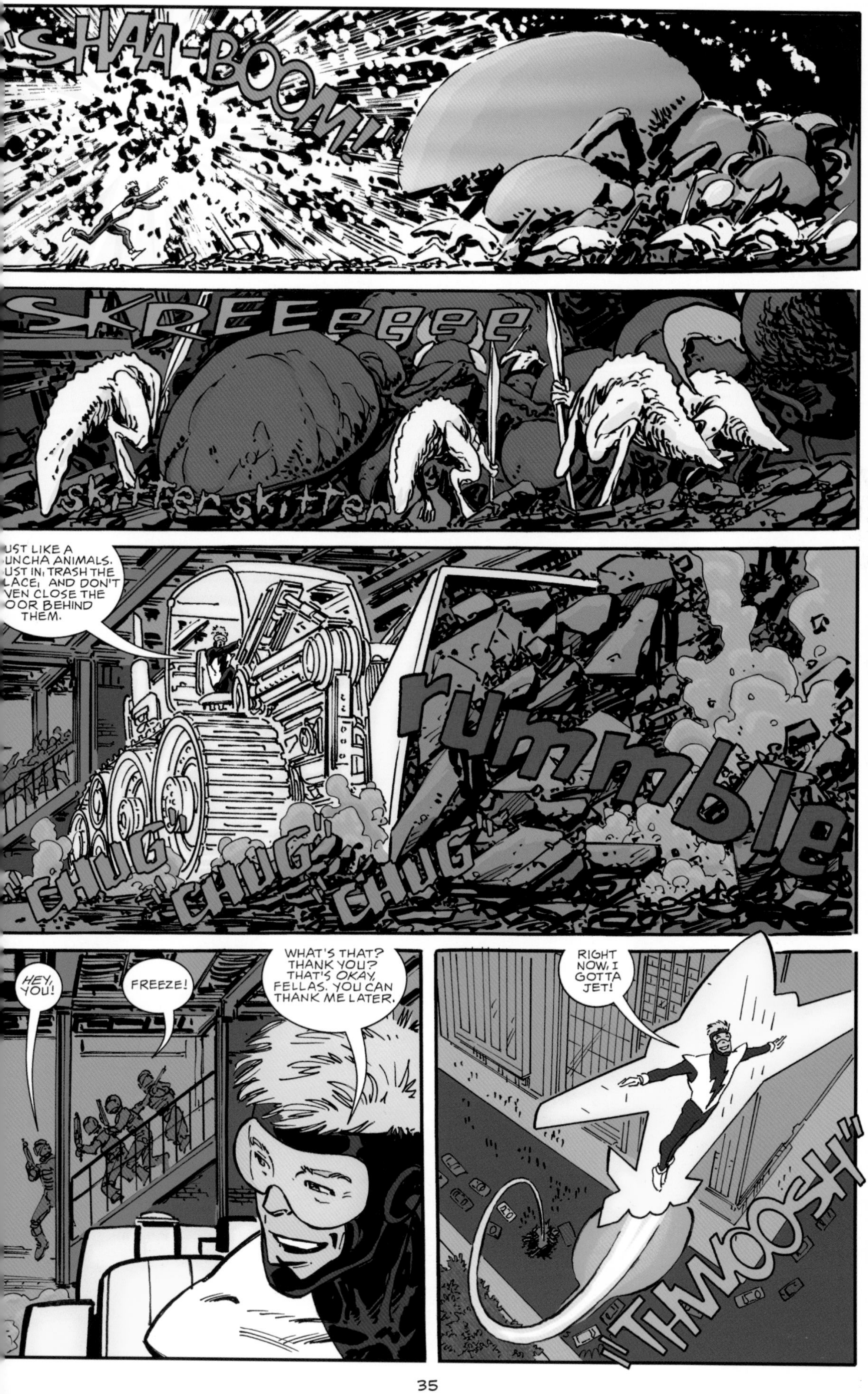
SHAA-BOOM!
SKREEeeee
skitter skitter
UST LIKE A
UNCHA ANIMALS.
UST IN, TRASH THE
LACE, AND DON'T
VEN CLOSE THE
OOR BEHIND
THEM.
rummble
CHUG CHUG CHUG
HEY, YOU!
FREEZE!
WHAT'S THAT? THANK YOU? THAT'S OKAY, FELLAS. YOU CAN THANK ME LATER.
RIGHT NOW, I GOTTA JET!
THWOOSH

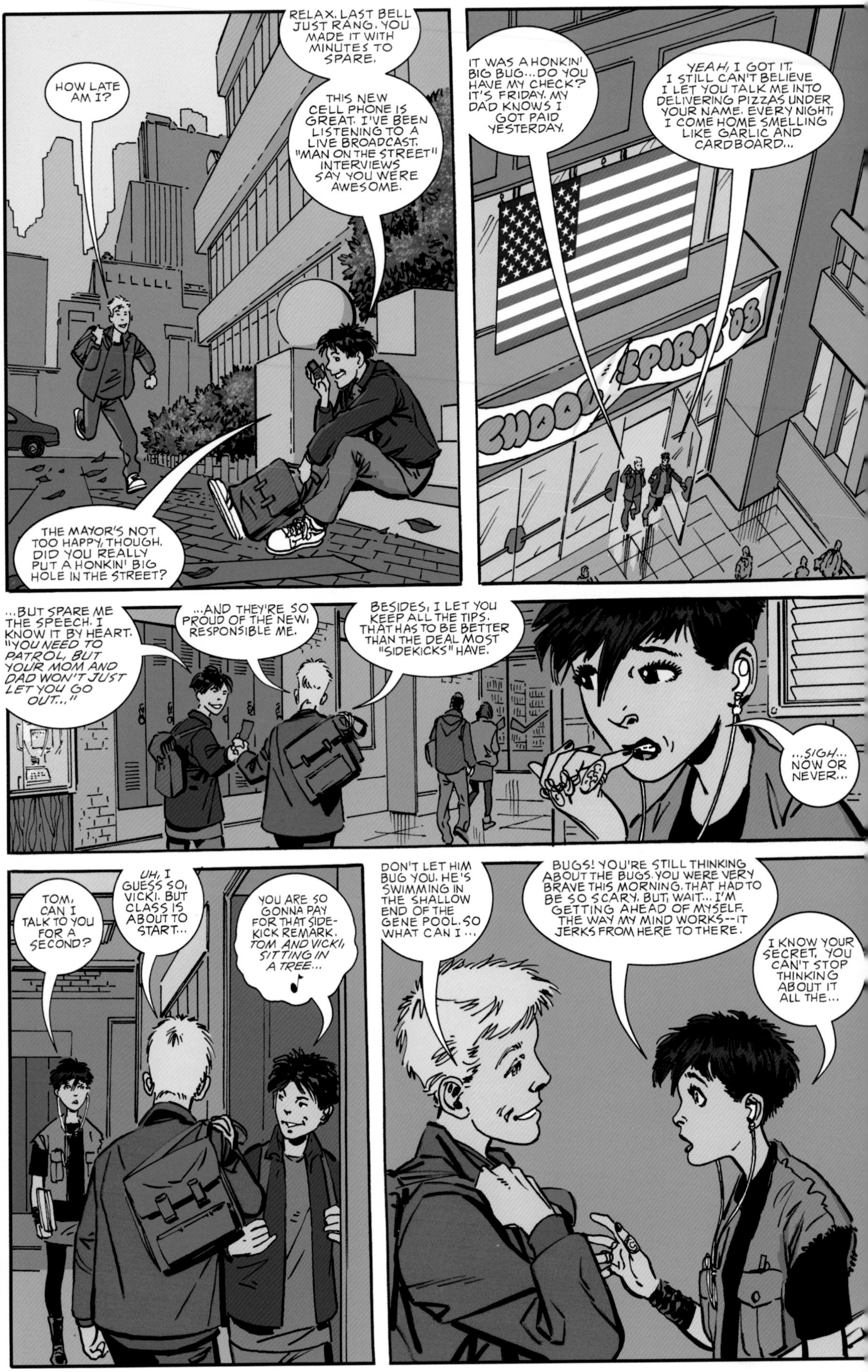
HOW LATE AM I?
RELAX. LAST BELL JUST RANG. YOU MADE IT WITH MINUTES TO SPARE.
THIS NEW CELL PHONE IS GREAT. I'VE BEEN LISTENING TO A LIVE BROADCAST. "MAN ON THE STREET" INTERVIEWS SAY YOU WERE AWESOME.
THE MAYOR'S NOT TOO HAPPY, THOUGH. DID YOU REALLY PUT A HONKIN' BIG HOLE IN THE STREET?
IT WAS A HONKIN' BIG BUG... DO YOU HAVE MY CHECK? IT'S FRIDAY. MY DAD KNOWS I GOT PAID YESTERDAY.
YEAH, I GOT IT. I STILL CAN'T BELIEVE I LET YOU TALK ME INTO DELIVERING PIZZAS UNDER YOUR NAME. EVERY NIGHT, I COME HOME SMELLING LIKE GARLIC AND CARDBOARD...
...BUT SPARE ME THE SPEECH. I KNOW IT BY HEART. "YOU NEED TO PATROL, BUT YOUR MOM AND DAD WON'T JUST LET YOU GO OUT..."
...AND THEY'RE SO PROUD OF THE NEW, RESPONSIBLE ME.
BESIDES, I LET YOU KEEP ALL THE TIPS. THAT HAS TO BE BETTER THAN THE DEAL MOST "SIDEKICKS" HAVE.
...SIGH... NOW OR NEVER...
TOM, CAN I TALK TO YOU FOR A SECOND?
UH, I GUESS SO, VICKI. BUT CLASS IS ABOUT TO START...
YOU ARE SO GONNA PAY FOR THAT SIDE-KICK REMARK. TOM AND VICKI, SITTING IN A TREE...
DON'T LET HIM BUG YOU. HE'S SWIMMING IN THE SHALLOW END OF THE GENE POOL. SO WHAT CAN I...
BUGS! YOU'RE STILL THINKING ABOUT THE BUGS. YOU WERE VERY BRAVE THIS MORNING. THAT HAD TO BE SO SCARY. BUT, WAIT... I'M GETTING AHEAD OF MYSELF. THE WAY MY MIND WORKS--IT JERKS FROM HERE TO THERE.
I KNOW YOUR SECRET. YOU CAN'T STOP THINKING ABOUT IT ALL THE...

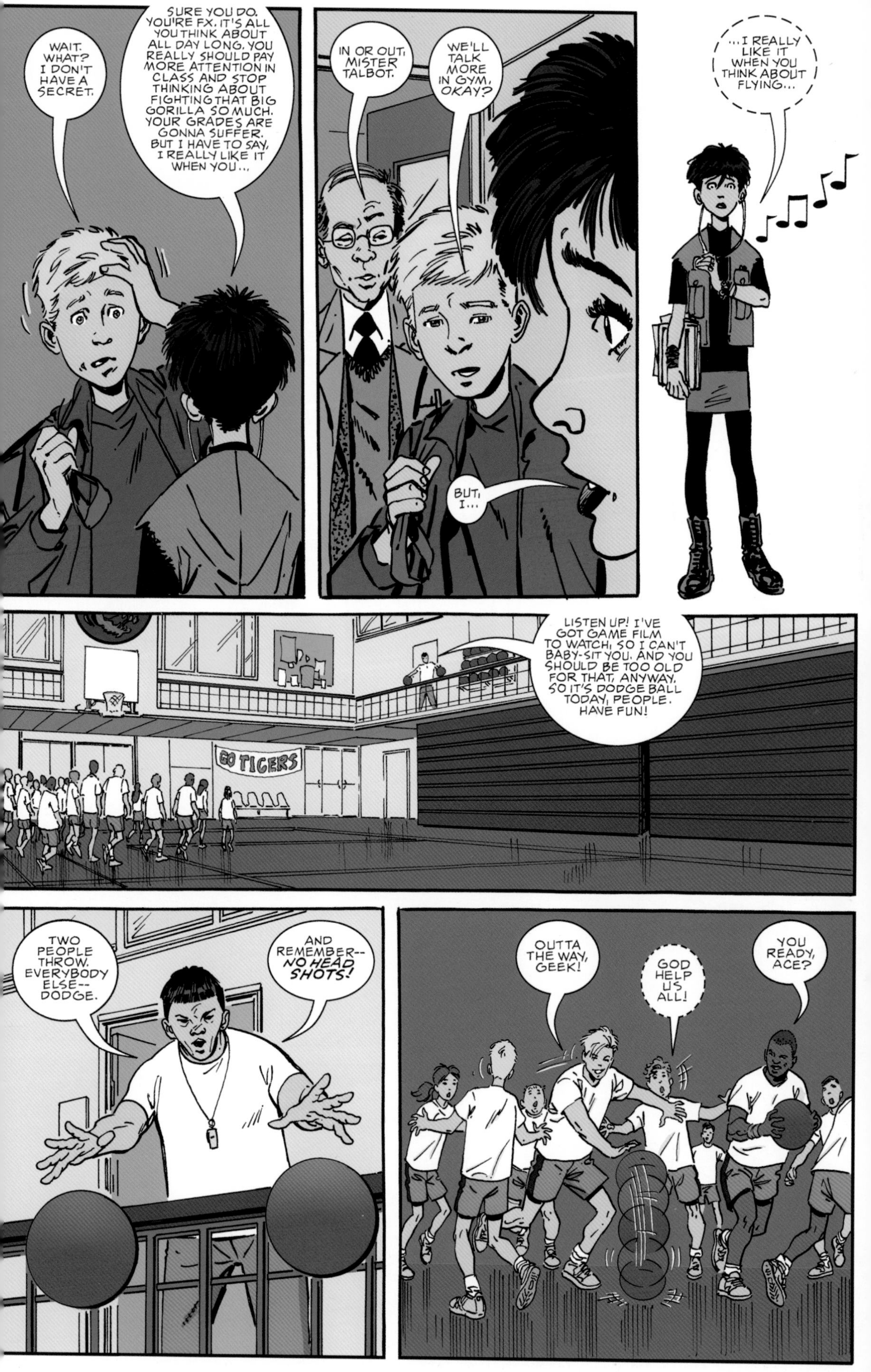

WAIT. WHAT? I DON'T HAVE A SECRET.
SURE YOU DO. YOU'RE FX. IT'S ALL YOU THINK ABOUT ALL DAY LONG. YOU REALLY SHOULD PAY MORE ATTENTION IN CLASS AND STOP THINKING ABOUT FIGHTING THAT BIG GORILLA SO MUCH. YOUR GRADES ARE GONNA SUFFER. BUT I HAVE TO SAY, I REALLY LIKE IT WHEN YOU...
IN OR OUT, MISTER TALBOT.
WE'LL TALK MORE IN GYM, OKAY?
BUT, I...
...I REALLY LIKE IT WHEN YOU THINK ABOUT FLYING...
GO TIGERS
LISTEN UP! I'VE GOT GAME FILM TO WATCH, SO I CAN'T BABY-SIT YOU. AND YOU SHOULD BE TOO OLD FOR THAT, ANYWAY. SO IT'S DODGE BALL TODAY, PEOPLE. HAVE FUN!
TWO PEOPLE THROW. EVERYBODY ELSE--DODGE.
AND REMEMBER--NO HEAD SHOTS!
OUTTA THE WAY, GEEK!
GOD HELP US ALL!
YOU READY, ACE?

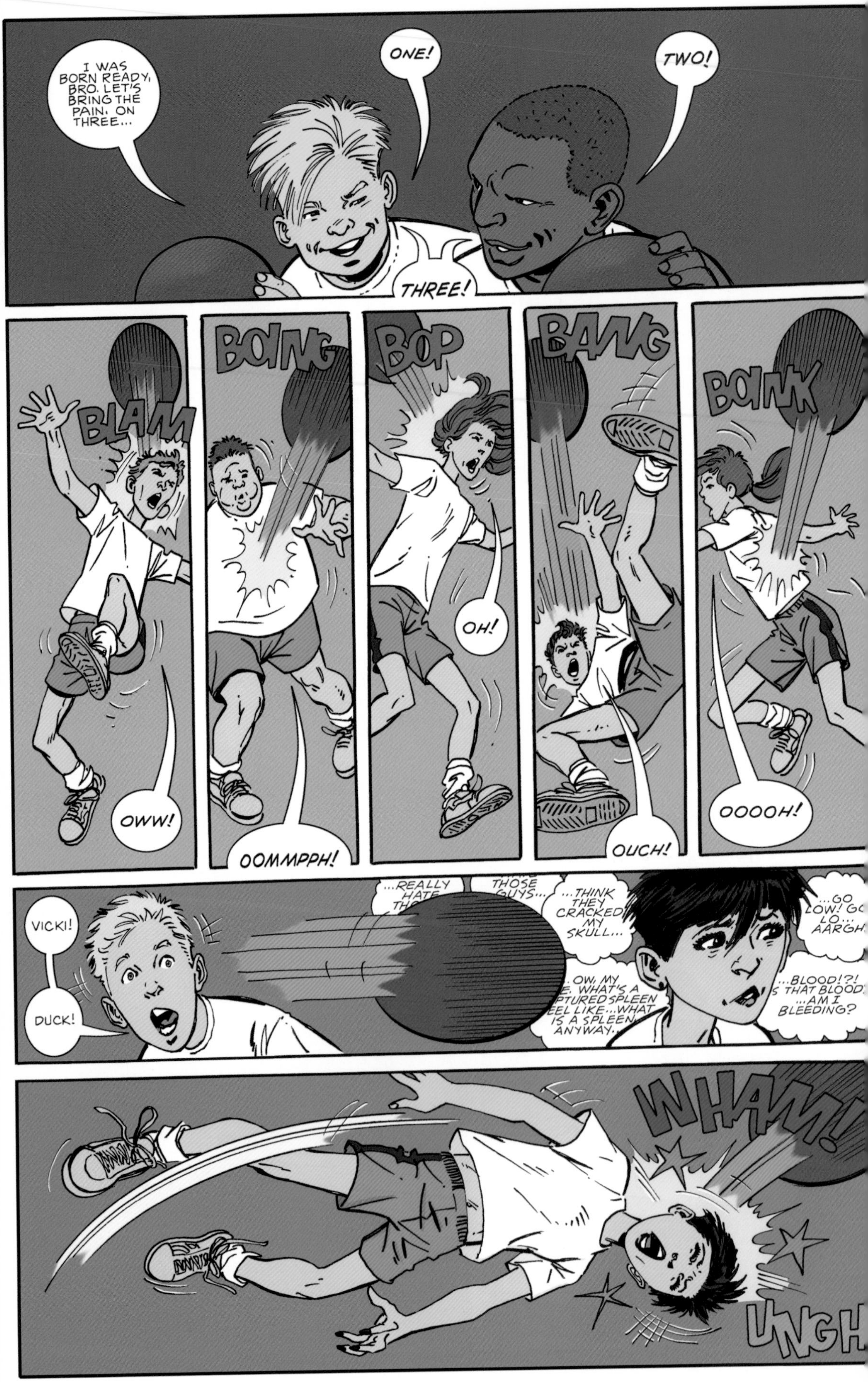

I WAS BORN READY, BRO. LET'S BRING THE PAIN. ON THREE...
ONE!
TWO!
THREE!
BLAM
OWW!
BOING
OOMMPPH!
BOP
OH!
BANG
OUCH!
BOINK
OOOOH!
VICKI!
DUCK!
...REALLY HATE
THOSE GUYS...
...THINK THEY CRACKED MY SKULL...
...GO LOW!
LO... AARGH
...BLOOD!?!
...AM I BLEEDING?
WHAT'S A
SPLEEN
...WHAT IS A SPLEEN ANYWAY...
WHAM!

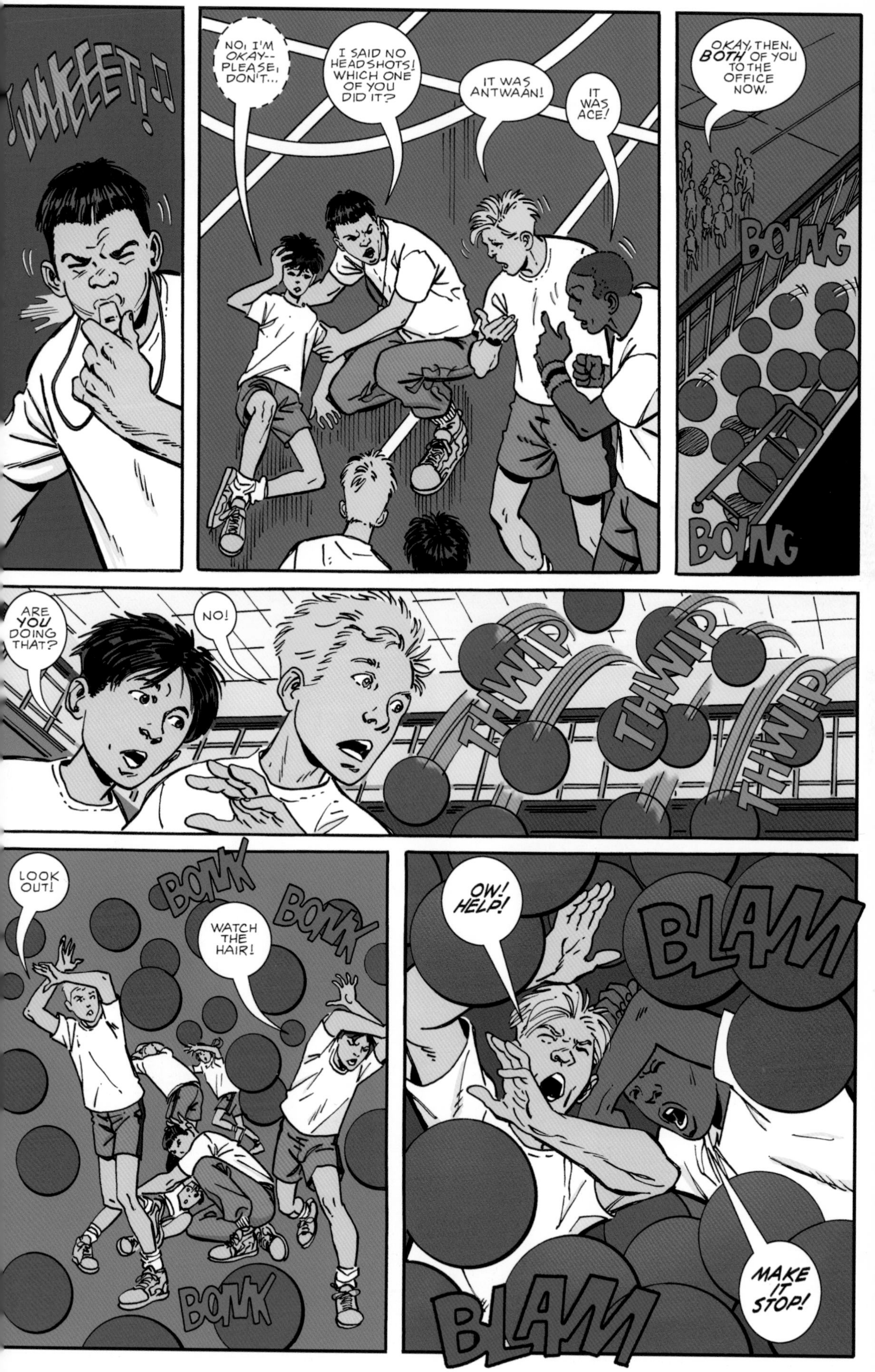
♪WHEEET!♫
NO, I'M OKAY-- PLEASE, DON'T...
I SAID NO HEADSHOTS! WHICH ONE OF YOU DID IT?
IT WAS ANTWAAN!
IT WAS ACE!
OKAY, THEN. BOTH OF YOU TO THE OFFICE NOW.
BOING
BOING
ARE YOU DOING THAT?
NO!
THWIP
THWIP
THWIP
LOOK OUT!
BONK
BONK
WATCH THE HAIR!
BONK
OW! HELP!
BLAM
MAKE IT STOP!
BLAM

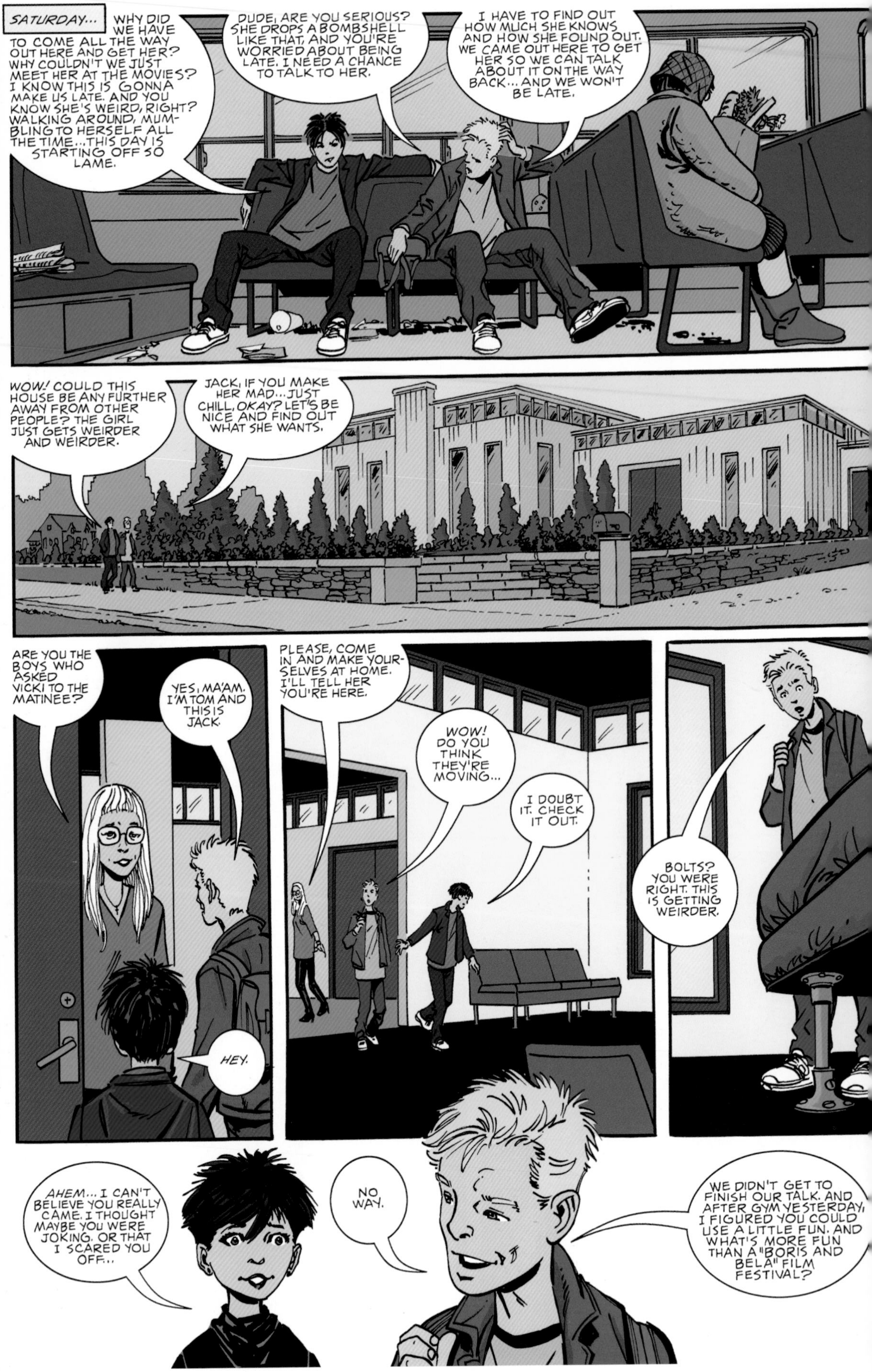
SATURDAY...
WHY DID WE HAVE TO COME ALL THE WAY OUT HERE AND GET HER? WHY COULDN'T WE JUST MEET HER AT THE MOVIES? I KNOW THIS IS GONNA MAKE US LATE. AND YOU KNOW SHE'S WEIRD, RIGHT? WALKING AROUND, MUMBLING TO HERSELF ALL THE TIME... THIS DAY IS STARTING OFF SO LAME.
DUDE, ARE YOU SERIOUS? SHE DROPS A BOMBSHELL LIKE THAT, AND YOU'RE WORRIED ABOUT BEING LATE. I NEED A CHANCE TO TALK TO HER.
I HAVE TO FIND OUT HOW MUCH SHE KNOWS AND HOW SHE FOUND OUT. WE CAME OUT HERE TO GET HER SO WE CAN TALK ABOUT IT ON THE WAY BACK... AND WE WON'T BE LATE.
WOW! COULD THIS HOUSE BE ANY FURTHER AWAY FROM OTHER PEOPLE? THE GIRL JUST GETS WEIRDER AND WEIRDER.
JACK, IF YOU MAKE HER MAD... JUST CHILL, OKAY? LET'S BE NICE AND FIND OUT WHAT SHE WANTS.
ARE YOU THE BOYS WHO ASKED VICKI TO THE MATINEE?
YES, MA'AM. I'M TOM AND THIS IS JACK.
HEY.
PLEASE, COME IN AND MAKE YOURSELVES AT HOME. I'LL TELL HER YOU'RE HERE.
WOW! DO YOU THINK THEY'RE MOVING...
I DOUBT IT. CHECK IT OUT.
BOLTS? YOU WERE RIGHT. THIS IS GETTING WEIRDER.
AHEM... I CAN'T BELIEVE YOU REALLY CAME. I THOUGHT MAYBE YOU WERE JOKING. OR THAT I SCARED YOU OFF...
NO WAY.
WE DIDN'T GET TO FINISH OUR TALK. AND AFTER GYM YESTERDAY, I FIGURED YOU COULD USE A LITTLE FUN. AND WHAT'S MORE FUN THAN A "BORIS AND BELA" FILM FESTIVAL?

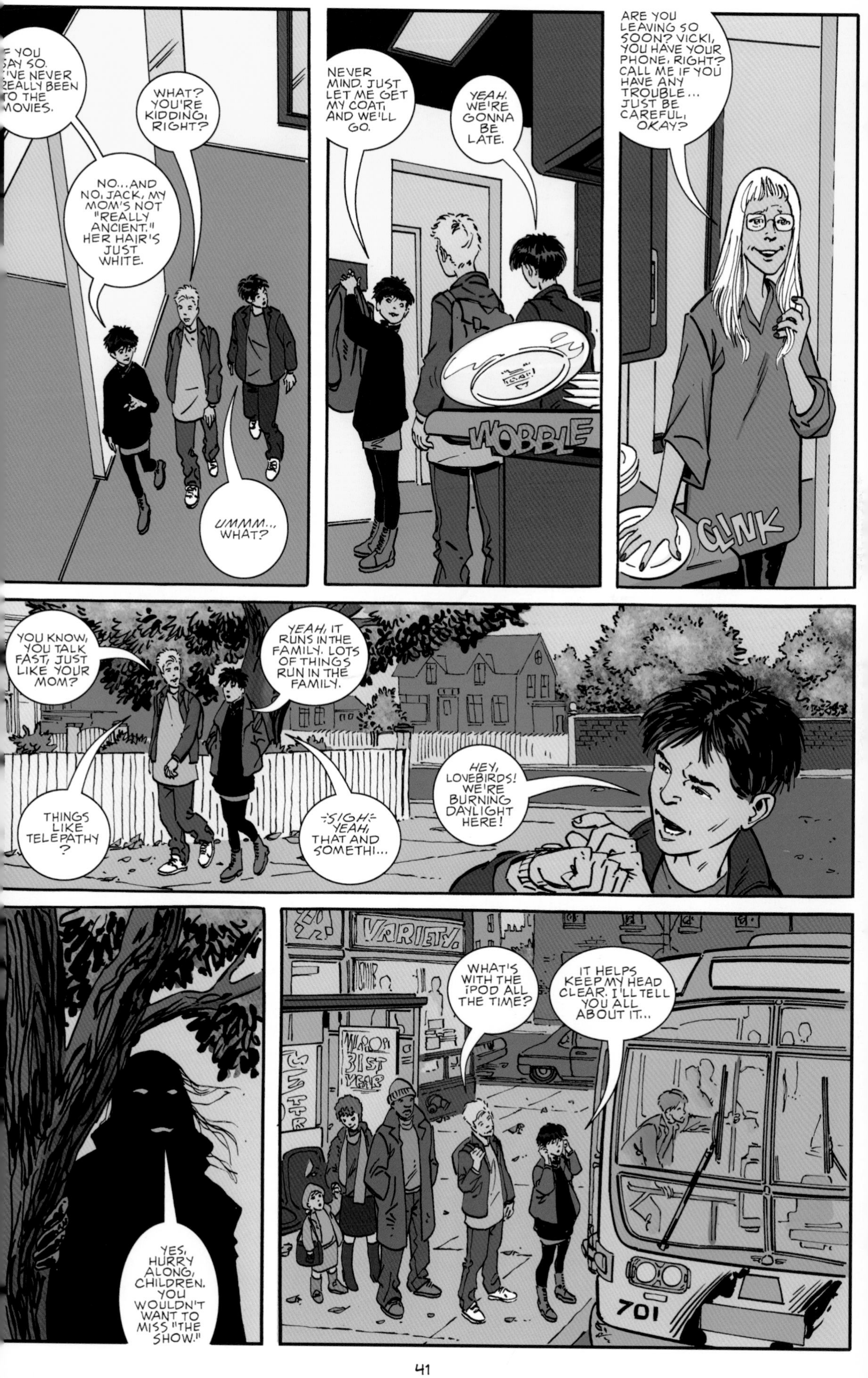
F YOU SAY SO. I'VE NEVER REALLY BEEN TO THE MOVIES.
WHAT? YOU'RE KIDDING, RIGHT?
NO... AND NO, JACK, MY MOM'S NOT "REALLY ANCIENT." HER HAIR'S JUST WHITE.
UMMM... WHAT?
NEVER MIND. JUST LET ME GET MY COAT, AND WE'LL GO.
YEAH. WE'RE GONNA BE LATE.
WOBBLE
ARE YOU LEAVING SO SOON? VICKI, YOU HAVE YOUR PHONE, RIGHT? CALL ME IF YOU HAVE ANY TROUBLE... JUST BE CAREFUL, OKAY?
CLINK
YOU KNOW, YOU TALK FAST, JUST LIKE YOUR MOM?
YEAH, IT RUNS IN THE FAMILY. LOTS OF THINGS RUN IN THE FAMILY.
THINGS LIKE TELEPATHY?
SIGH YEAH, THAT AND SOMETHI...
HEY, LOVEBIRDS! WE'RE BURNING DAYLIGHT HERE!
YES, HURRY ALONG, CHILDREN. YOU WOULDN'T WANT TO MISS "THE SHOW."
VARIETY
31 ST YEAR
WHAT'S WITH THE iPOD ALL THE TIME?
IT HELPS KEEP MY HEAD CLEAR. I'LL TELL YOU ALL ABOUT IT...
701

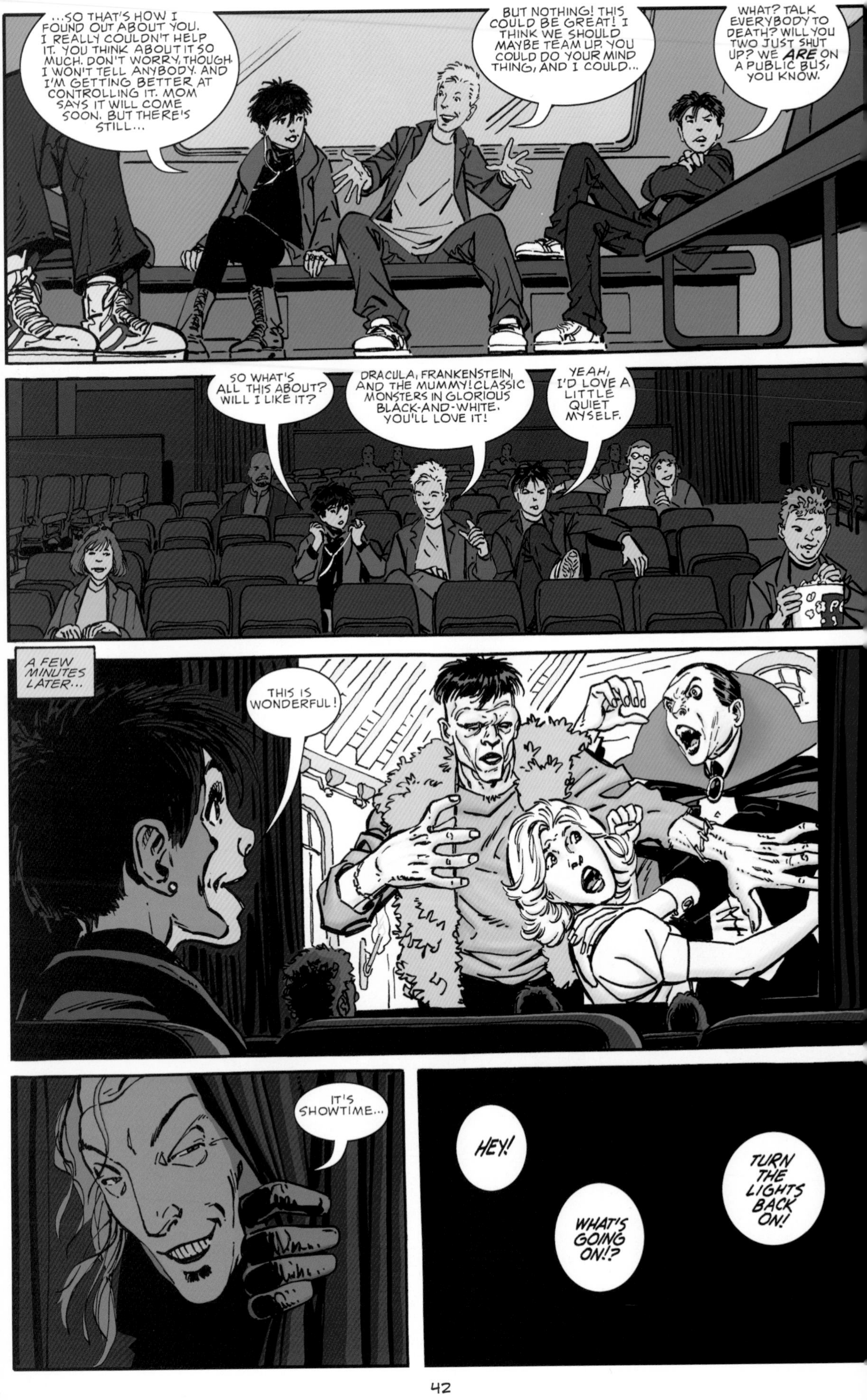
...SO THAT'S HOW I FOUND OUT ABOUT YOU. I REALLY COULDN'T HELP IT. YOU THINK ABOUT IT SO MUCH. DON'T WORRY, THOUGH. I WON'T TELL ANYBODY. AND I'M GETTING BETTER AT CONTROLLING IT. MOM SAYS IT WILL COME SOON. BUT THERE'S STILL...
BUT NOTHING! THIS COULD BE GREAT! I THINK WE SHOULD MAYBE TEAM UP. YOU COULD DO YOUR MIND THING, AND I COULD...
WHAT? TALK EVERYBODY TO DEATH? WILL YOU TWO JUST SHUT UP? WE ARE ON A PUBLIC BUS, YOU KNOW.
SO WHAT'S ALL THIS ABOUT? WILL I LIKE IT?
DRACULA, FRANKENSTEIN, AND THE MUMMY! CLASSIC MONSTERS IN GLORIOUS BLACK-AND-WHITE. YOU'LL LOVE IT!
YEAH, I'D LOVE A LITTLE QUIET MYSELF.
A FEW MINUTES LATER...
THIS IS WONDERFUL!
IT'S SHOWTIME...
HEY!
WHAT'S GOING ON!?
TURN THE LIGHTS BACK ON!

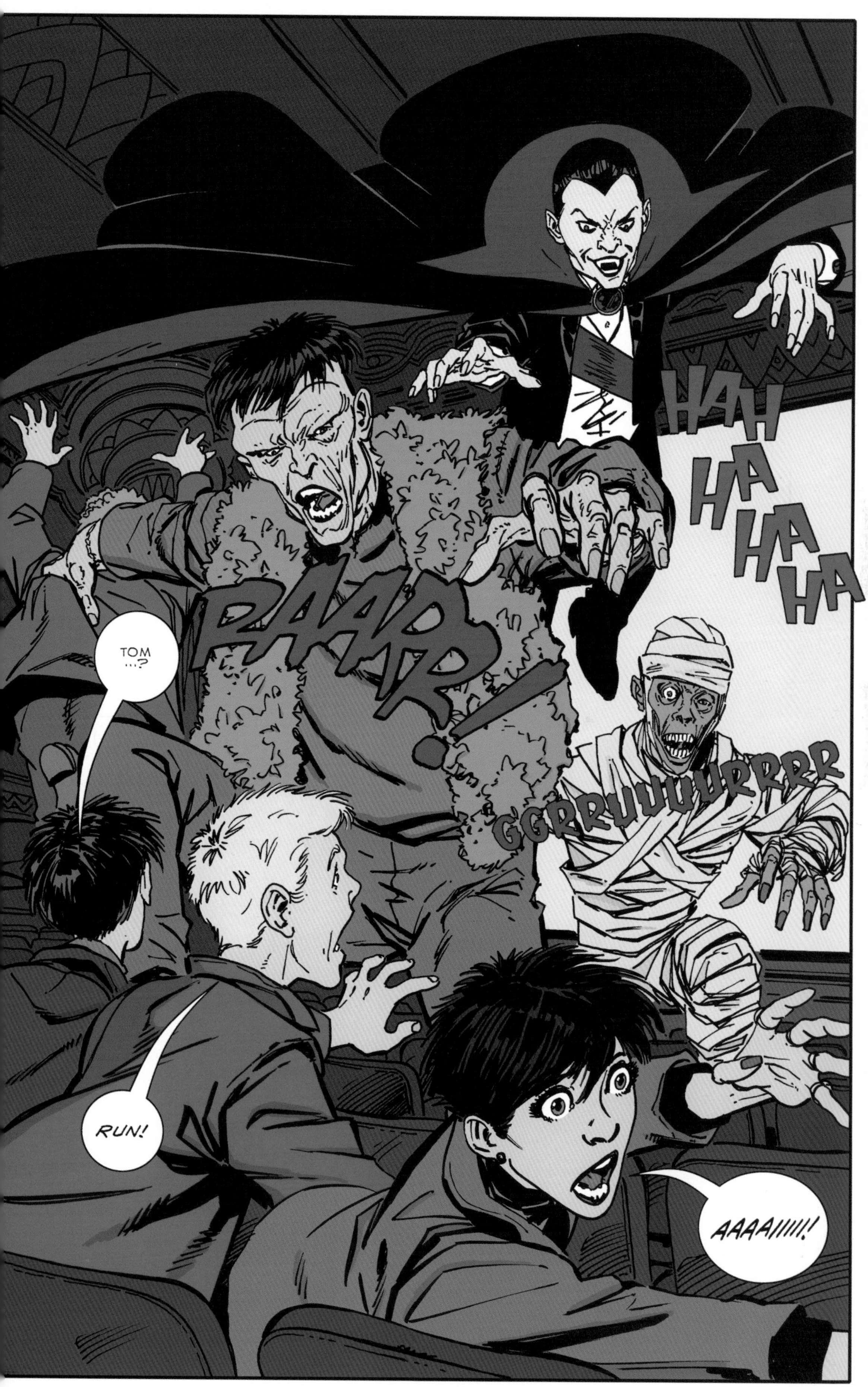
HAH HA HA HA HA
RAARR!
GGRRUUUURRRR
TOM ...?
RUN!
AAAAI!!!!!

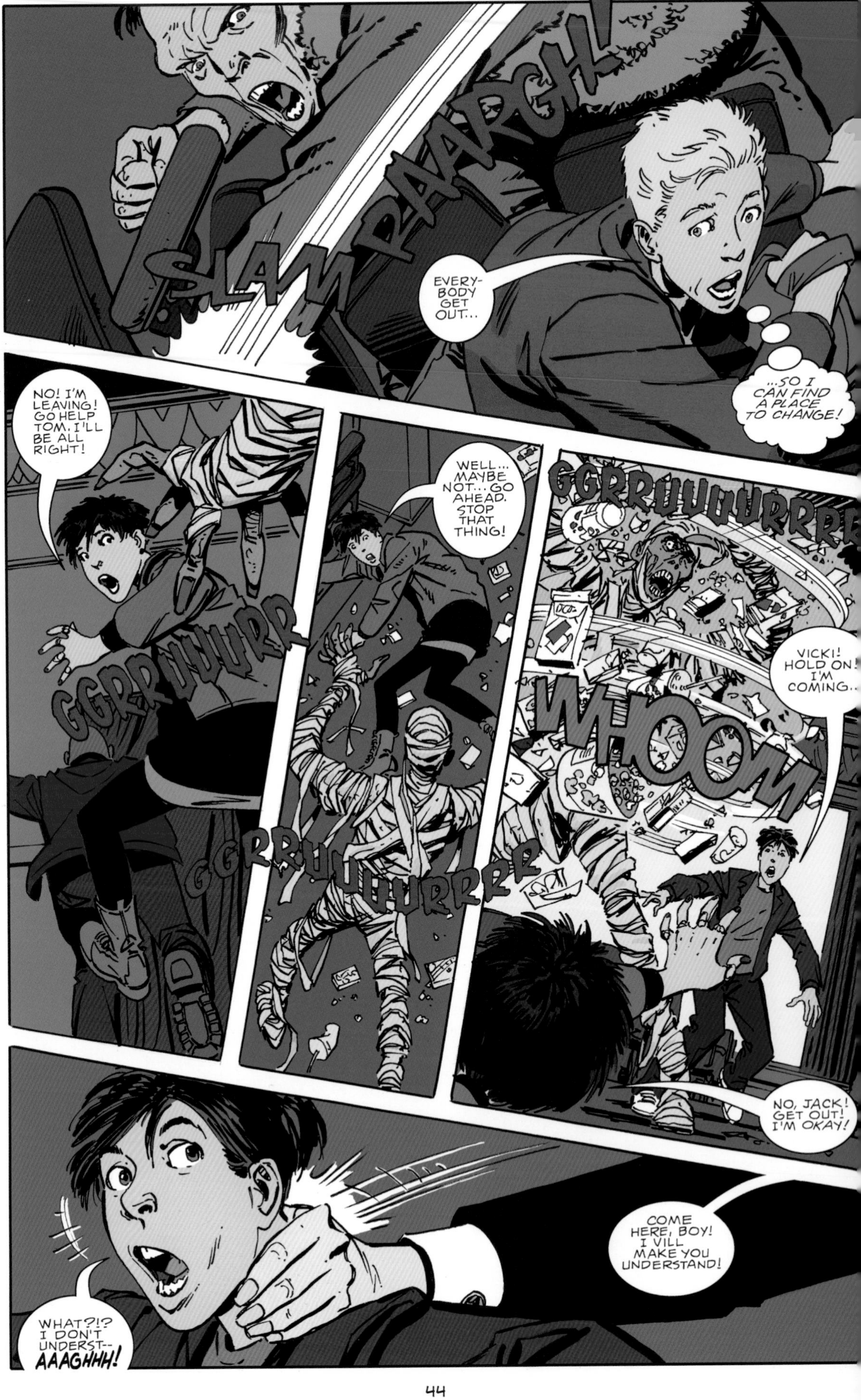
SLAM
RAAARGH!
EVERY-BODY GET OUT...
...SO I CAN FIND A PLACE TO CHANGE!
NO! I'M LEAVING! GO HELP TOM. I'LL BE ALL RIGHT!
GGRRUUURR
WELL... MAYBE NOT... GO AHEAD. STOP THAT THING!
GGRRUUUURRRR
GGRRUUUUURRRR
VICKI! HOLD ON! I'M COMING...
WHOOM
NO, JACK! GET OUT! I'M OKAY!
COME HERE, BOY! I VILL MAKE YOU UNDERSTAND!
WHAT?!? I DON'T UNDERST-- AAAGHHH!

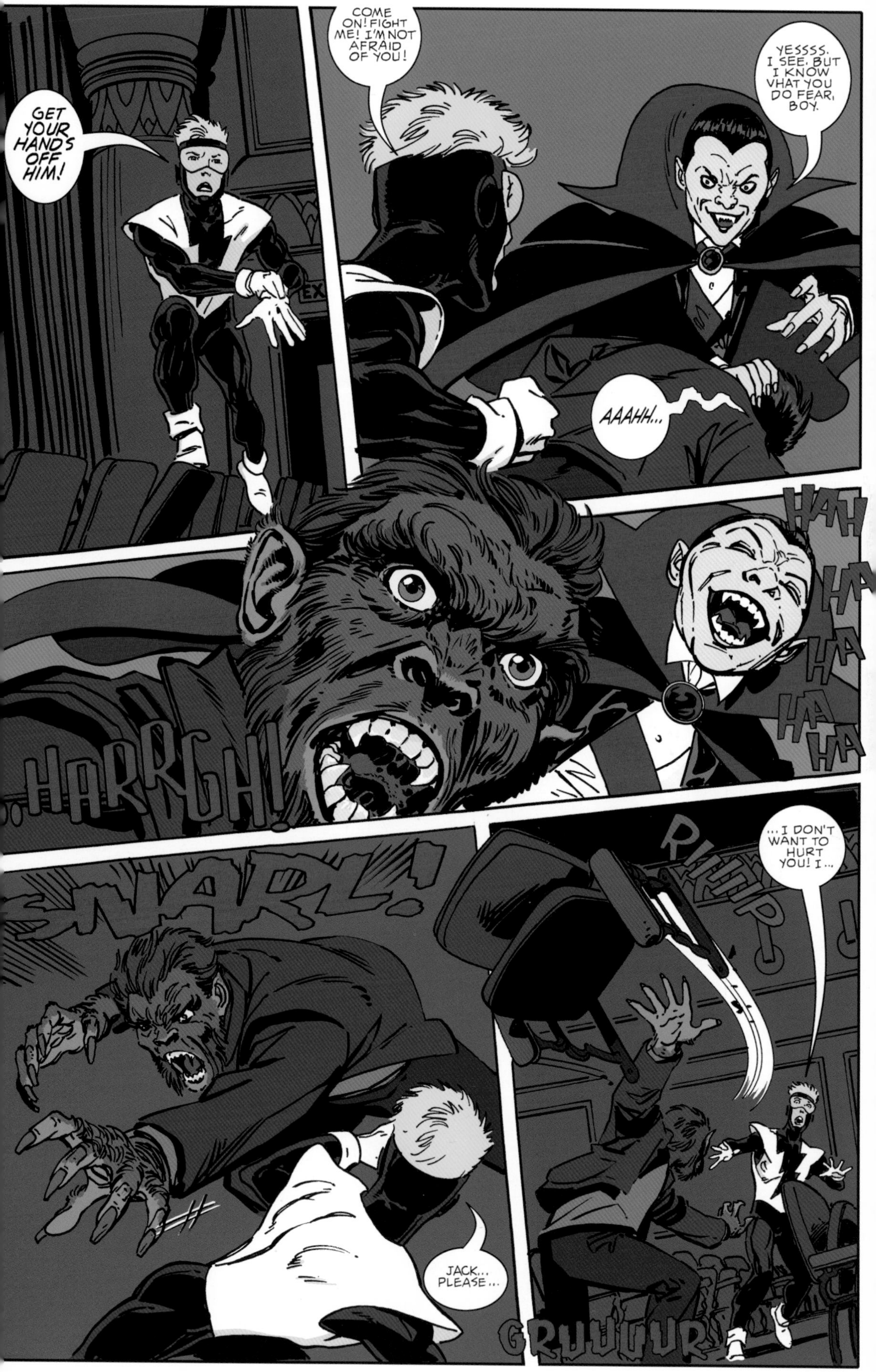
GET YOUR HAND'S OFF HIM!
COME ON! FIGHT ME! I'M NOT AFRAID OF YOU!
YESSSS. I SEE, BUT I KNOW VHAT YOU DO FEAR, BOY.
AAAHH...
HAH HA HA HA HA HA HA
HARRGH!
SNARL!
RHUMP
...I DON'T WANT TO HURT YOU! I...
JACK... PLEASE...
GRUUUUR

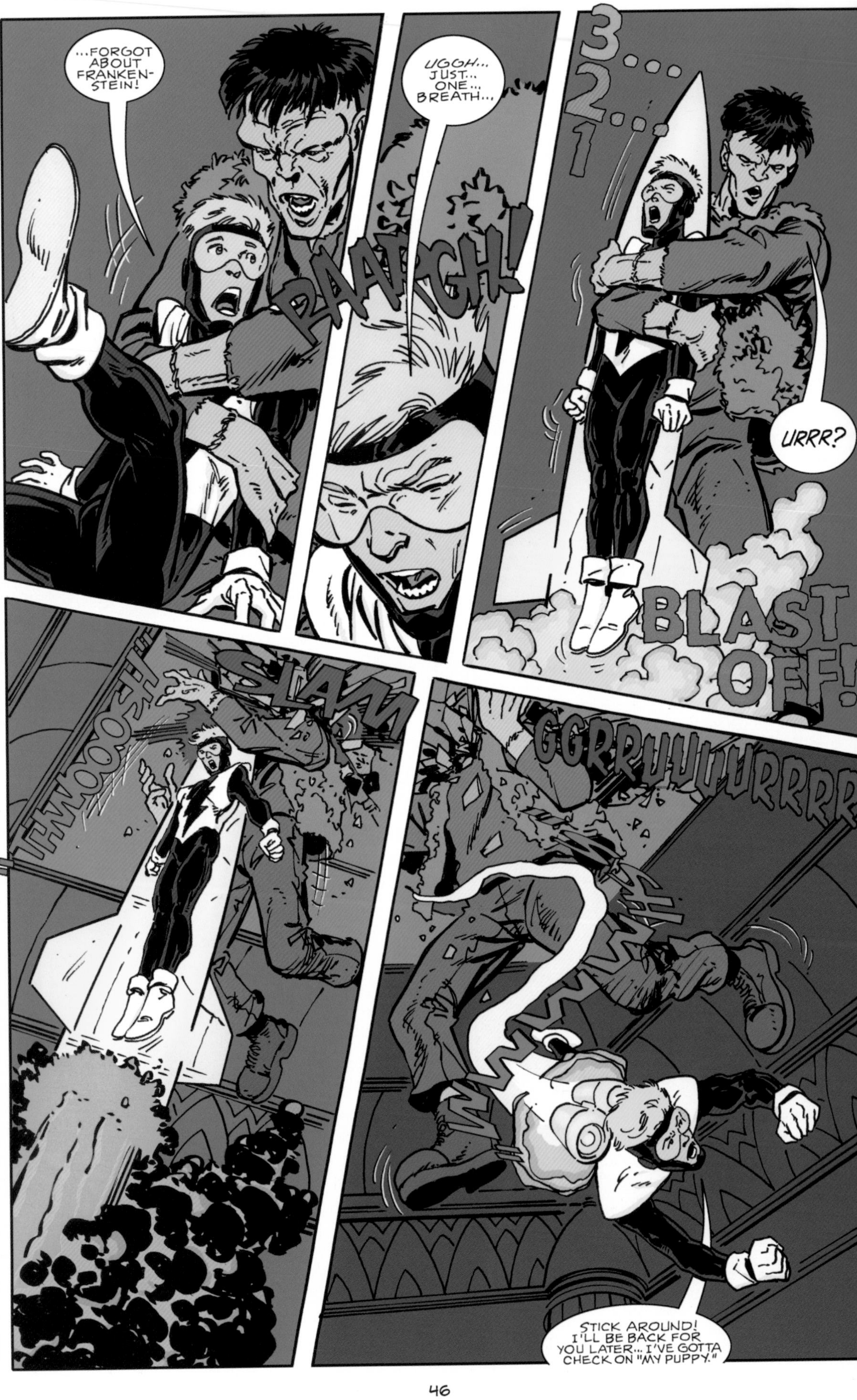
...FORGOT ABOUT FRANKEN-STEIN!
RAAARGH!
UGGH... JUST... ONE... BREATH...
3... 2... 1
URRR?
BLAST OFF!
THWOOOSH
SLAM
GGRRUUUUURRRR
STICK AROUND! I'LL BE BACK FOR YOU LATER... I'VE GOTTA CHECK ON "MY PUPPY."

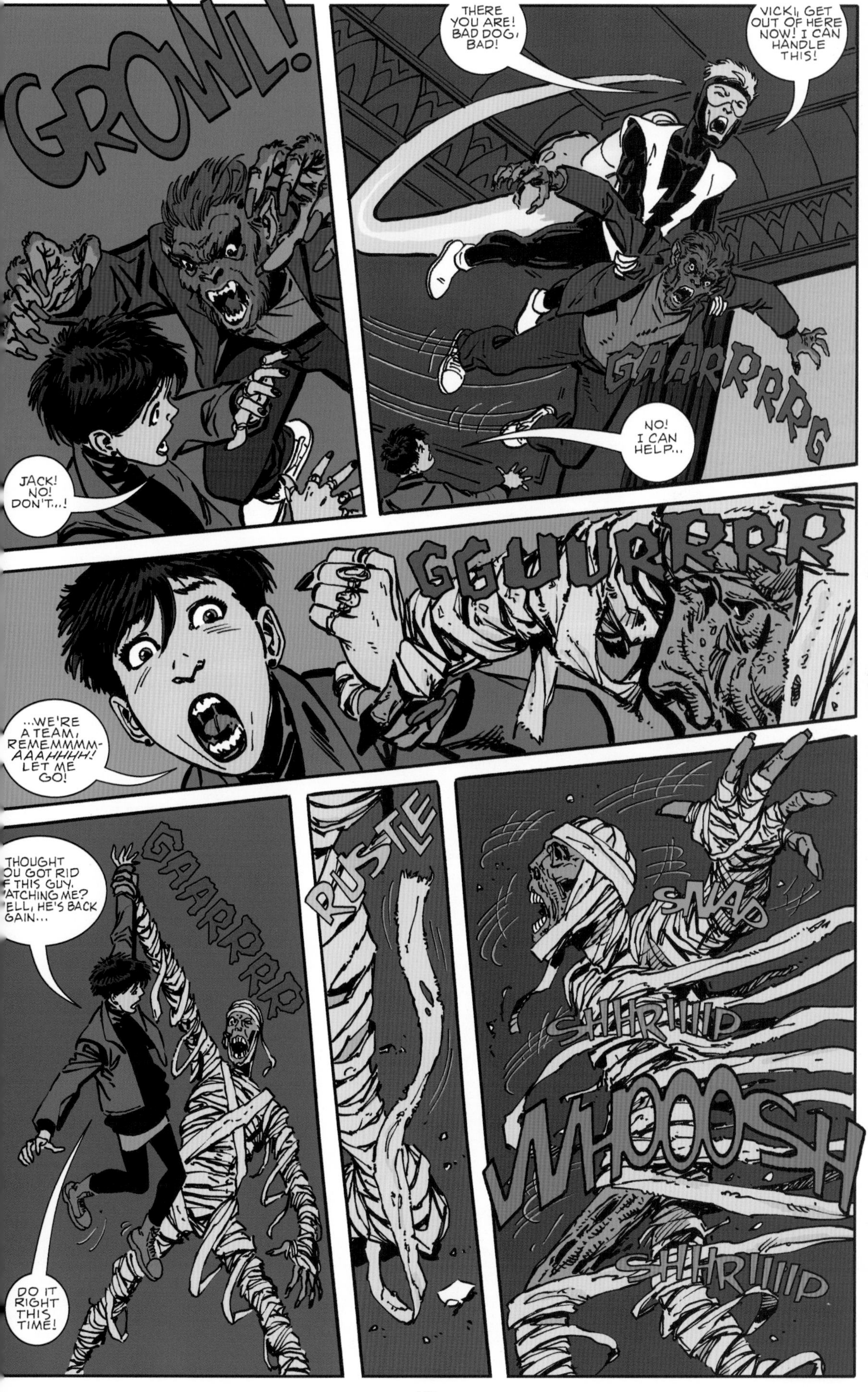
GROWL!
JACK! NO! DON'T...!
THERE YOU ARE! BAD DOG, BAD!
VICKI, GET OUT OF HERE NOW! I CAN HANDLE THIS!
GAARRRRG
NO! I CAN HELP...
GGUURRRR
...WE'RE A TEAM, REMEMMMM-AAAHHHH! LET ME GO!
THOUGHT OU GOT RID F THIS GUY, ATCHING ME? ELL, HE'S BACK GAIN...
GAARRRRR
DO IT RIGHT THIS TIME!
RUSTLE
SNAP
SHHRIIIP
WHOOOSH
SHHRIIIP

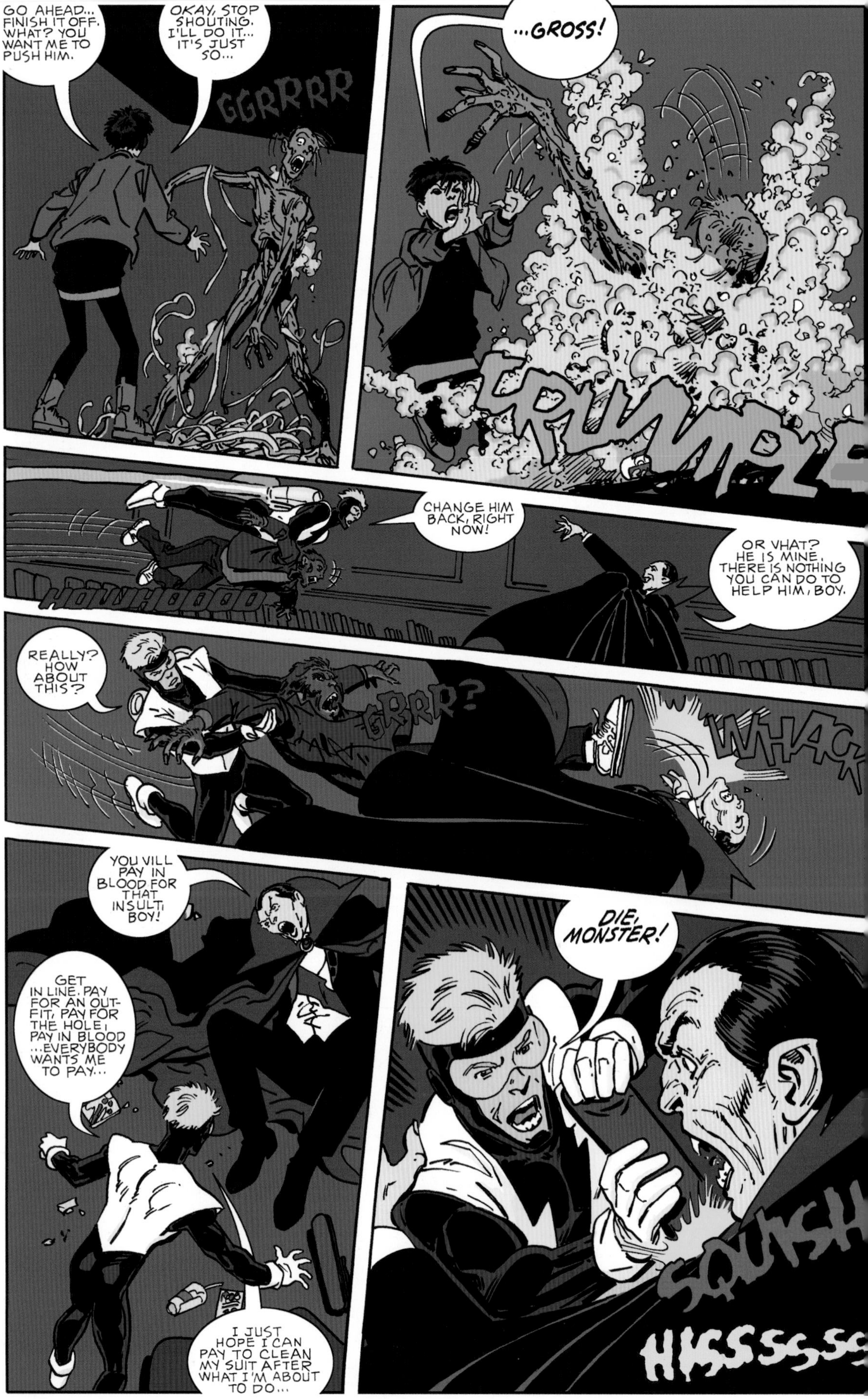

GO AHEAD... FINISH IT OFF. WHAT? YOU WANT ME TO PUSH HIM.
OKAY, STOP SHOUTING. I'LL DO IT... IT'S JUST SO...
GGRRRR
...GROSS!
CRUMPLE
CHANGE HIM BACK, RIGHT NOW!
HOWHOOOO
OR VHAT? HE IS MINE. THERE IS NOTHING YOU CAN DO TO HELP HIM, BOY.
REALLY? HOW ABOUT THIS?
GRRR?
WHACK
YOU VILL PAY IN BLOOD FOR THAT INSULT, BOY!
GET IN LINE. PAY FOR AN OUTFIT, PAY FOR THE HOLE, PAY IN BLOOD ...EVERYBODY WANTS ME TO PAY...
I JUST HOPE I CAN PAY TO CLEAN MY SUIT AFTER WHAT I'M ABOUT TO DO...
DIE, MONSTER!
SQUISH
HISSSSSS

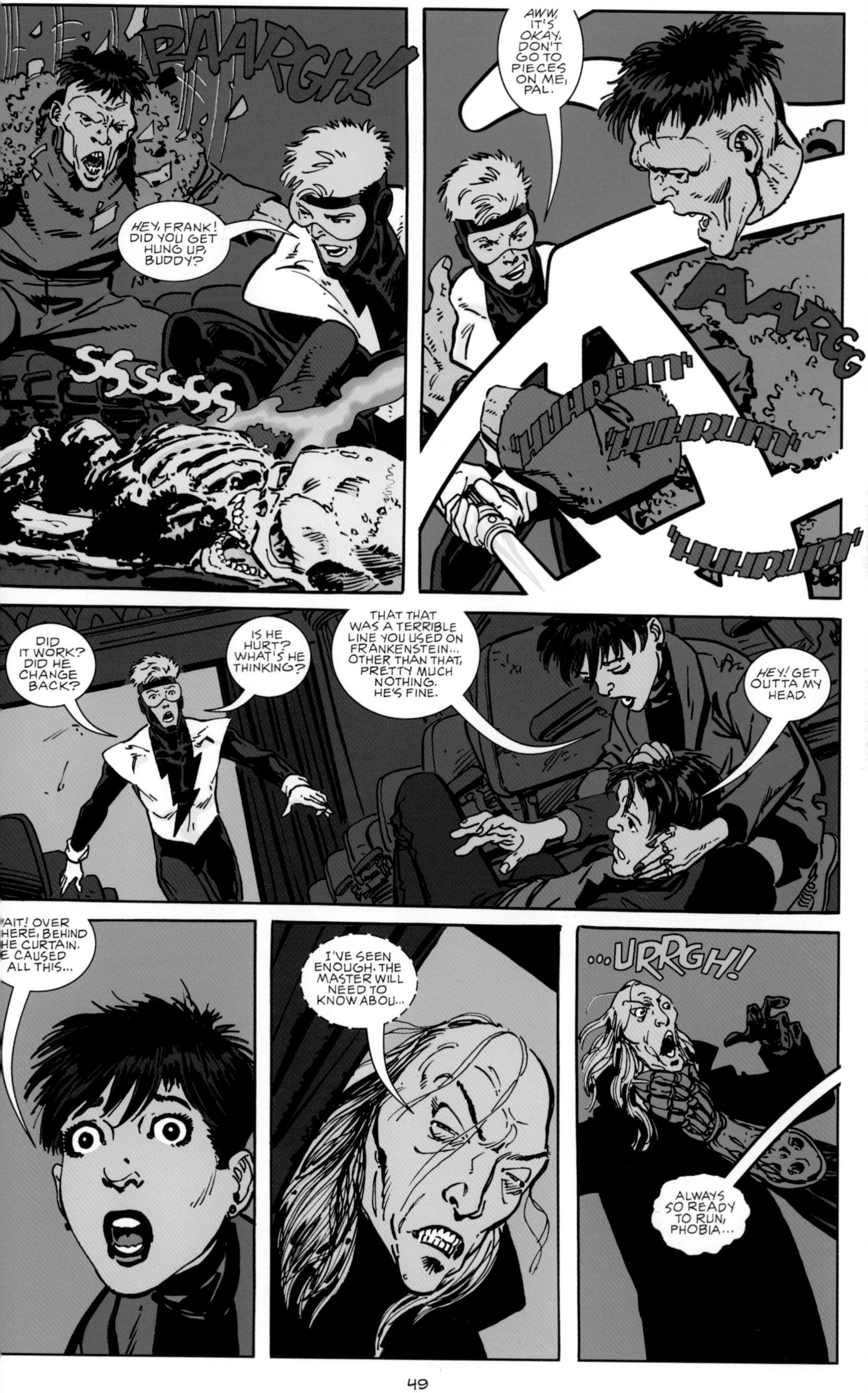
RAARGH!
HEY, FRANK! DID YOU GET HUNG UP, BUDDY?
SSSSSS
AWW, IT'S OKAY. DON'T GO TO PIECES ON ME, PAL.
AARGG
"HUHRUM"
"HUHRUM"
"HUHRUM"
DID IT WORK? DID HE CHANGE BACK?
IS HE HURT? WHAT'S HE THINKING?
THAT THAT WAS A TERRIBLE LINE YOU USED ON FRANKENSTEIN... OTHER THAN THAT, PRETTY MUCH NOTHING. HE'S FINE.
HEY! GET OUTTA MY HEAD.
AIT! OVER HERE, BEHIND HE CURTAIN. E CAUSED ALL THIS...
I'VE SEEN ENOUGH. THE MASTER WILL NEED TO KNOW ABOU...
...URRGH!
ALWAYS SO READY TO RUN, PHOBIA...

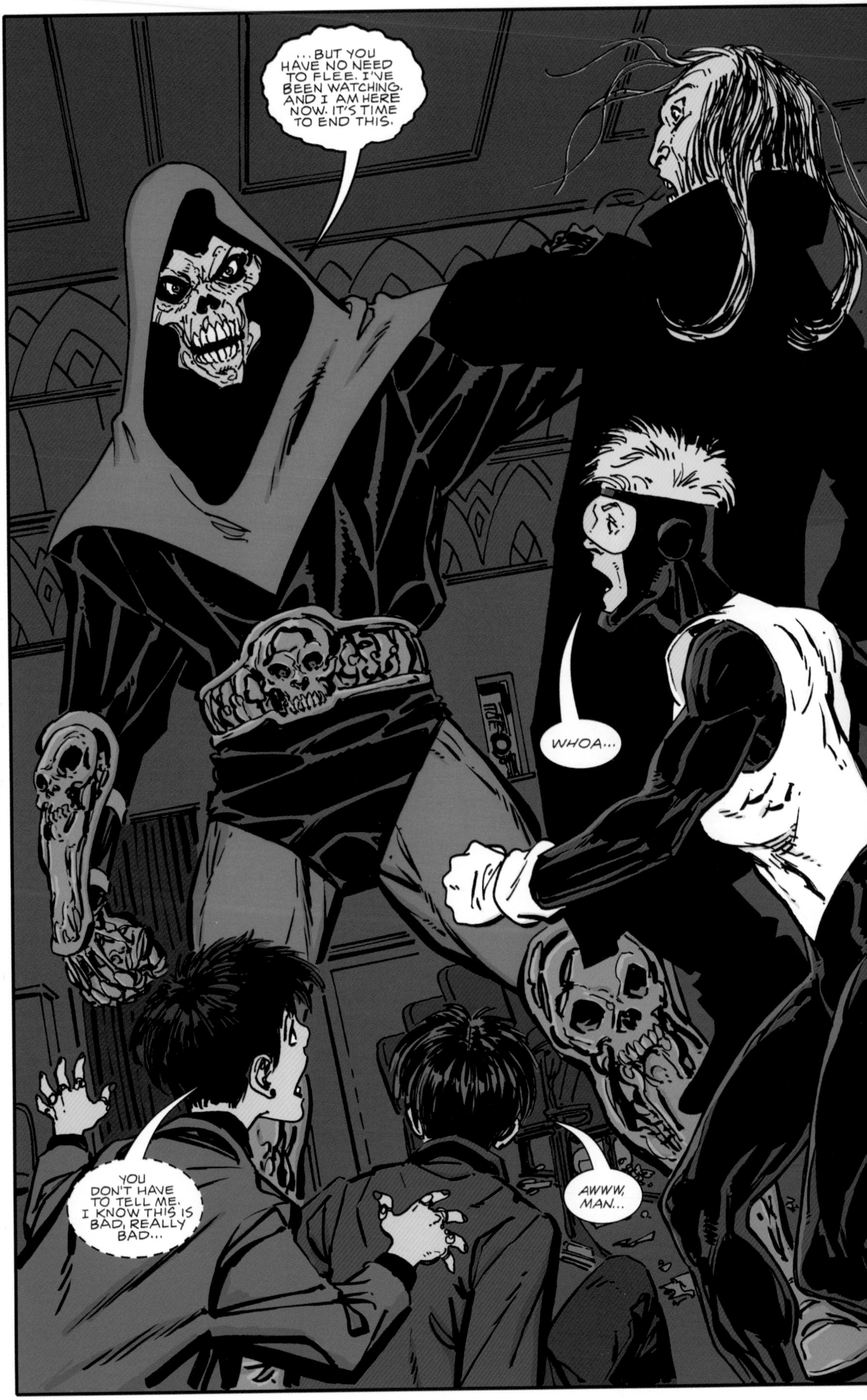

...BUT YOU HAVE NO NEED TO FLEE. I'VE BEEN WATCHING. AND I AM HERE NOW. IT'S TIME TO END THIS.
WHOA...
YOU DON'T HAVE TO TELL ME. I KNOW THIS IS BAD, REALLY BAD...
AWWW, MAN...

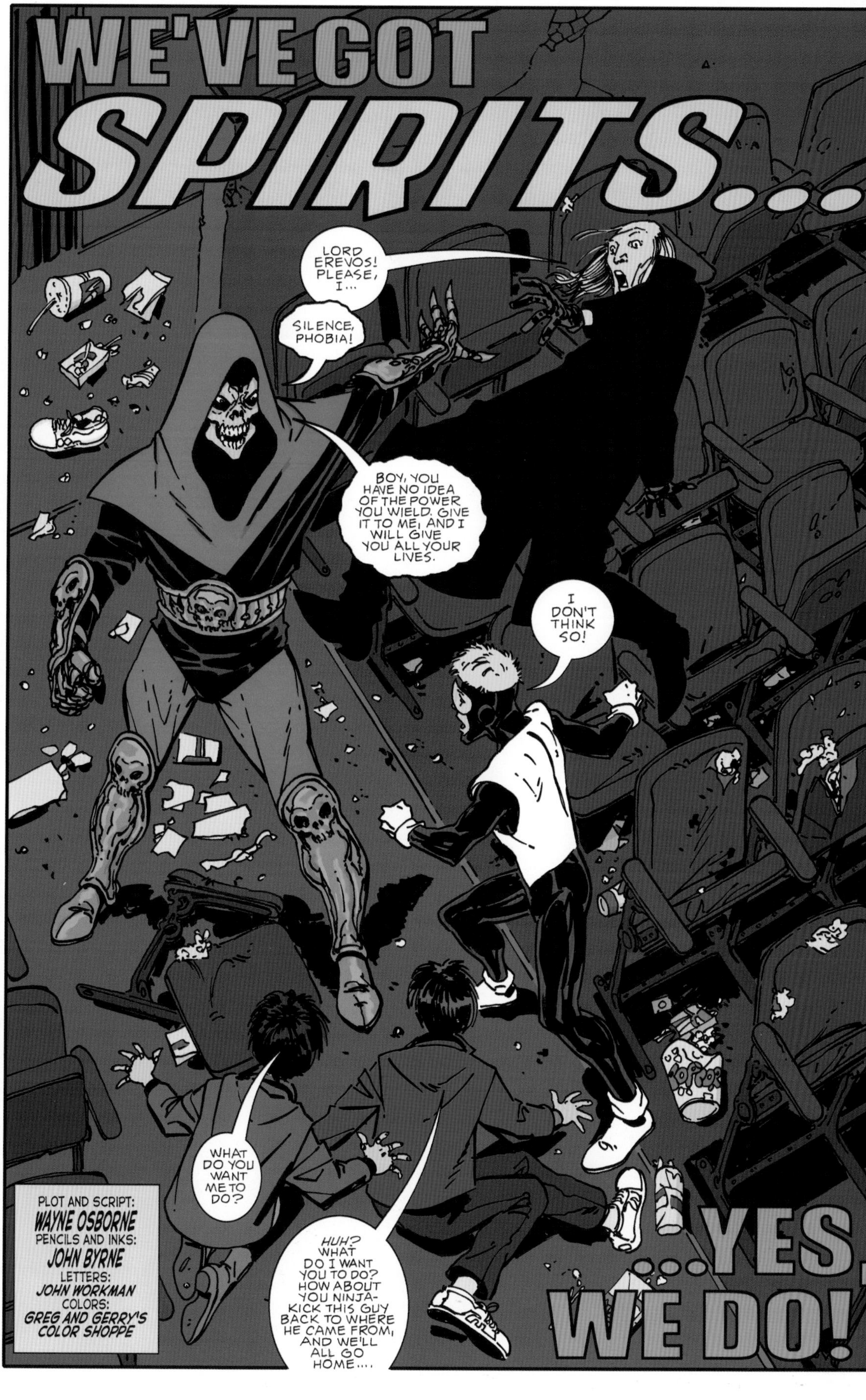
WE'VE GOT SPIRITS...
LORD EREVOS! PLEASE, I...
SILENCE, PHOBIA!
BOY, YOU HAVE NO IDEA OF THE POWER YOU WIELD. GIVE IT TO ME, AND I WILL GIVE YOU ALL YOUR LIVES.
I DON'T THINK SO!
WHAT DO YOU WANT ME TO DO?
HUH? WHAT DO I WANT YOU TO DO? HOW ABOUT YOU NINJA-KICK THIS GUY BACK TO WHERE HE CAME FROM, AND WE'LL ALL GO HOME....
...YES, WE DO!
PLOT AND SCRIPT: WAYNE OSBORNE
PENCILS AND INKS: JOHN BYRNE
LETTERS: JOHN WORKMAN
COLORS: GREG AND GERRY'S COLOR SHOPPE

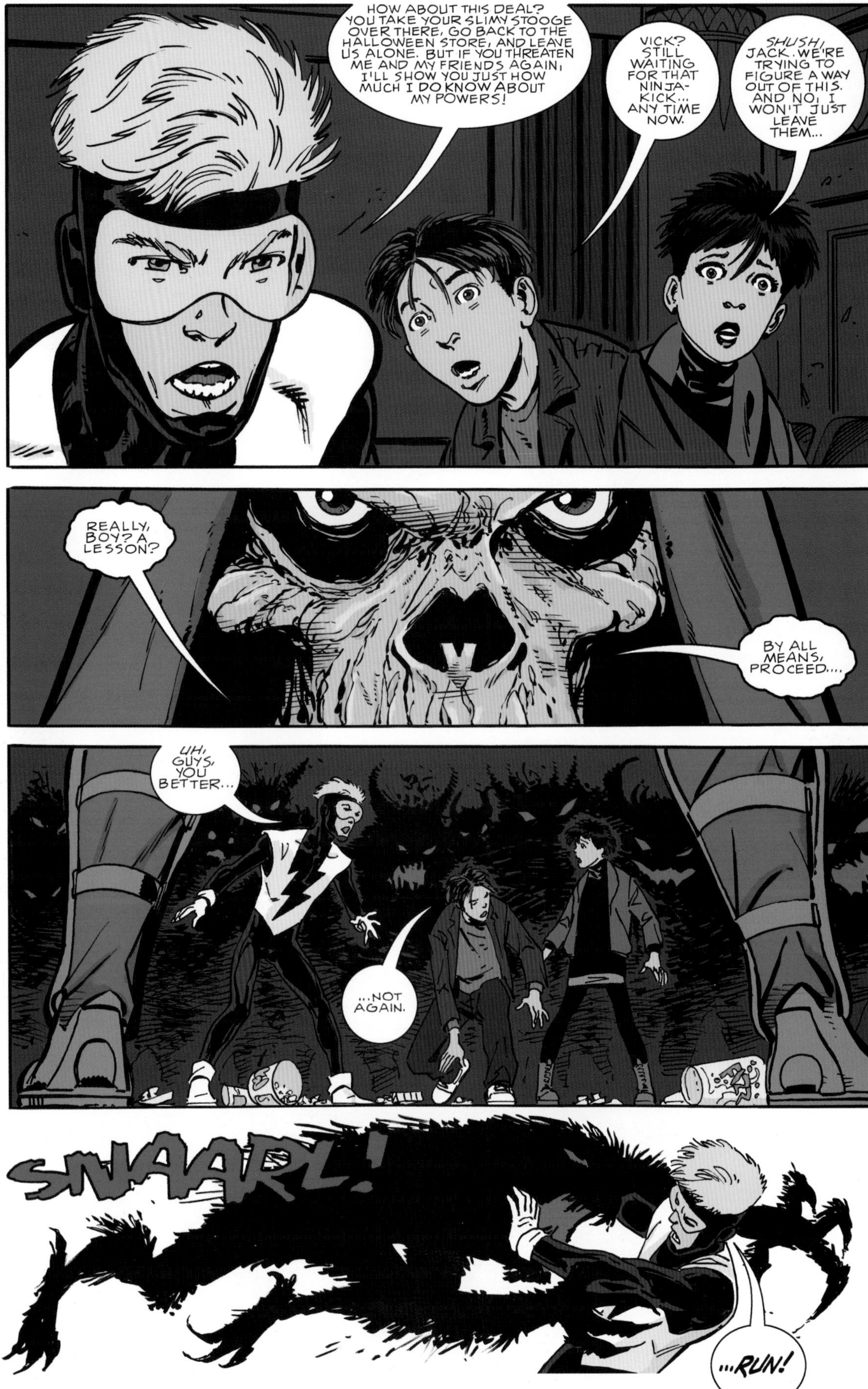

HOW ABOUT THIS DEAL? YOU TAKE YOUR SLIMY STOOGE OVER THERE, GO BACK TO THE HALLOWEEN STORE, AND LEAVE US ALONE. BUT IF YOU THREATEN ME AND MY FRIENDS AGAIN, I'LL SHOW YOU JUST HOW MUCH I DO KNOW ABOUT MY POWERS!
VICK? STILL WAITING FOR THAT NINJA-KICK... ANY TIME NOW.
SHUSH, JACK. WE'RE TRYING TO FIGURE A WAY OUT OF THIS. AND NO, I WON'T JUST LEAVE THEM...
REALLY, BOY? A LESSON?
BY ALL MEANS, PROCEED....
UH, GUYS, YOU BETTER...
...NOT AGAIN.
SNAARL!
...RUN!

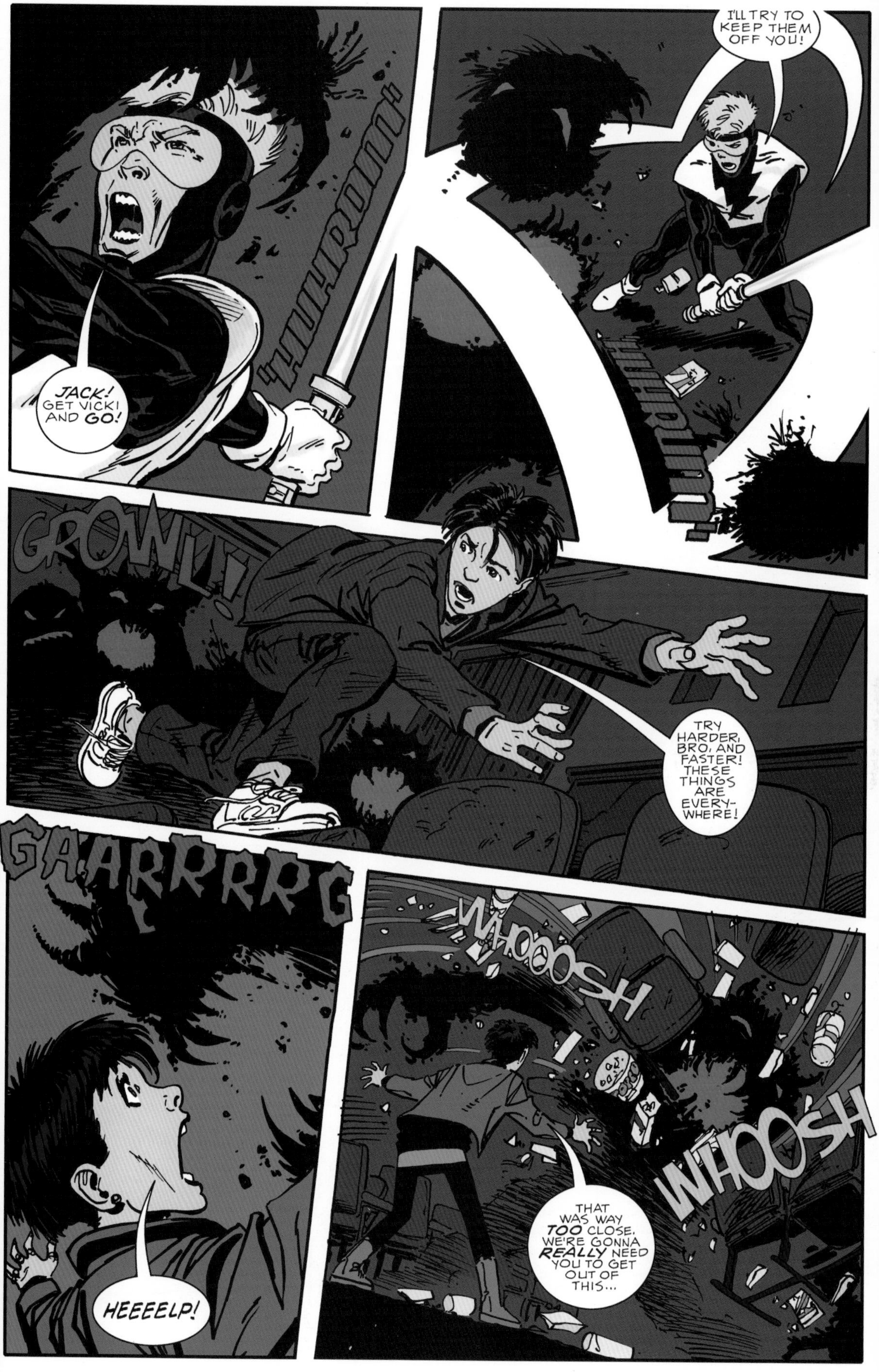
JACK! GET VICKI AND GO!
I'LL TRY TO KEEP THEM OFF YOU!
GROWL!!
TRY HARDER, BRO, AND FASTER! THESE THINGS ARE EVERY-WHERE!
GAARRRRG
HEEEELP!
WHOOOSH
WHOOSH
THAT WAS WAY TOO CLOSE. WE'RE GONNA REALLY NEED YOU TO GET OUT OF THIS...

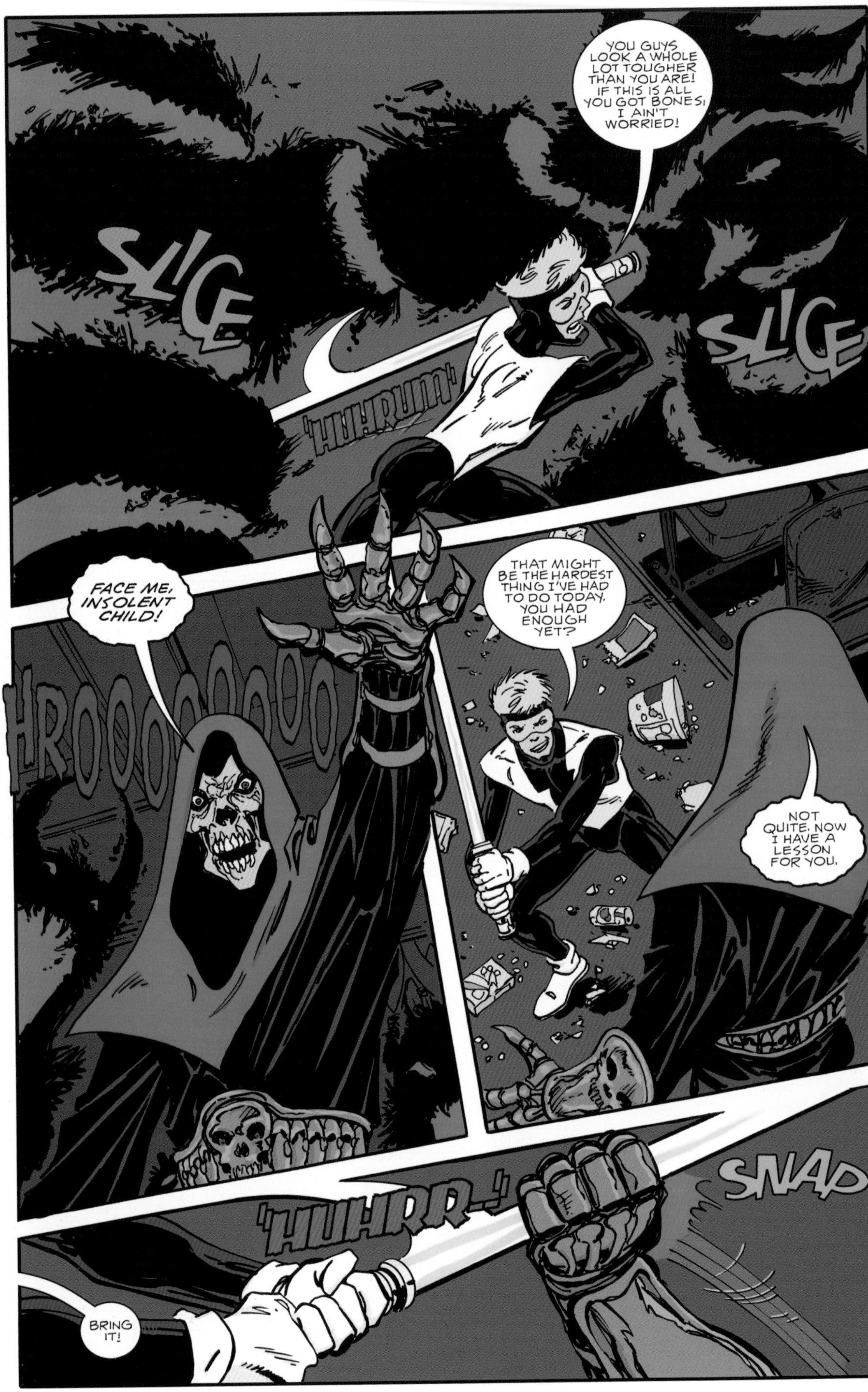

YOU GUYS LOOK A WHOLE LOT TOUGHER THAN YOU ARE! IF THIS IS ALL YOU GOT BONES, I AIN'T WORRIED!
SLICE
SLICE
HUHRUMM
FACE ME, INSOLENT CHILD!
HROOOOOOOO
THAT MIGHT BE THE HARDEST THING I'VE HAD TO DO TODAY. YOU HAD ENOUGH YET?
NOT QUITE. NOW I HAVE A LESSON FOR YOU.
SNAP
HUHRR
BRING IT!

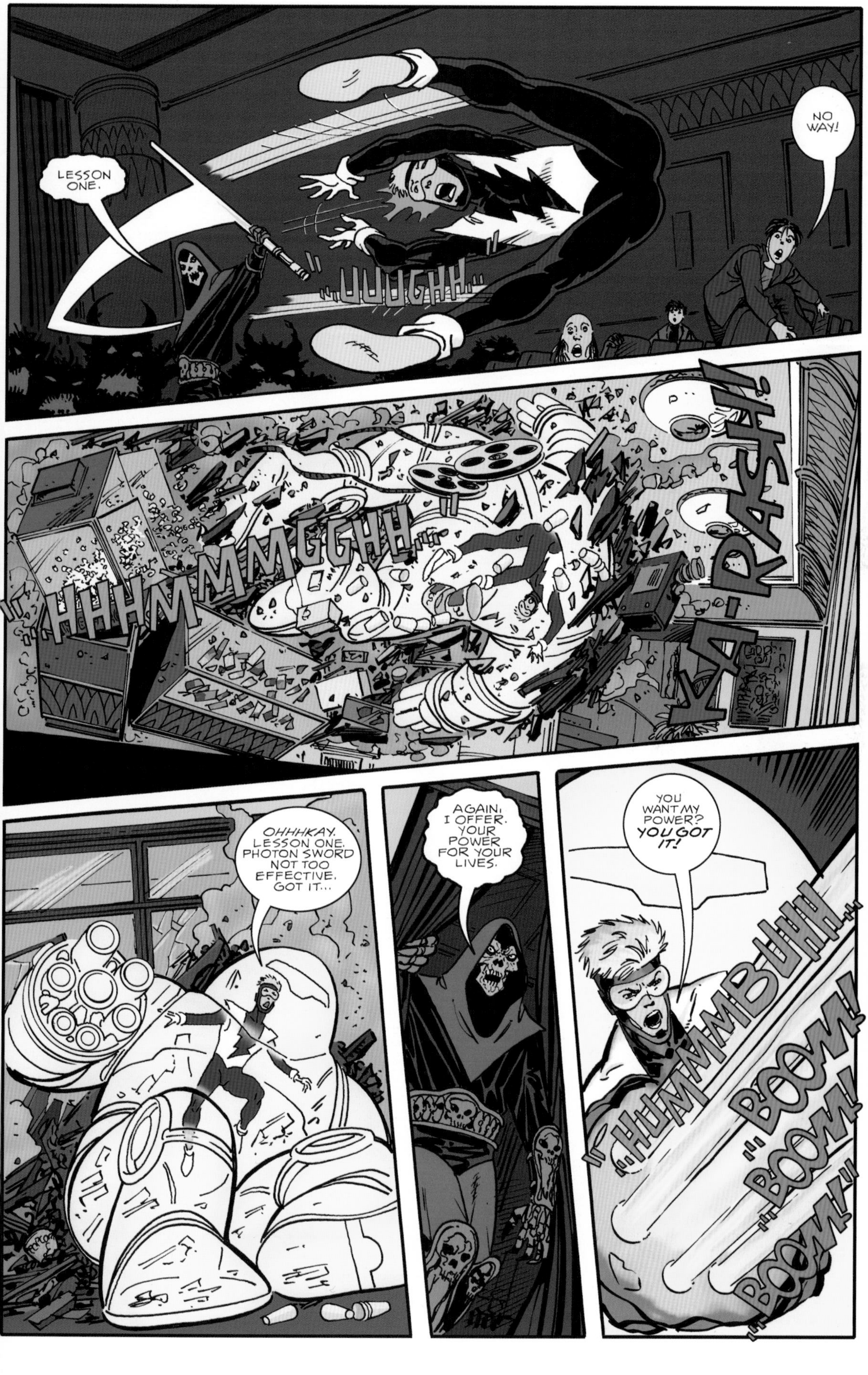
LESSON ONE.
NO WAY!
"UUUGHH"
"HHHMMMMGGHH"
KA-RASH!
OHHHKAY. LESSON ONE. PHOTON SWORD NOT TOO EFFECTIVE. GOT IT...
AGAIN, I OFFER. YOUR POWER FOR YOUR LIVES.
YOU WANT MY POWER? YOU GOT IT!
"HUMMMBUHH"
"BOOM!"
"BOOM!"
"BOOM!"

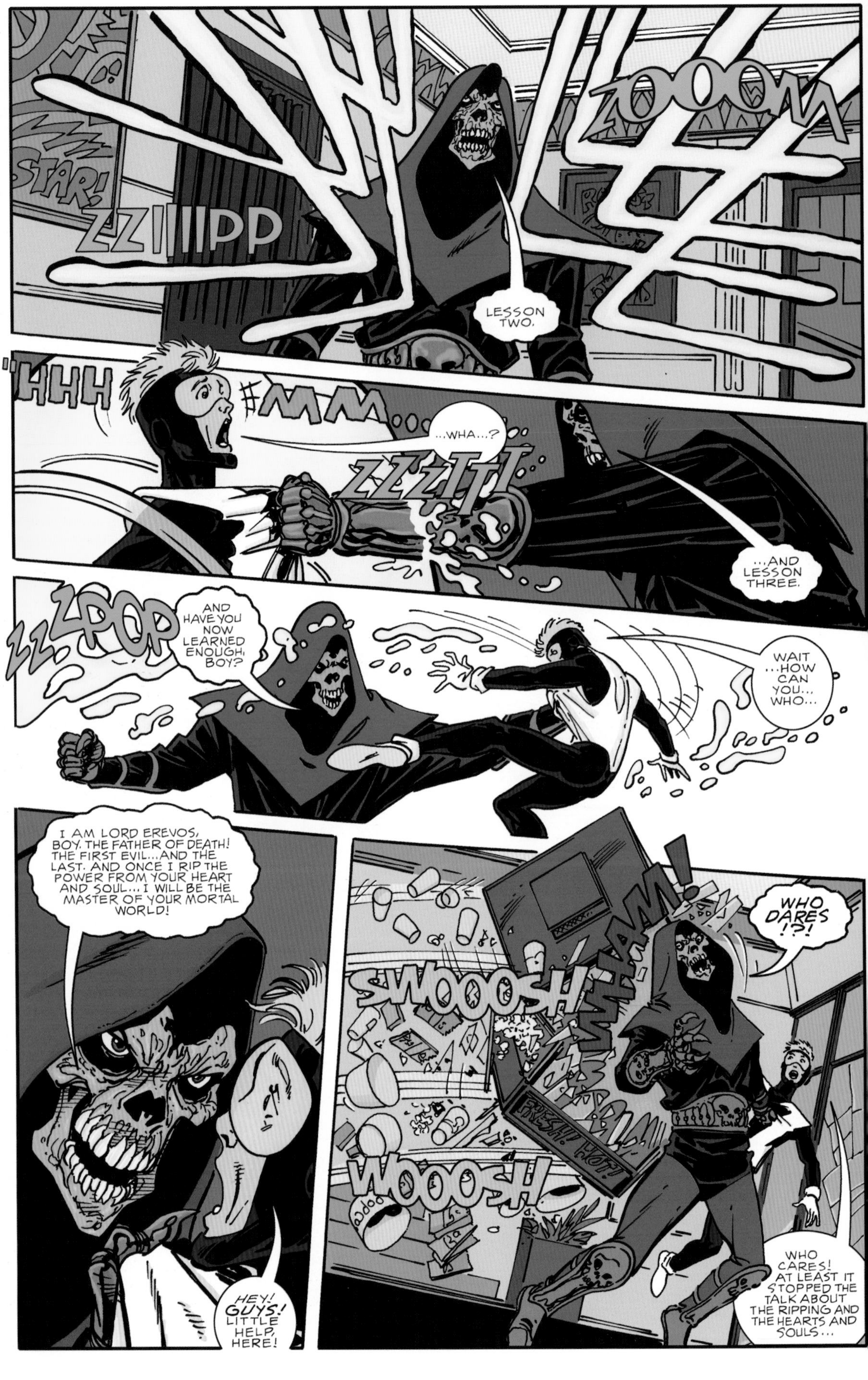
STAR!
ZZIIIPP
ZOOOM
LESSON TWO.
HHHMM...
...WHA...?
ZZZITT!
...AND LESSON THREE.
ZZZPOP
AND HAVE YOU NOW LEARNED ENOUGH, BOY?
WAIT ...HOW CAN YOU... WHO...
I AM LORD EREVOS, BOY. THE FATHER OF DEATH! THE FIRST EVIL...AND THE LAST. AND ONCE I RIP THE POWER FROM YOUR HEART AND SOUL... I WILL BE THE MASTER OF YOUR MORTAL WORLD!
HEY! GUYS! LITTLE HELP, HERE!
WHAM!
WHO DARES !?!
SWOOOSH!
FRESH! HOT!
WOOOSH!
WHO CARES! AT LEAST IT STOPPED THE TALK ABOUT THE RIPPING AND THE HEARTS AND SOULS...

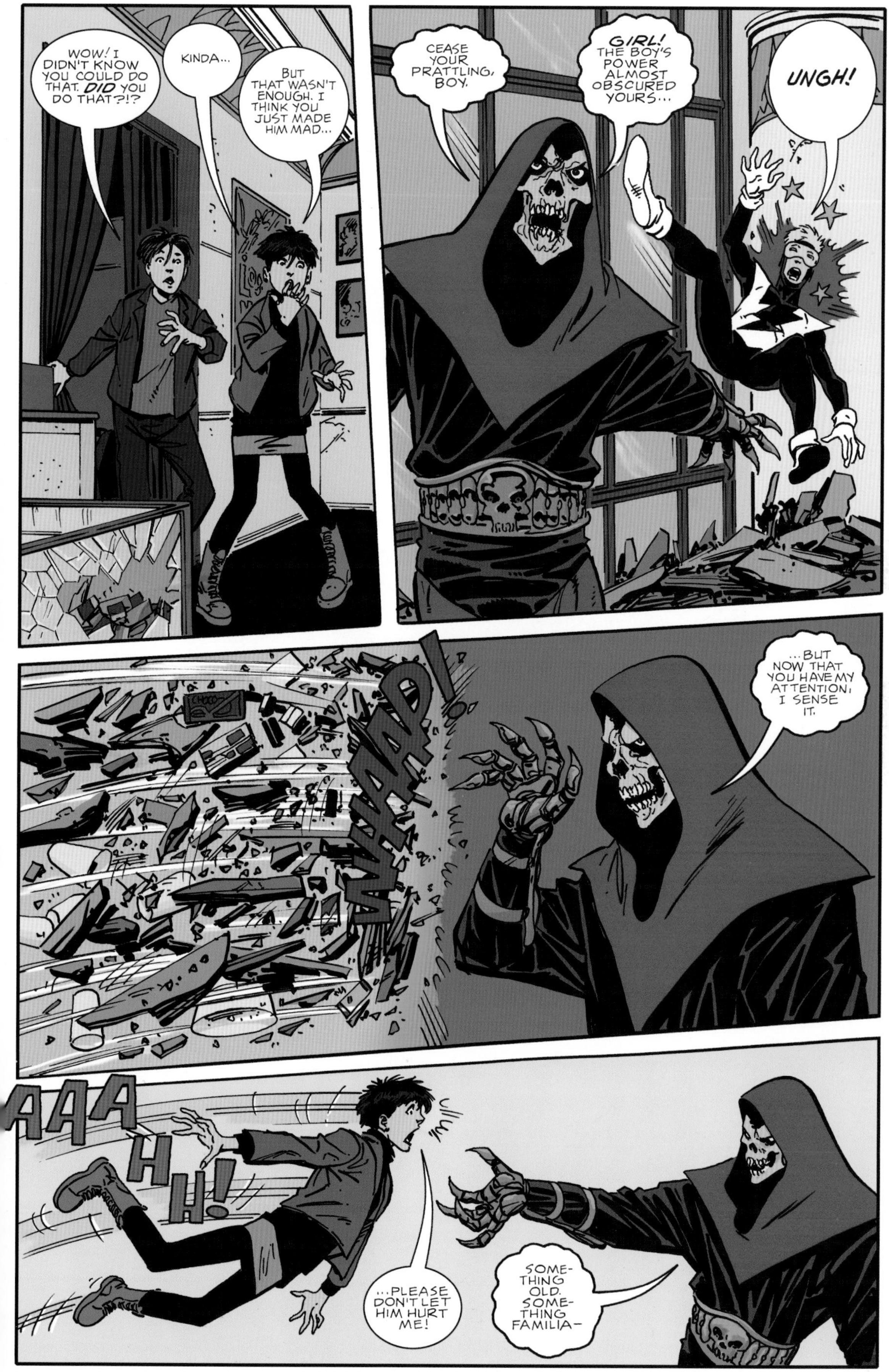
WOW! I DIDN'T KNOW YOU COULD DO THAT. DID YOU DO THAT?!?
KINDA...
BUT THAT WASN'T ENOUGH. I THINK YOU JUST MADE HIM MAD...
CEASE YOUR PRATTLING, BOY.
GIRL! THE BOY'S POWER ALMOST OBSCURED YOURS...
UNGH!
WHAAP!
...BUT NOW THAT YOU HAVE MY ATTENTION, I SENSE IT.
AAAHH!
...PLEASE DON'T LET HIM HURT ME!
SOME-THING OLD. SOME-THING FAMILIA-

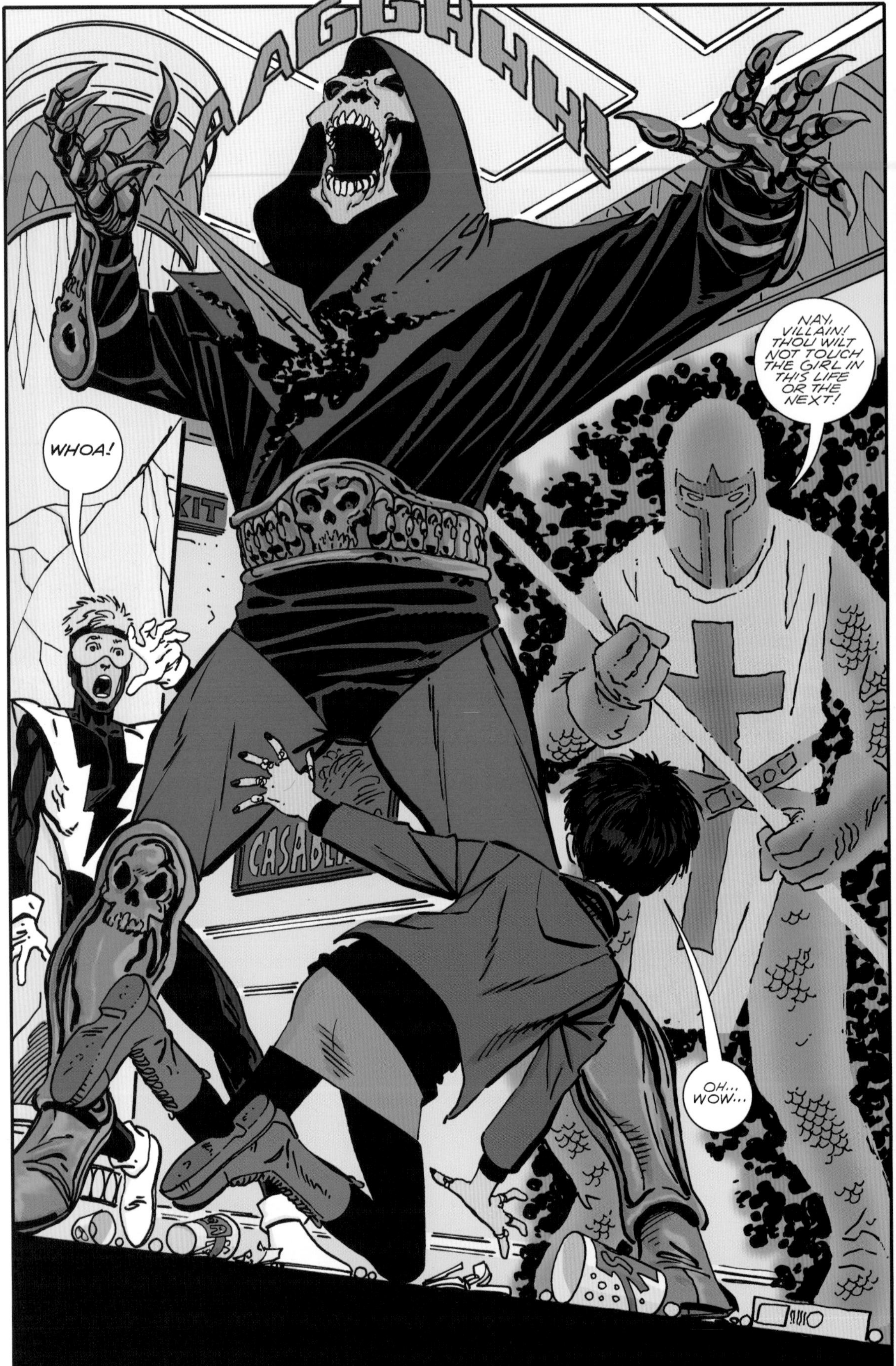
AAGGHHH!
NAY, VILLAIN! THOU WILT NOT TOUCH THE GIRL IN THIS LIFE OR THE NEXT!
WHOA!
OH... WOW...
CASABL
XIT

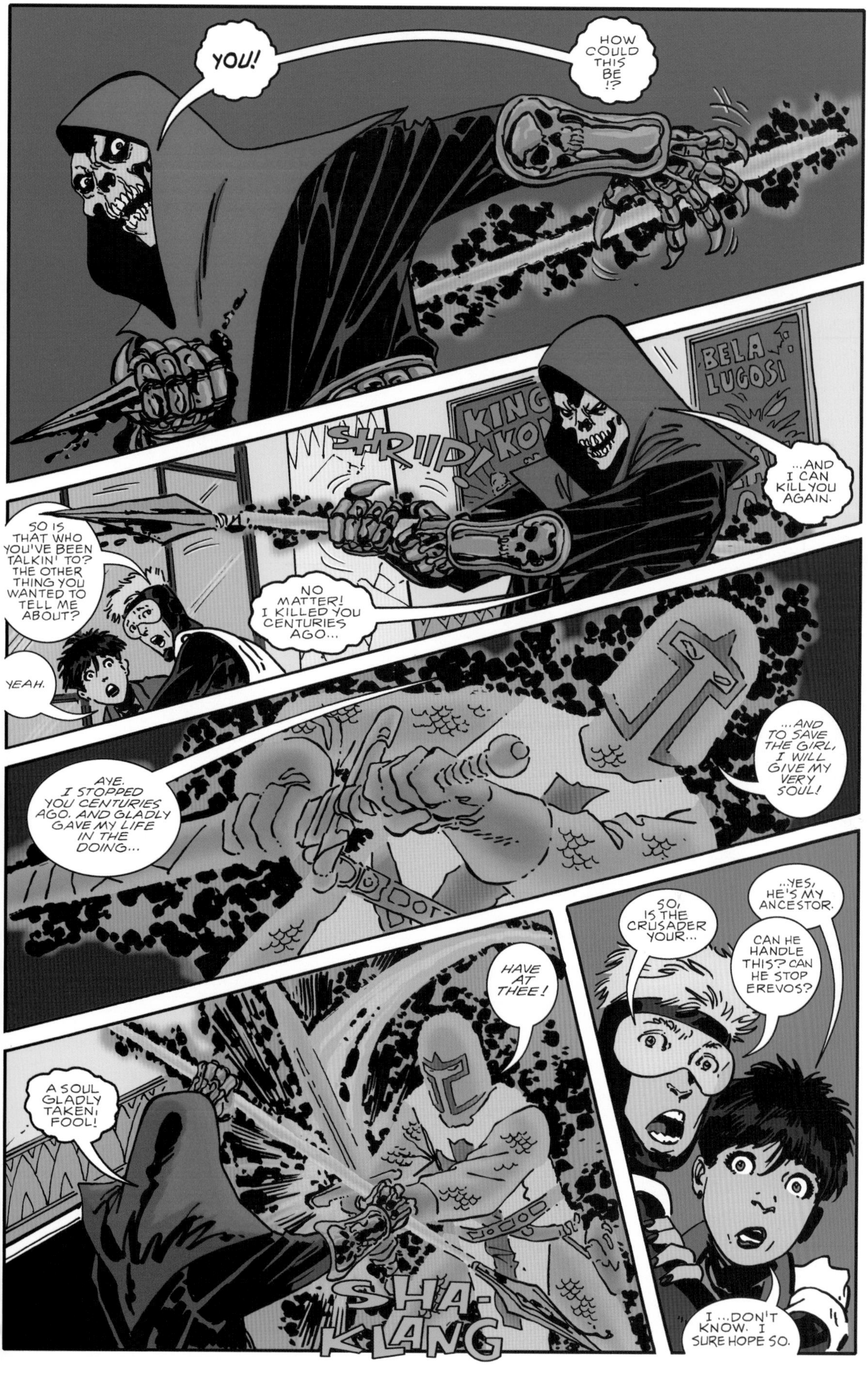
YOU!
HOW COULD THIS BE !?
BELA LUGOSI
KING KONG
SHRIID!
...AND I CAN KILL YOU AGAIN.
SO IS THAT WHO YOU'VE BEEN TALKIN' TO? THE OTHER THING YOU WANTED TO TELL ME ABOUT?
NO MATTER! I KILLED YOU CENTURIES AGO...
YEAH.
...AND TO SAVE THE GIRL, I WILL GIVE MY VERY SOUL!
AYE. I STOPPED YOU CENTURIES AGO. AND GLADLY GAVE MY LIFE IN THE DOING...
SO, IS THE CRUSADER YOUR...
...YES, HE'S MY ANCESTOR.
CAN HE HANDLE THIS? CAN HE STOP EREVOS?
HAVE AT THEE!
A SOUL GLADLY TAKEN, FOOL!
SHA-KLANG
I ...DON'T KNOW. I SURE HOPE SO.

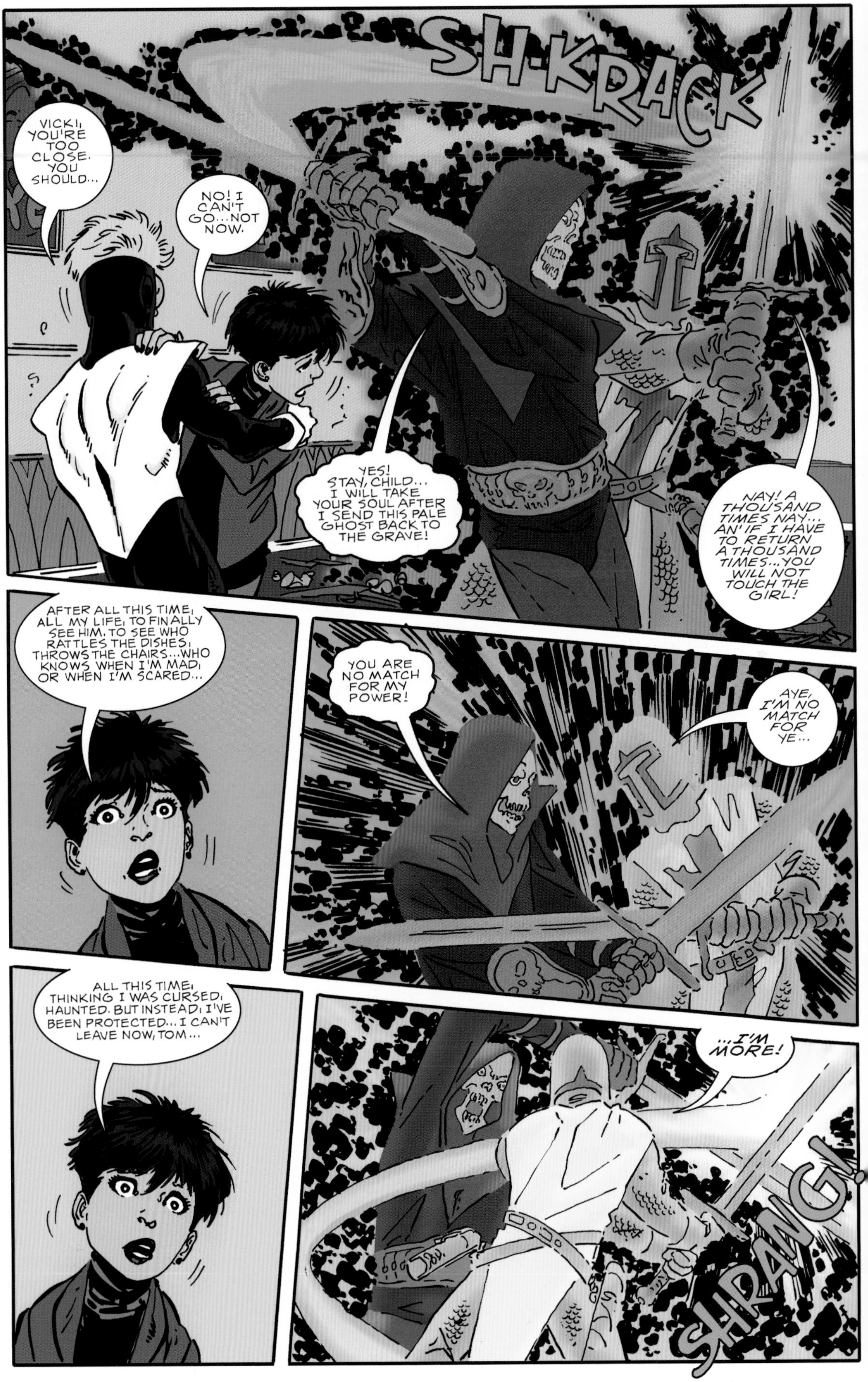
SH-KRACK
VICKI, YOU'RE TOO CLOSE. YOU SHOULD...
NO! I CAN'T GO...NOT NOW.
YES! STAY, CHILD... I WILL TAKE YOUR SOUL AFTER I SEND THIS PALE GHOST BACK TO THE GRAVE!
NAY! A THOUSAND TIMES NAY... AN' IF I HAVE TO RETURN A THOUSAND TIMES...YOU WILL NOT TOUCH THE GIRL!
AFTER ALL THIS TIME, ALL MY LIFE, TO FINALLY SEE HIM, TO SEE WHO RATTLES THE DISHES, THROWS THE CHAIRS...WHO KNOWS WHEN I'M MAD, OR WHEN I'M SCARED...
YOU ARE NO MATCH FOR MY POWER!
AYE, I'M NO MATCH FOR YE...
ALL THIS TIME, THINKING I WAS CURSED, HAUNTED. BUT INSTEAD, I'VE BEEN PROTECTED... I CAN'T LEAVE NOW, TOM...
...I'M MORE!
SHRANG!

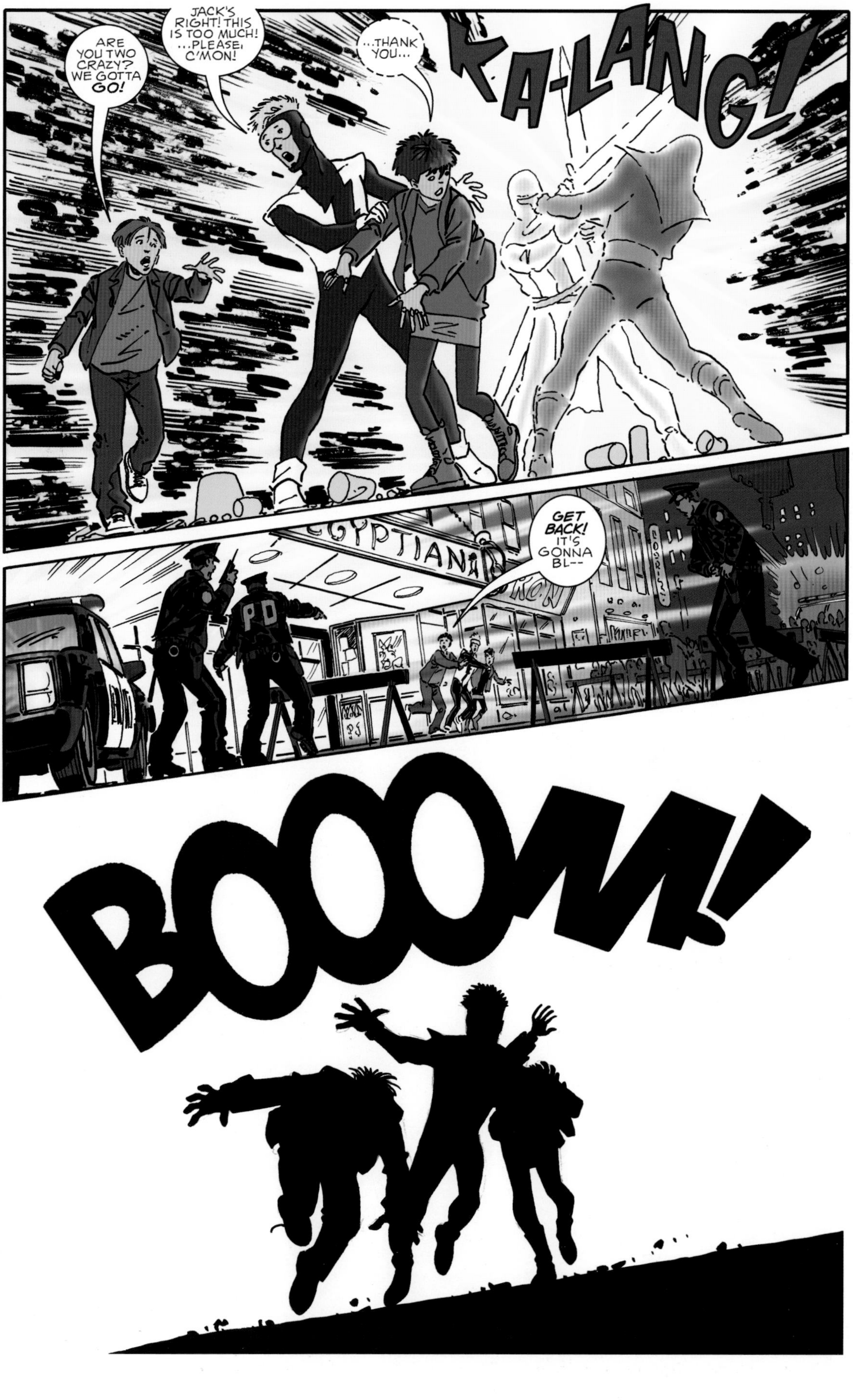
ARE YOU TWO CRAZY? WE GOTTA GO!
JACK'S RIGHT! THIS IS TOO MUCH! ...PLEASE, C'MON!
...THANK YOU...
KA-LANG!
GET BACK! IT'S GONNA BL--
BOOOM!

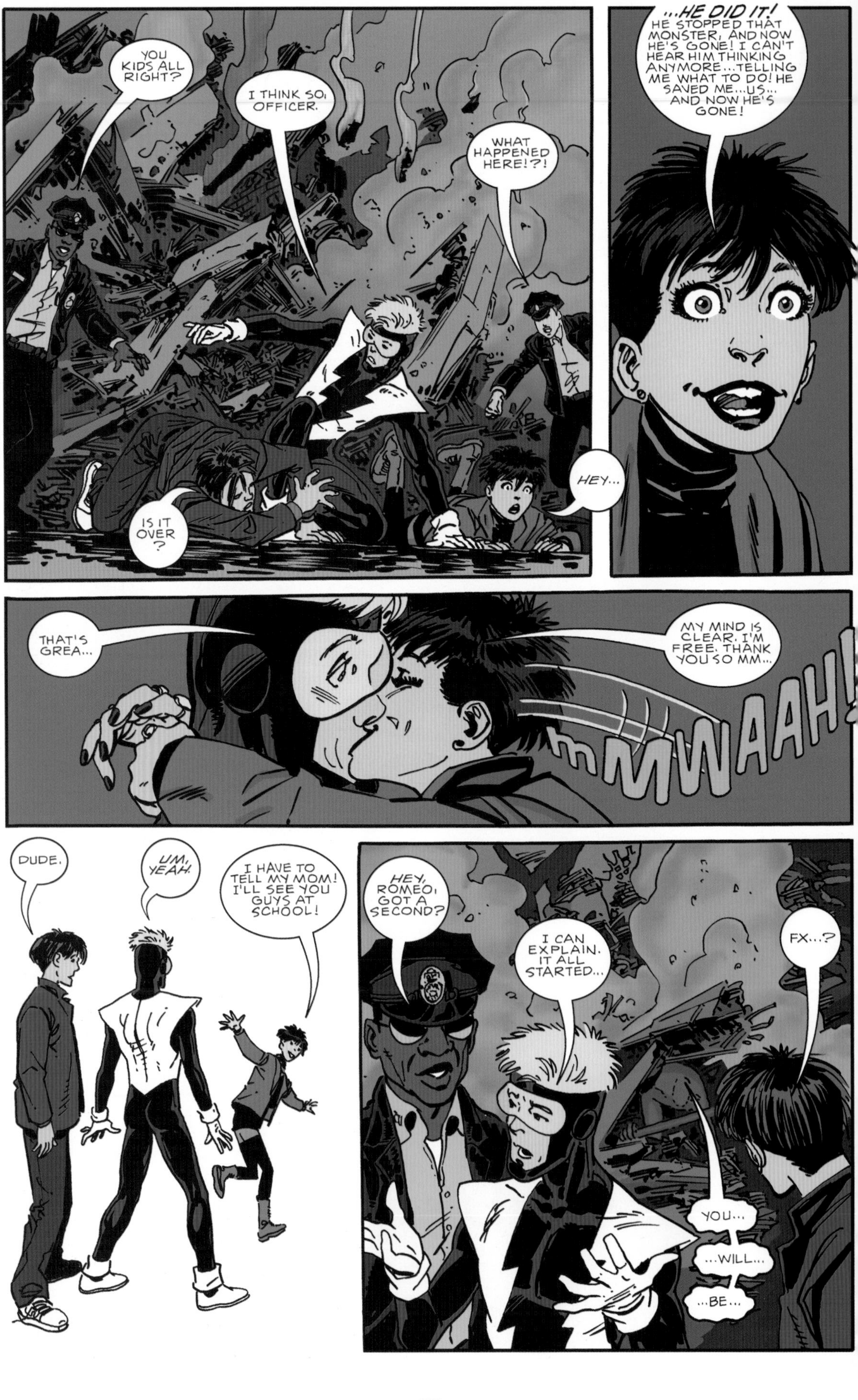
YOU KIDS ALL RIGHT?
I THINK SO, OFFICER.
WHAT HAPPENED HERE!?!
IS IT OVER?
HEY...
...HE DID IT! HE STOPPED THAT MONSTER, AND NOW HE'S GONE! I CAN'T HEAR HIM THINKING ANYMORE... TELLING ME WHAT TO DO! HE SAVED ME... US... AND NOW HE'S GONE!
THAT'S GREA...
MY MIND IS CLEAR. I'M FREE. THANK YOU SO MM...
mMWAAH!
DUDE.
UM, YEAH.
I HAVE TO TELL MY MOM! I'LL SEE YOU GUYS AT SCHOOL!
HEY, ROMEO, GOT A SECOND?
I CAN EXPLAIN. IT ALL STARTED...
FX...?
YOU...
...WILL...
...BE...

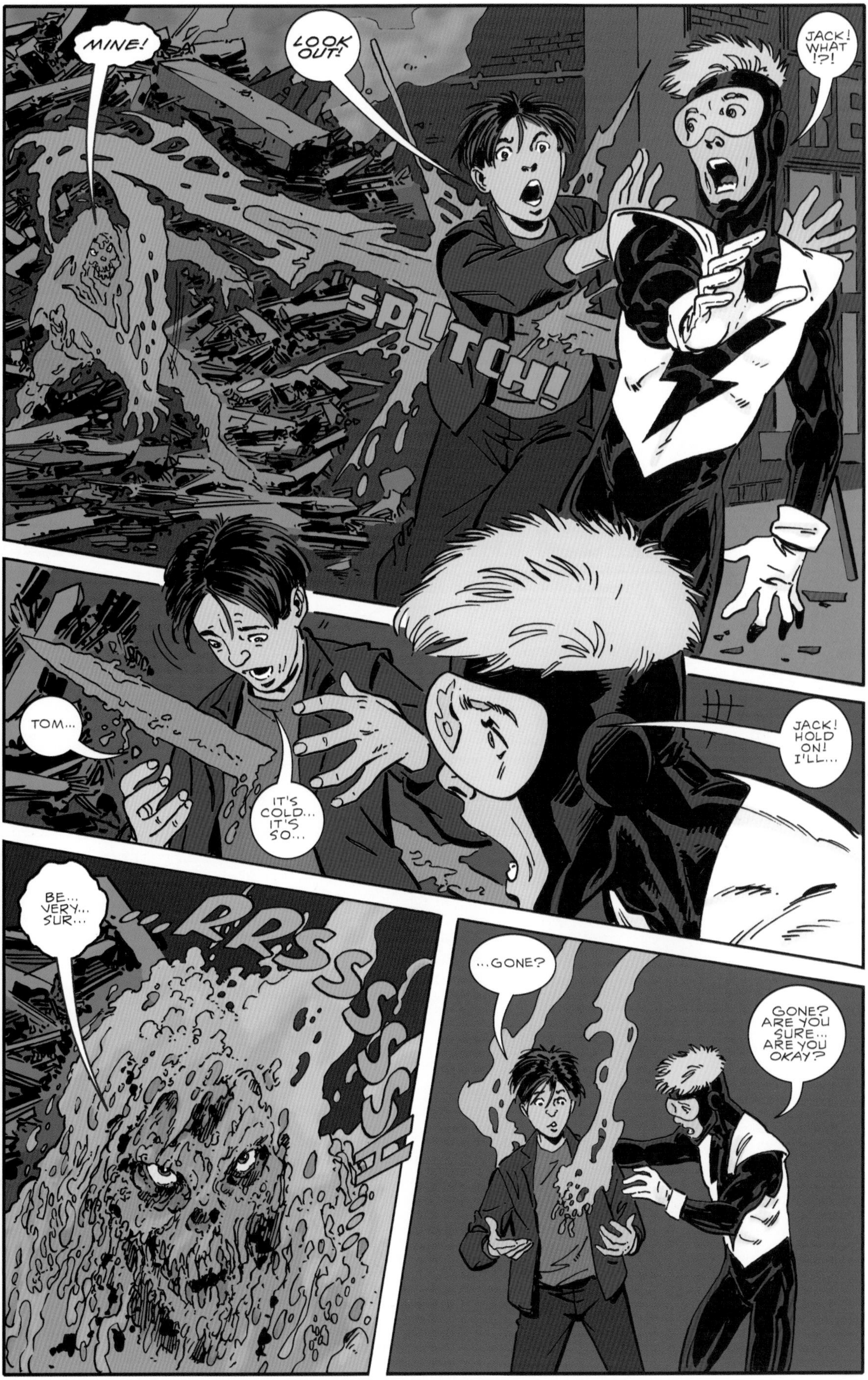
MINE!
LOOK OUT!
JACK! WHAT !?!
SPLITCH!
TOM...
IT'S COLD... IT'S SO...
JACK! HOLD ON! I'LL...
BE... VERY... SUR...
RRSSSSSH
...GONE?
GONE? ARE YOU SURE... ARE YOU OKAY?

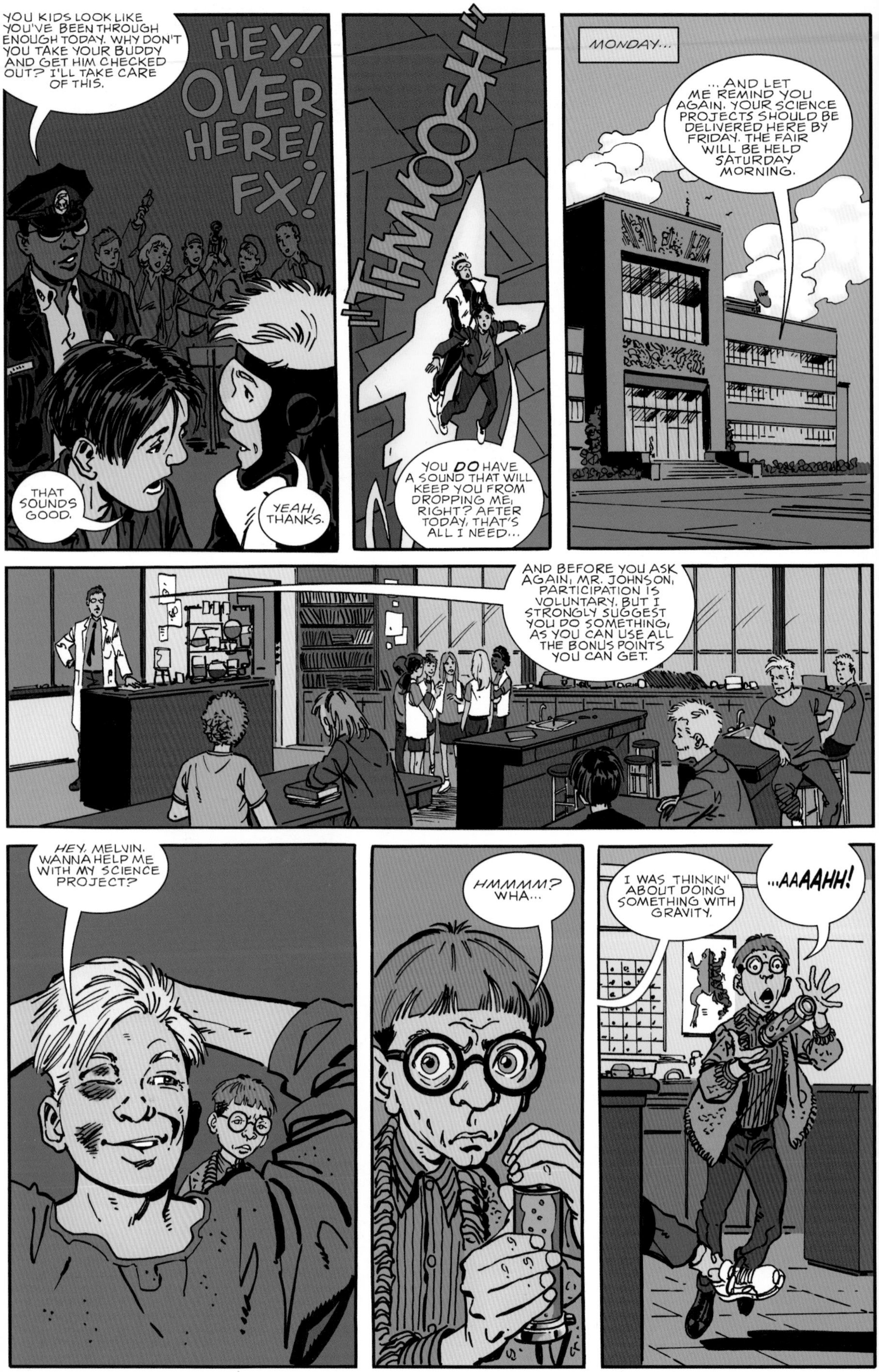
YOU KIDS LOOK LIKE YOU'VE BEEN THROUGH ENOUGH TODAY. WHY DON'T YOU TAKE YOUR BUDDY AND GET HIM CHECKED OUT? I'LL TAKE CARE OF THIS.
HEY! OVER HERE! FX!
THAT SOUNDS GOOD.
YEAH, THANKS.
THWOOSH
YOU DO HAVE A SOUND THAT WILL KEEP YOU FROM DROPPING ME, RIGHT? AFTER TODAY, THAT'S ALL I NEED...
MONDAY...
...AND LET ME REMIND YOU AGAIN. YOUR SCIENCE PROJECTS SHOULD BE DELIVERED HERE BY FRIDAY. THE FAIR WILL BE HELD SATURDAY MORNING.
AND BEFORE YOU ASK AGAIN, MR. JOHNSON, PARTICIPATION IS VOLUNTARY. BUT I STRONGLY SUGGEST YOU DO SOMETHING, AS YOU CAN USE ALL THE BONUS POINTS YOU CAN GET.
HEY, MELVIN. WANNA HELP ME WITH MY SCIENCE PROJECT?
HMMMM? WHA...
I WAS THINKIN' ABOUT DOING SOMETHING WITH GRAVITY.
...AAAAHH!

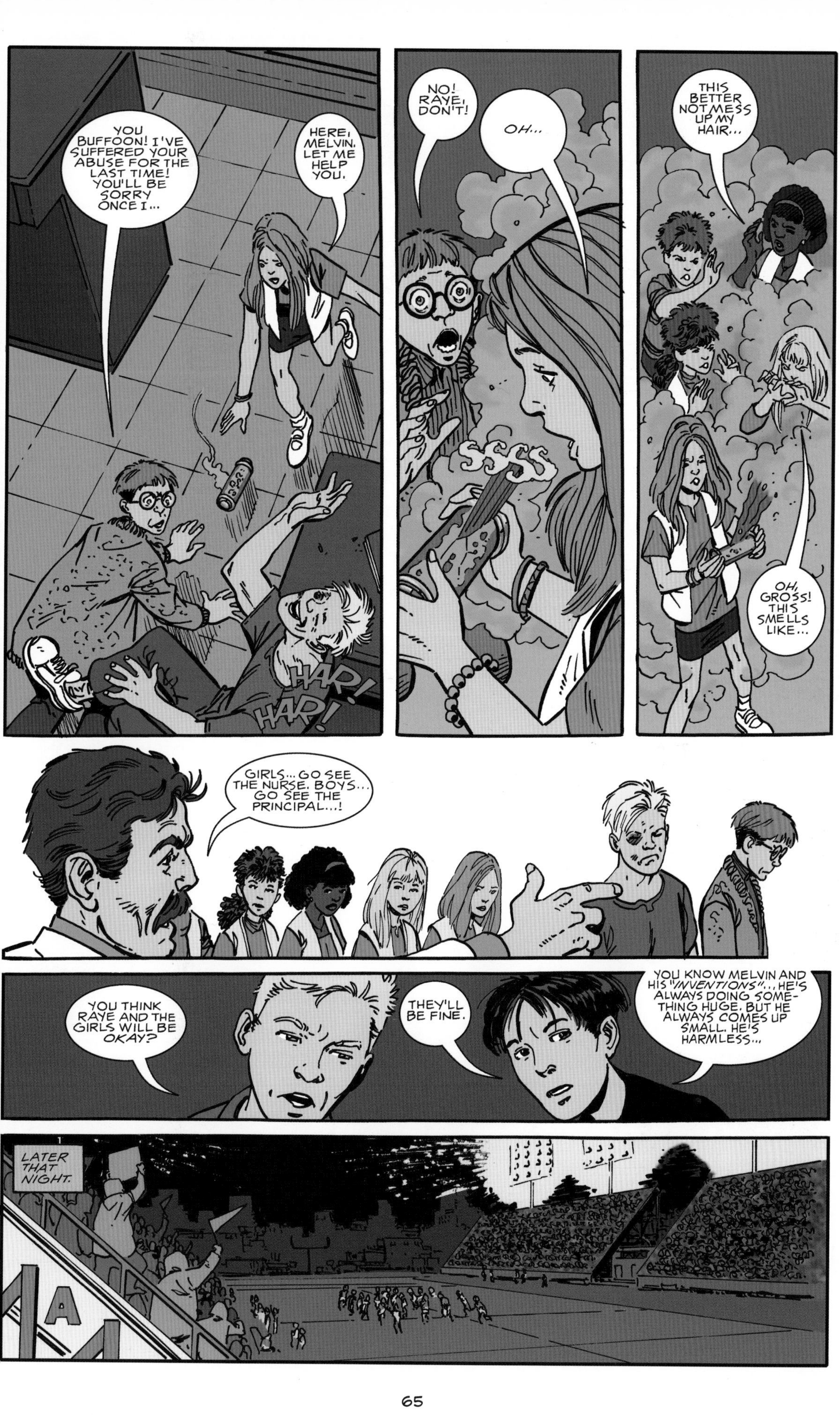
YOU BUFFOON! I'VE SUFFERED YOUR ABUSE FOR THE LAST TIME! YOU'LL BE SORRY ONCE I...
HERE, MELVIN. LET ME HELP YOU.
HAR! HAR!
NO! RAYE, DON'T!
OH...
SSSS
THIS BETTER NOT MESS UP MY HAIR...
OH, GROSS! THIS SMELLS LIKE...
GIRLS... GO SEE THE NURSE. BOYS... GO SEE THE PRINCIPAL...!
YOU THINK RAYE AND THE GIRLS WILL BE OKAY?
THEY'LL BE FINE.
YOU KNOW MELVIN AND HIS "INVENTIONS"... HE'S ALWAYS DOING SOMETHING HUGE. BUT HE ALWAYS COMES UP SMALL. HE'S HARMLESS...
LATER THAT NIGHT.

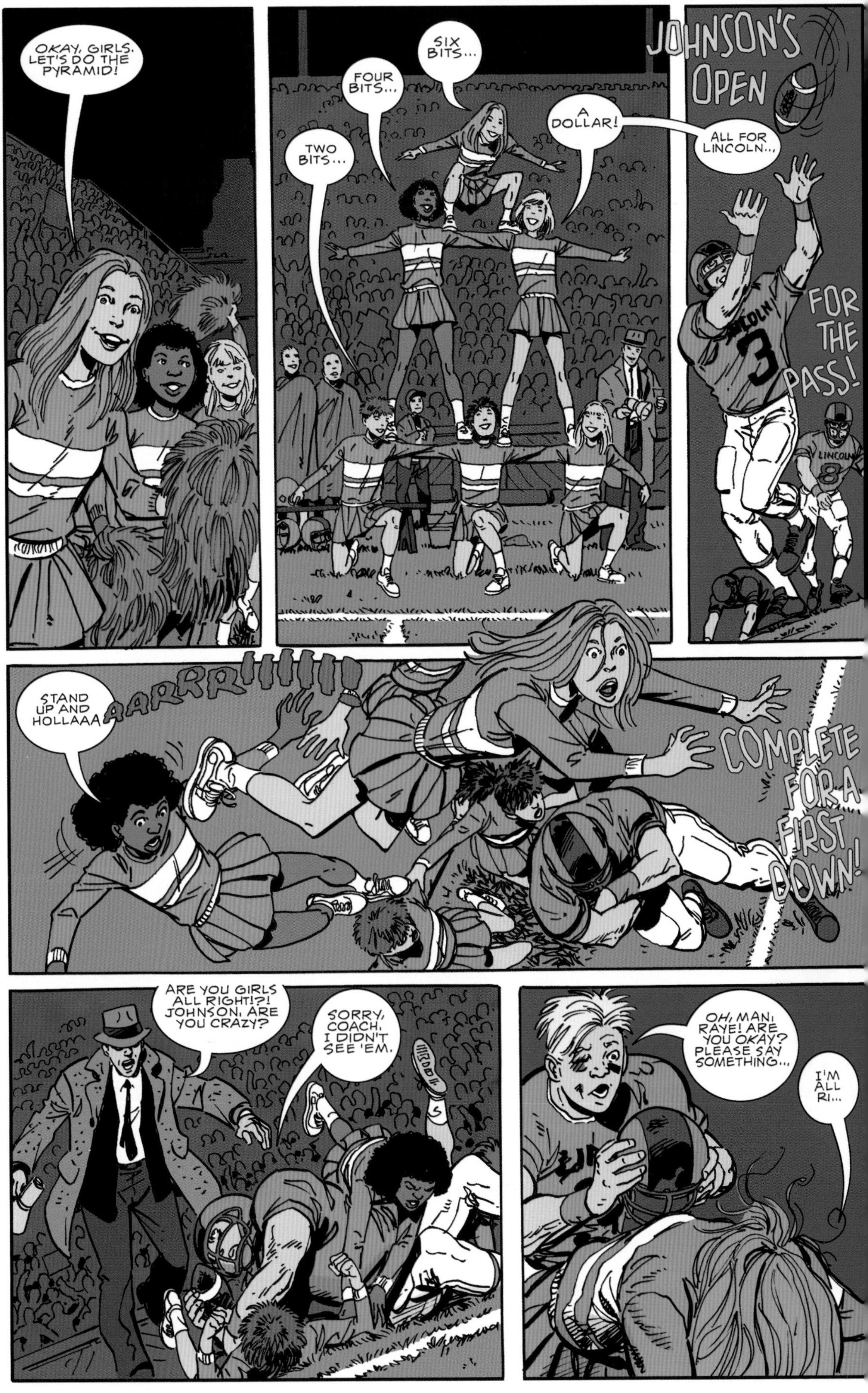

OKAY, GIRLS. LET'S DO THE PYRAMID!
TWO BITS...
FOUR BITS...
SIX BITS...
A DOLLAR!
ALL FOR LINCOLN...
JOHNSON'S OPEN
FOR THE PASS!
STAND UP AND HOLLAAA
AARRRIIIIII
COMPLETE FOR A FIRST DOWN!
ARE YOU GIRLS ALL RIGHT!?! JOHNSON, ARE YOU CRAZY?
SORRY, COACH. I DIDN'T SEE 'EM.
OH, MAN, RAYE! ARE YOU OKAY? PLEASE SAY SOMETHING...
I'M ALL RI...

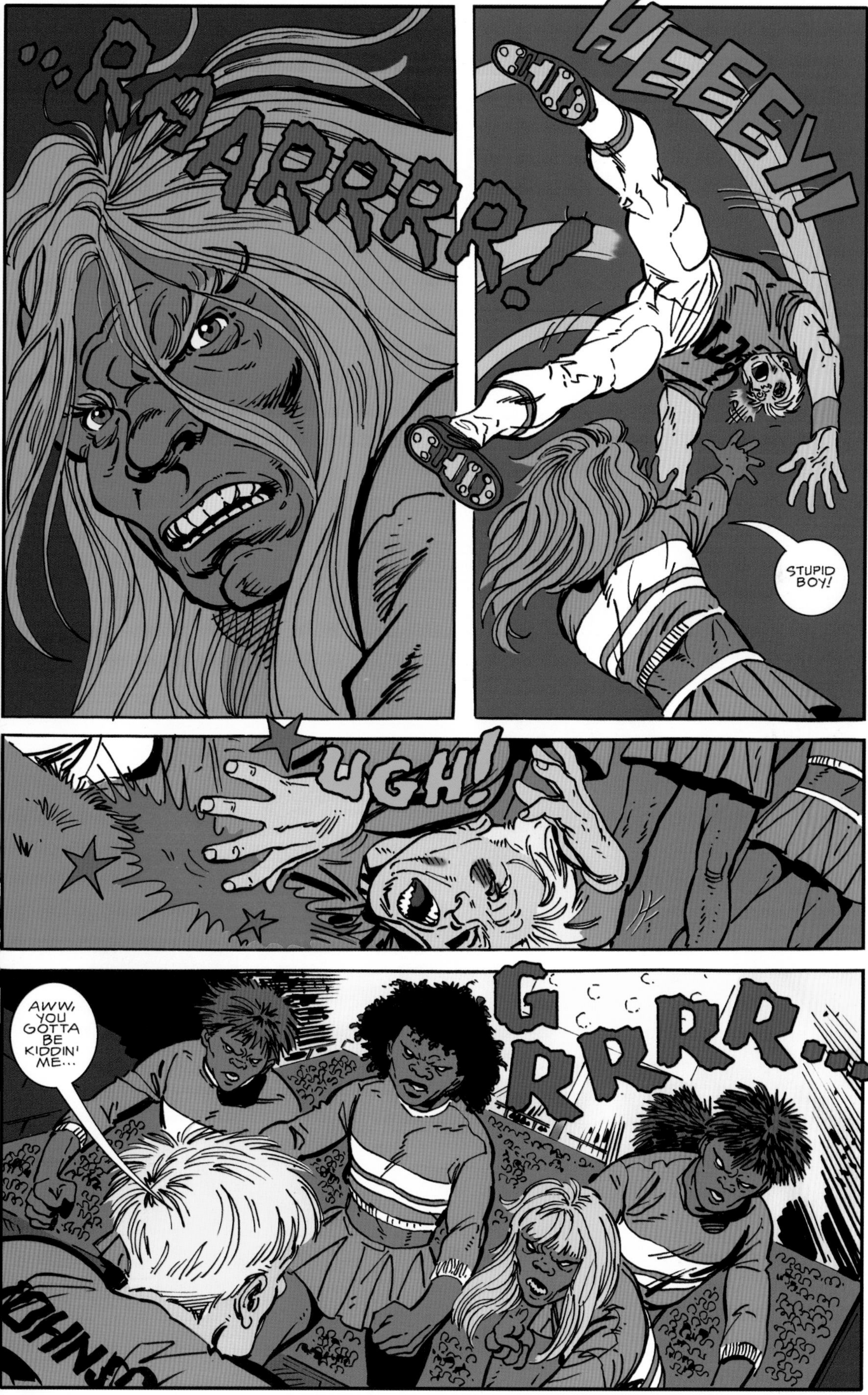
..RAARRRRR!
HEEEY!
STUPID BOY!
UGH!
AWW, YOU GOTTA BE KIDDIN' ME...
GRRRR...

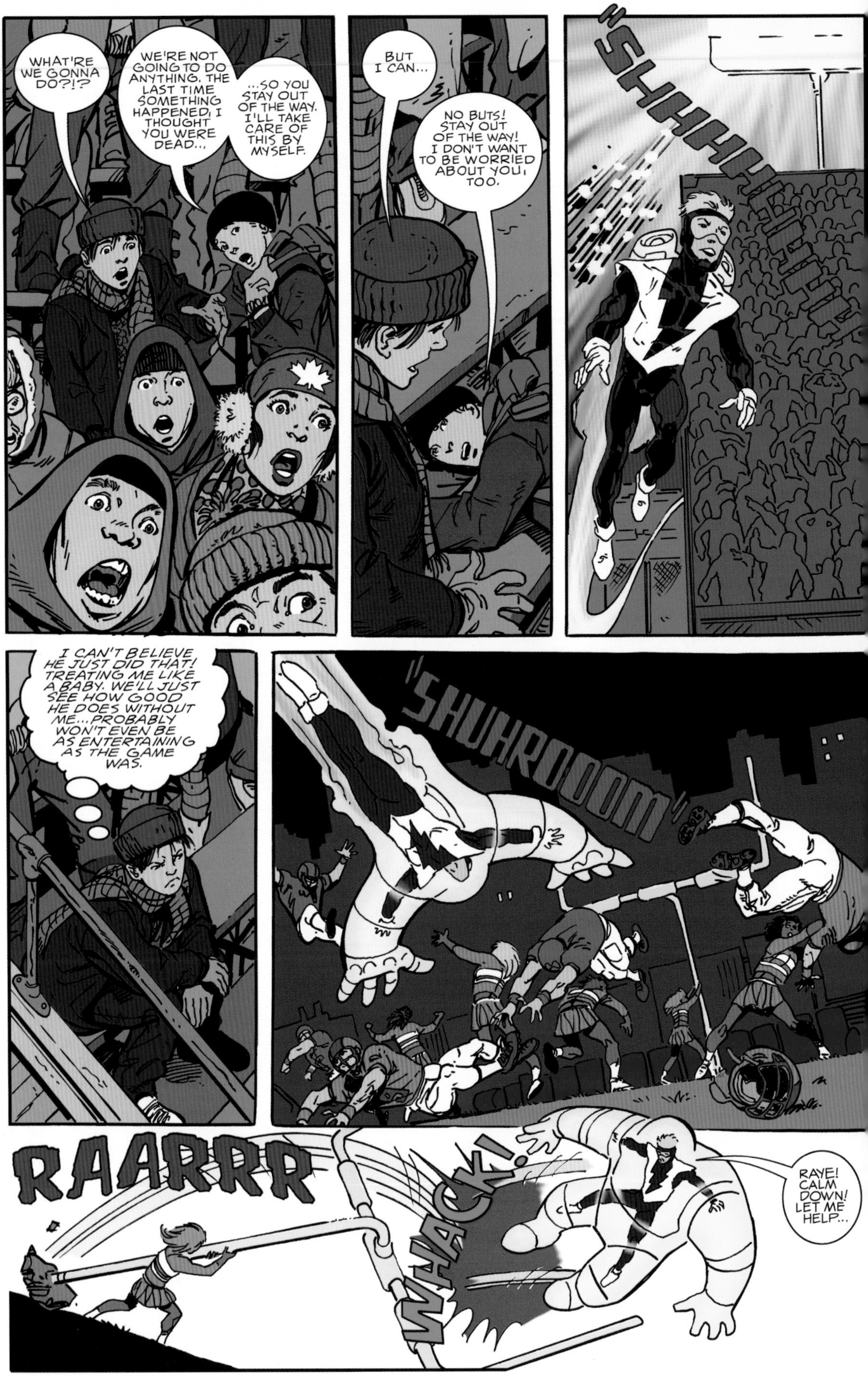
WHAT'RE WE GONNA DO?!?
WE'RE NOT GOING TO DO ANYTHING. THE LAST TIME SOMETHING HAPPENED, I THOUGHT YOU WERE DEAD...
...SO YOU STAY OUT OF THE WAY. I'LL TAKE CARE OF THIS BY MYSELF.
BUT I CAN...
NO BUTS! STAY OUT OF THE WAY! I DON'T WANT TO BE WORRIED ABOUT YOU, TOO.
"SHHHHHHHHH!"
I CAN'T BELIEVE HE JUST DID THAT! TREATING ME LIKE A BABY. WE'LL JUST SEE HOW GOOD HE DOES WITHOUT ME...PROBABLY WON'T EVEN BE AS ENTERTAINING AS THE GAME WAS.
"SHUHROOOM"
RAARRR
WHACK!
RAYE! CALM DOWN! LET ME HELP...

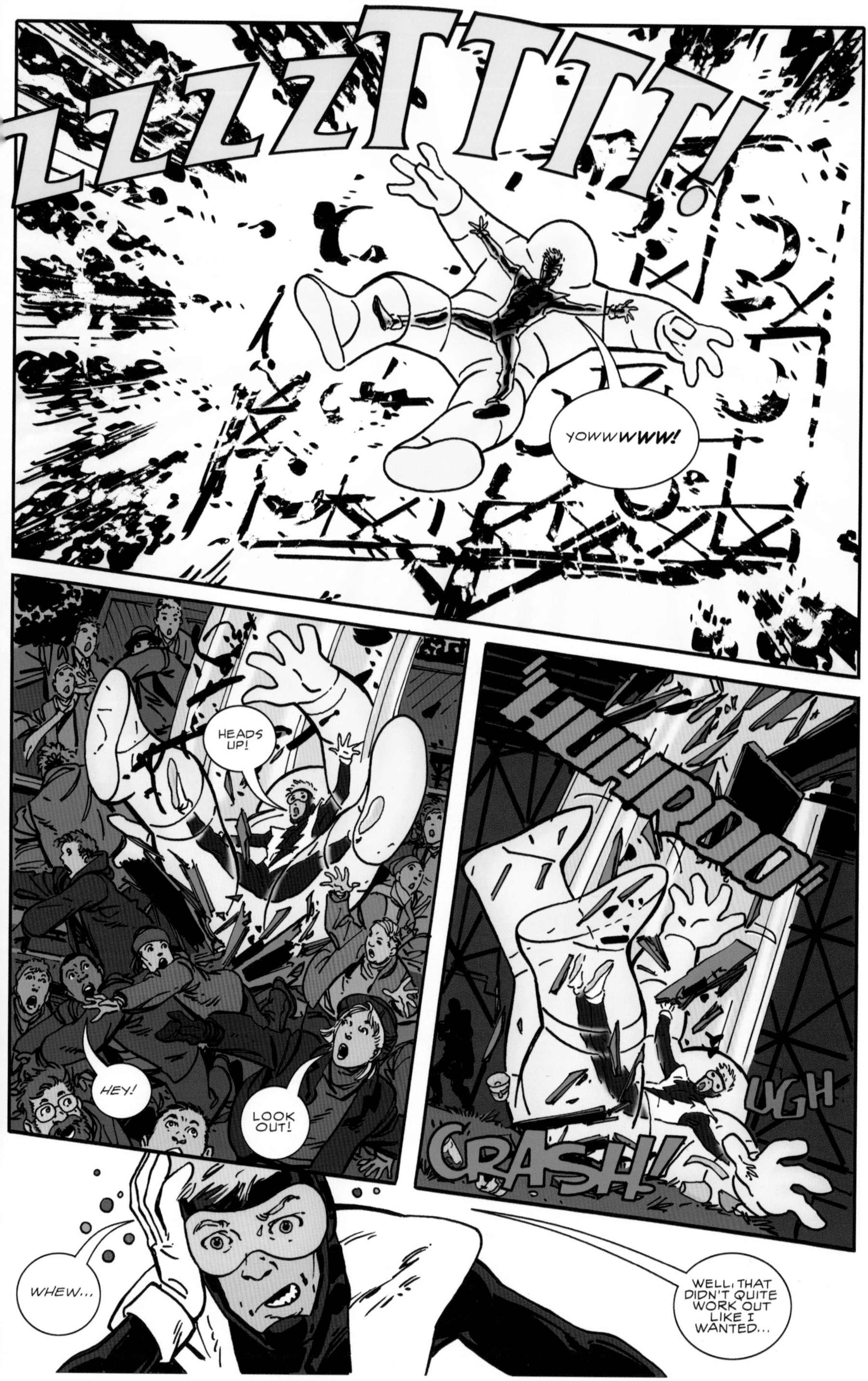
ZZZZTTTT!
YOWWWWW!
HEADS UP!
HEY!
LOOK OUT!
UGH
CRASH!
WHEW...
WELL, THAT DIDN'T QUITE WORK OUT LIKE I WANTED...

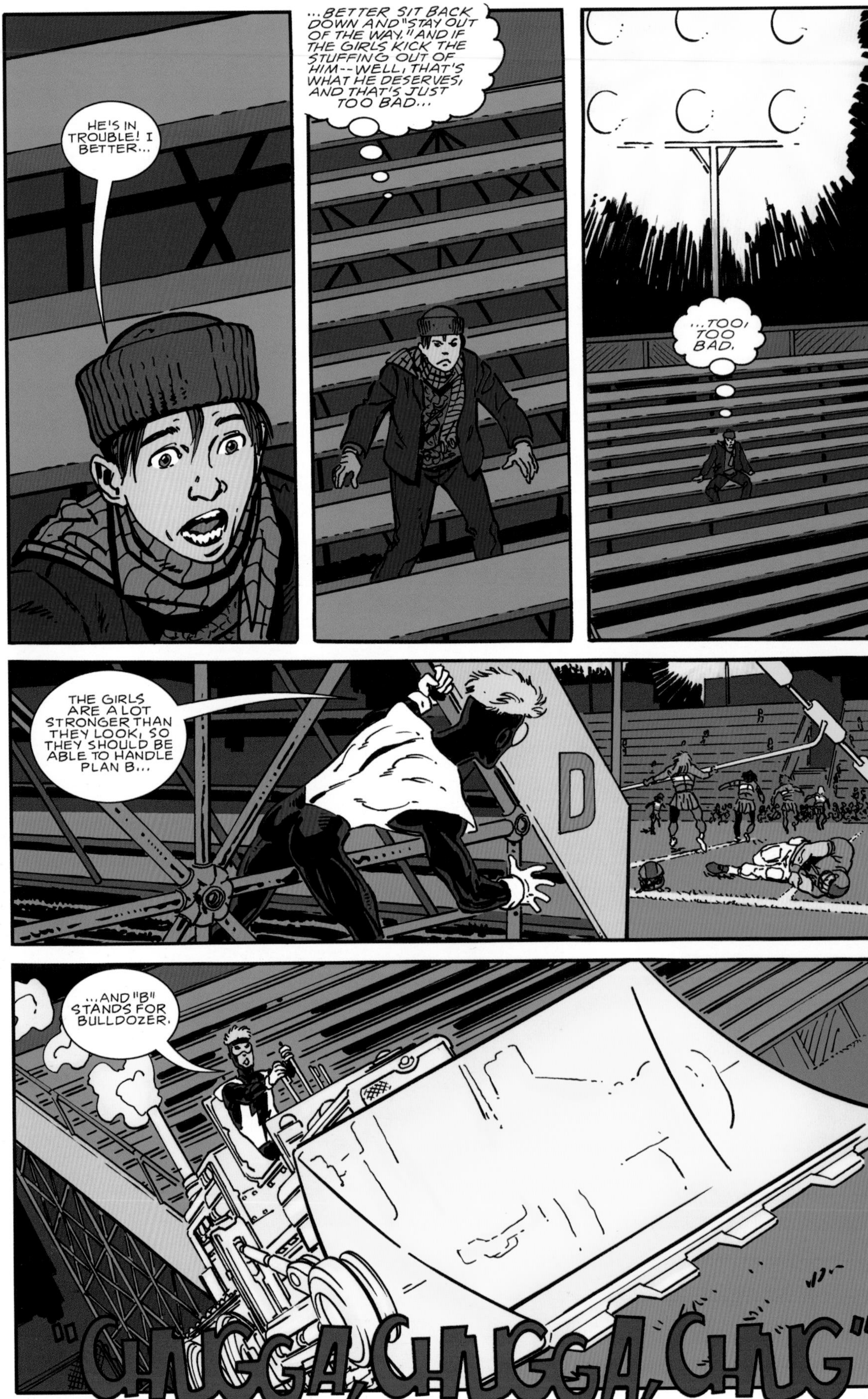
HE'S IN TROUBLE! I BETTER...
...BETTER SIT BACK DOWN AND "STAY OUT OF THE WAY." AND IF THE GIRLS KICK THE STUFFING OUT OF HIM--WELL, THAT'S WHAT HE DESERVES, AND THAT'S JUST TOO BAD...
...TOO, TOO BAD.
THE GIRLS ARE A LOT STRONGER THAN THEY LOOK, SO THEY SHOULD BE ABLE TO HANDLE PLAN B...
D
...AND "B" STANDS FOR BULLDOZER.
"CHUGGA, CHUGGA, CHUG"

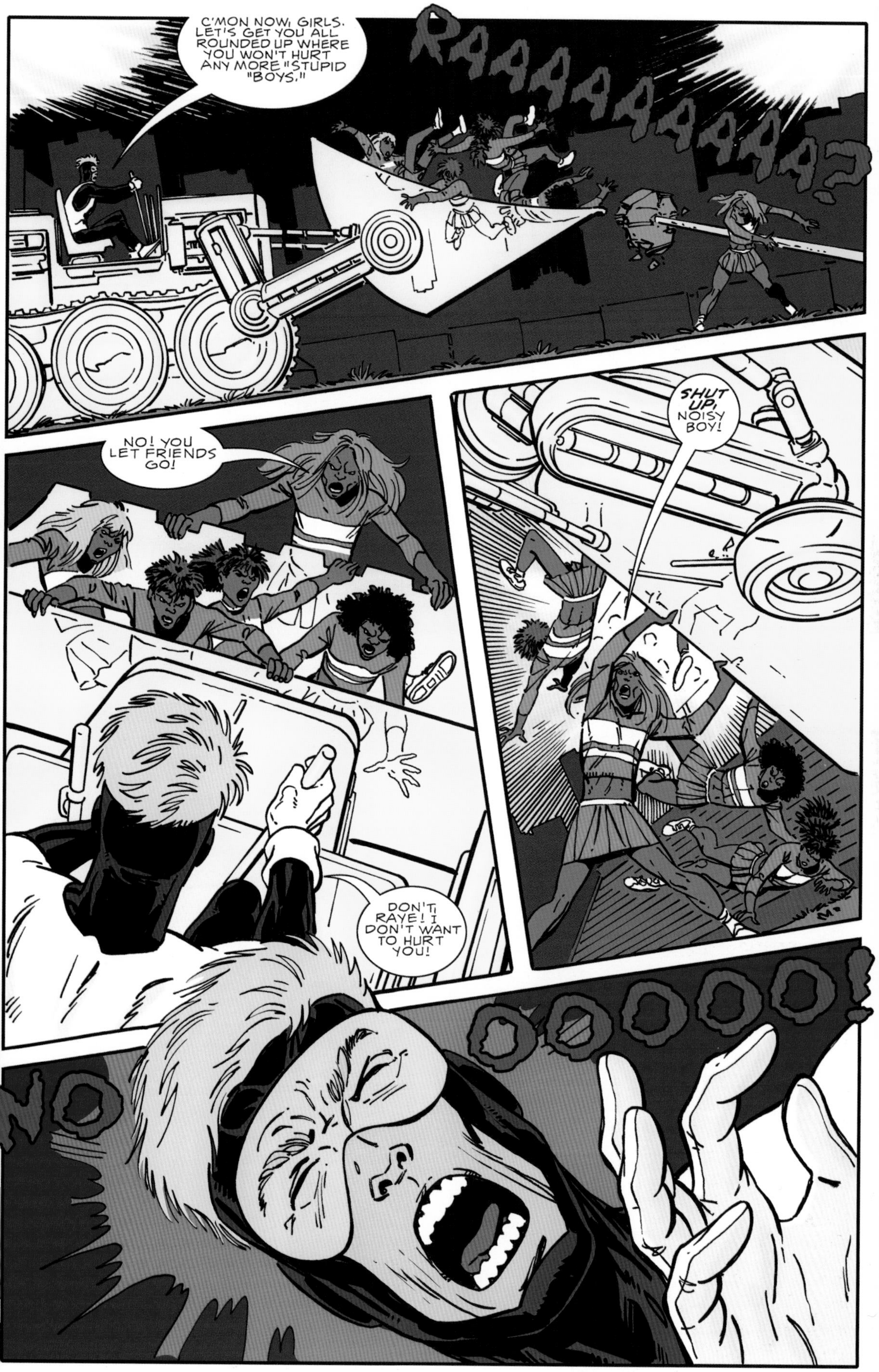
C'MON NOW, GIRLS. LET'S GET YOU ALL ROUNDED UP WHERE YOU WON'T HURT ANY MORE "STUPID "BOYS."
RAAAAAAAAAA?
NO! YOU LET FRIENDS GO!
SHUT UP, NOISY BOY!
DON'T, RAYE! I DON'T WANT TO HURT YOU!
NOOOOOO!

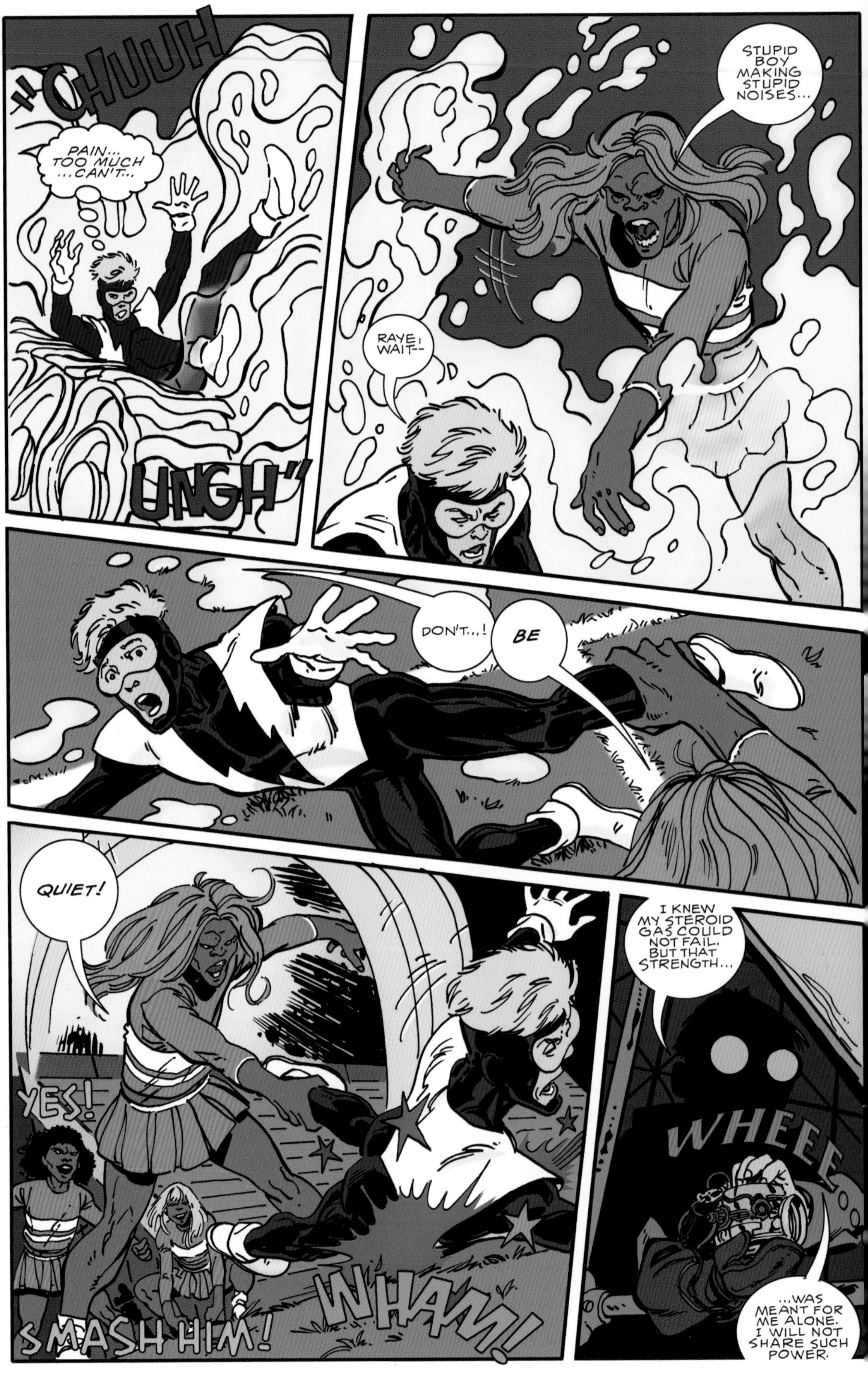
"CHUUUH
PAIN... TOO MUCH ...CAN'T...
UNGH"
STUPID BOY MAKING STUPID NOISES...
RAYE! WAIT--
DON'T...!
BE
QUIET!
YES!
SMASH HIM!
WHAM!
I KNEW MY STEROID GAS COULD NOT FAIL. BUT THAT STRENGTH...
WHEEE...
...WAS MEANT FOR ME ALONE. I WILL NOT SHARE SUCH POWER.

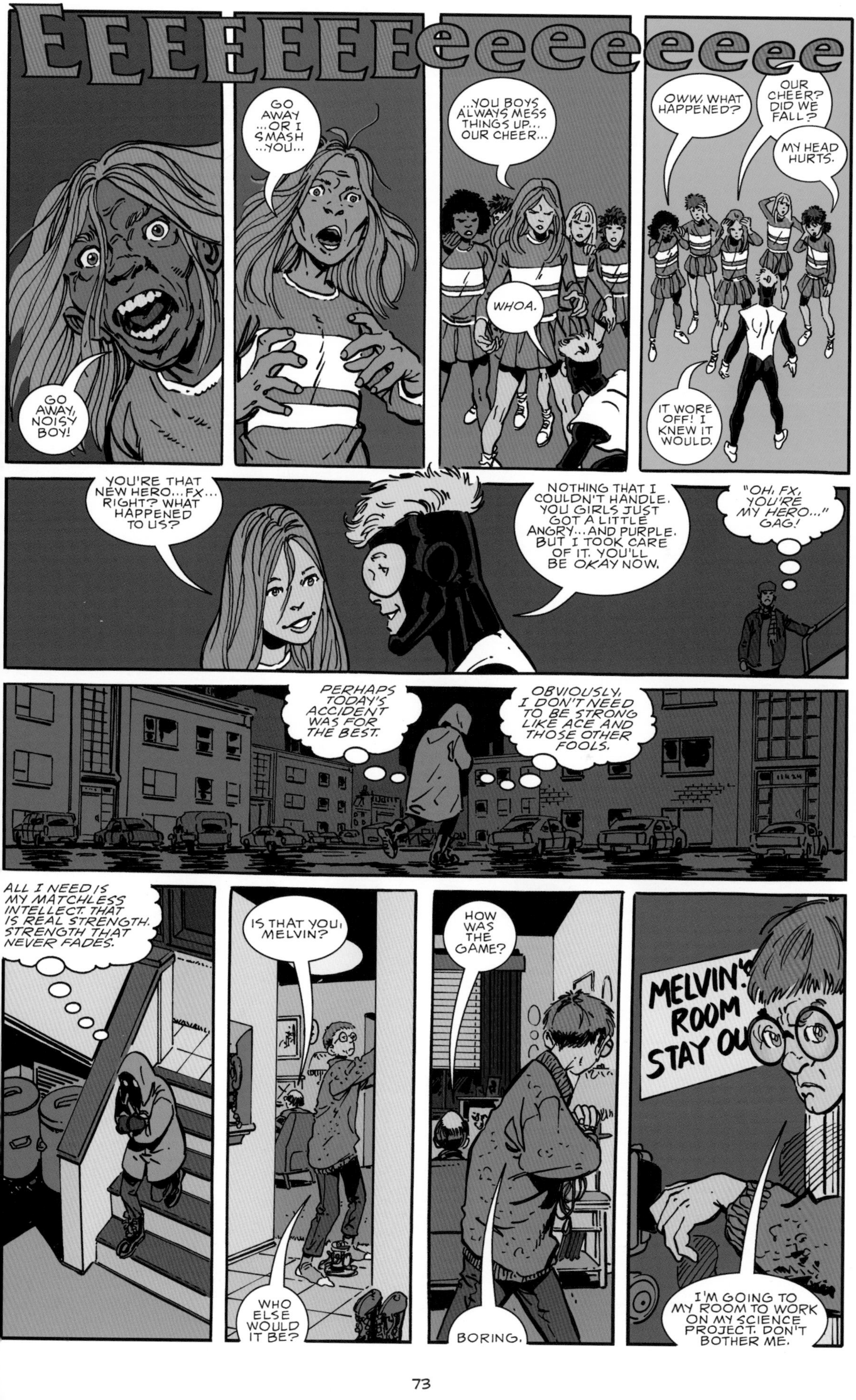

EEEEEEEeeeeeeeee
GO AWAY, NOISY BOY!
GO AWAY ...OR I SMASH ...YOU...
...YOU BOYS ALWAYS MESS THINGS UP... OUR CHEER...
WHOA.
OWW, WHAT HAPPENED?
OUR CHEER? DID WE FALL?
MY HEAD HURTS.
IT WORE OFF! I KNEW IT WOULD.
YOU'RE THAT NEW HERO...FX... RIGHT? WHAT HAPPENED TO US?
NOTHING THAT I COULDN'T HANDLE. YOU GIRLS JUST GOT A LITTLE ANGRY...AND PURPLE. BUT I TOOK CARE OF IT. YOU'LL BE OKAY NOW.
"OH, FX, YOU'RE MY HERO..." GAG!
PERHAPS TODAY'S ACCIDENT WAS FOR THE BEST.
OBVIOUSLY, I DON'T NEED TO BE STRONG LIKE ACE AND THOSE OTHER FOOLS.
ALL I NEED IS MY MATCHLESS INTELLECT. THAT IS REAL STRENGTH. STRENGTH THAT NEVER FADES.
IS THAT YOU, MELVIN?
WHO ELSE WOULD IT BE?
HOW WAS THE GAME?
BORING.
MELVIN'S ROOM STAY OU
I'M GOING TO MY ROOM TO WORK ON MY SCIENCE PROJECT. DON'T BOTHER ME.

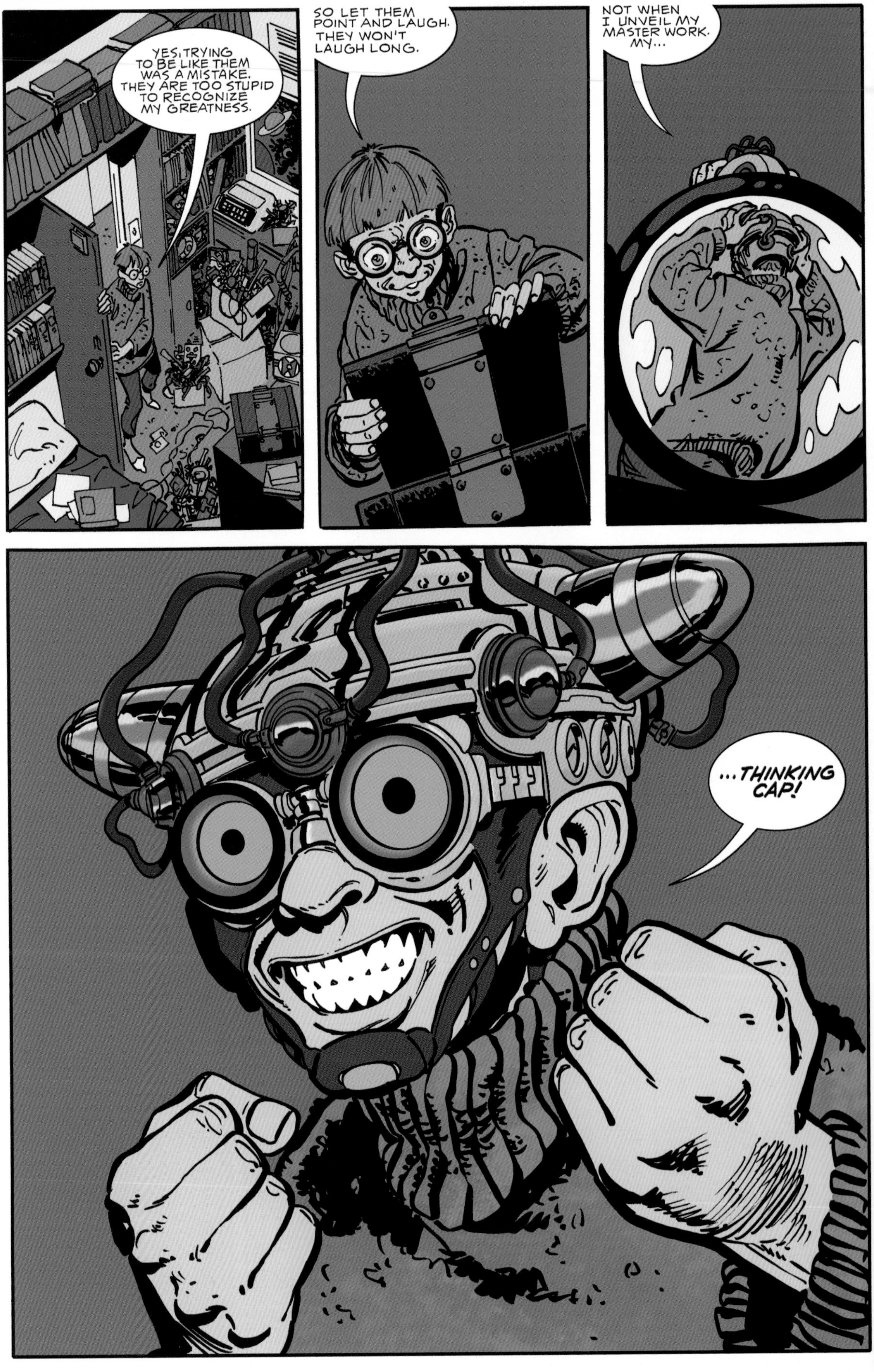
YES, TRYING TO BE LIKE THEM WAS A MISTAKE. THEY ARE TOO STUPID TO RECOGNIZE MY GREATNESS.
SO LET THEM POINT AND LAUGH. THEY WON'T LAUGH LONG.
NOT WHEN I UNVEIL MY MASTER WORK. MY...
...THINKING CAP!

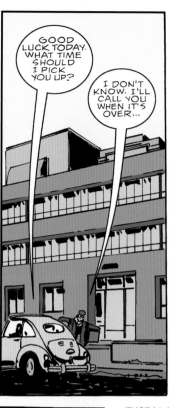

GOOD LUCK TODAY. WHAT TIME SHOULD I PICK YOU UP?

I DON'T KNOW. I'LL CALL YOU WHEN IT'S OVER...

...MAYBE. BUT IF THINGS GO AS PLANNED, I WILL MOVE BEYOND SUCH PETTY CONCERNS AS NEEDING A RIDE HOME. OR EVEN NEEDING A HOME. THE ENTIRE WORLD WILL BE AT MY BECK AND CALL.

HEY, MELVIN. IS THAT THE FIRST-PLACE PROJECT THERE?

OF COURSE IT IS.

JUST LOOK AT MY COMPETITION. BAKING SODA VOLCANO, STYRO-FOAM SOLAR SYSTEM, ANT FARMS...

...THIS WOULD BE HUMOROUS IF IT WASN'T SO PATHETIC.

ALL THE LAUGHTER AND MOCKING STOPS TODAY...OR ELSE.

SCOTT, MITCH...? PAY ATTENTION. YOU MIGHT WANT TO BE THE FIRST TO WORSHIP YOUR NEW GOD...

GAAAH!

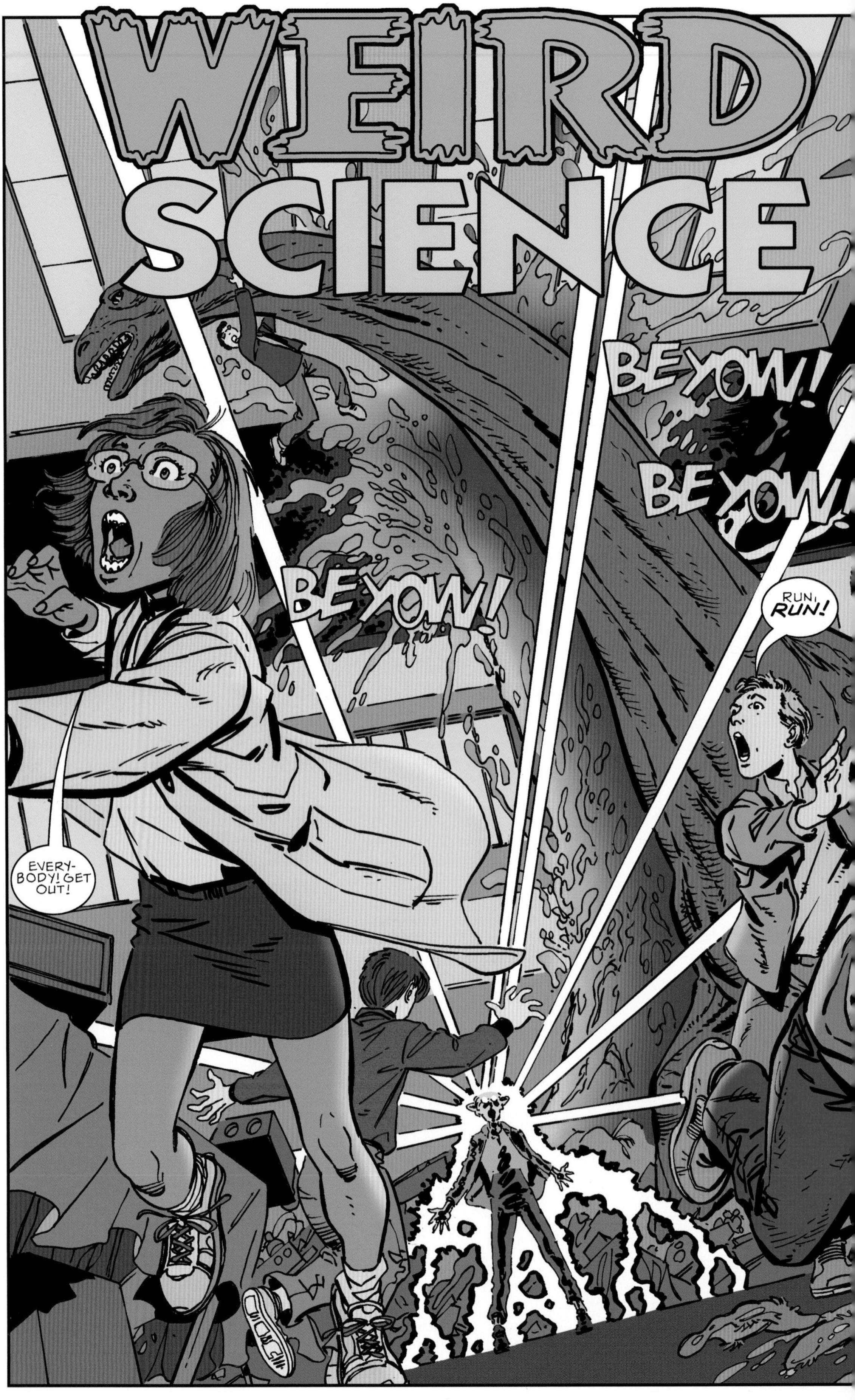
WEIRD SCIENCE
BEYOW!
BEYOW!
BEYOW!
RUN, RUN!
EVERY-BODY! GET OUT!

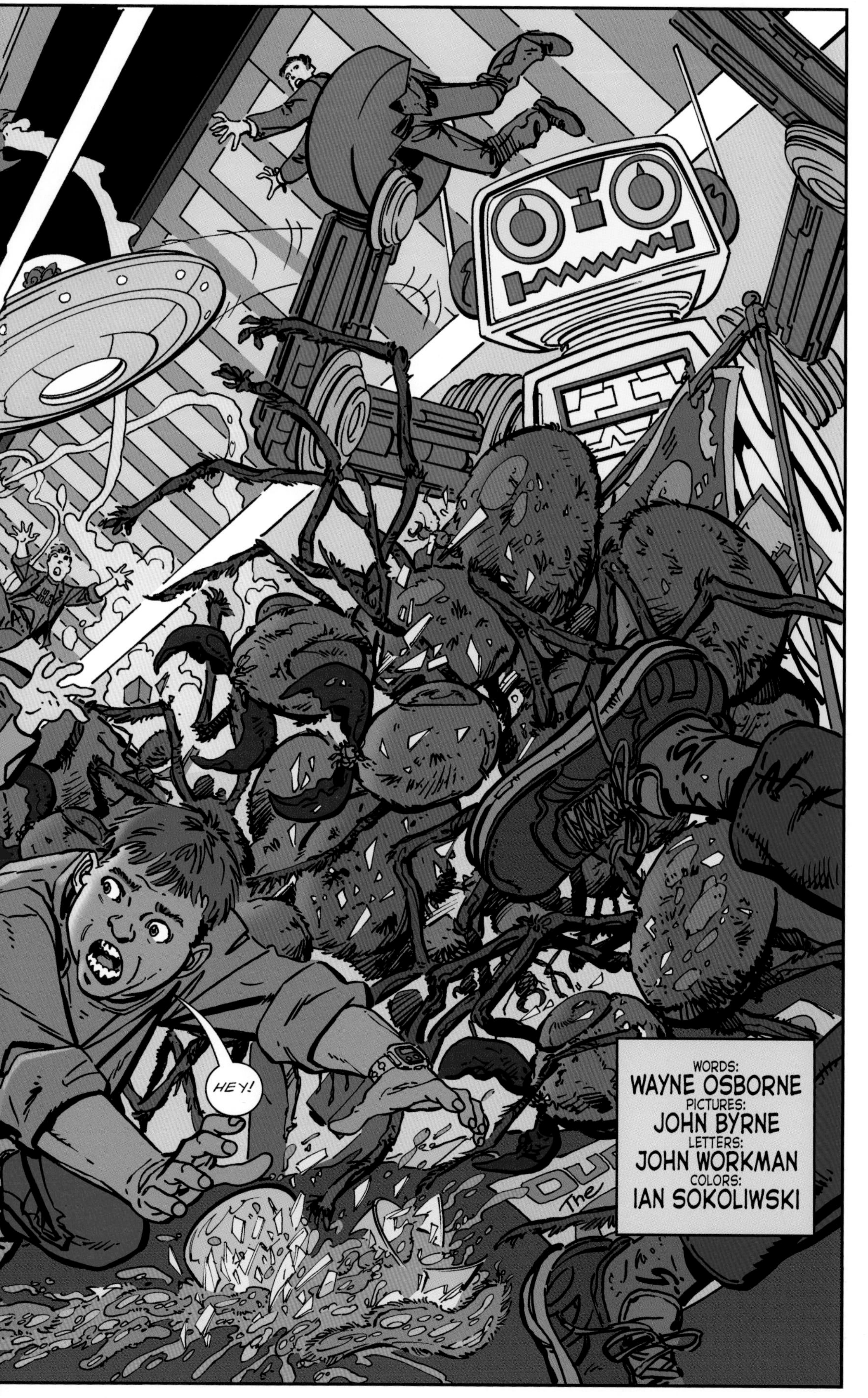
HEY!
WORDS:
WAYNE OSBORNE
PICTURES:
JOHN BYRNE
LETTERS:
JOHN WORKMAN
COLORS:
IAN SOKOLIWSKI

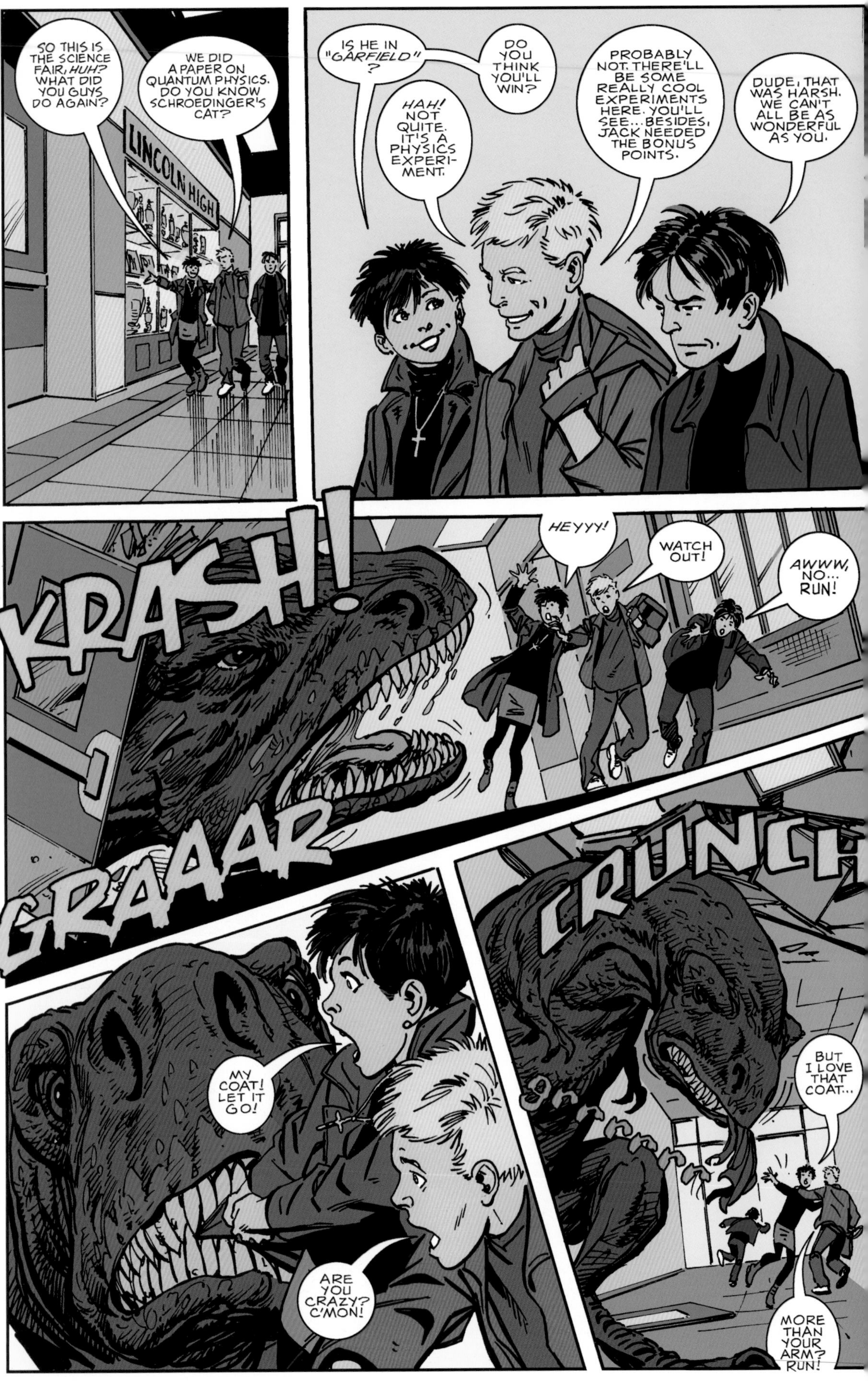
SO THIS IS THE SCIENCE FAIR, HUH? WHAT DID YOU GUYS DO AGAIN?
WE DID A PAPER ON QUANTUM PHYSICS. DO YOU KNOW SCHROEDINGER'S CAT?
LINCOLN HIGH
IS HE IN "GARFIELD"?
HAH! NOT QUITE. IT'S A PHYSICS EXPERIMENT.
DO YOU THINK YOU'LL WIN?
PROBABLY NOT. THERE'LL BE SOME REALLY COOL EXPERIMENTS HERE. YOU'LL SEE... BESIDES, JACK NEEDED THE BONUS POINTS.
DUDE, THAT WAS HARSH. WE CAN'T ALL BE AS WONDERFUL AS YOU.
KRASH!
HEYYY!
WATCH OUT!
AWWW, NO... RUN!
GRAAAR
CRUNCH
MY COAT! LET IT GO!
ARE YOU CRAZY? C'MON!
BUT I LOVE THAT COAT...
MORE THAN YOUR ARM? RUN!

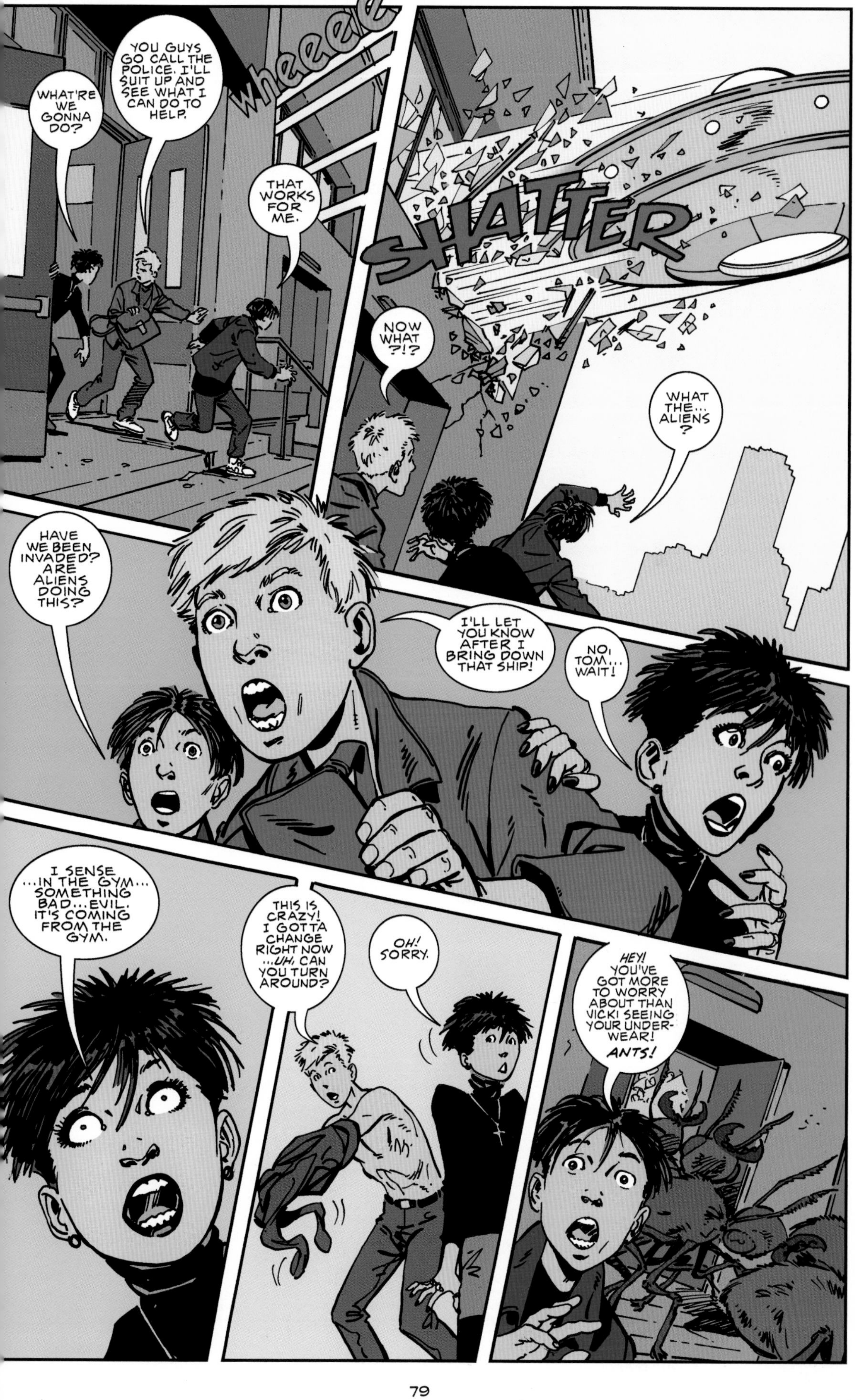
WHEEEE
WHAT'RE WE GONNA DO?
YOU GUYS GO CALL THE POLICE. I'LL SUIT UP AND SEE WHAT I CAN DO TO HELP.
THAT WORKS FOR ME.
SHATTER
NOW WHAT ?!?
WHAT THE... ALIENS?
HAVE WE BEEN INVADED? ARE ALIENS DOING THIS?
I'LL LET YOU KNOW AFTER I BRING DOWN THAT SHIP!
NO, TOM... WAIT!
I SENSE ...IN THE GYM... SOMETHING BAD...EVIL. IT'S COMING FROM THE GYM.
THIS IS CRAZY! I GOTTA CHANGE RIGHT NOW ...UH, CAN YOU TURN AROUND?
OH! SORRY.
HEY! YOU'VE GOT MORE TO WORRY ABOUT THAN VICKI SEEING YOUR UNDER-WEAR! ANTS!

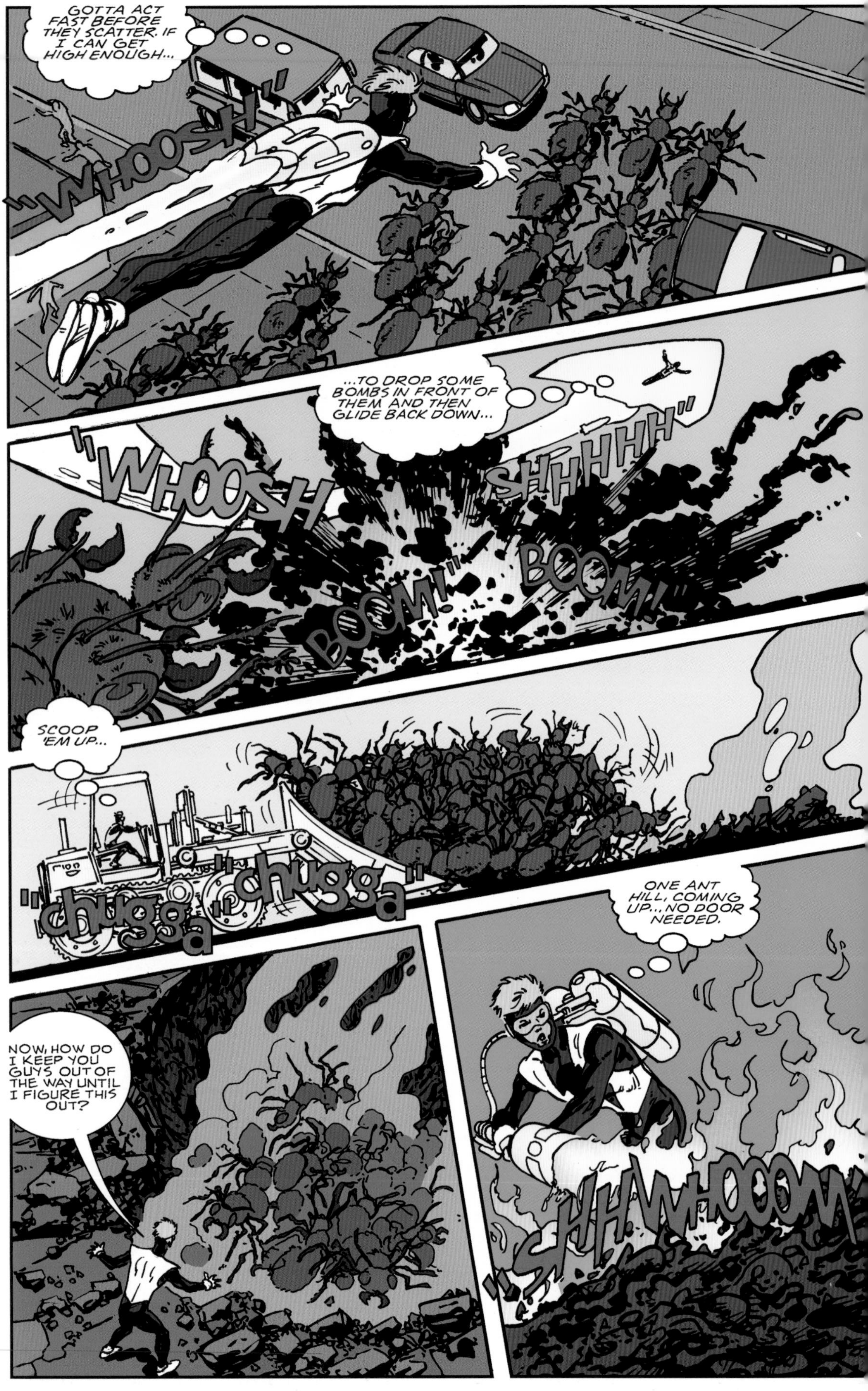

GOTTA ACT FAST BEFORE THEY SCATTER. IF I CAN GET HIGH ENOUGH...
"WHOOSH"
...TO DROP SOME BOMBS IN FRONT OF THEM AND THEN GLIDE BACK DOWN...
"WHOOSH"
"SHHHHHH"
"BOOM!"
"BOOM!"
SCOOP 'EM UP...
"chugga" "chugga"
ONE ANT HILL, COMING UP... NO DOOR NEEDED.
NOW, HOW DO I KEEP YOU GUYS OUT OF THE WAY UNTIL I FIGURE THIS OUT?
"SHHWHOOOM"

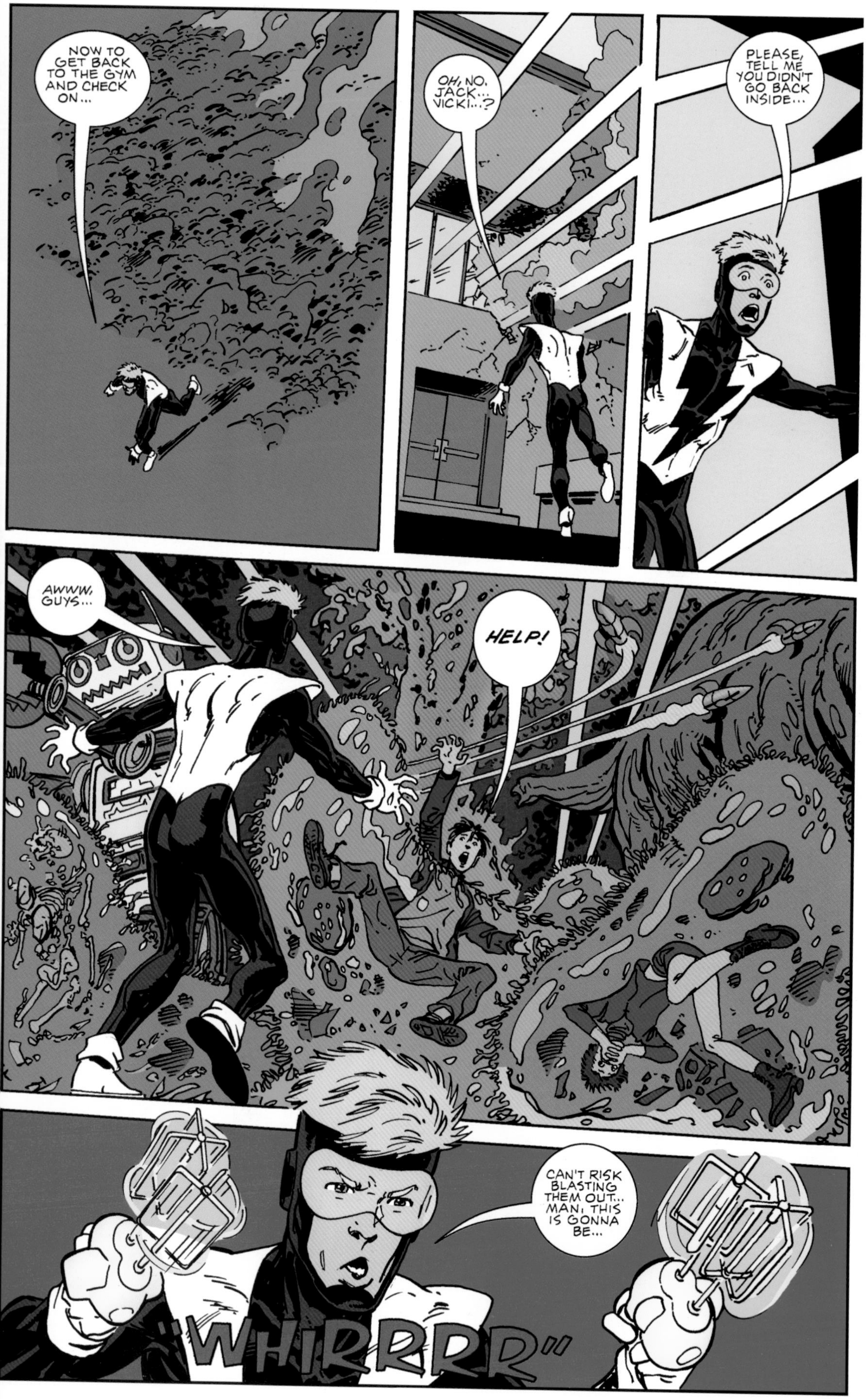
NOW TO GET BACK TO THE GYM AND CHECK ON...
OH, NO. JACK... VICKI...?
PLEASE, TELL ME YOU DIDN'T GO BACK INSIDE...
AWWW, GUYS...
HELP!
CAN'T RISK BLASTING THEM OUT... MAN, THIS IS GONNA BE...
"WHIRRRR"

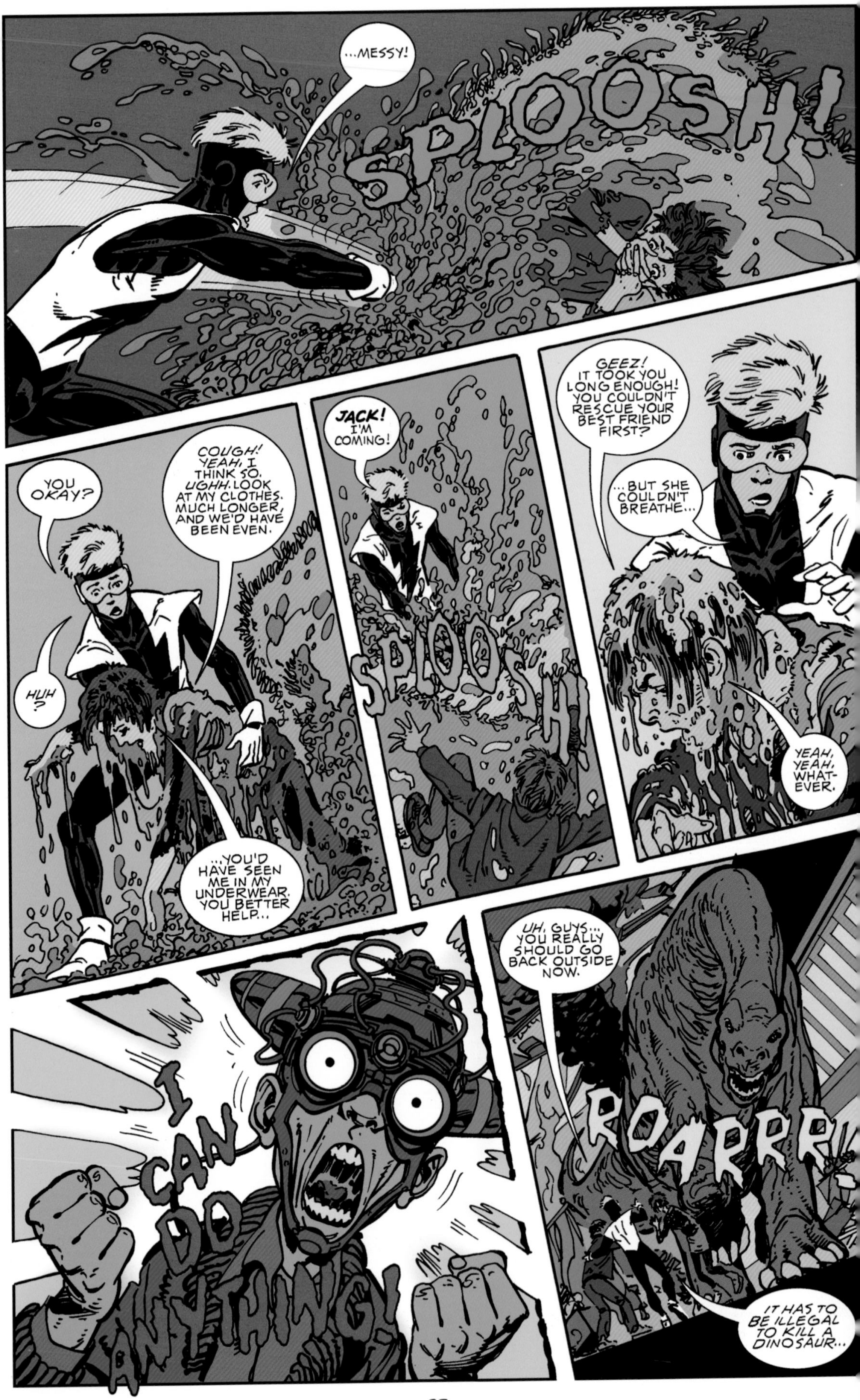
...MESSY!
SPLOOSH!
YOU OKAY?
COUGH! YEAH, I THINK SO. UGHH. LOOK AT MY CLOTHES. MUCH LONGER, AND WE'D HAVE BEEN EVEN.
HUH?
...YOU'D HAVE SEEN ME IN MY UNDERWEAR. YOU BETTER HELP...
JACK! I'M COMING!
SPLOOSH
GEEZ! IT TOOK YOU LONG ENOUGH! YOU COULDN'T RESCUE YOUR BEST FRIEND FIRST?
...BUT SHE COULDN'T BREATHE...
YEAH, YEAH, WHAT-EVER.
I CAN DO ANYTHING!
UH, GUYS... YOU REALLY SHOULD GO BACK OUTSIDE NOW.
ROARRR
IT HAS TO BE ILLEGAL TO KILL A DINOSAUR...

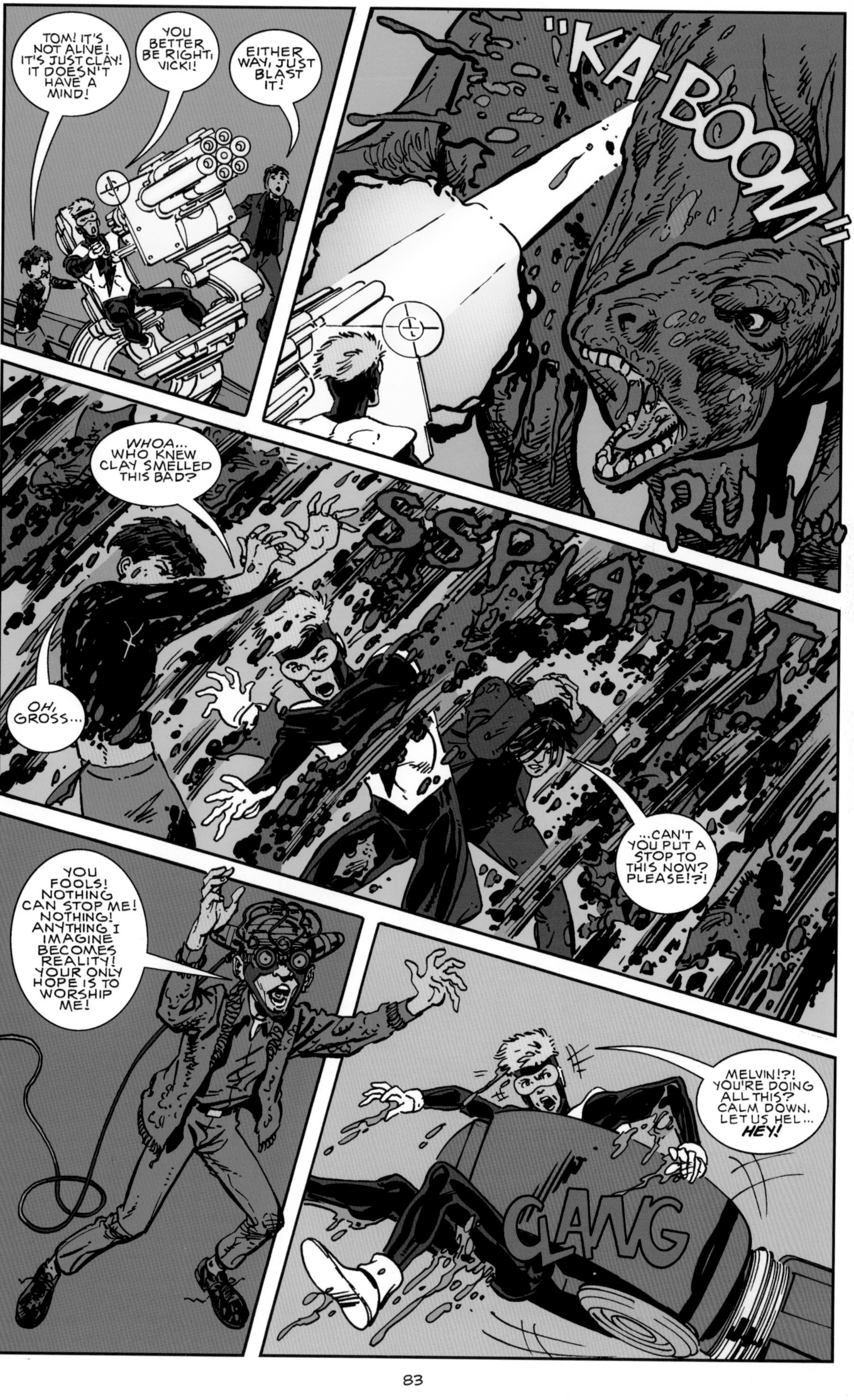
TOM! IT'S NOT ALIVE! IT'S JUST CLAY! IT DOESN'T HAVE A MIND!
YOU BETTER BE RIGHT, VICKI!
EITHER WAY, JUST BLAST IT!
"KA-BOOM!!"
RUH...
WHOA... WHO KNEW CLAY SMELLED THIS BAD?
SSPLAAAT
OH, GROSS...
...CAN'T YOU PUT A STOP TO THIS NOW? PLEASE!?!
YOU FOOLS! NOTHING CAN STOP ME! NOTHING! ANYTHING I IMAGINE BECOMES REALITY! YOUR ONLY HOPE IS TO WORSHIP ME!
MELVIN!?! YOU'RE DOING ALL THIS? CALM DOWN. LET US HEL... HEY!
CLANG

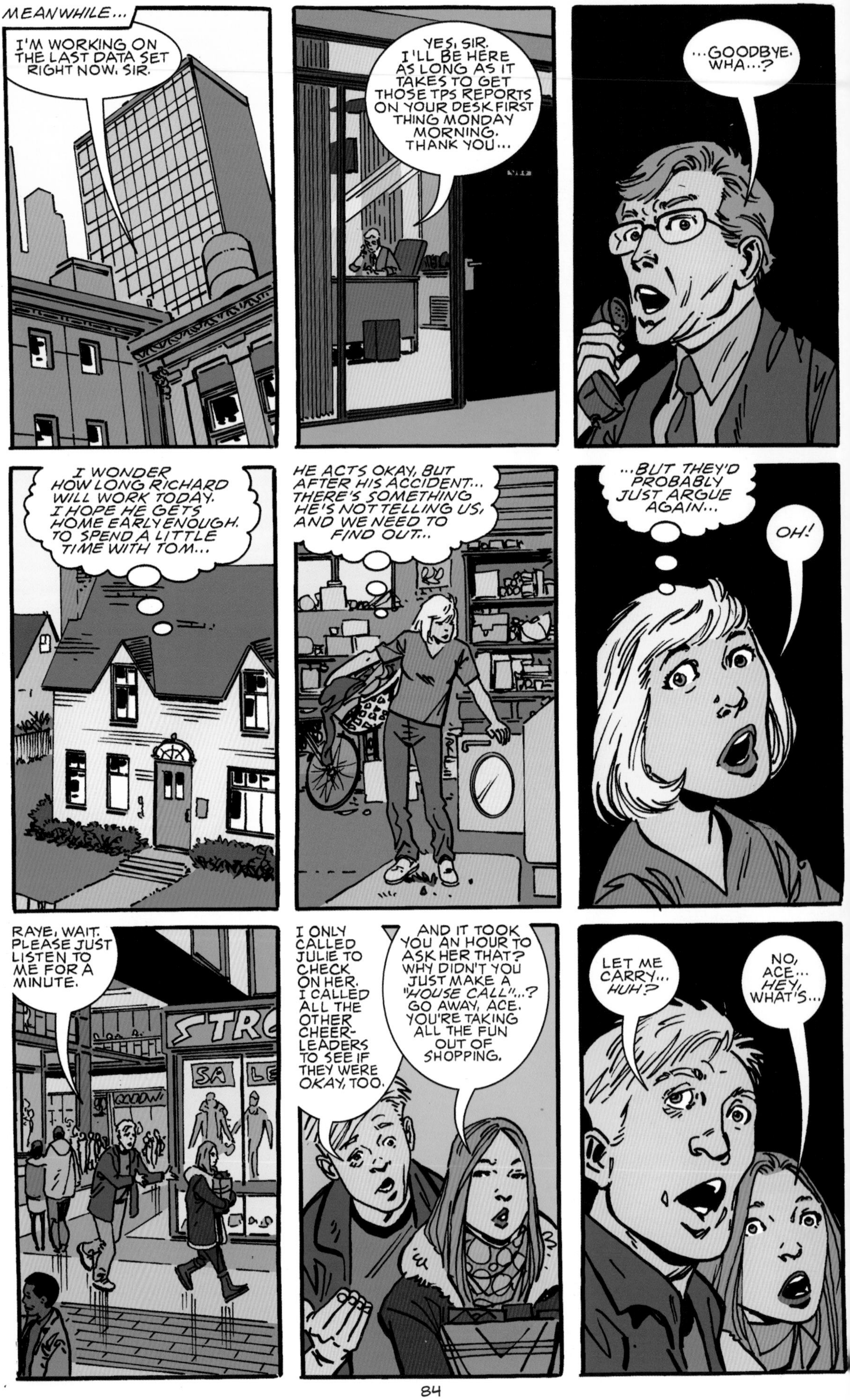
MEANWHILE...
I'M WORKING ON THE LAST DATA SET RIGHT NOW, SIR.
YES, SIR. I'LL BE HERE AS LONG AS IT TAKES TO GET THOSE TPS REPORTS ON YOUR DESK FIRST THING MONDAY MORNING. THANK YOU...
...GOODBYE. WHA...?
I WONDER HOW LONG RICHARD WILL WORK TODAY. I HOPE HE GETS HOME EARLY ENOUGH. TO SPEND A LITTLE TIME WITH TOM...
HE ACTS OKAY, BUT AFTER HIS ACCIDENT... THERE'S SOMETHING HE'S NOT TELLING US, AND WE NEED TO FIND OUT...
...BUT THEY'D PROBABLY JUST ARGUE AGAIN...
OH!
RAYE, WAIT. PLEASE JUST LISTEN TO ME FOR A MINUTE.
I ONLY CALLED JULIE TO CHECK ON HER. I CALLED ALL THE OTHER CHEER-LEADERS TO SEE IF THEY WERE OKAY, TOO.
AND IT TOOK YOU AN HOUR TO ASK HER THAT? WHY DIDN'T YOU JUST MAKE A "HOUSE CALL"...? GO AWAY, ACE. YOU'RE TAKING ALL THE FUN OUT OF SHOPPING.
LET ME CARRY... HUH?
NO, ACE... HEY, WHAT'S...

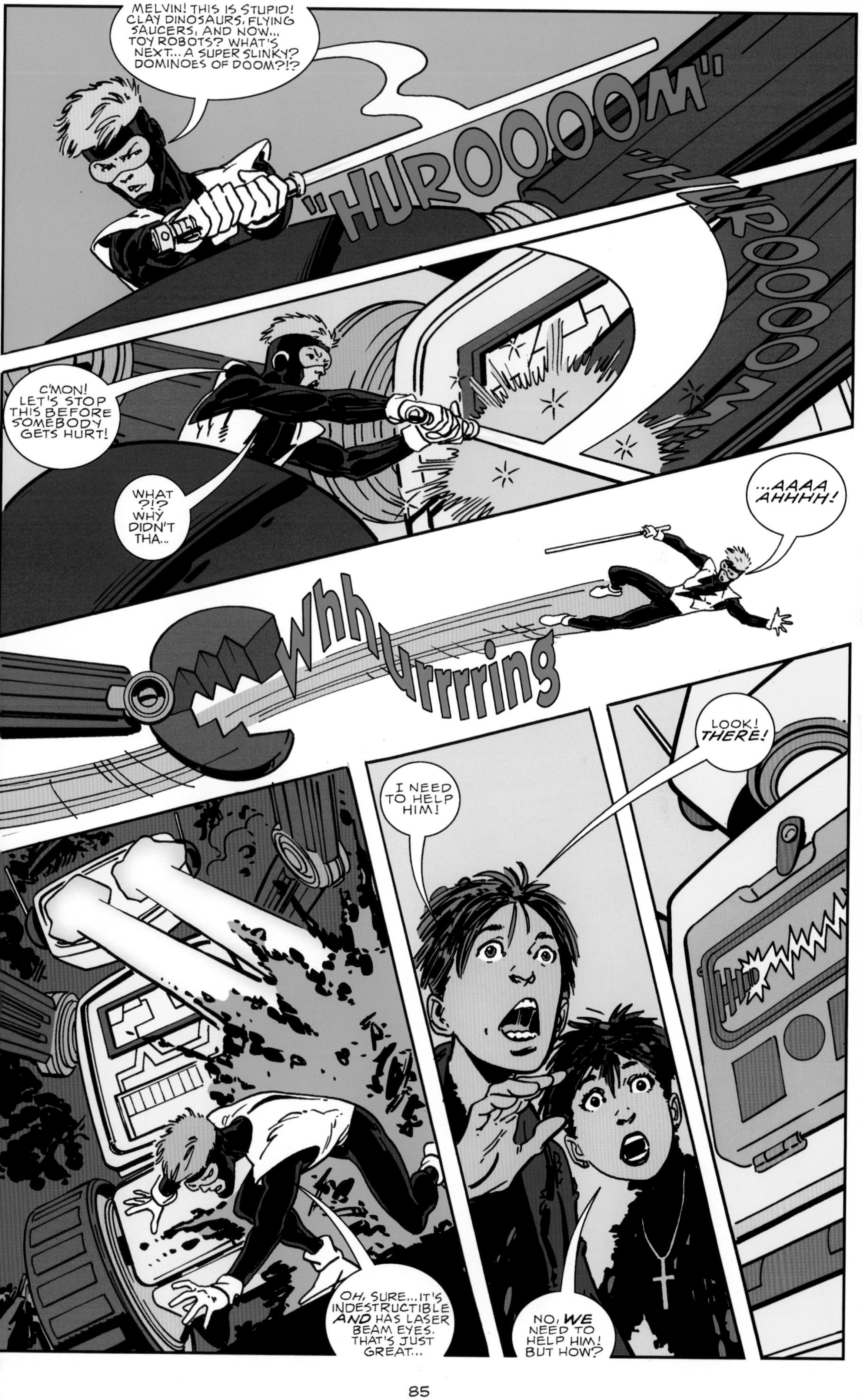
MELVIN! THIS IS STUPID! CLAY DINOSAURS, FLYING SAUCERS, AND NOW... TOY ROBOTS? WHAT'S NEXT... A SUPER SLINKY? DOMINOES OF DOOM?!?
"HUROOOOM"
"HUROOOON"
C'MON! LET'S STOP THIS BEFORE SOMEBODY GETS HURT!
WHAT?!? WHY DIDN'T THA...
...AAAA AHHHH!
Whhurrrring
I NEED TO HELP HIM!
LOOK! THERE!
OH, SURE... IT'S INDESTRUCTIBLE AND HAS LASER BEAM EYES. THAT'S JUST GREAT...
NO, WE NEED TO HELP HIM! BUT HOW?

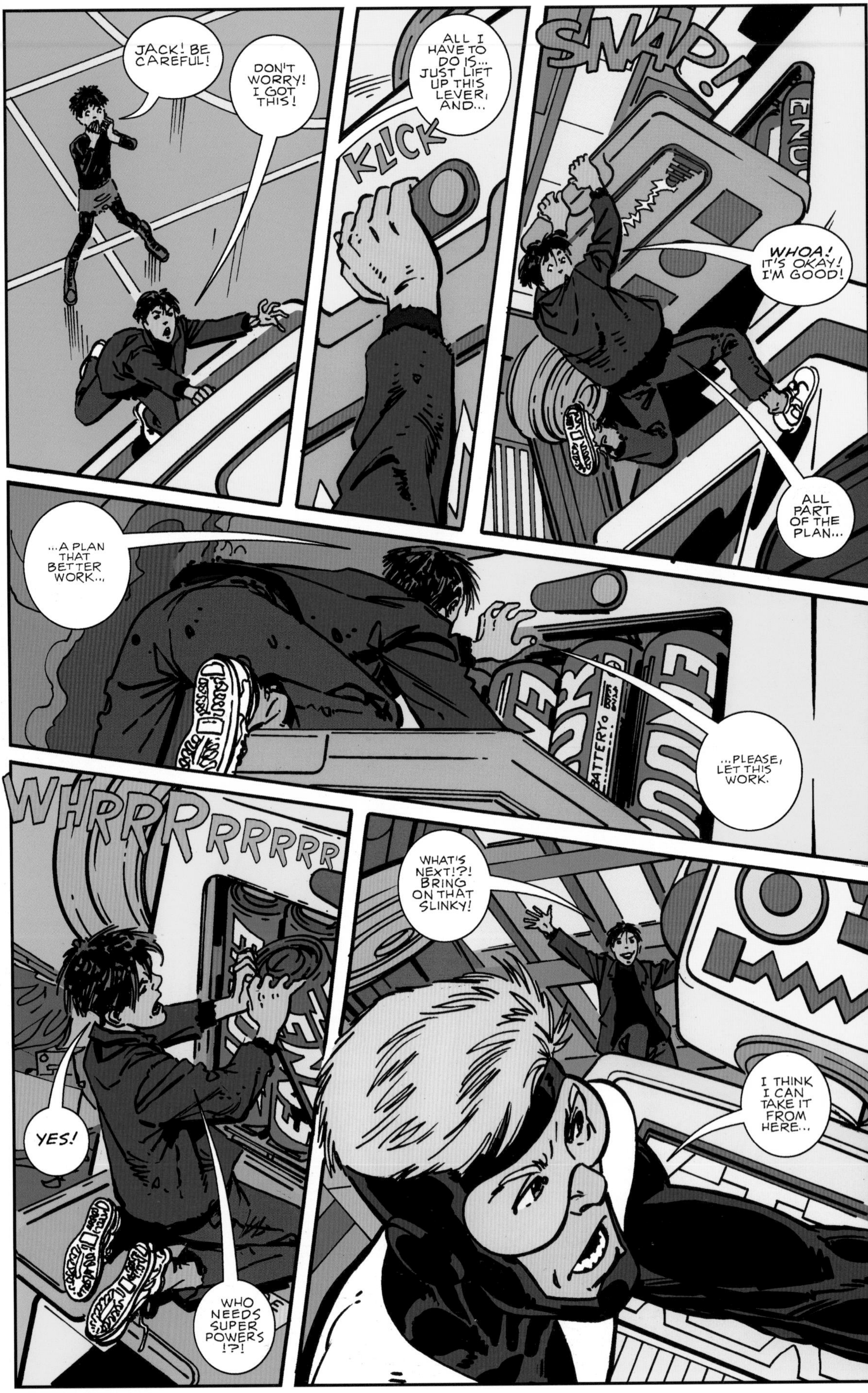
JACK! BE CAREFUL!
DON'T WORRY! I GOT THIS!
ALL I HAVE TO DO IS... JUST LIFT UP THIS LEVER, AND...
KLICK
SNAP!
WHOA! IT'S OKAY! I'M GOOD!
ALL PART OF THE PLAN...
...A PLAN THAT BETTER WORK...
...PLEASE, LET THIS WORK.
BATTERY
WHRRRRRRRR
YES!
WHO NEEDS SUPER POWERS !?!
WHAT'S NEXT!?! BRING ON THAT SLINKY!
I THINK I CAN TAKE IT FROM HERE...

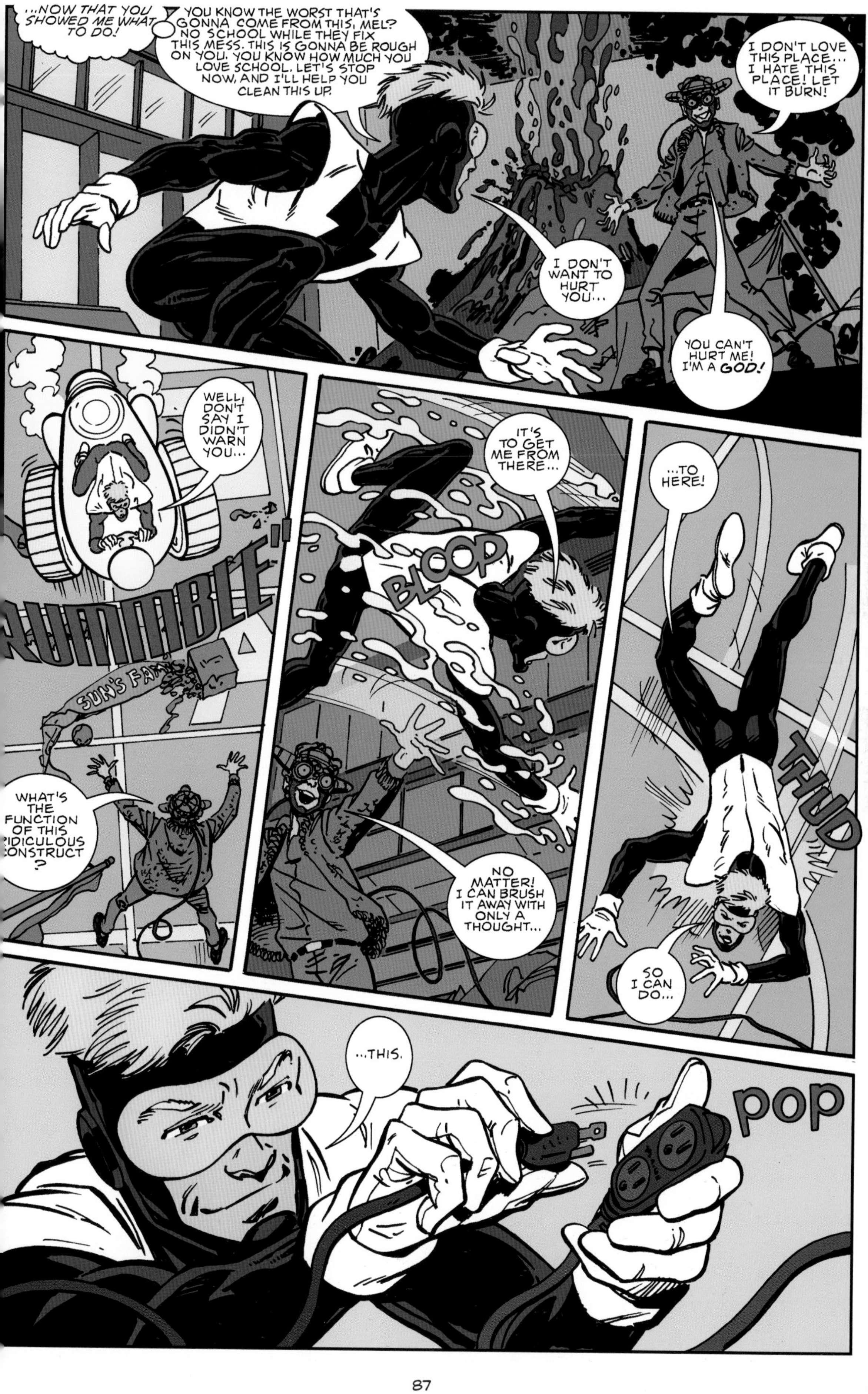
...NOW THAT YOU SHOWED ME WHAT TO DO!
YOU KNOW THE WORST THAT'S GONNA COME FROM THIS, MEL? NO SCHOOL WHILE THEY FIX THIS MESS. THIS IS GONNA BE ROUGH ON YOU. YOU KNOW HOW MUCH YOU LOVE SCHOOL. LET'S STOP NOW, AND I'LL HELP YOU CLEAN THIS UP.
I DON'T LOVE THIS PLACE... I HATE THIS PLACE! LET IT BURN!
I DON'T WANT TO HURT YOU...
YOU CAN'T HURT ME! I'M A GOD!
WELL, DON'T SAY I DIDN'T WARN YOU...
RUMBLE
SUN'S FARM
WHAT'S THE FUNCTION OF THIS RIDICULOUS CONSTRUCT?
IT'S TO GET ME FROM THERE...
BLOOP
NO MATTER! I CAN BRUSH IT AWAY WITH ONLY A THOUGHT...
...TO HERE!
THUD
SO I CAN DO...
...THIS.
pop

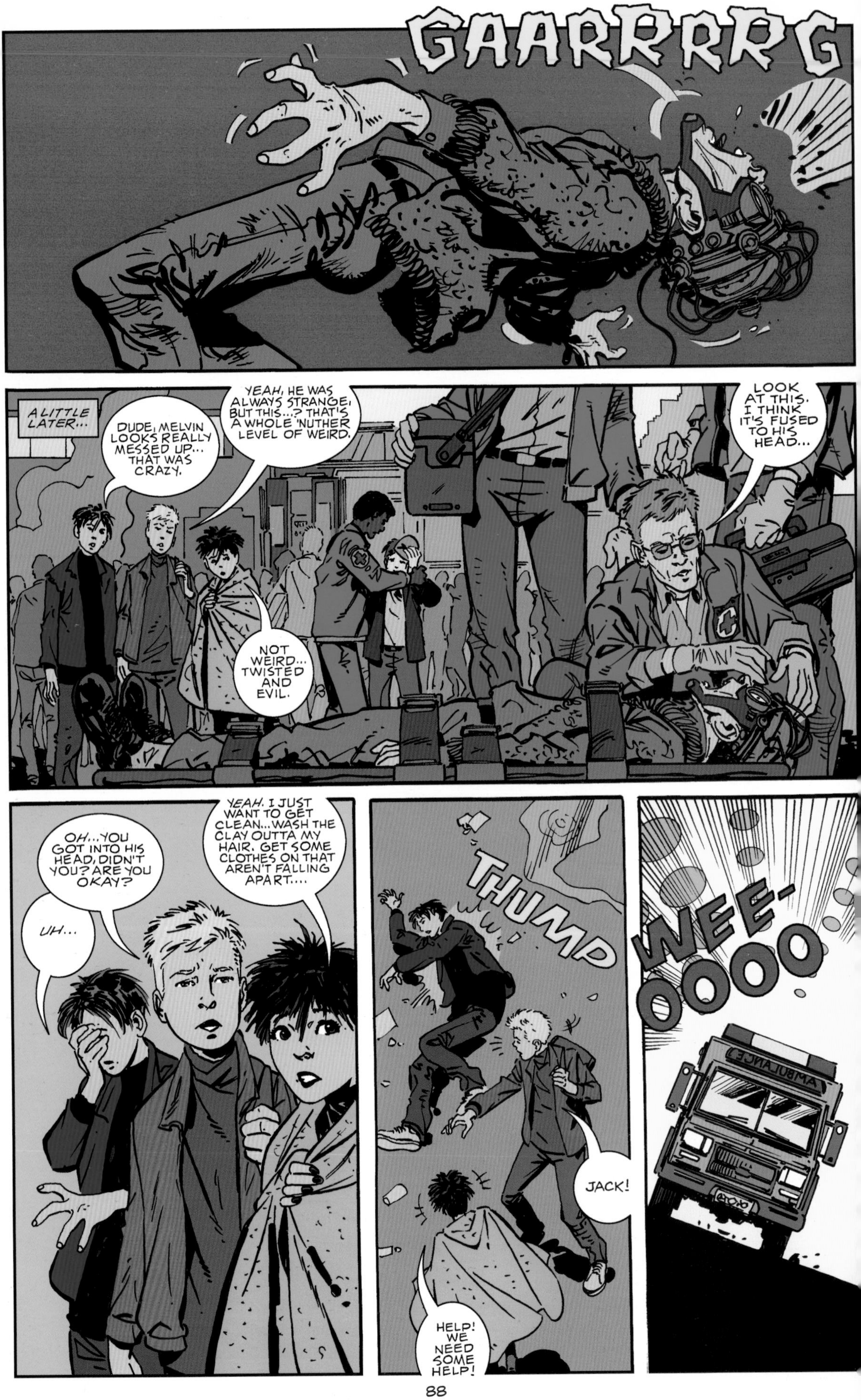
GAARRRRG
A LITTLE LATER...
DUDE, MELVIN LOOKS REALLY MESSED UP... THAT WAS CRAZY.
YEAH, HE WAS ALWAYS STRANGE, BUT THIS...? THAT'S A WHOLE 'NUTHER LEVEL OF WEIRD.
NOT WEIRD... TWISTED AND EVIL.
LOOK AT THIS. I THINK IT'S FUSED TO HIS HEAD...
OH... YOU GOT INTO HIS HEAD, DIDN'T YOU? ARE YOU OKAY?
UH...
YEAH. I JUST WANT TO GET CLEAN... WASH THE CLAY OUTTA MY HAIR. GET SOME CLOTHES ON THAT AREN'T FALLING APART....
THUMP
JACK!
HELP! WE NEED SOME HELP!
WEE-OOOO
AMBULANCE

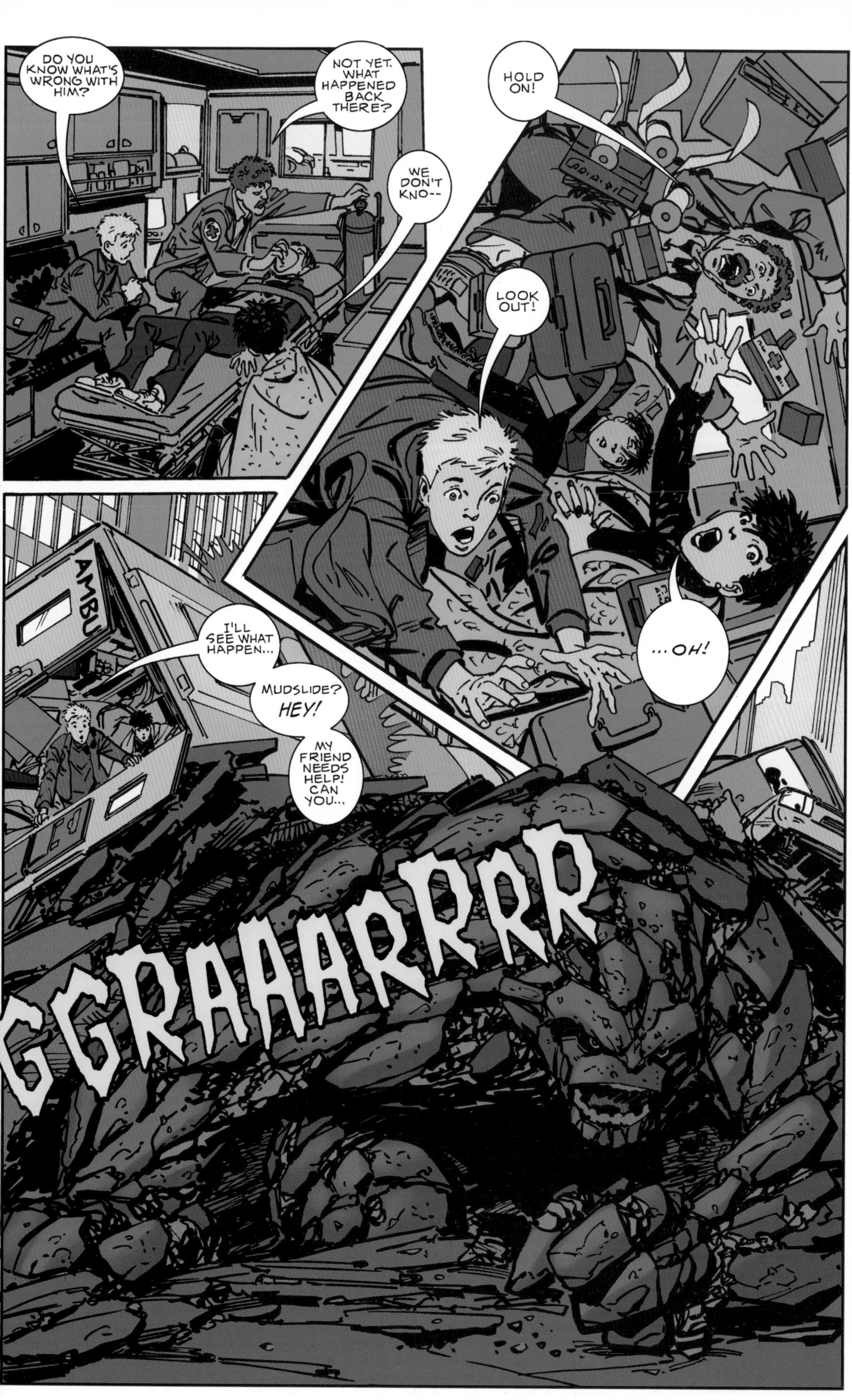
DO YOU KNOW WHAT'S WRONG WITH HIM?
NOT YET. WHAT HAPPENED BACK THERE?
WE DON'T KNO--
HOLD ON!
LOOK OUT!
...OH!
AMBU
I'LL SEE WHAT HAPPEN...
MUDSLIDE? HEY!
MY FRIEND NEEDS HELP! CAN YOU...
GGRAAARRRR

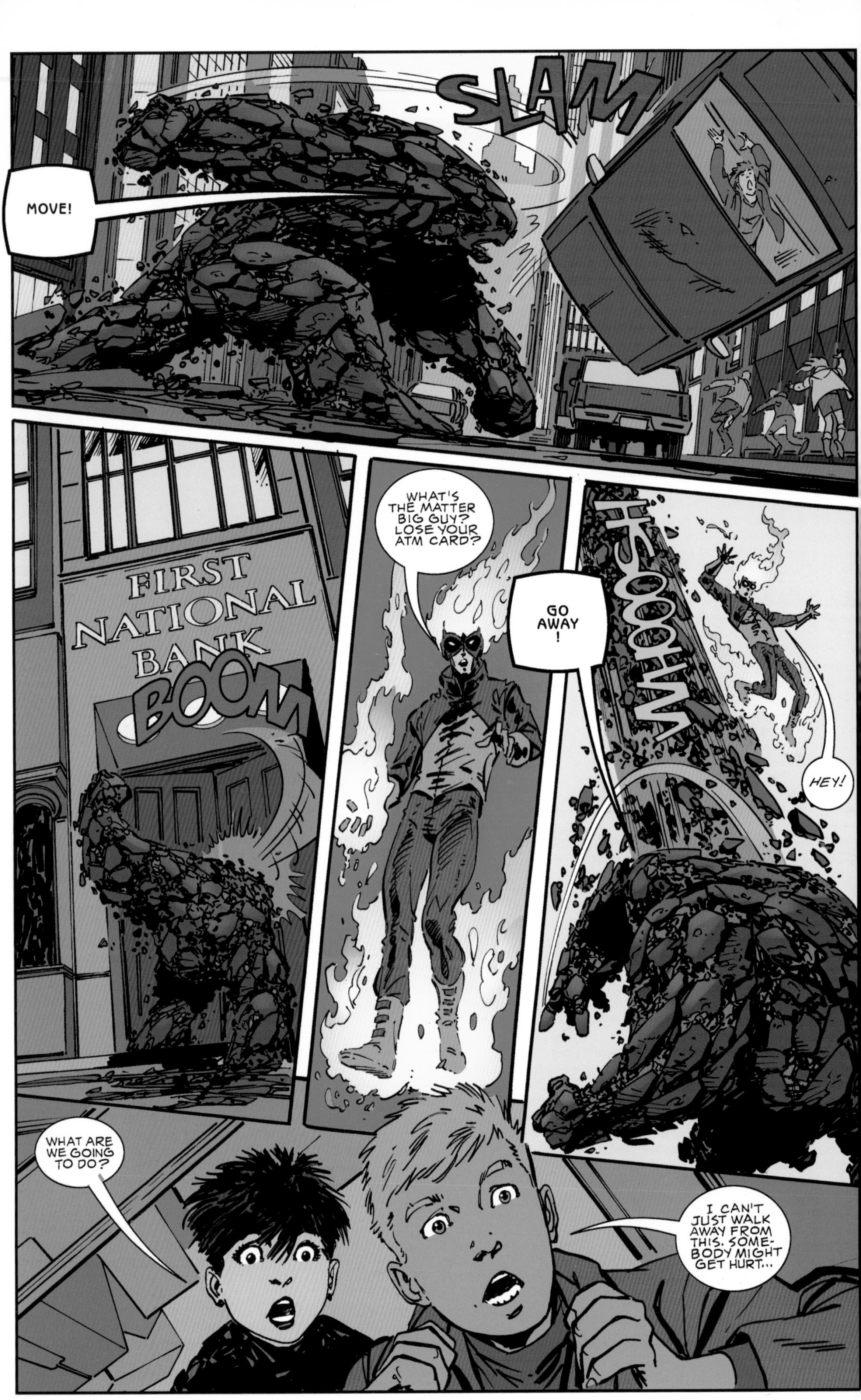
SLAM
MOVE!
FIRST NATIONAL BANK
BOOM
WHAT'S THE MATTER BIG GUY? LOSE YOUR ATM CARD?
GO AWAY!
WHOOOM
HEY!
WHAT ARE WE GOING TO DO?
I CAN'T JUST WALK AWAY FROM THIS. SOMEBODY MIGHT GET HURT...

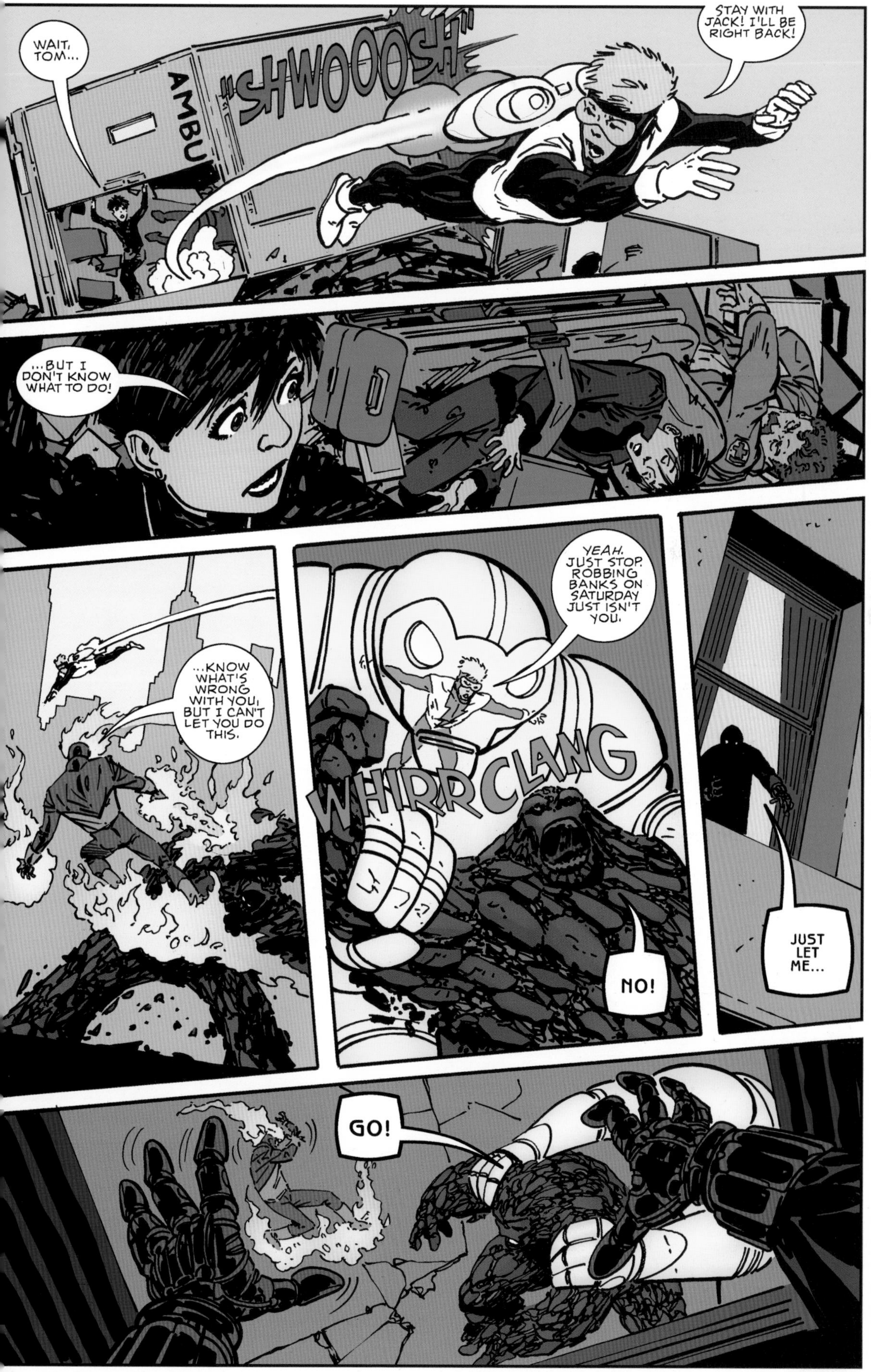
WAIT, TOM...
"SHWOOOSH"
AMBU
STAY WITH JACK! I'LL BE RIGHT BACK!
...BUT I DON'T KNOW WHAT TO DO!
...KNOW WHAT'S WRONG WITH YOU, BUT I CAN'T LET YOU DO THIS.
YEAH. JUST STOP. ROBBING BANKS ON SATURDAY JUST ISN'T YOU.
WHIRRCLANG
NO!
JUST LET ME...
GO!

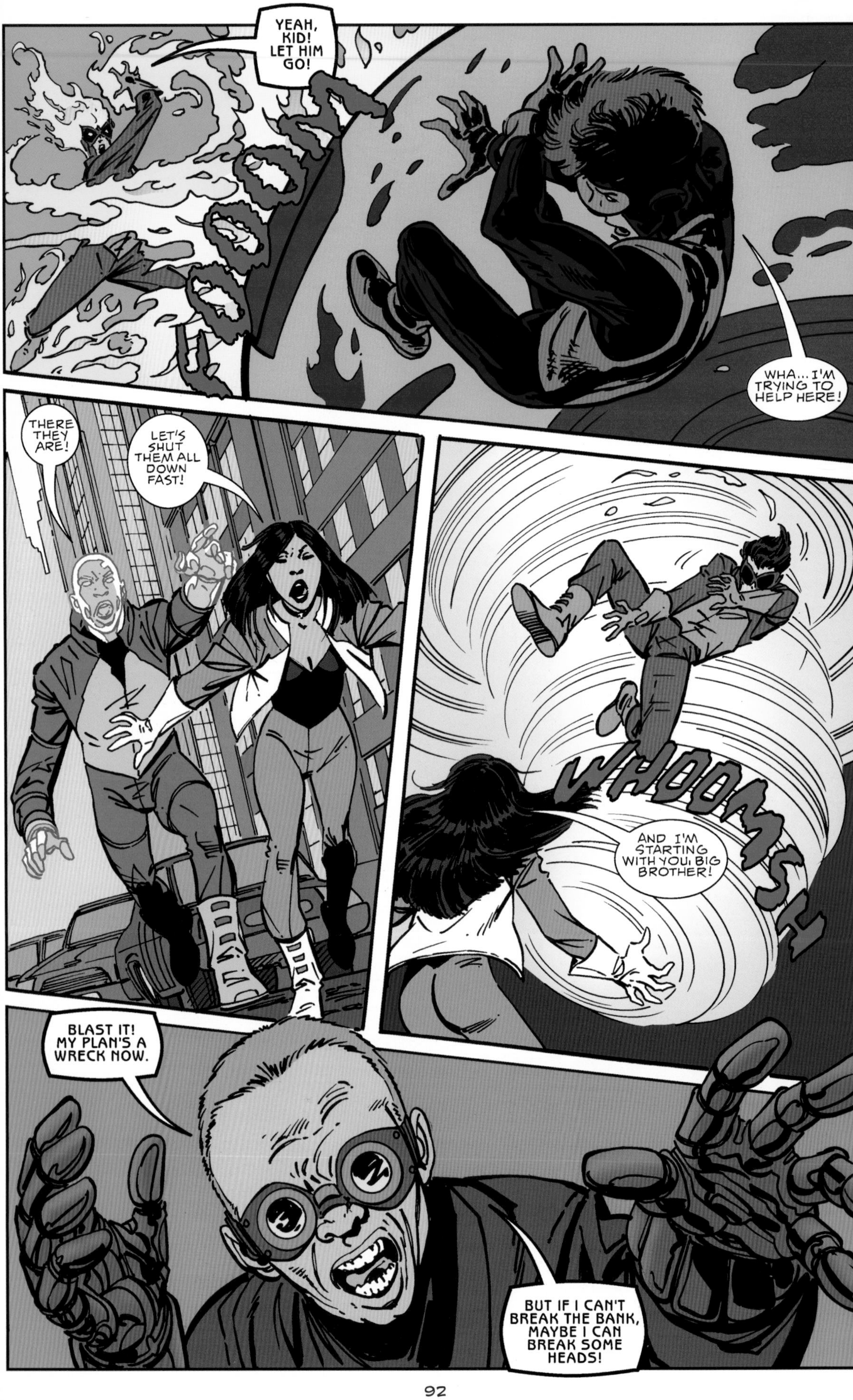
YEAH, KID! LET HIM GO!
WHA... I'M TRYING TO HELP HERE!
THERE THEY ARE!
LET'S SHUT THEM ALL DOWN FAST!
WHOOMSH
AND I'M STARTING WITH YOU, BIG BROTHER!
BLAST IT! MY PLAN'S A WRECK NOW.
BUT IF I CAN'T BREAK THE BANK, MAYBE I CAN BREAK SOME HEADS!

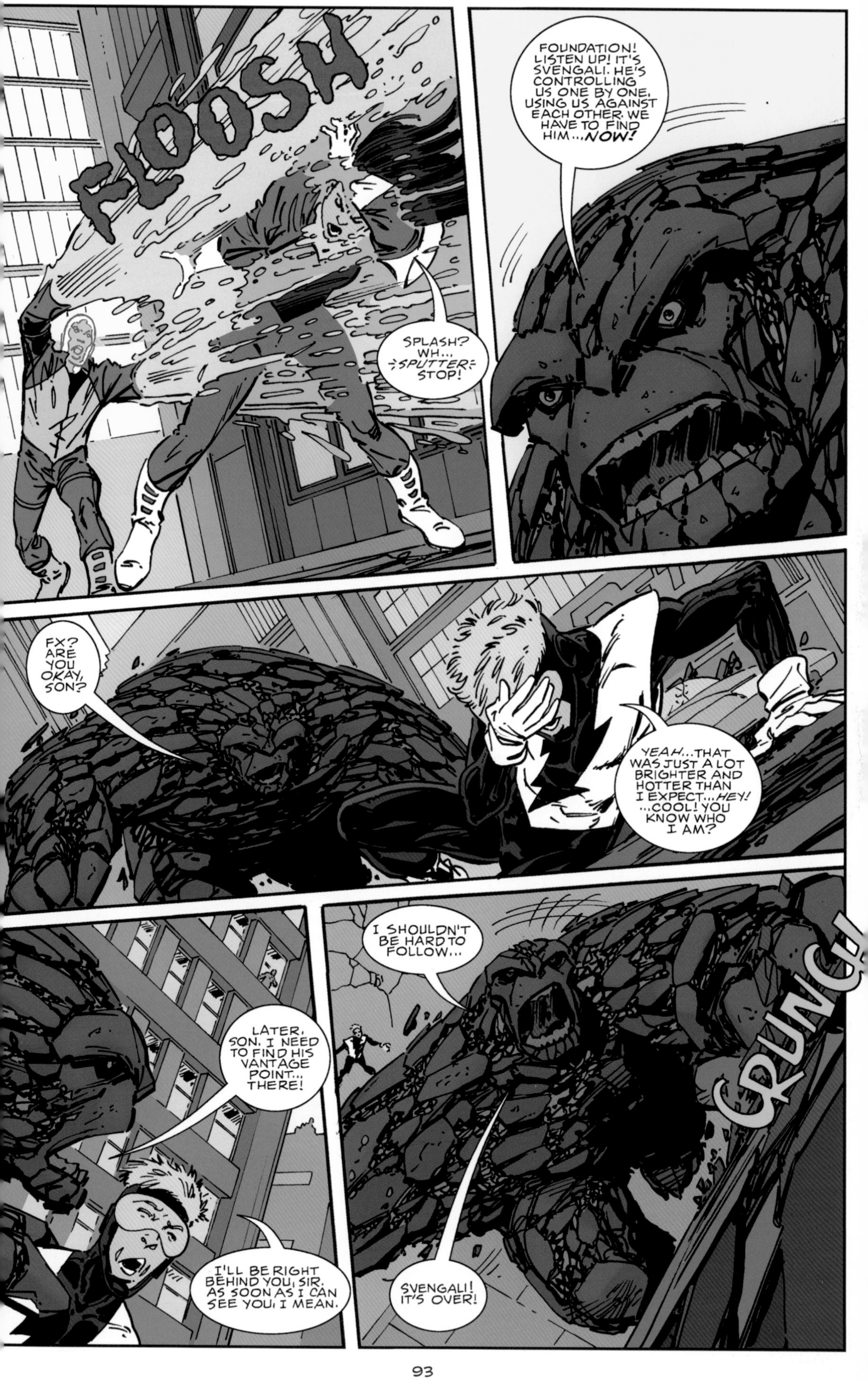
FLOOSH
SPLASH? WH... ~SPUTTER~ STOP!
FOUNDATION! LISTEN UP! IT'S SVENGALI. HE'S CONTROLLING US ONE BY ONE, USING US AGAINST EACH OTHER. WE HAVE TO FIND HIM...NOW!
FX? ARE YOU OKAY, SON?
YEAH...THAT WAS JUST A LOT BRIGHTER AND HOTTER THAN I EXPECT...HEY! ...COOL! YOU KNOW WHO I AM?
LATER, SON. I NEED TO FIND HIS VANTAGE POINT... THERE!
I'LL BE RIGHT BEHIND YOU, SIR. AS SOON AS I CAN SEE YOU, I MEAN.
I SHOULDN'T BE HARD TO FOLLOW...
CRUNCH
SVENGALI! IT'S OVER!

YOUR PLAN WAS FLAWED FROM THE BEGINNING. YOUR GLOVES DON'T MAKE YOU STRONG ENOUGH TO CONTROL US ALL.

I DON'T NEED ALL OF YOU... JUST ONE. AND THIS IS A LONG WAY FROM OVER.

JUST LIKE IT'S A LONG WAY...

MISTY!?! FIGHT HIM!

...DOWN MUDSLIDE!

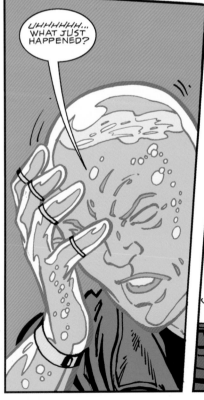

UHHHHHH... WHAT JUST HAPPENED?

SHAKE IT OFF, SPLASH! IT'S SVENGALI! HE'S GOT MISTY.

MUDSLIDE WENT AFTER HIM... BUT MISTY JUST BLASTED HIM OFF THE BUILDING. I'M GONNA TRY TO DISTRACT HER. C'MON!

"VARROOM"

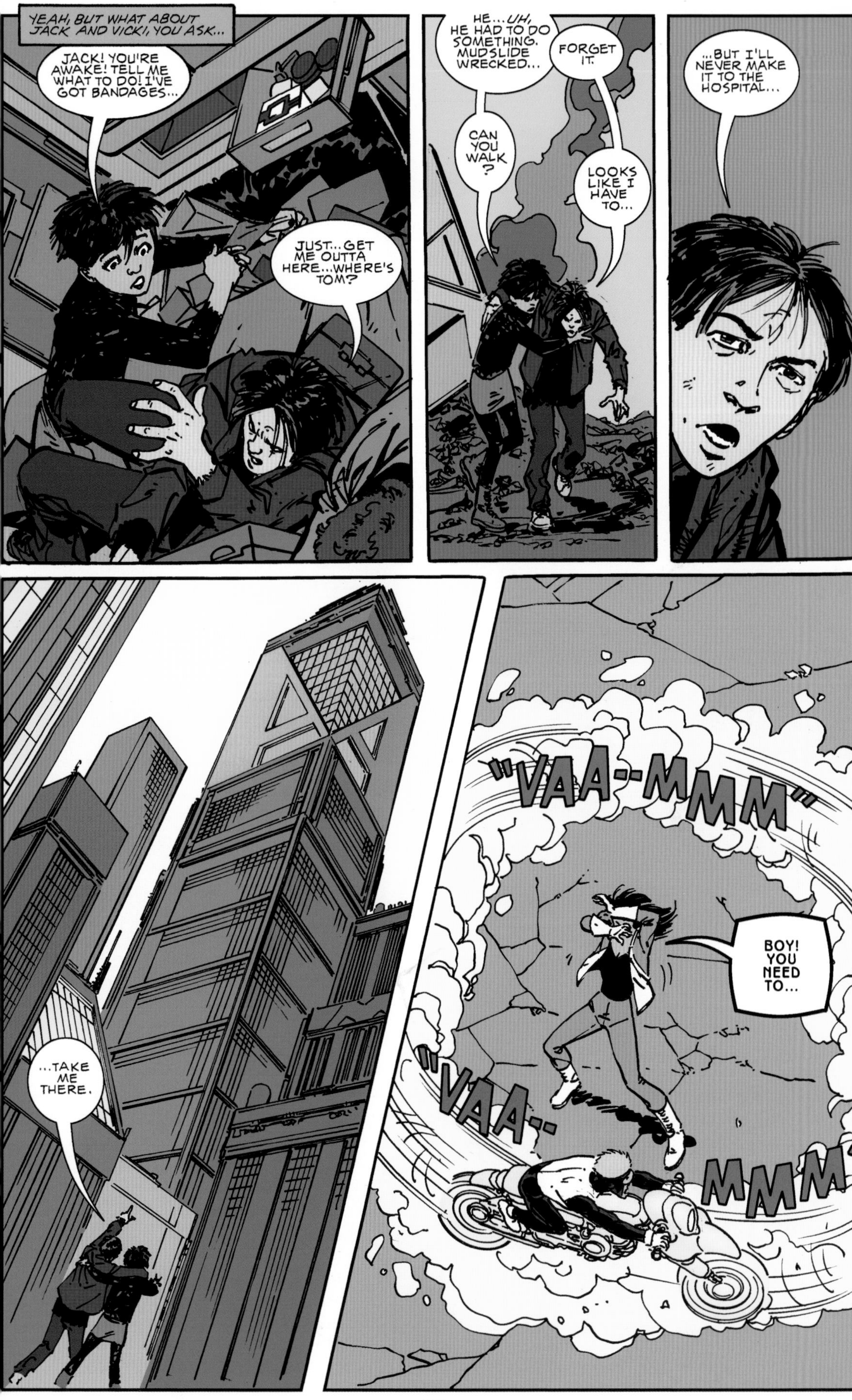
YEAH, BUT WHAT ABOUT JACK AND VICKI, YOU ASK...
JACK! YOU'RE AWAKE! TELL ME WHAT TO DO! I'VE GOT BANDAGES...
JUST...GET ME OUTTA HERE...WHERE'S TOM?
HE...UH, HE HAD TO DO SOMETHING. MUDSLIDE WRECKED...
FORGET IT.
CAN YOU WALK?
LOOKS LIKE I HAVE TO...
...BUT I'LL NEVER MAKE IT TO THE HOSPITAL...
...TAKE ME THERE.
"VAA--MMM"
BOY! YOU NEED TO...
"VAA--
MMM"

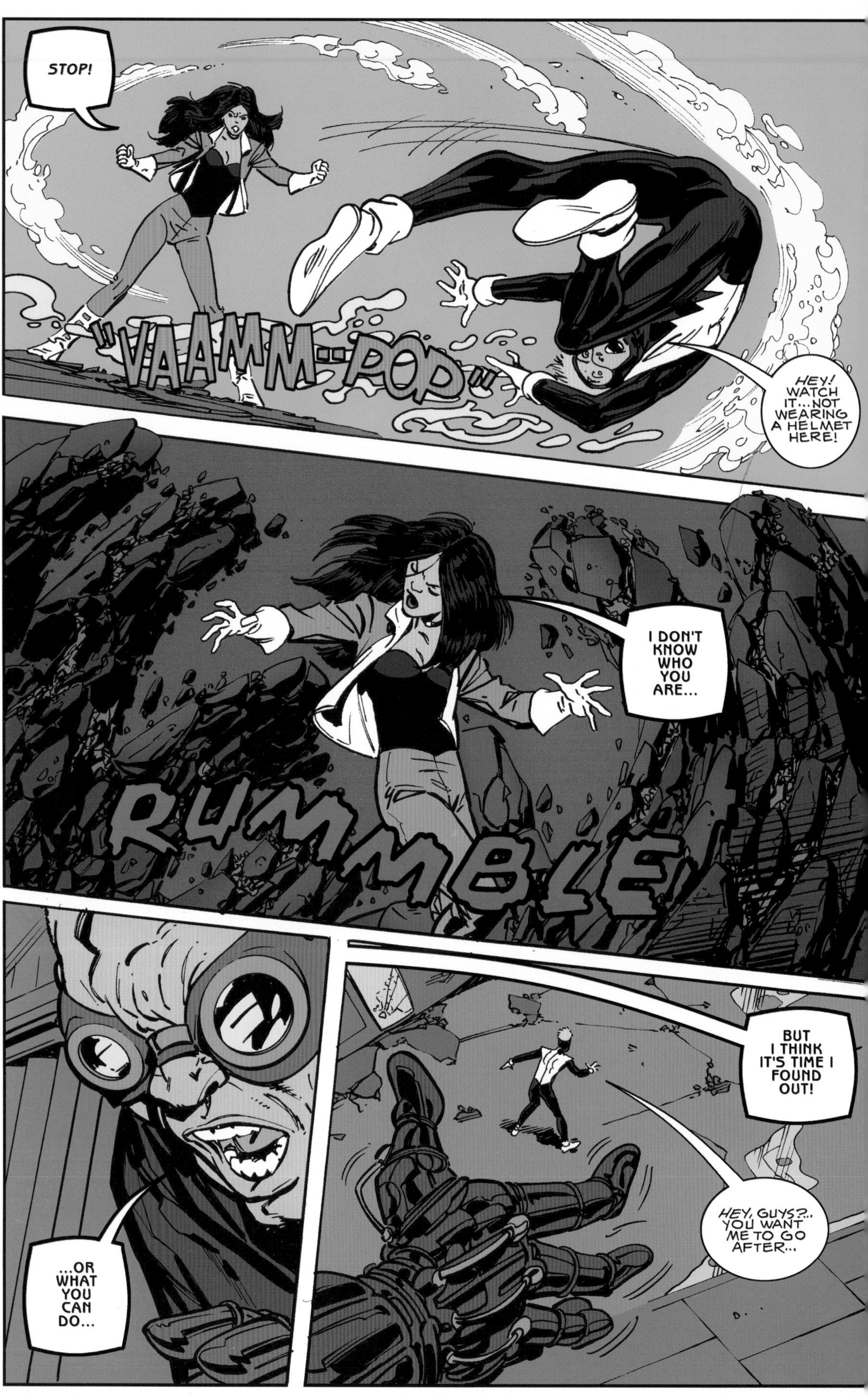
STOP!
"VAAMM--POP"
HEY! WATCH IT...NOT WEARING A HELMET HERE!
I DON'T KNOW WHO YOU ARE...
RUMMBLE
BUT I THINK IT'S TIME I FOUND OUT!
HEY, GUYS?.. YOU WANT ME TO GO AFTER...
...OR WHAT YOU CAN DO...

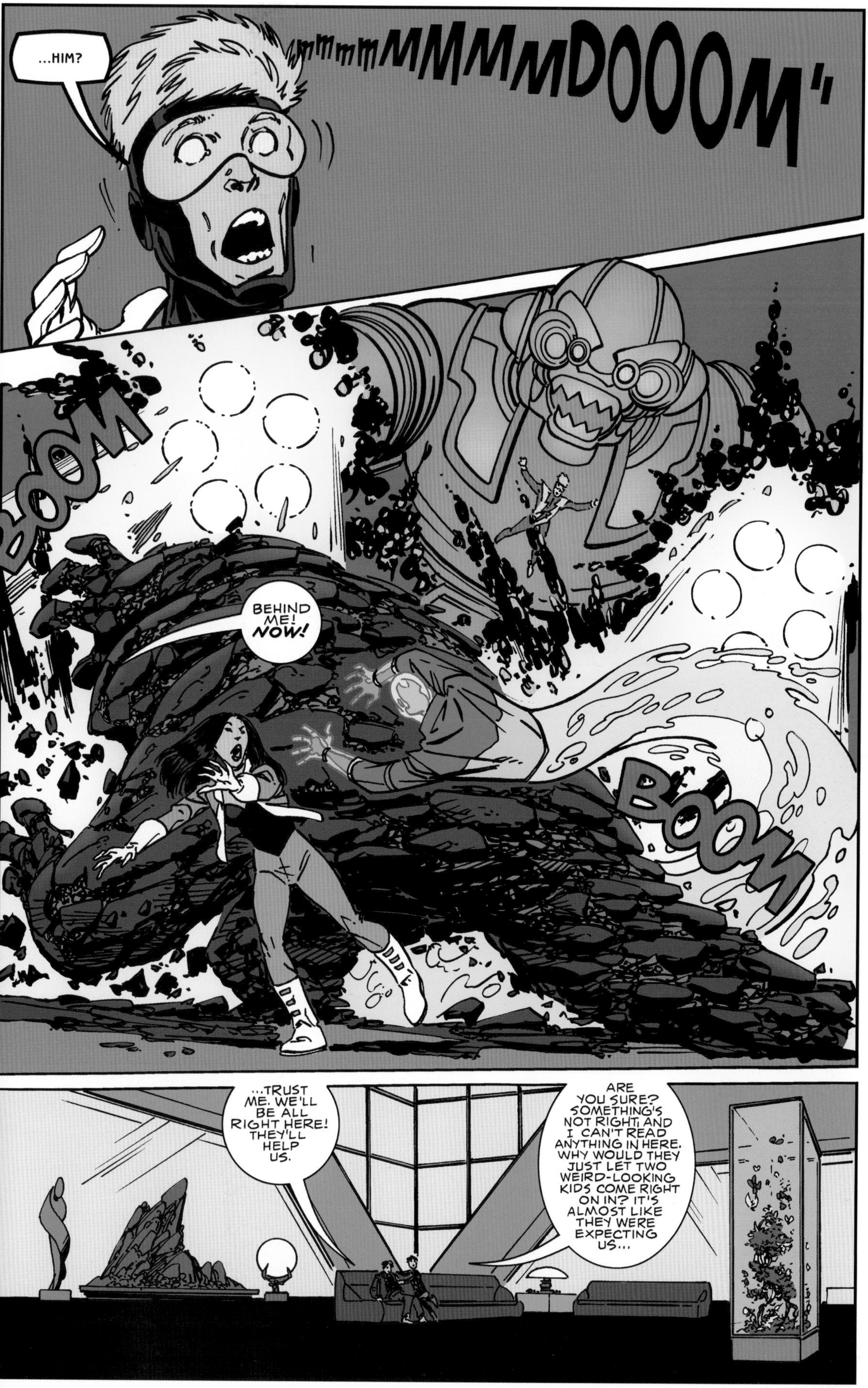
...HIM?
mmmmmMMMMMDOOOM
BOOM
BEHIND ME! NOW!
BOOM
...TRUST ME. WE'LL BE ALL RIGHT HERE! THEY'LL HELP US.
ARE YOU SURE? SOMETHING'S NOT RIGHT, AND I CAN'T READ ANYTHING IN HERE. WHY WOULD THEY JUST LET TWO WEIRD-LOOKING KIDS COME RIGHT ON IN? IT'S ALMOST LIKE THEY WERE EXPECTING US...

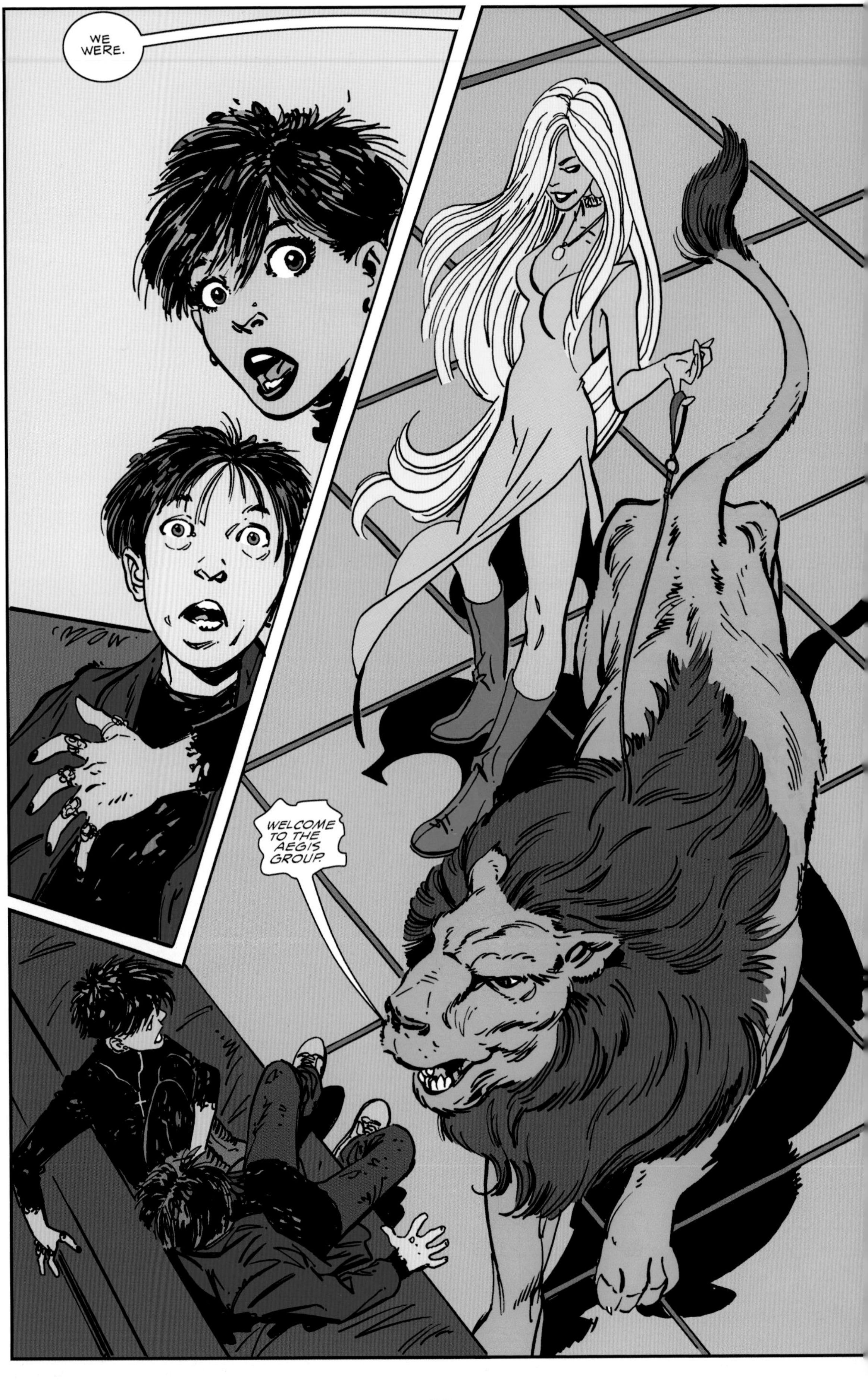
WE WERE.
WELCOME TO THE AEGIS GROUP.

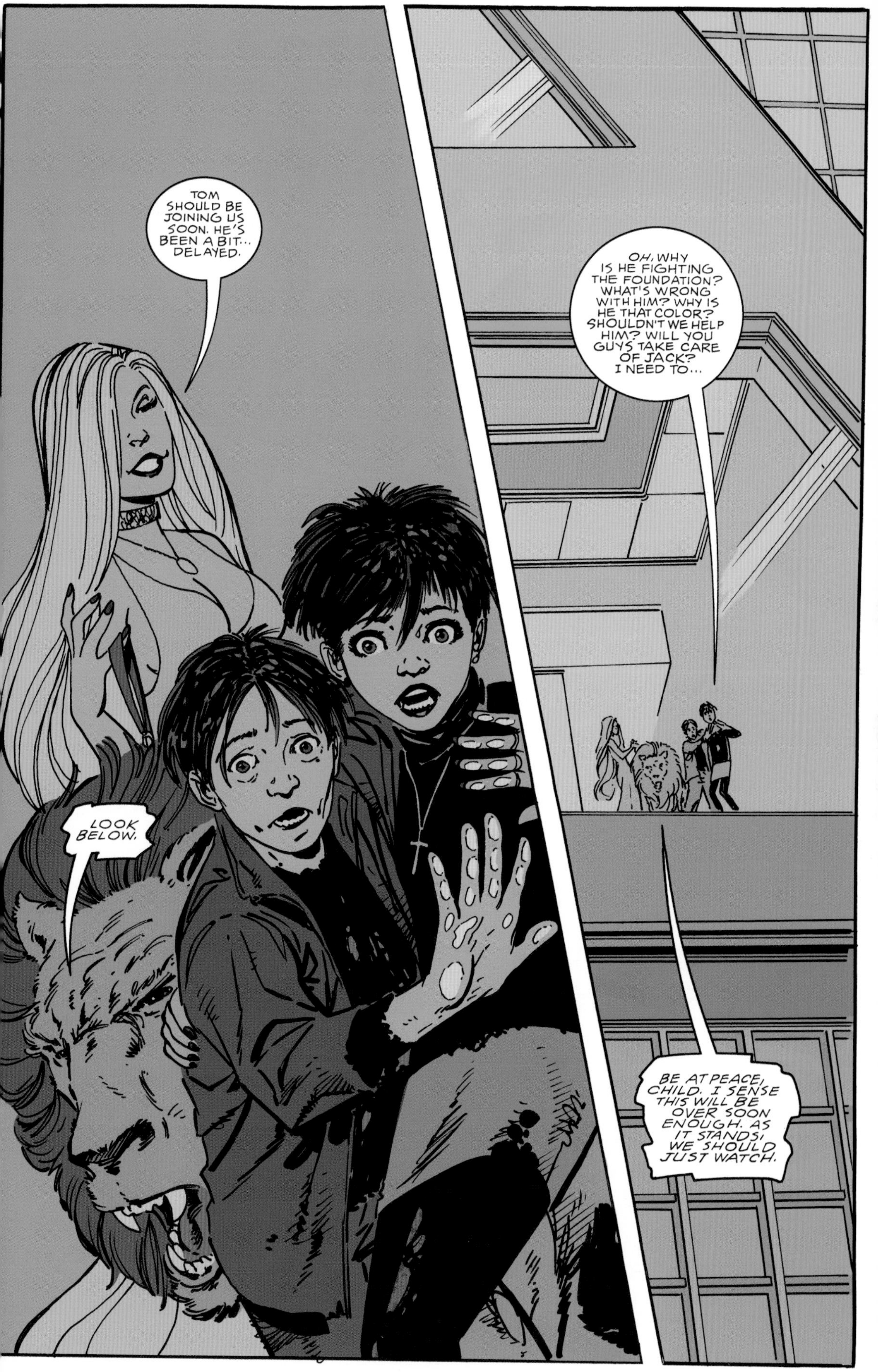
TOM SHOULD BE JOINING US SOON. HE'S BEEN A BIT... DELAYED.
LOOK BELOW.
OH, WHY IS HE FIGHTING THE FOUNDATION? WHAT'S WRONG WITH HIM? WHY IS HE THAT COLOR? SHOULDN'T WE HELP HIM? WILL YOU GUYS TAKE CARE OF JACK? I NEED TO...
BE AT PEACE, CHILD. I SENSE THIS WILL BE OVER SOON ENOUGH. AS IT STANDS, WE SHOULD JUST WATCH.

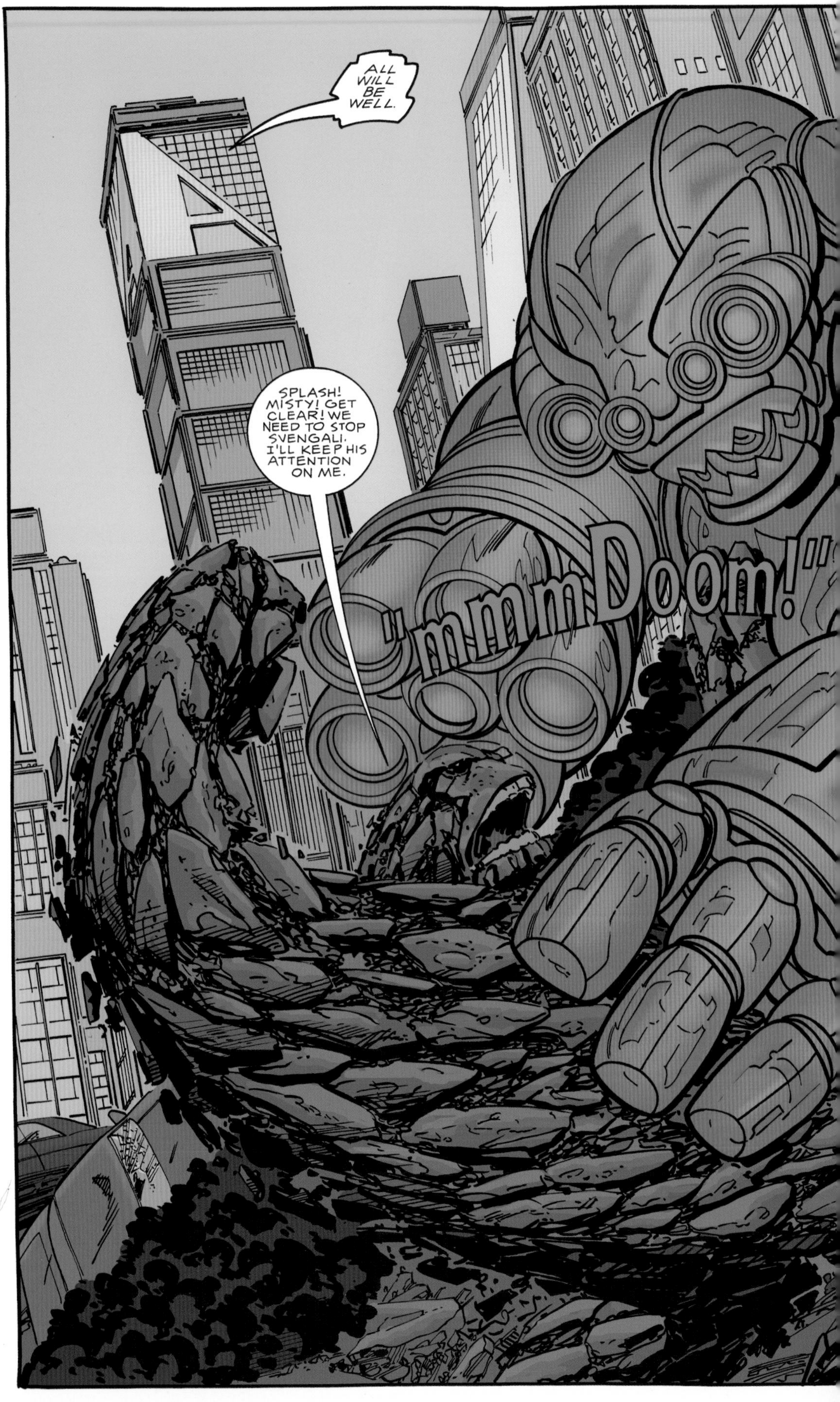
ALL WILL BE WELL.
SPLASH! MISTY! GET CLEAR! WE NEED TO STOP SVENGALI. I'LL KEEP HIS ATTENTION ON ME.
"mmmDoom!"

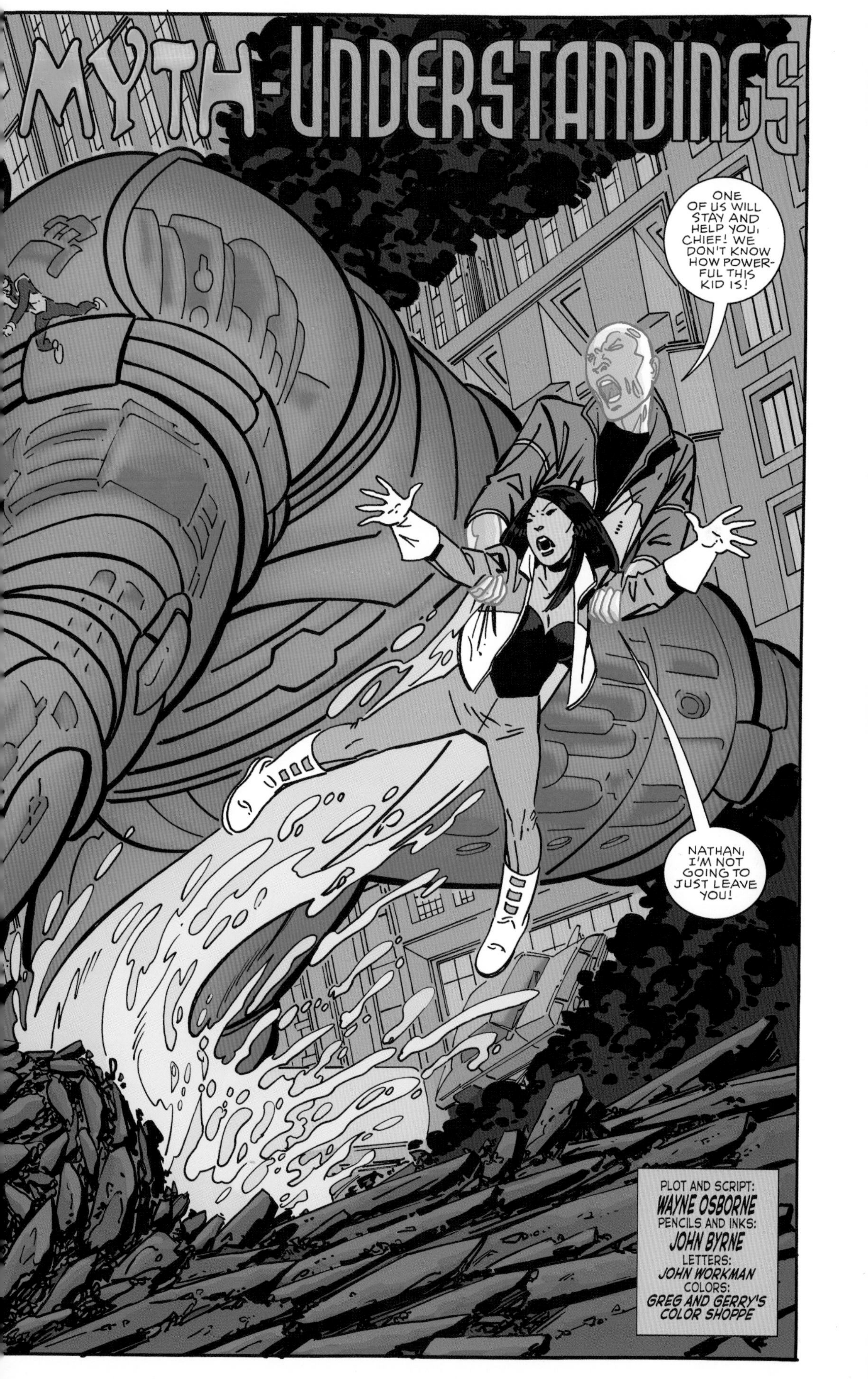
MYTH-UNDERSTANDINGS
ONE OF US WILL STAY AND HELP YOU, CHIEF! WE DON'T KNOW HOW POWER-FUL THIS KID IS!
NATHAN, I'M NOT GOING TO JUST LEAVE YOU!
PLOT AND SCRIPT: WAYNE OSBORNE
PENCILS AND INKS: JOHN BYRNE
LETTERS: JOHN WORKMAN
COLORS: GREG AND GERRY'S COLOR SHOPPE

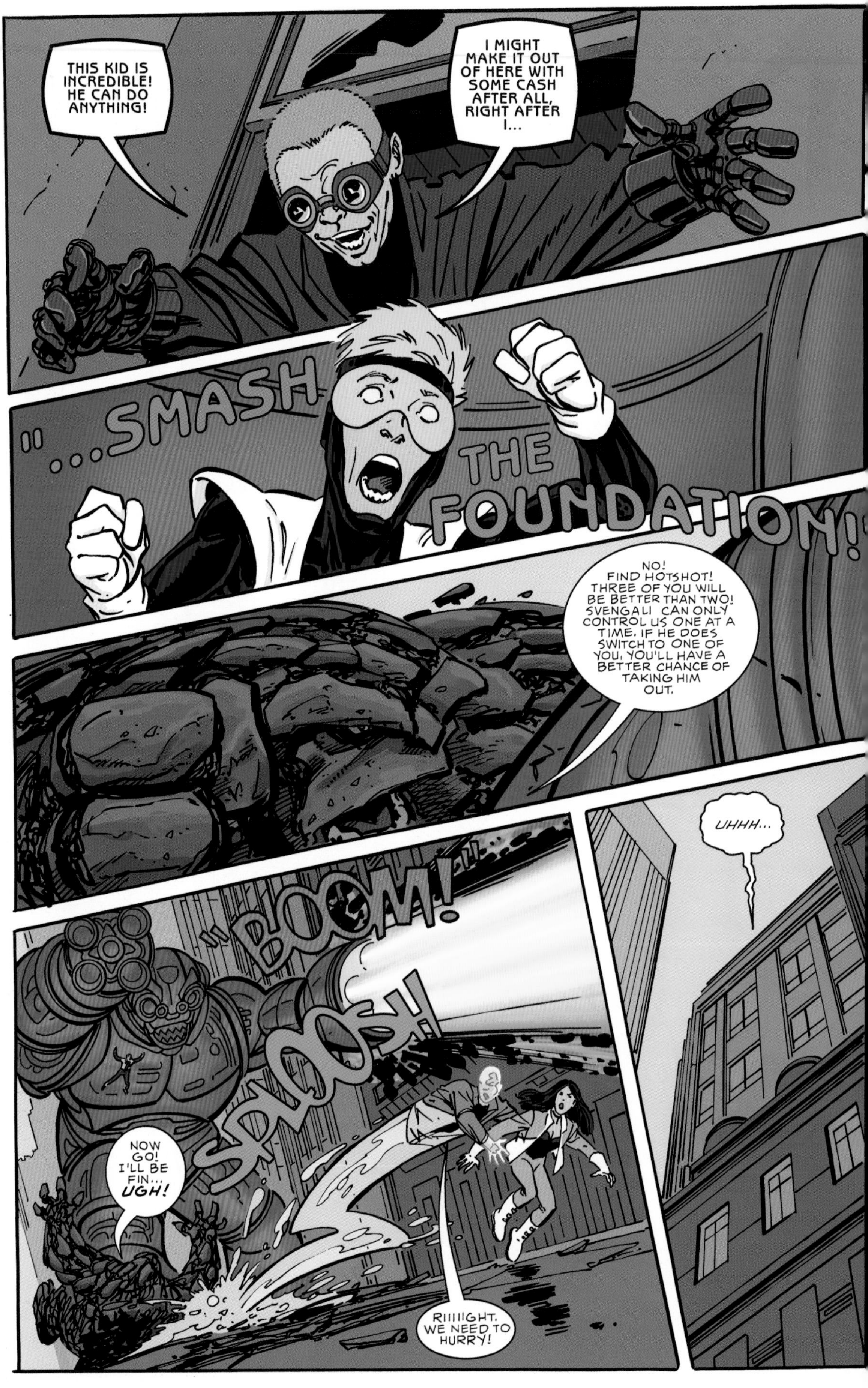
THIS KID IS INCREDIBLE! HE CAN DO ANYTHING!
I MIGHT MAKE IT OUT OF HERE WITH SOME CASH AFTER ALL, RIGHT AFTER I...
"...SMASH THE FOUNDATION!"
NO! FIND HOTSHOT! THREE OF YOU WILL BE BETTER THAN TWO! SVENGALI CAN ONLY CONTROL US ONE AT A TIME. IF HE DOES SWITCH TO ONE OF YOU, YOU'LL HAVE A BETTER CHANCE OF TAKING HIM OUT.
"BOOM!"
SPLOOSH!
NOW GO! I'LL BE FIN... UGH!
RIIIIGHT. WE NEED TO HURRY!
UHHH...

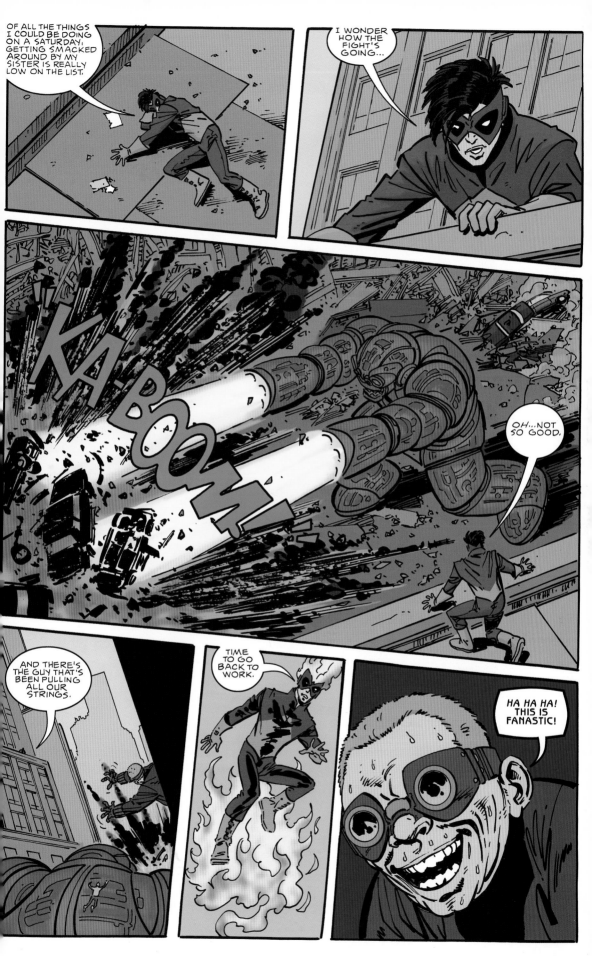

OF ALL THE THINGS I COULD BE DOING ON A SATURDAY, GETTING SMACKED AROUND BY MY SISTER IS REALLY LOW ON THE LIST.

I WONDER HOW THE FIGHT'S GOING...

KABOOM

OH...NOT SO GOOD.

AND THERE'S THE GUY THAT'S BEEN PULLING ALL OUR STRINGS.

TIME TO GO BACK TO WORK.

HA HA HA! THIS IS FANASTIC!

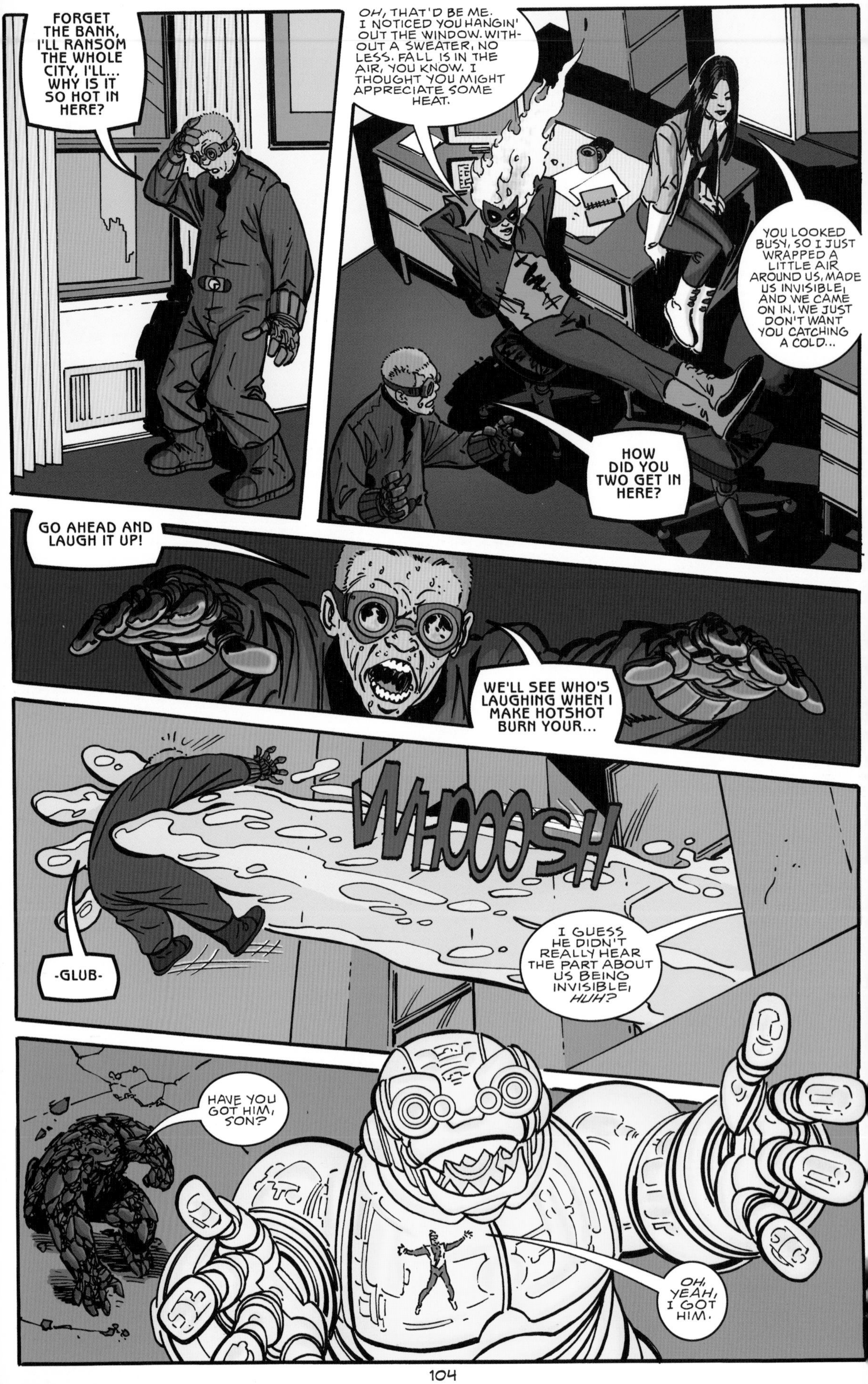

FORGET THE BANK, I'LL RANSOM THE WHOLE CITY, I'LL... WHY IS IT SO HOT IN HERE?
OH, THAT'D BE ME. I NOTICED YOU HANGIN' OUT THE WINDOW. WITHOUT A SWEATER, NO LESS. FALL IS IN THE AIR, YOU KNOW. I THOUGHT YOU MIGHT APPRECIATE SOME HEAT.
YOU LOOKED BUSY, SO I JUST WRAPPED A LITTLE AIR AROUND US, MADE US INVISIBLE, AND WE CAME ON IN. WE JUST DON'T WANT YOU CATCHING A COLD...
HOW DID YOU TWO GET IN HERE?
GO AHEAD AND LAUGH IT UP!
WE'LL SEE WHO'S LAUGHING WHEN I MAKE HOTSHOT BURN YOUR...
WHOOOSH
-GLUB-
I GUESS HE DIDN'T REALLY HEAR THE PART ABOUT US BEING INVISIBLE, HUH?
HAVE YOU GOT HIM, SON?
OH, YEAH, I GOT HIM.

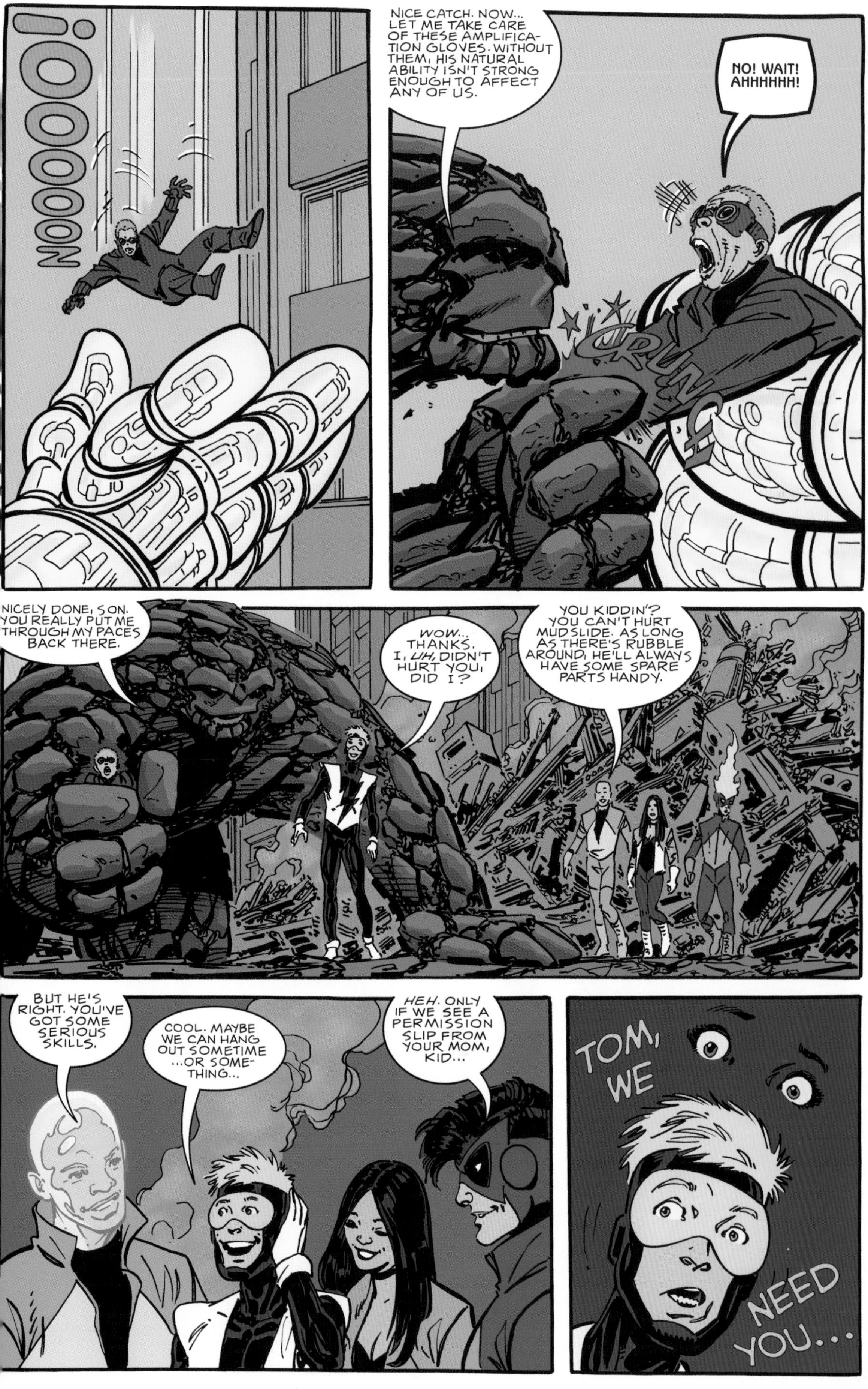
NOOOOOO!
NICE CATCH. NOW... LET ME TAKE CARE OF THESE AMPLIFICATION GLOVES. WITHOUT THEM, HIS NATURAL ABILITY ISN'T STRONG ENOUGH TO AFFECT ANY OF US.
NO! WAIT! AHHHHHH!
CRUNCH
NICELY DONE, SON. YOU REALLY PUT ME THROUGH MY PACES BACK THERE.
WOW... THANKS. I, UH, DIDN'T HURT YOU, DID I?
YOU KIDDIN'? YOU CAN'T HURT MUDSLIDE. AS LONG AS THERE'S RUBBLE AROUND, HE'LL ALWAYS HAVE SOME SPARE PARTS HANDY.
BUT HE'S RIGHT. YOU'VE GOT SOME SERIOUS SKILLS.
COOL. MAYBE WE CAN HANG OUT SOMETIME ...OR SOMETHING...
HEH. ONLY IF WE SEE A PERMISSION SLIP FROM YOUR MOM, KID...
TOM, WE NEED YOU...

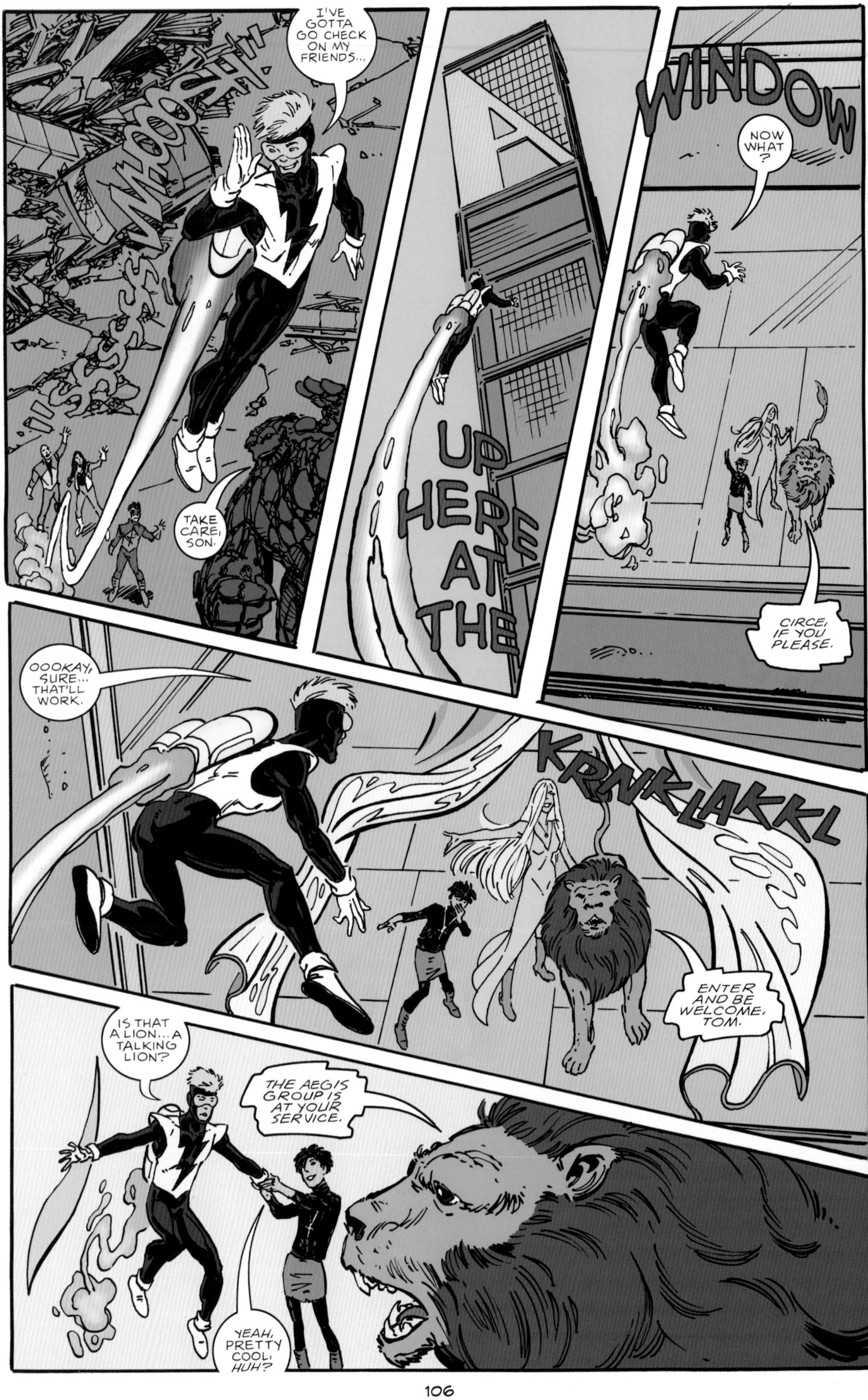

I'VE GOTTA GO CHECK ON MY FRIENDS...
WHOOSH!!
SSS
TAKE CARE, SON.
UP HERE AT THE
WINDOW
NOW WHAT?
CIRCE, IF YOU PLEASE.
OOOKAY, SURE... THAT'LL WORK.
KRNKLAKKL
ENTER AND BE WELCOME, TOM.
IS THAT A LION... A TALKING LION?
THE AEGIS GROUP IS AT YOUR SERVICE.
YEAH, PRETTY COOL, HUH?

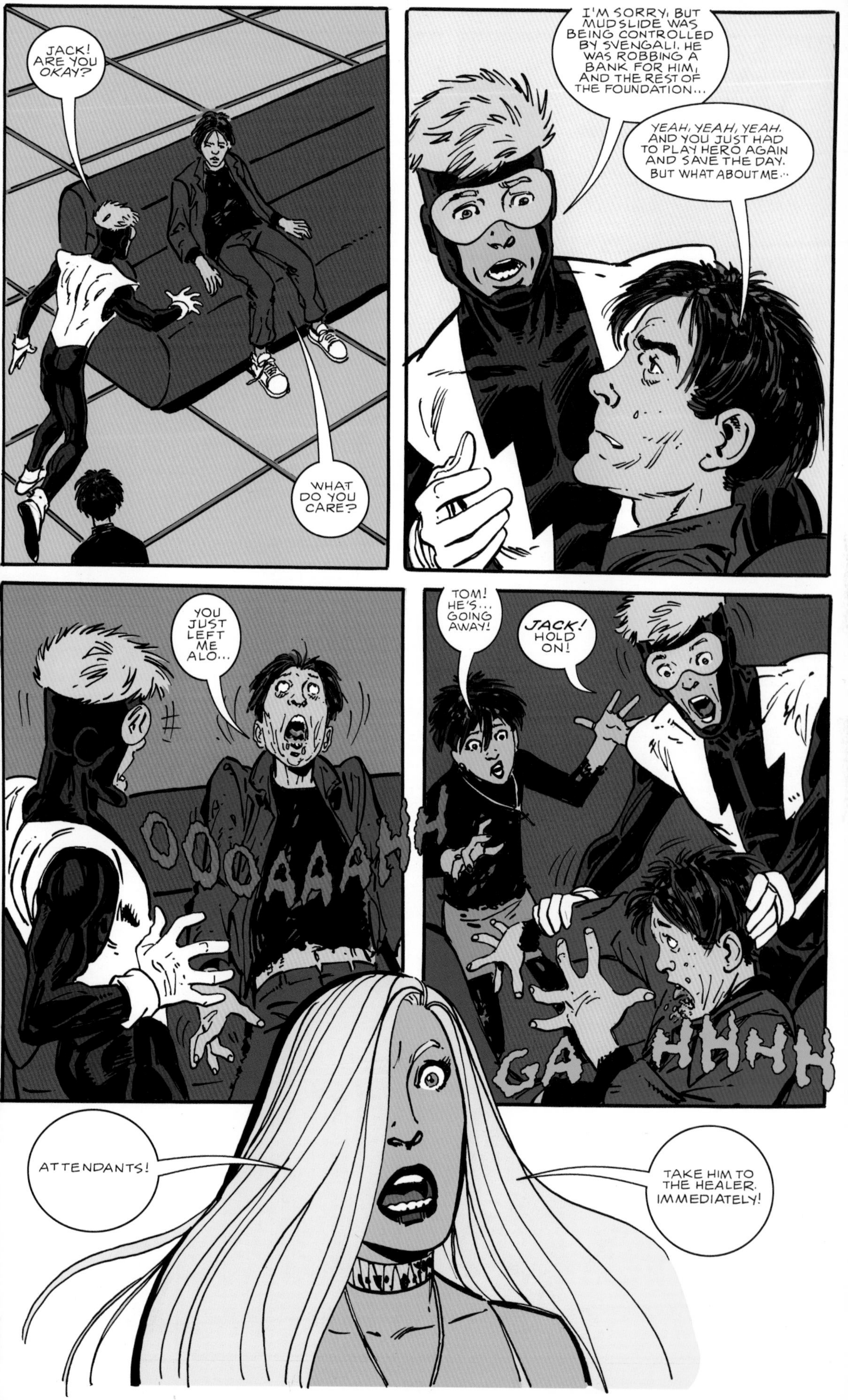
JACK! ARE YOU OKAY?
WHAT DO YOU CARE?
I'M SORRY, BUT MUDSLIDE WAS BEING CONTROLLED BY SVENGALI. HE WAS ROBBING A BANK FOR HIM, AND THE REST OF THE FOUNDATION...
YEAH, YEAH, YEAH. AND YOU JUST HAD TO PLAY HERO AGAIN AND SAVE THE DAY. BUT WHAT ABOUT ME...
YOU JUST LEFT ME ALO...
OOOAAAAHH
TOM! HE'S... GOING AWAY!
JACK! HOLD ON!
GAHHHH
ATTENDANTS!
TAKE HIM TO THE HEALER. IMMEDIATELY!

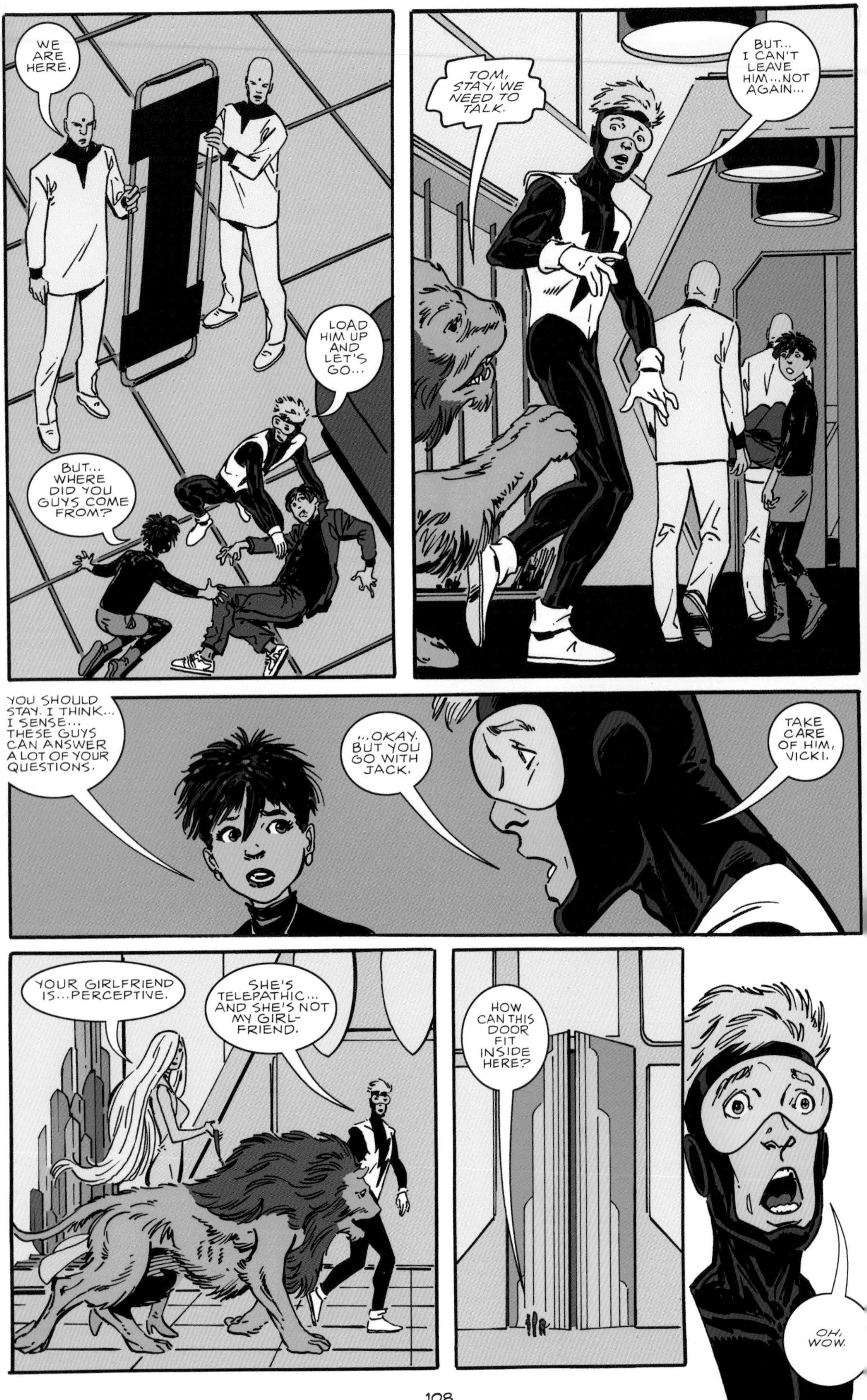
WE ARE HERE.
LOAD HIM UP AND LET'S GO...
BUT... WHERE DID YOU GUYS COME FROM?
TOM, STAY, WE NEED TO TALK.
BUT... I CAN'T LEAVE HIM... NOT AGAIN...
YOU SHOULD STAY. I THINK... I SENSE... THESE GUYS CAN ANSWER A LOT OF YOUR QUESTIONS.
...OKAY. BUT YOU GO WITH JACK.
TAKE CARE OF HIM, VICKI.
YOUR GIRLFRIEND IS...PERCEPTIVE.
SHE'S TELEPATHIC... AND SHE'S NOT MY GIRL-FRIEND.
HOW CAN THIS DOOR FIT INSIDE HERE?
OH, WOW.

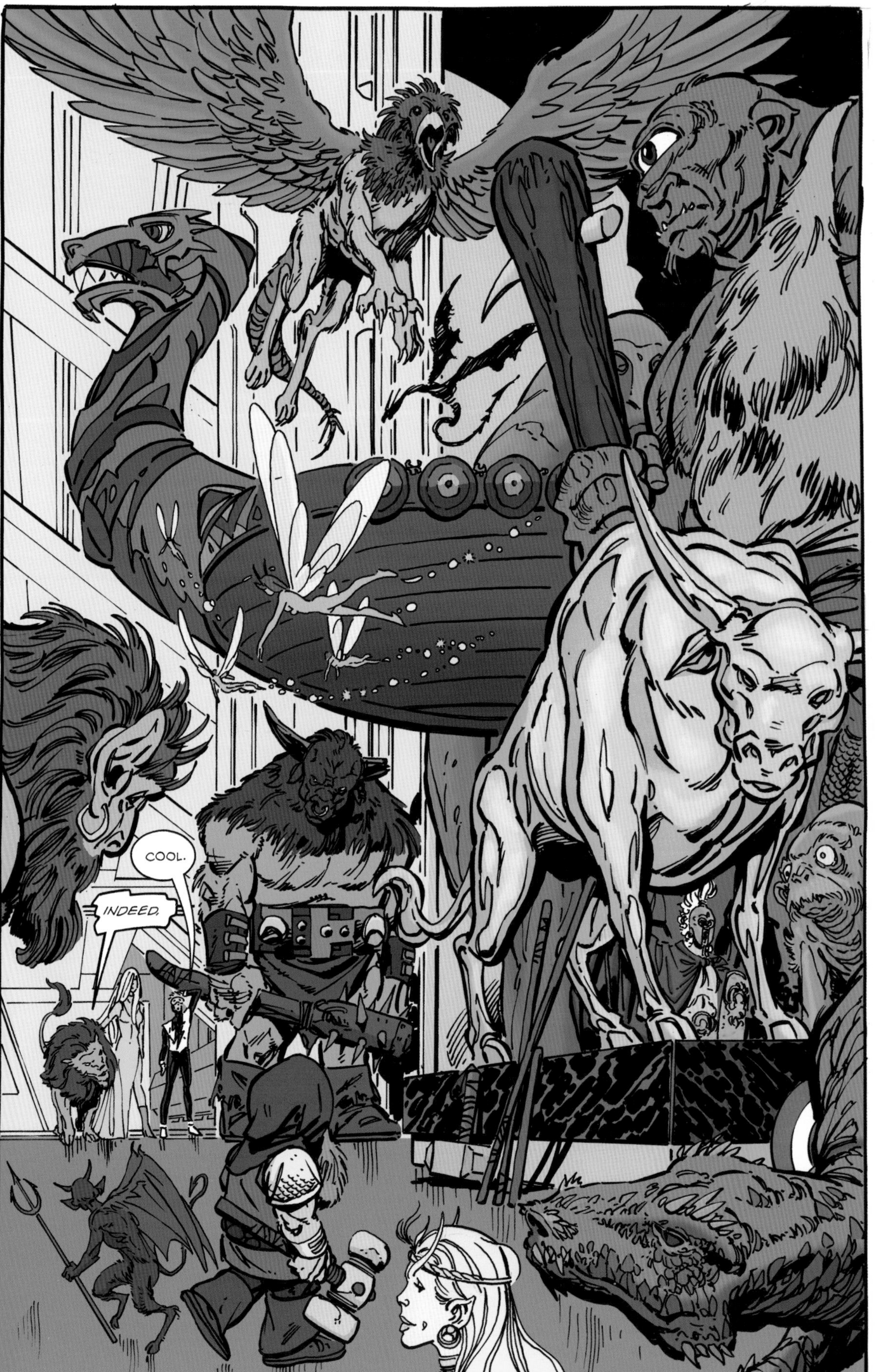
COOL.
INDEED.

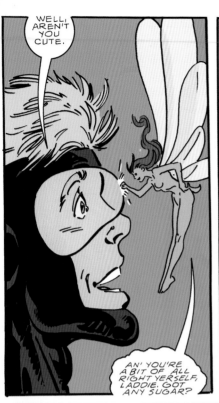

WELL, AREN'T YOU CUTE.

AN' YOU'RE A BIT OF ALL RIGHT YERSELF, LADDIE. GOT ANY SUGAR?

ALL THE MYTHS, ALL THE LEGENDS...

...THINGS I USED TO DREAM ABOUT SEEING, AND THINGS I COULD NEVER IMAGINE... ALL OF IT REAL. HOW CAN THIS BE...

..TRU... WOO HOO HOO. UH, HEY, THERE.

OH, WON'T YOU SWIM WITH US, BOY... ♪

FOLLOW OUR SONG AND FIND YOUR HEART'S JOY... ♪

UH, THAT'S OKAY. ÷GULP÷ I LEFT MY TRUNKS AT HOME...MAYBE NEXT TIME.

CAREFUL OF THE SIRENS, TOM.

MOST OF THE MAGIC LEFT IN THE WORLD, BOTH GOOD AND BAD, WE HAVE GATHERED HERE. THE AEGIS GROUP STANDS GUARD AT THE DOORWAY BETWEEN THE WORLDS.

hee

hee

hee

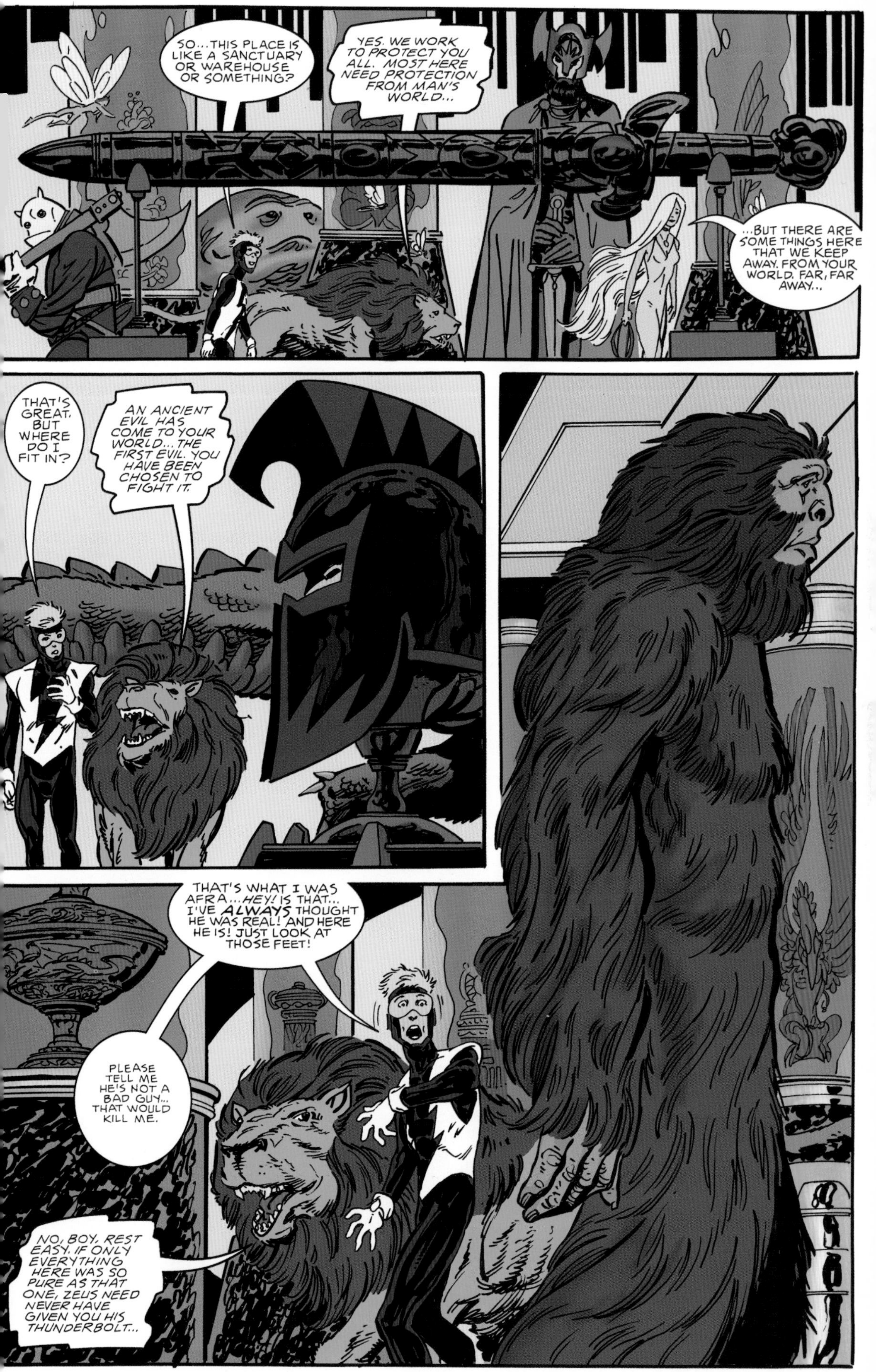

SO... THIS PLACE IS LIKE A SANCTUARY OR WAREHOUSE OR SOMETHING?
YES. WE WORK TO PROTECT YOU ALL. MOST HERE NEED PROTECTION FROM MAN'S WORLD...
...BUT THERE ARE SOME THINGS HERE THAT WE KEEP AWAY. FROM YOUR WORLD. FAR, FAR AWAY...
THAT'S GREAT. BUT WHERE DO I FIT IN?
AN ANCIENT EVIL HAS COME TO YOUR WORLD... THE FIRST EVIL. YOU HAVE BEEN CHOSEN TO FIGHT IT.
THAT'S WHAT I WAS AFRA... HEY! IS THAT... I'VE ALWAYS THOUGHT HE WAS REAL! AND HERE HE IS! JUST LOOK AT THOSE FEET!
PLEASE TELL ME HE'S NOT A BAD GUY... THAT WOULD KILL ME.
NO, BOY. REST EASY. IF ONLY EVERYTHING HERE WAS SO PURE AS THAT ONE, ZEUS NEED NEVER HAVE GIVEN YOU HIS THUNDERBOLT...

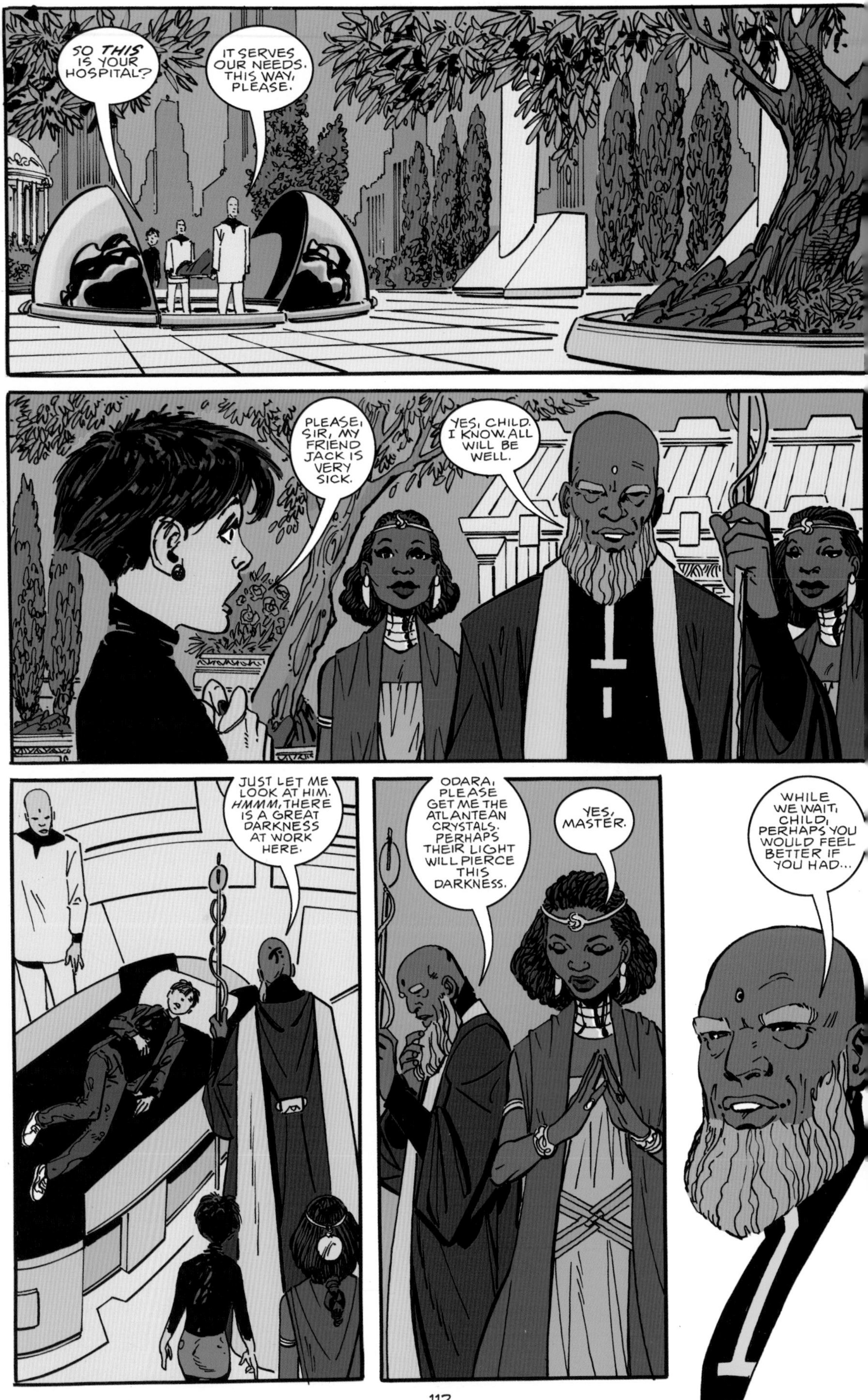
SO THIS IS YOUR HOSPITAL?
IT SERVES OUR NEEDS. THIS WAY, PLEASE.
PLEASE, SIR, MY FRIEND JACK IS VERY SICK.
YES, CHILD. I KNOW. ALL WILL BE WELL.
JUST LET ME LOOK AT HIM. HMMM, THERE IS A GREAT DARKNESS AT WORK HERE.
ODARA, PLEASE GET ME THE ATLANTEAN CRYSTALS. PERHAPS THEIR LIGHT WILL PIERCE THIS DARKNESS.
YES, MASTER.
WHILE WE WAIT, CHILD, PERHAPS YOU WOULD FEEL BETTER IF YOU HAD...

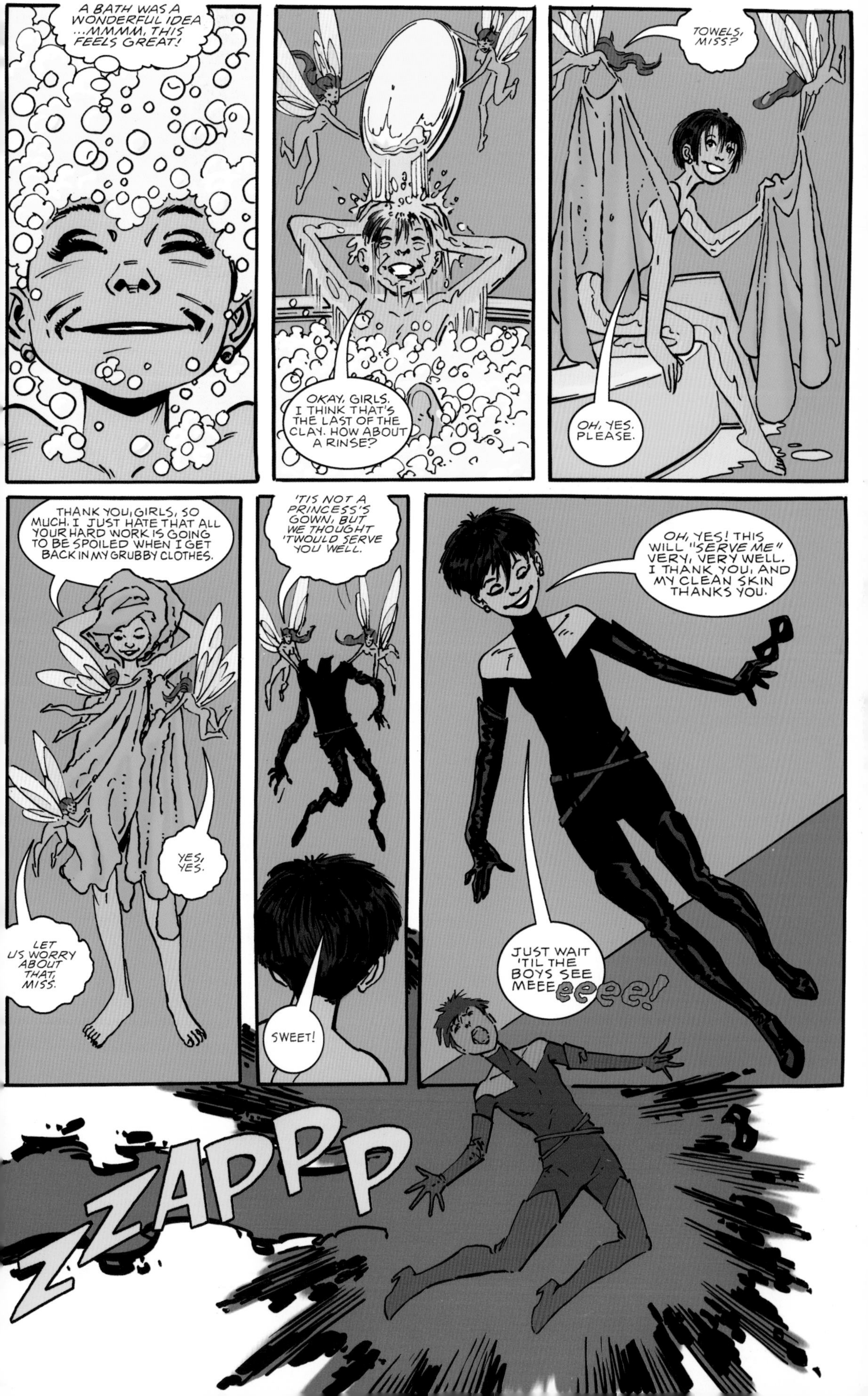
A BATH WAS A WONDERFUL IDEA ...MMMM, THIS FEELS GREAT!
OKAY, GIRLS. I THINK THAT'S THE LAST OF THE CLAY. HOW ABOUT A RINSE?
TOWELS, MISS?
OH, YES. PLEASE.
THANK YOU, GIRLS, SO MUCH. I JUST HATE THAT ALL YOUR HARD WORK IS GOING TO BE SPOILED WHEN I GET BACK IN MY GRUBBY CLOTHES.
YES, YES.
LET US WORRY ABOUT THAT, MISS.
'TIS NOT A PRINCESS'S GOWN, BUT WE THOUGHT 'TWOULD SERVE YOU WELL.
SWEET!
OH, YES! THIS WILL "SERVE ME" VERY, VERY WELL. I THANK YOU, AND MY CLEAN SKIN THANKS YOU.
JUST WAIT 'TIL THE BOYS SEE MEEEeeee!
ZZZAPPP

COOL THREADS, VICK. I WONDER IF THEY HAVE SOMETHING IN MY SIZE...

WAIT...WHAT? ZEUS GAVE ME HIS THUNDER-BOLT???

SURELY YOU KNOW THIS. THE SCENT OF HIS POWER ON YOU IS OVERWHELMING.

LOOK, ALL I KNOW IS I SAW A LIGHT, AND THEN JACK HIT ME IN THE HEAD WITH A STICK. THAT PUT ME IN A COMA...AND IN THE HOSPITAL. THEN I WOKE UP LIKE THIS.

THAT IS DISTRESSING ...AND DANGEROUS. THE POWER OF A GOD WITH NO KNOWLEDGE OF ITS USE.

THAT WOULD EXPLAIN YOUR RATHER "UNIQUE" WAY OF USING THE THUNDERBOLT. PERHAPS THE HEALER CAN HELP YOU, TOO.

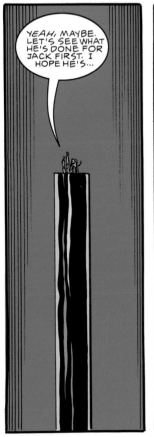

YEAH, MAYBE. LET'S SEE WHAT HE'S DONE FOR JACK FIRST. I HOPE HE'S...

...OKAY?

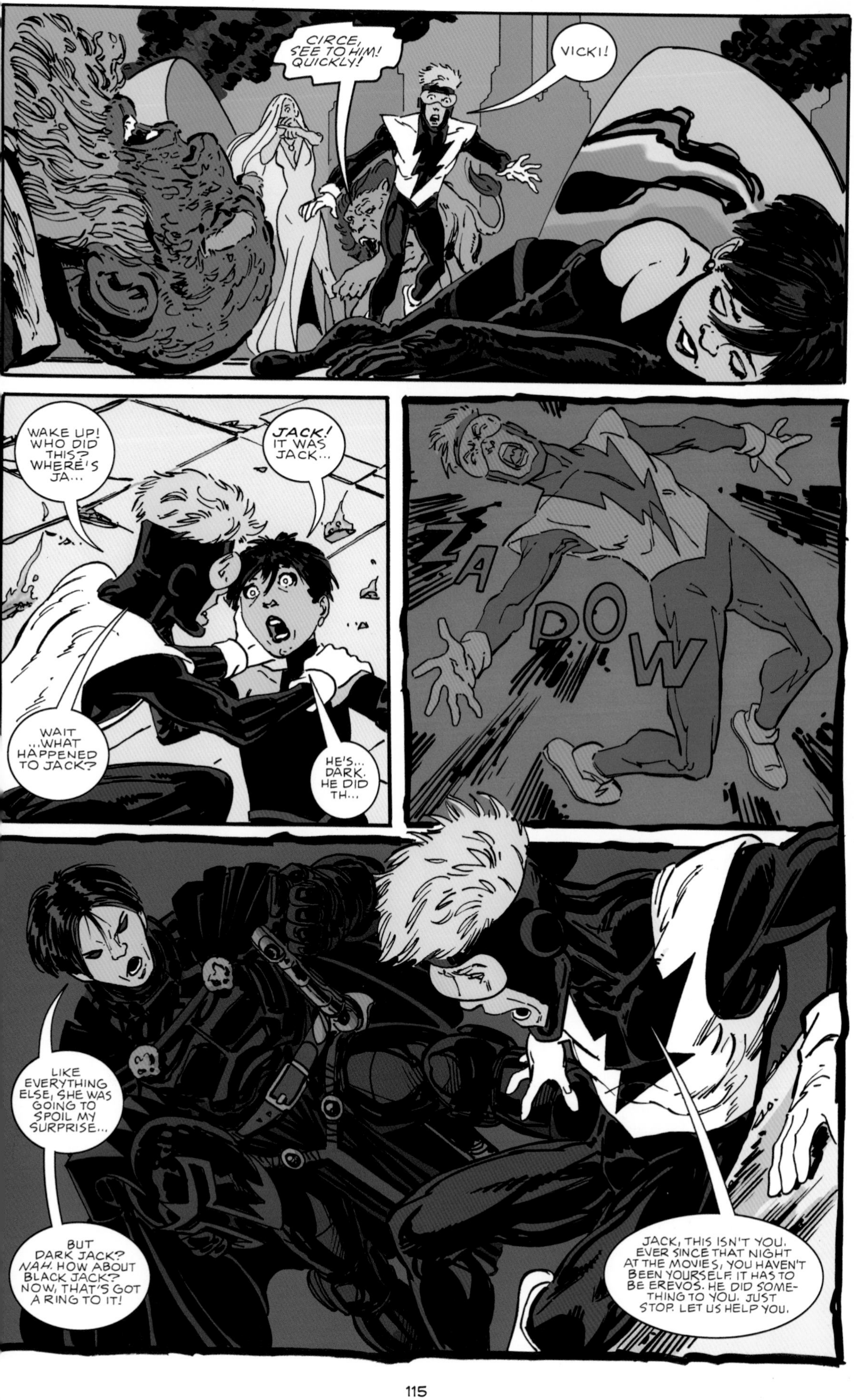

CIRCE, SEE TO HIM! QUICKLY!
VICKI!
WAKE UP! WHO DID THIS? WHERE'S JA...
JACK! IT WAS JACK...
WAIT ...WHAT HAPPENED TO JACK?
HE'S... DARK. HE DID TH...
ZA DOW
LIKE EVERYTHING ELSE, SHE WAS GOING TO SPOIL MY SURPRISE...
BUT DARK JACK? NAH. HOW ABOUT BLACK JACK? NOW, THAT'S GOT A RING TO IT!
JACK, THIS ISN'T YOU. EVER SINCE THAT NIGHT AT THE MOVIES, YOU HAVEN'T BEEN YOURSELF. IT HAS TO BE EREVOS. HE DID SOMETHING TO YOU. JUST STOP. LET US HELP YOU.

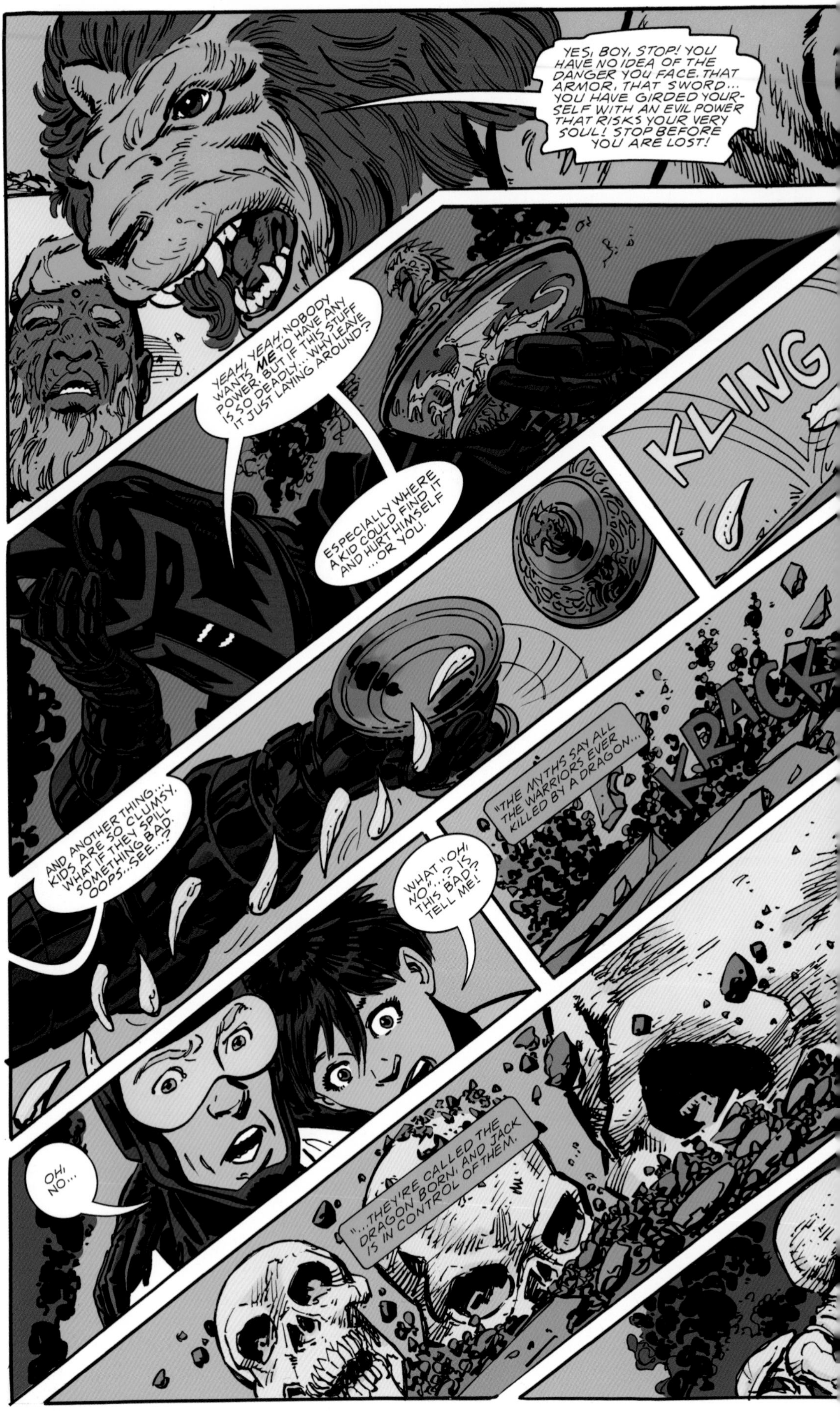
YES, BOY, STOP! YOU HAVE NO IDEA OF THE DANGER YOU FACE. THAT ARMOR, THAT SWORD... YOU HAVE GIRDED YOURSELF WITH AN EVIL POWER THAT RISKS YOUR VERY SOUL! STOP BEFORE YOU ARE LOST!
YEAH, YEAH. NOBODY WANTS ME TO HAVE ANY POWER. BUT IF THIS STUFF IS SO DEADLY... WHY LEAVE IT JUST LAYING AROUND?
ESPECIALLY WHERE A KID COULD FIND IT AND HURT HIMSELF ...OR YOU.
KLING
AND ANOTHER THING... KIDS ARE SO CLUMSY. WHAT IF THEY SPILL SOMETHING BAD. OOPS...SEE...?
"THE MYTHS SAY ALL THE WARRIORS EVER KILLED BY A DRAGON...
KRACK
WHAT "OH, NO"...? IS THIS BAD? TELL ME!
OH, NO...
"...THEY'RE CALLED THE DRAGON BORN, AND JACK IS IN CONTROL OF THEM.

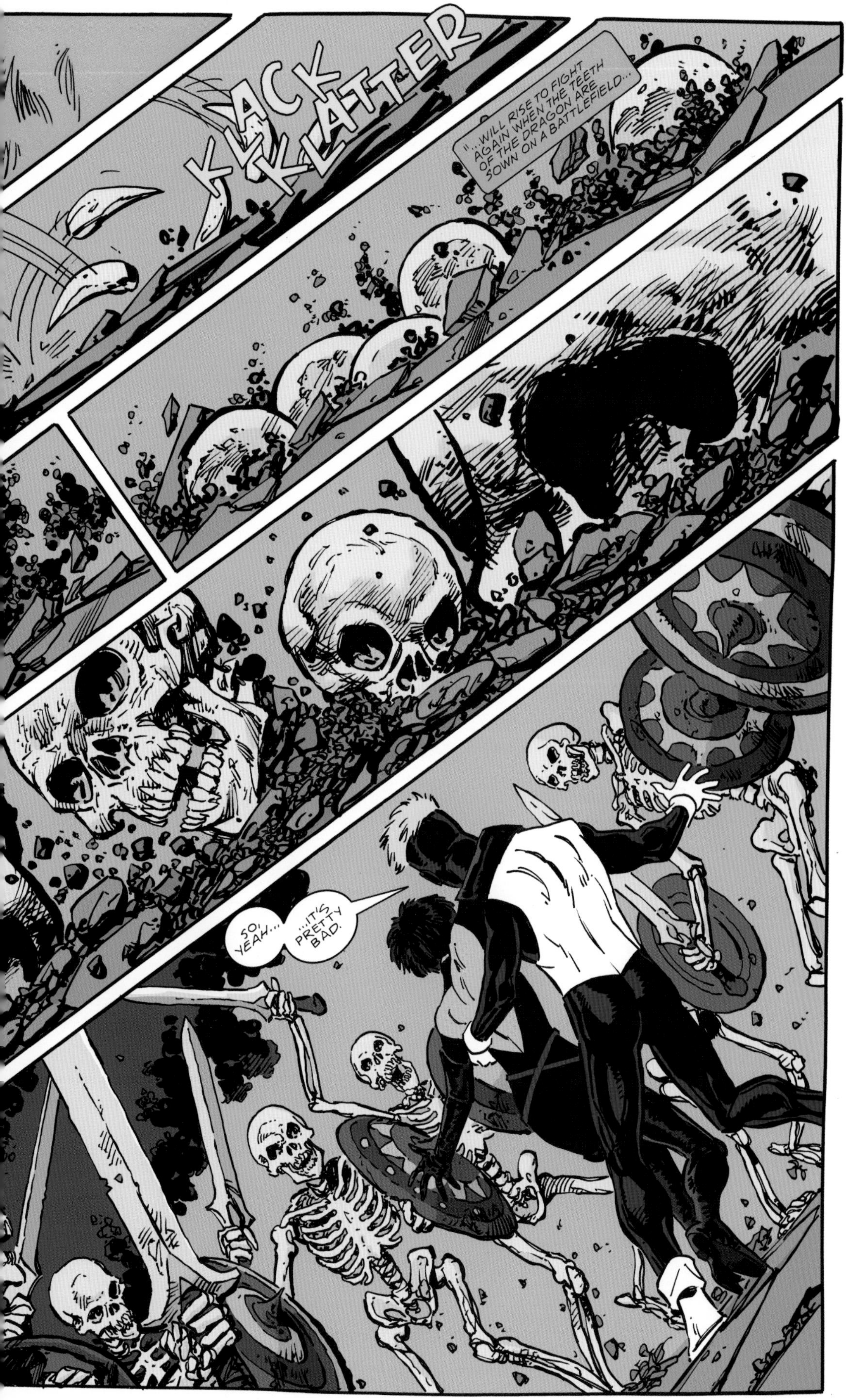
KLACK KLATTER
"...WILL RISE TO FIGHT AGAIN WHEN THE TEETH OF THE DRAGON ARE SOWN ON A BATTLEFIELD..."
SO, YEAH...
...IT'S PRETTY BAD.

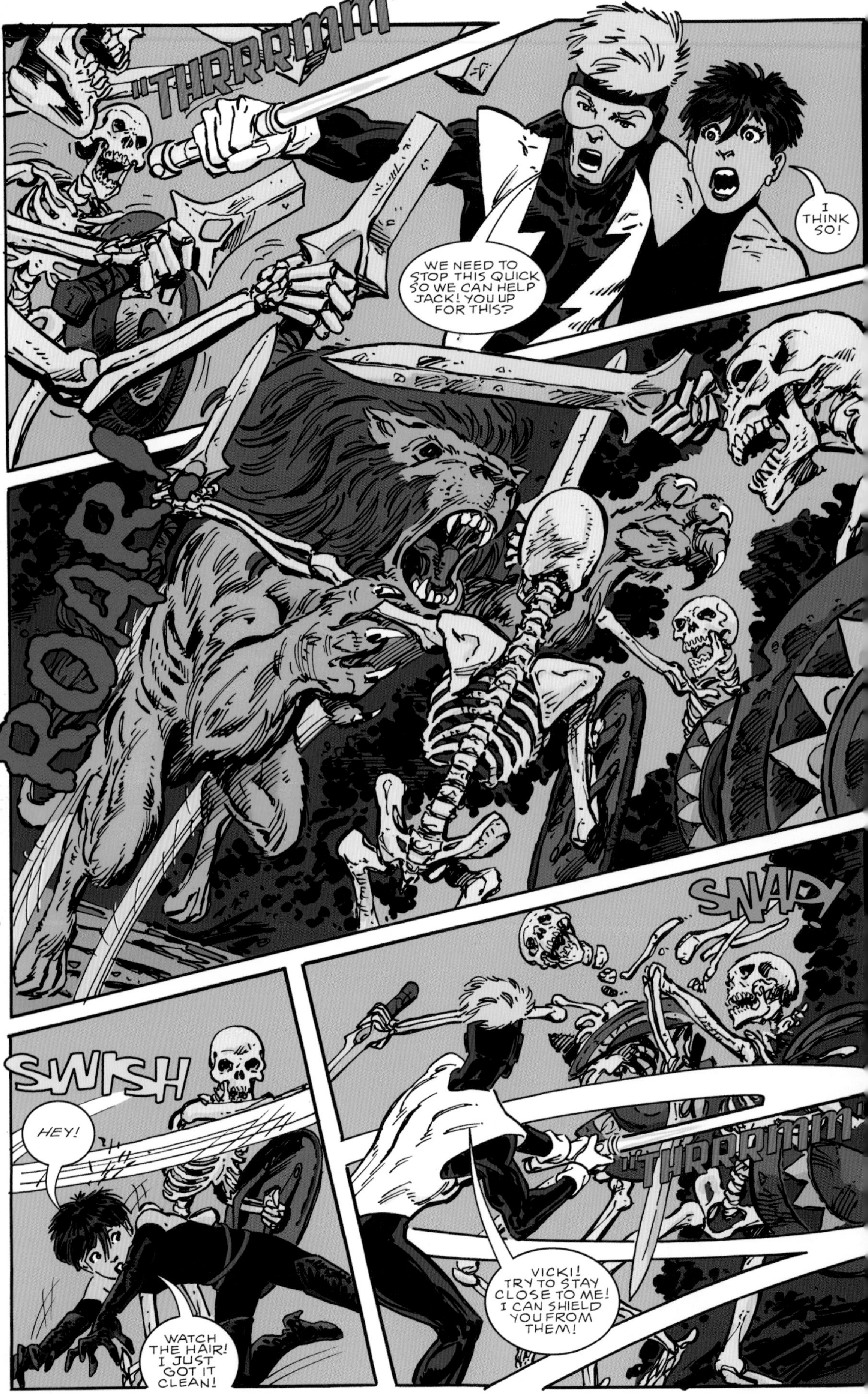
"THRRRMMM"
WE NEED TO STOP THIS QUICK SO WE CAN HELP JACK! YOU UP FOR THIS?
I THINK SO!
ROAR
SNAP!
SWISH
HEY!
WATCH THE HAIR! I JUST GOT IT CLEAN!
"THRRRMMM"
VICKI! TRY TO STAY CLOSE TO ME! I CAN SHIELD YOU FROM THEM!

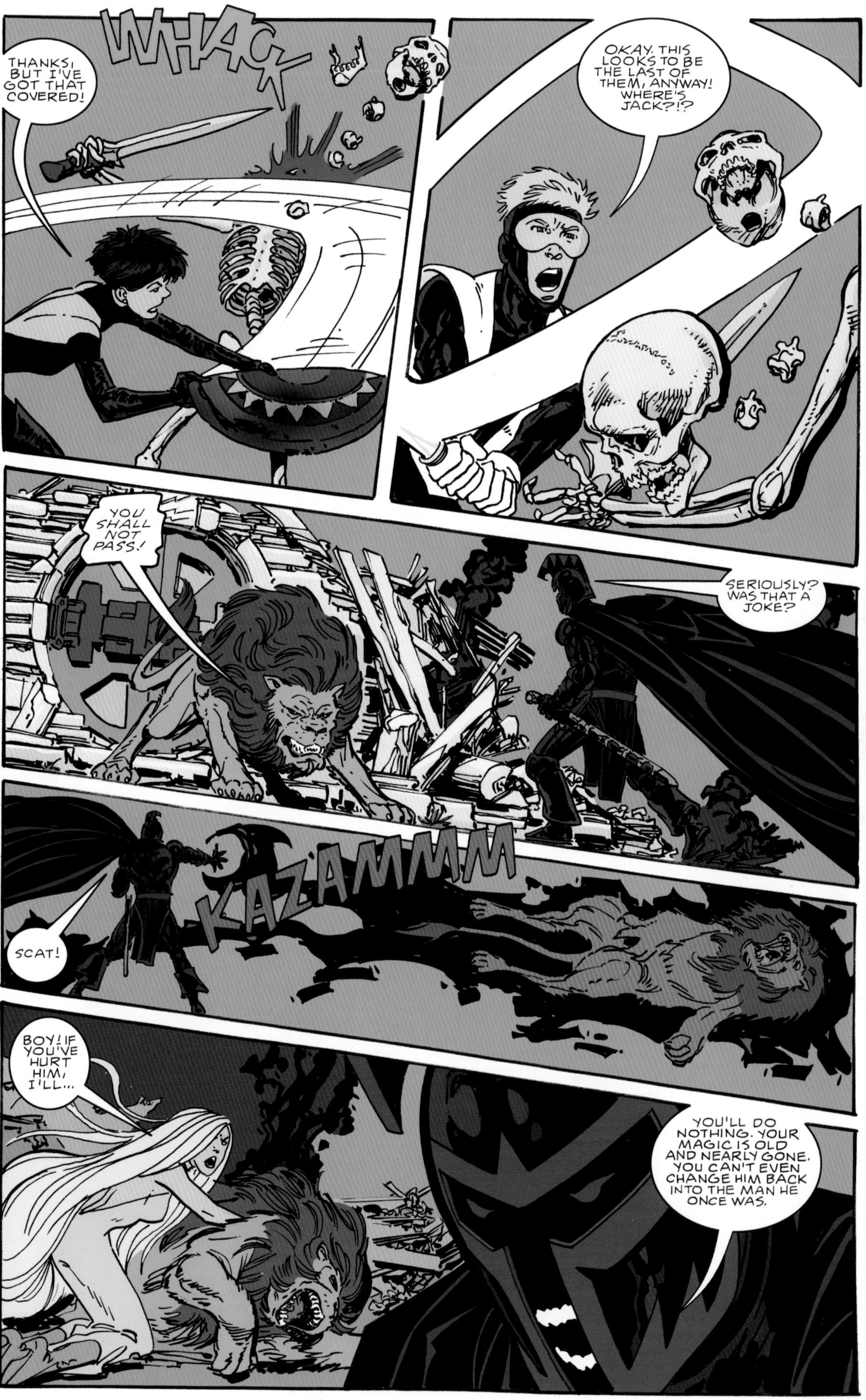
WHACK
THANKS, BUT I'VE GOT THAT COVERED!
OKAY. THIS LOOKS TO BE THE LAST OF THEM, ANYWAY! WHERE'S JACK?!?
YOU SHALL NOT PASS!
SERIOUSLY? WAS THAT A JOKE?
KAZAMMM
SCAT!
BOY! IF YOU'VE HURT HIM, I'LL...
YOU'LL DO NOTHING. YOUR MAGIC IS OLD AND NEARLY GONE. YOU CAN'T EVEN CHANGE HIM BACK INTO THE MAN HE ONCE WAS.

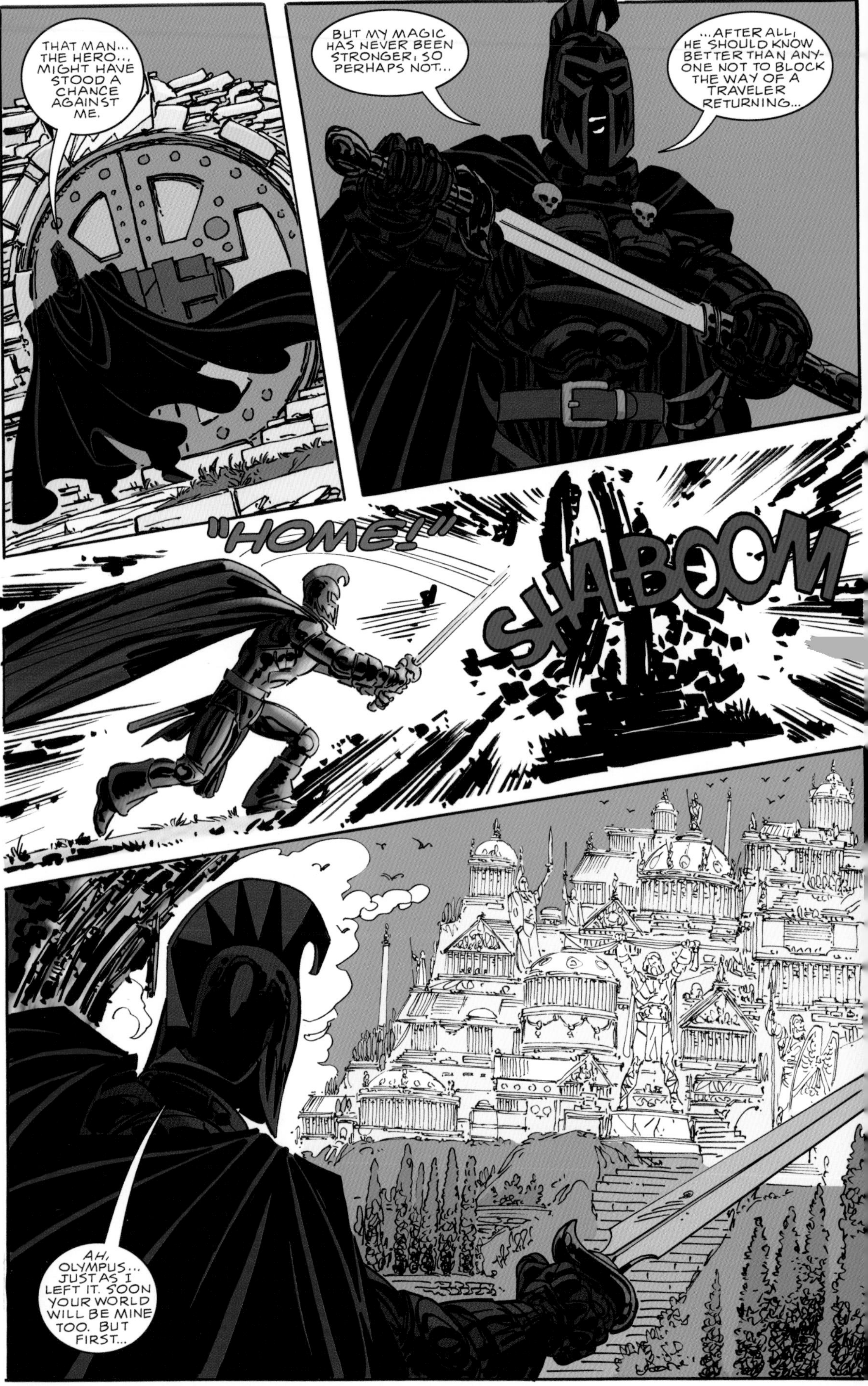
THAT MAN... THE HERO... MIGHT HAVE STOOD A CHANCE AGAINST ME.
BUT MY MAGIC HAS NEVER BEEN STRONGER, SO PERHAPS NOT...
...AFTER ALL, HE SHOULD KNOW BETTER THAN ANYONE NOT TO BLOCK THE WAY OF A TRAVELER RETURNING...
"HOME!"
SHABOOM
AH, OLYMPUS... JUST AS I LEFT IT. SOON YOUR WORLD WILL BE MINE TOO. BUT FIRST...

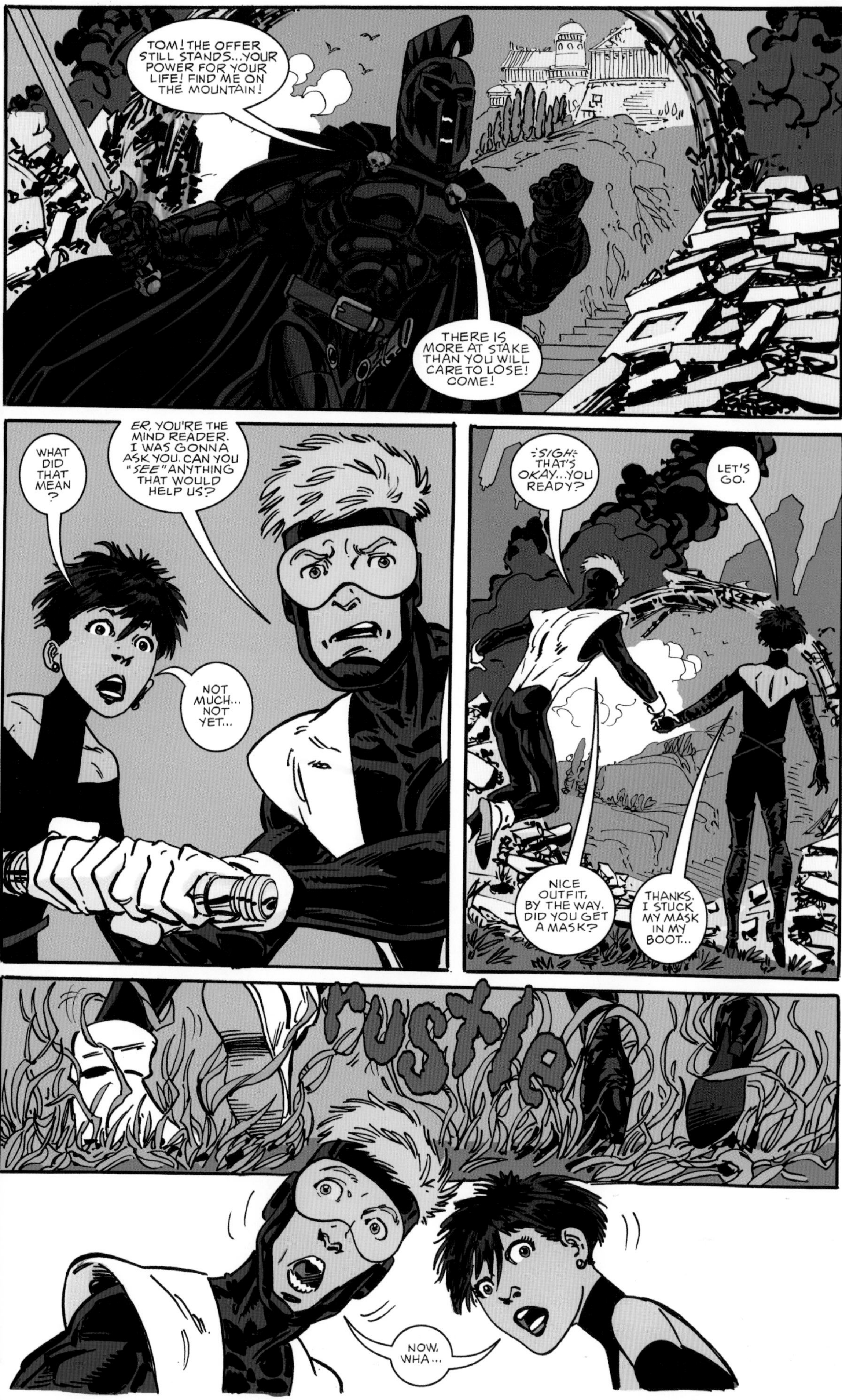
TOM! THE OFFER STILL STANDS... YOUR POWER FOR YOUR LIFE! FIND ME ON THE MOUNTAIN!
THERE IS MORE AT STAKE THAN YOU WILL CARE TO LOSE! COME!
WHAT DID THAT MEAN?
ER, YOU'RE THE MIND READER. I WAS GONNA ASK YOU. CAN YOU "SEE" ANYTHING THAT WOULD HELP US?
NOT MUCH... NOT YET...
SIGH THAT'S OKAY... YOU READY?
LET'S GO.
NICE OUTFIT, BY THE WAY. DID YOU GET A MASK?
THANKS. I STUCK MY MASK IN MY BOOT...
rustle
NOW, WHA...

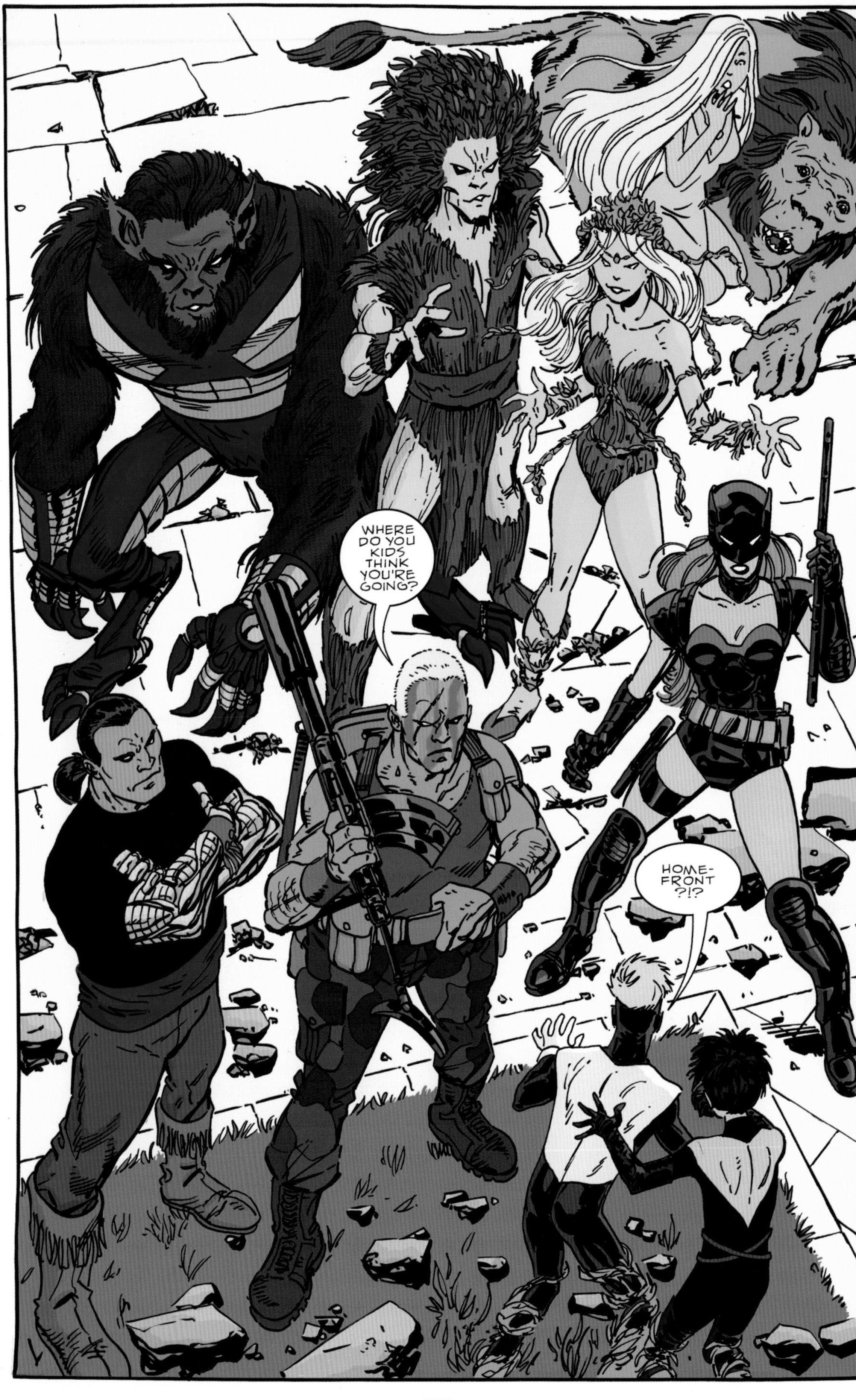
WHERE DO YOU KIDS THINK YOU'RE GOING?
HOME-FRONT?!?

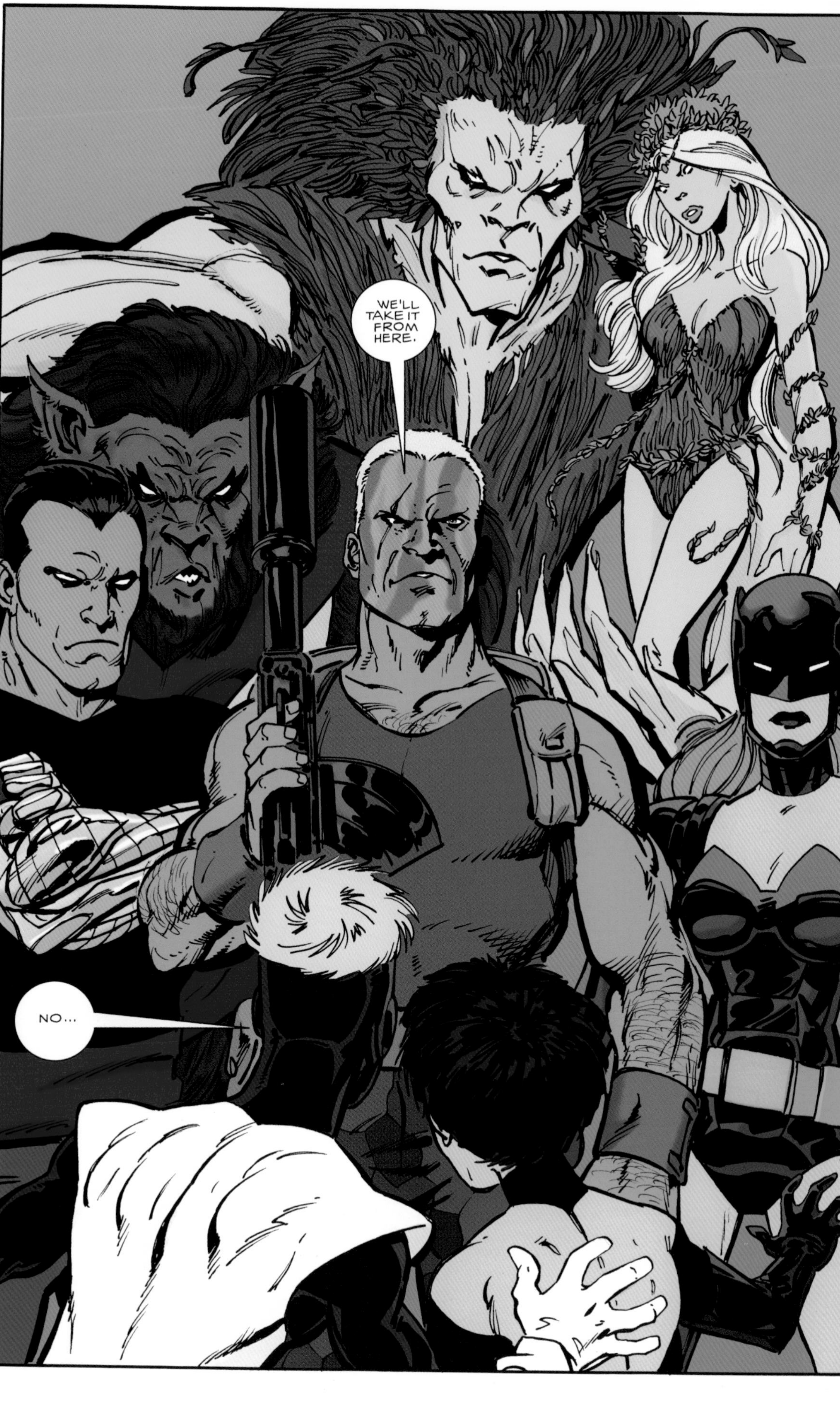
WE'LL TAKE IT FROM HERE.
NO...

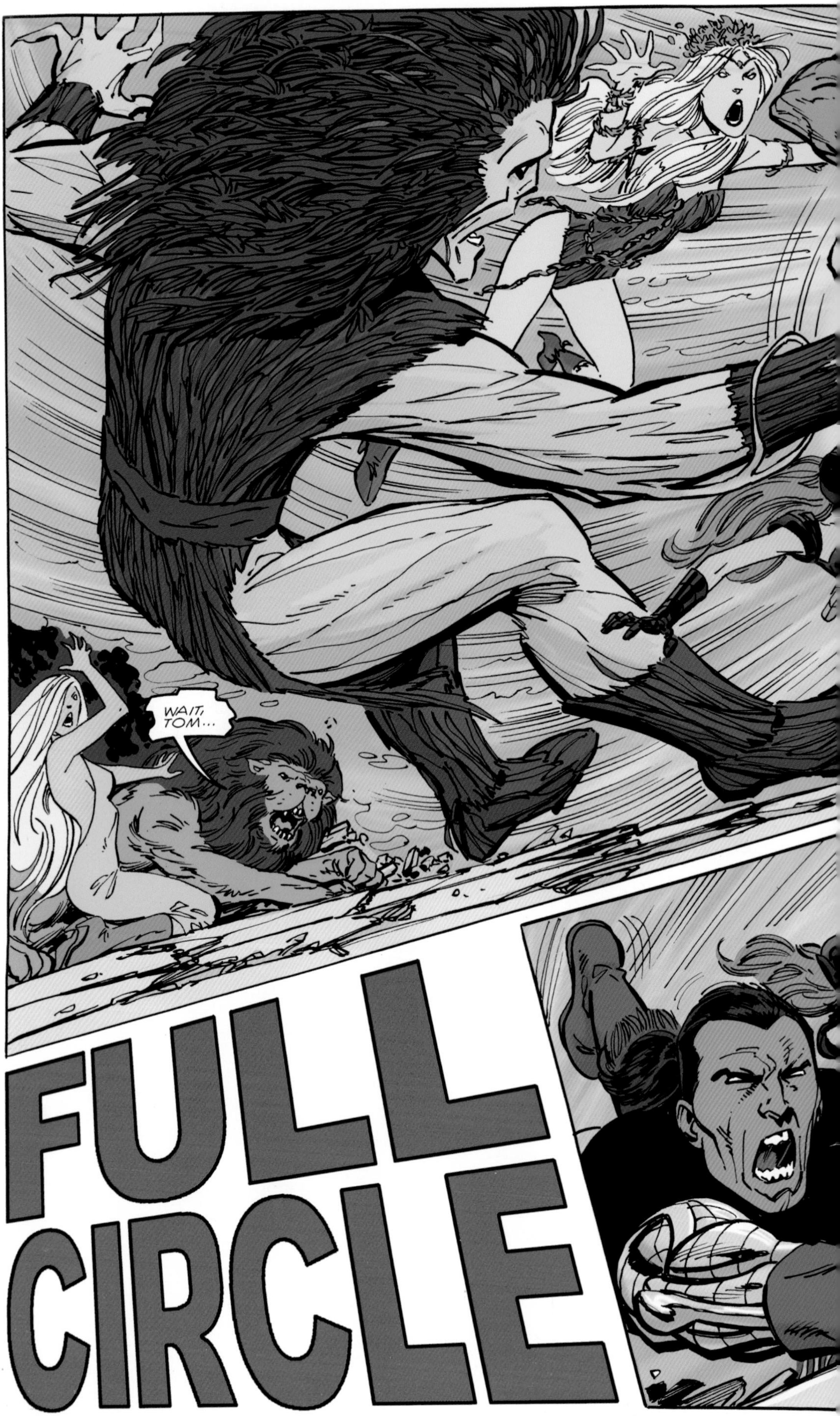
WAIT, TOM...
FULL CIRCLE

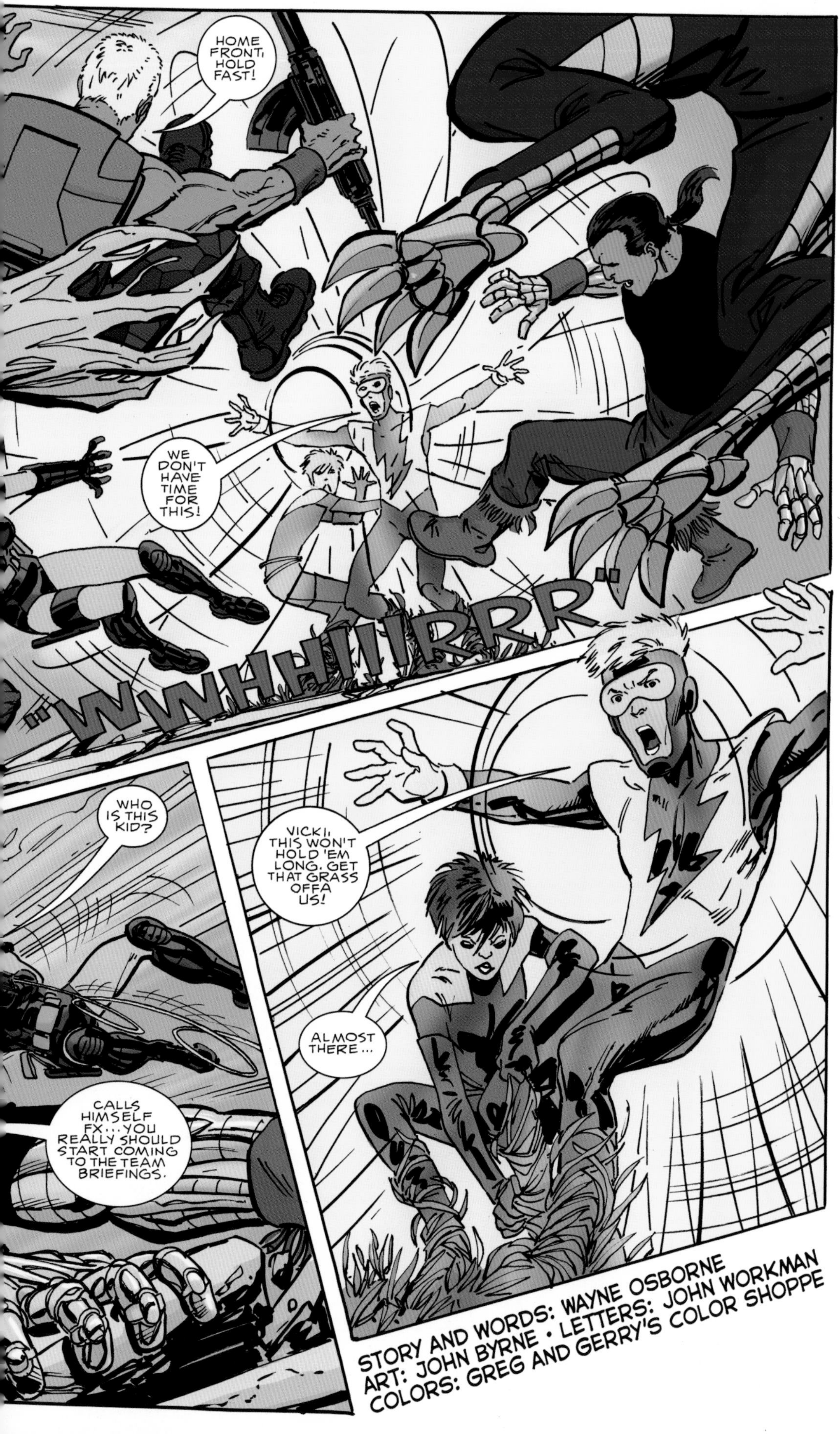
HOME FRONT, HOLD FAST!
WE DON'T HAVE TIME FOR THIS!
"WWHHIIIRRR"
WHO IS THIS KID?
CALLS HIMSELF FX... YOU REALLY SHOULD START COMING TO THE TEAM BRIEFINGS.
VICKI, THIS WON'T HOLD 'EM LONG. GET THAT GRASS OFFA US!
ALMOST THERE...
STORY AND WORDS: WAYNE OSBORNE
ART: JOHN BYRNE • LETTERS: JOHN WORKMAN
COLORS: GREG AND GERRY'S COLOR SHOPPE

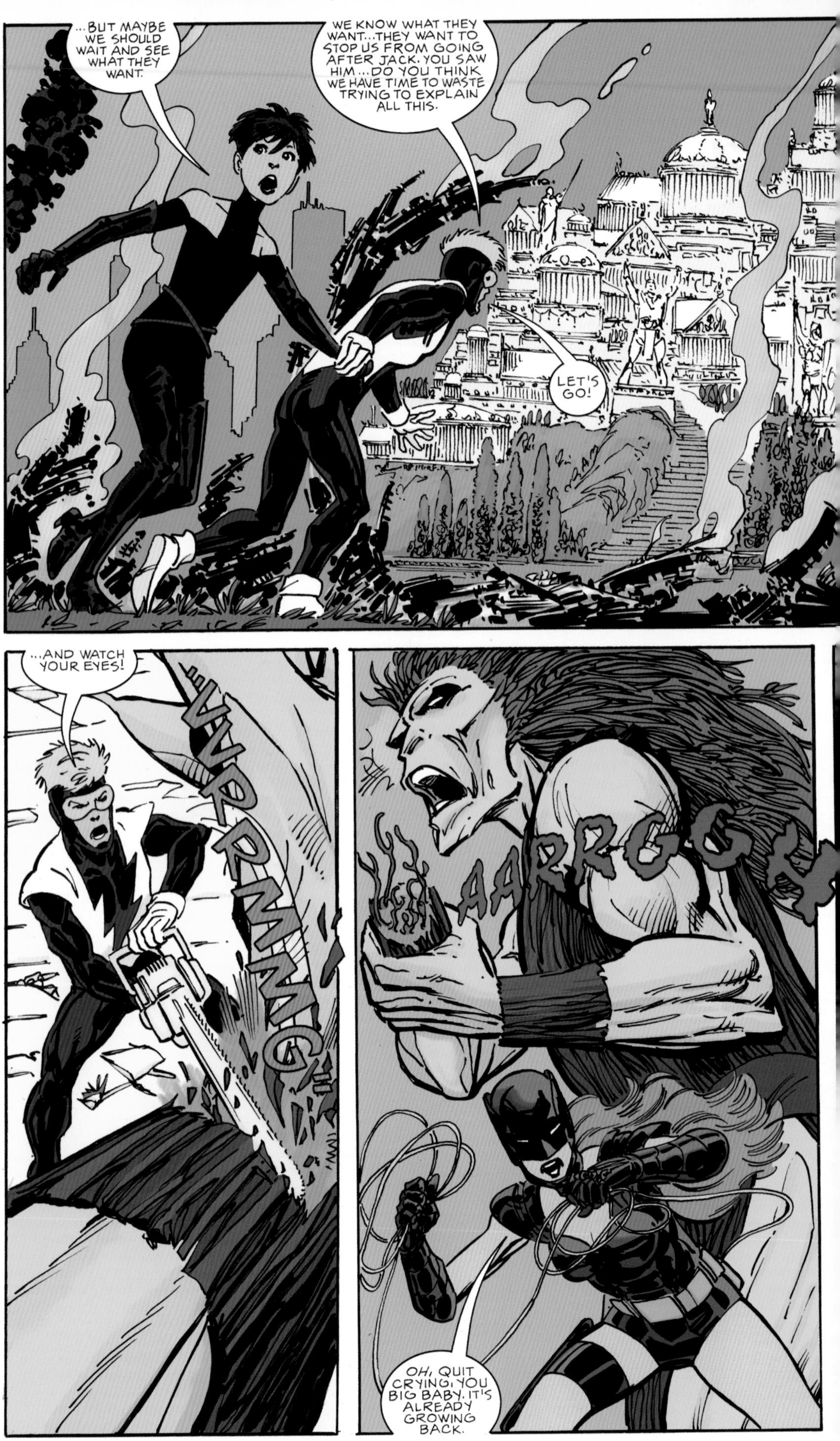
...BUT MAYBE WE SHOULD WAIT AND SEE WHAT THEY WANT.
WE KNOW WHAT THEY WANT...THEY WANT TO STOP US FROM GOING AFTER JACK. YOU SAW HIM...DO YOU THINK WE HAVE TIME TO WASTE TRYING TO EXPLAIN ALL THIS.
LET'S GO!
...AND WATCH YOUR EYES!
VVRRMMG
AARRGGH
OH, QUIT CRYING, YOU BIG BABY. IT'S ALREADY GROWING BACK.

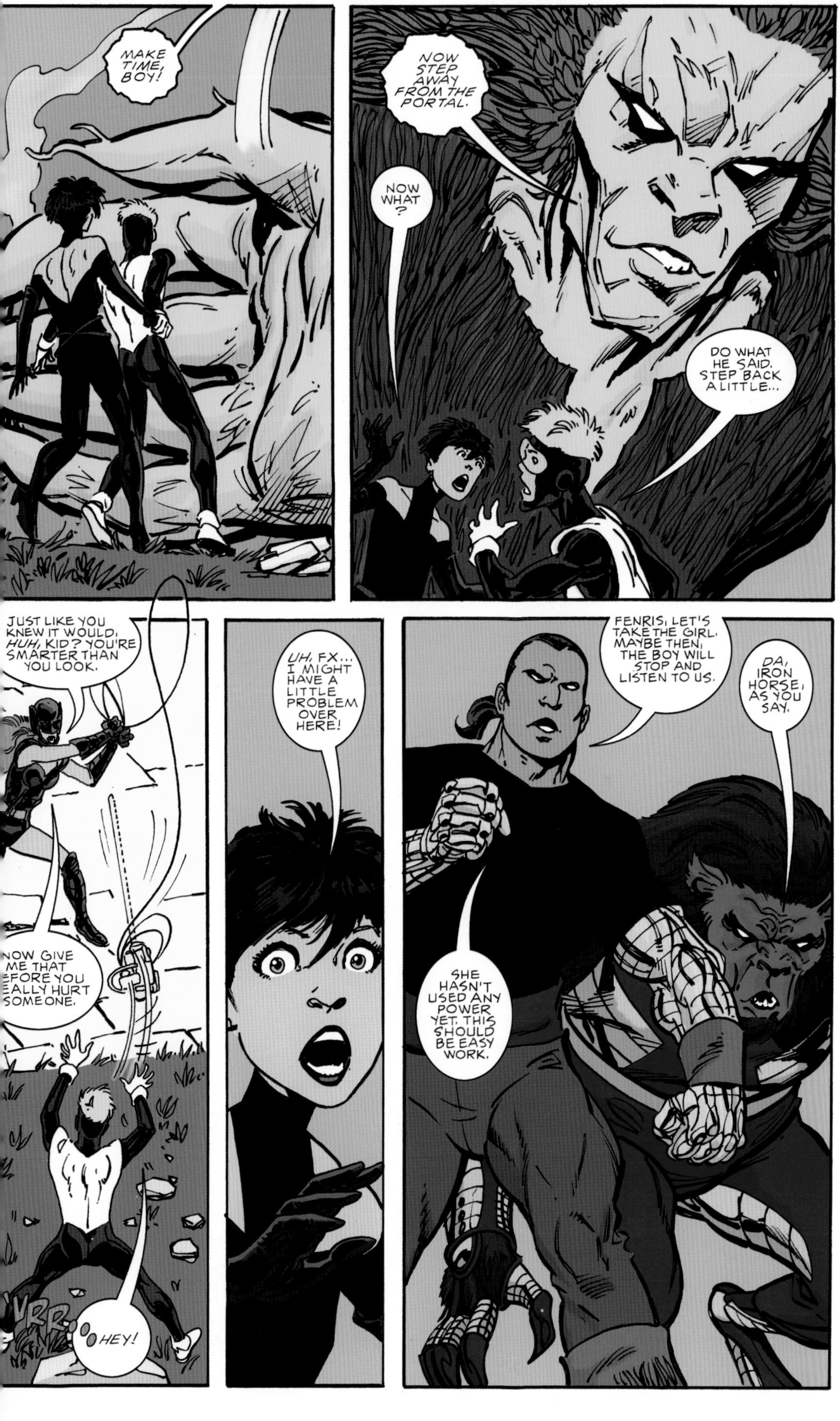
MAKE TIME, BOY!
NOW STEP AWAY FROM THE PORTAL.
NOW WHAT?
DO WHAT HE SAID. STEP BACK A LITTLE...
JUST LIKE YOU KNEW IT WOULD, HUH, KID? YOU'RE SMARTER THAN YOU LOOK.
NOW GIVE ME THAT EFORE YOU EALLY HURT SOMEONE.
VRR
HEY!
UH, FX... I MIGHT HAVE A LITTLE PROBLEM OVER HERE!
FENRIS, LET'S TAKE THE GIRL. MAYBE THEN, THE BOY WILL STOP AND LISTEN TO US.
DA, IRON HORSE, AS YOU SAY.
SHE HASN'T USED ANY POWER YET. THIS SHOULD BE EASY WORK.

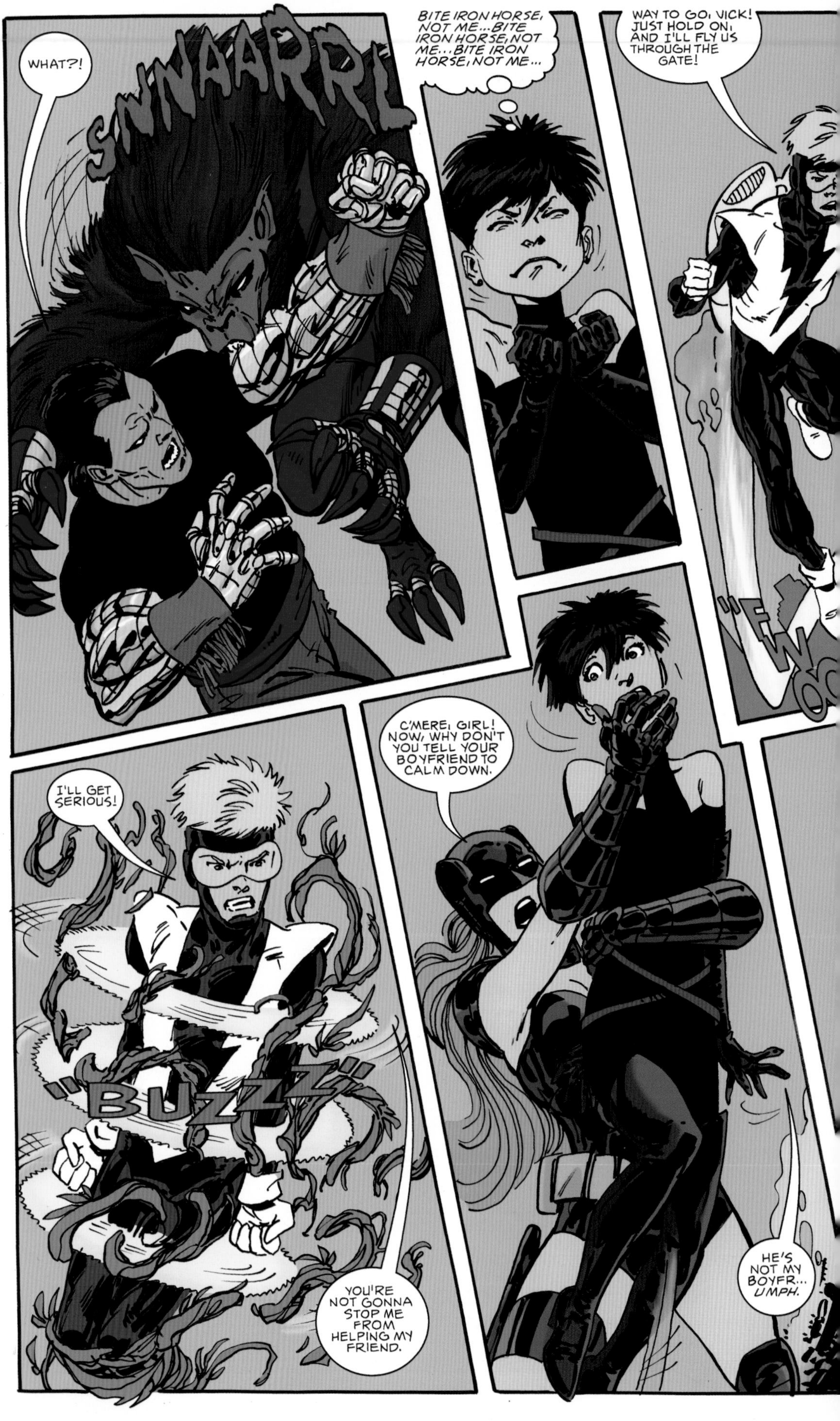
WHAT?!
SNNAARRL
BITE IRON HORSE, NOT ME... BITE IRON HORSE, NOT ME... BITE IRON HORSE, NOT ME...
WAY TO GO, VICK! JUST HOLD ON, AND I'LL FLY US THROUGH THE GATE!
C'MERE, GIRL! NOW, WHY DON'T YOU TELL YOUR BOYFRIEND TO CALM DOWN.
I'LL GET SERIOUS!
"BUZZZ"
YOU'RE NOT GONNA STOP ME FROM HELPING MY FRIEND.
HE'S NOT MY BOYFR... *UMPH.*

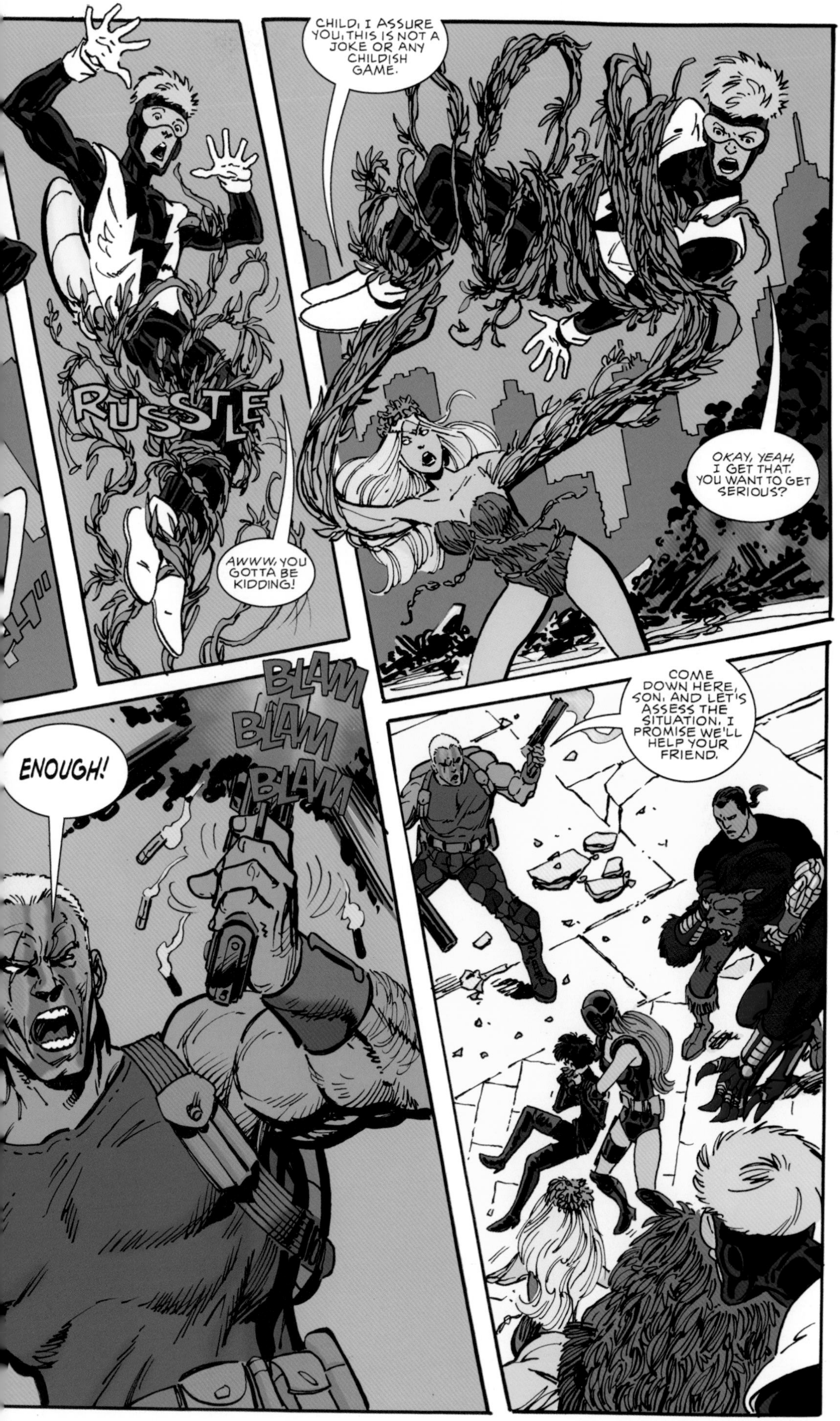
RUSSTLE
AWWW, YOU GOTTA BE KIDDING!
CHILD, I ASSURE YOU, THIS IS NOT A JOKE OR ANY CHILDISH GAME.
OKAY, YEAH, I GET THAT. YOU WANT TO GET SERIOUS?
ENOUGH!
BLAM BLAM BLAM
COME DOWN HERE, SON, AND LET'S ASSESS THE SITUATION. I PROMISE WE'LL HELP YOUR FRIEND.

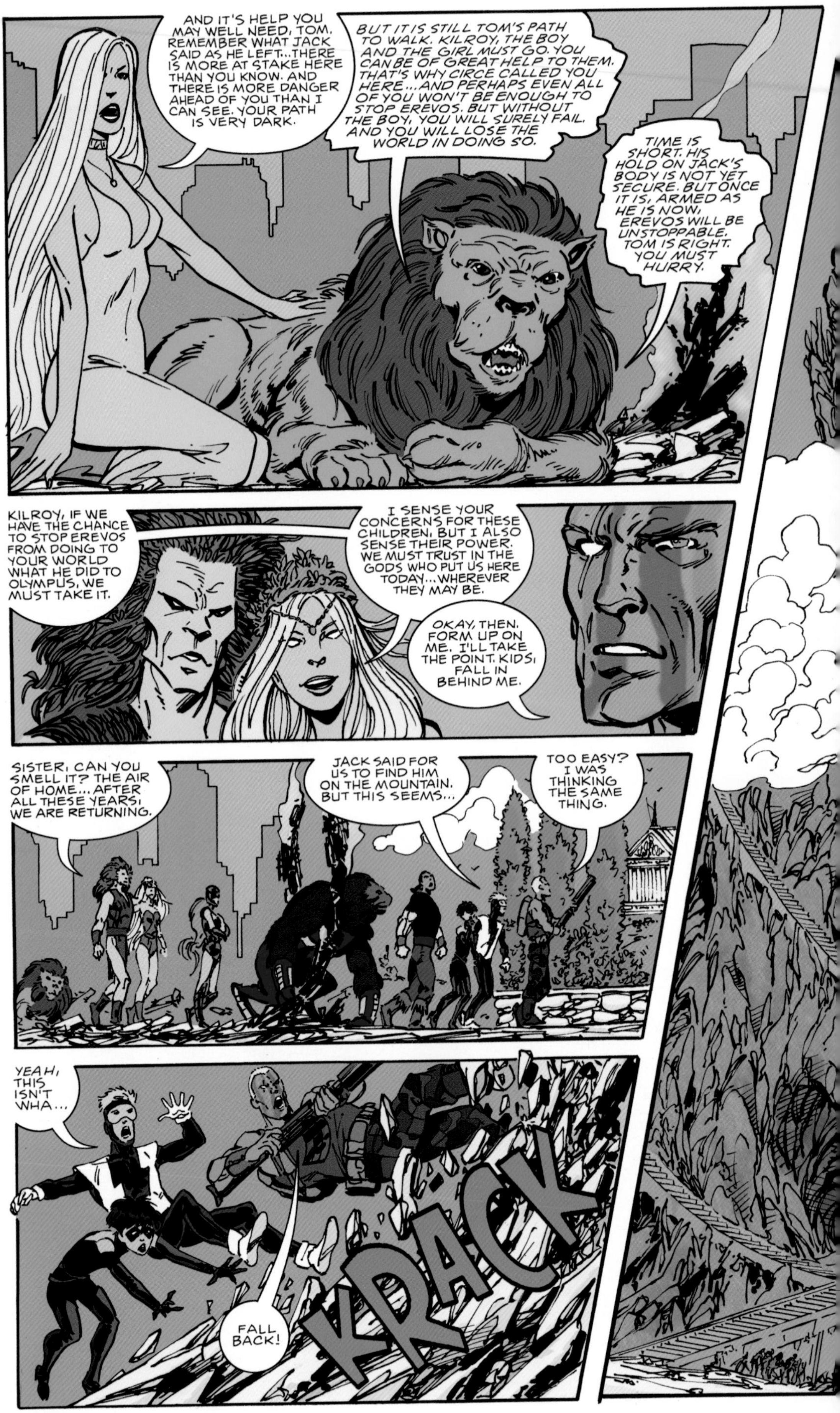
AND IT'S HELP YOU MAY WELL NEED, TOM. REMEMBER WHAT JACK SAID AS HE LEFT... THERE IS MORE AT STAKE HERE THAN YOU KNOW. AND THERE IS MORE DANGER AHEAD OF YOU THAN I CAN SEE. YOUR PATH IS VERY DARK.
BUT IT IS STILL TOM'S PATH TO WALK. KILROY, THE BOY AND THE GIRL MUST GO. YOU CAN BE OF GREAT HELP TO THEM. THAT'S WHY CIRCE CALLED YOU HERE... AND PERHAPS EVEN ALL OF YOU WON'T BE ENOUGH TO STOP EREVOS. BUT WITHOUT THE BOY, YOU WILL SURELY FAIL. AND YOU WILL LOSE THE WORLD IN DOING SO.
TIME IS SHORT. HIS HOLD ON JACK'S BODY IS NOT YET SECURE. BUT ONCE IT IS, ARMED AS HE IS NOW, EREVOS WILL BE UNSTOPPABLE. TOM IS RIGHT. YOU MUST HURRY.
KILROY, IF WE HAVE THE CHANCE TO STOP EREVOS FROM DOING TO YOUR WORLD WHAT HE DID TO OLYMPUS, WE MUST TAKE IT.
I SENSE YOUR CONCERNS FOR THESE CHILDREN, BUT I ALSO SENSE THEIR POWER. WE MUST TRUST IN THE GODS WHO PUT US HERE TODAY... WHEREVER THEY MAY BE.
OKAY, THEN. FORM UP ON ME. I'LL TAKE THE POINT. KIDS, FALL IN BEHIND ME.
SISTER, CAN YOU SMELL IT? THE AIR OF HOME... AFTER ALL THESE YEARS, WE ARE RETURNING.
JACK SAID FOR US TO FIND HIM ON THE MOUNTAIN. BUT THIS SEEMS...
TOO EASY? I WAS THINKING THE SAME THING.
YEAH, THIS ISN'T WHA...
FALL BACK!
KRACK

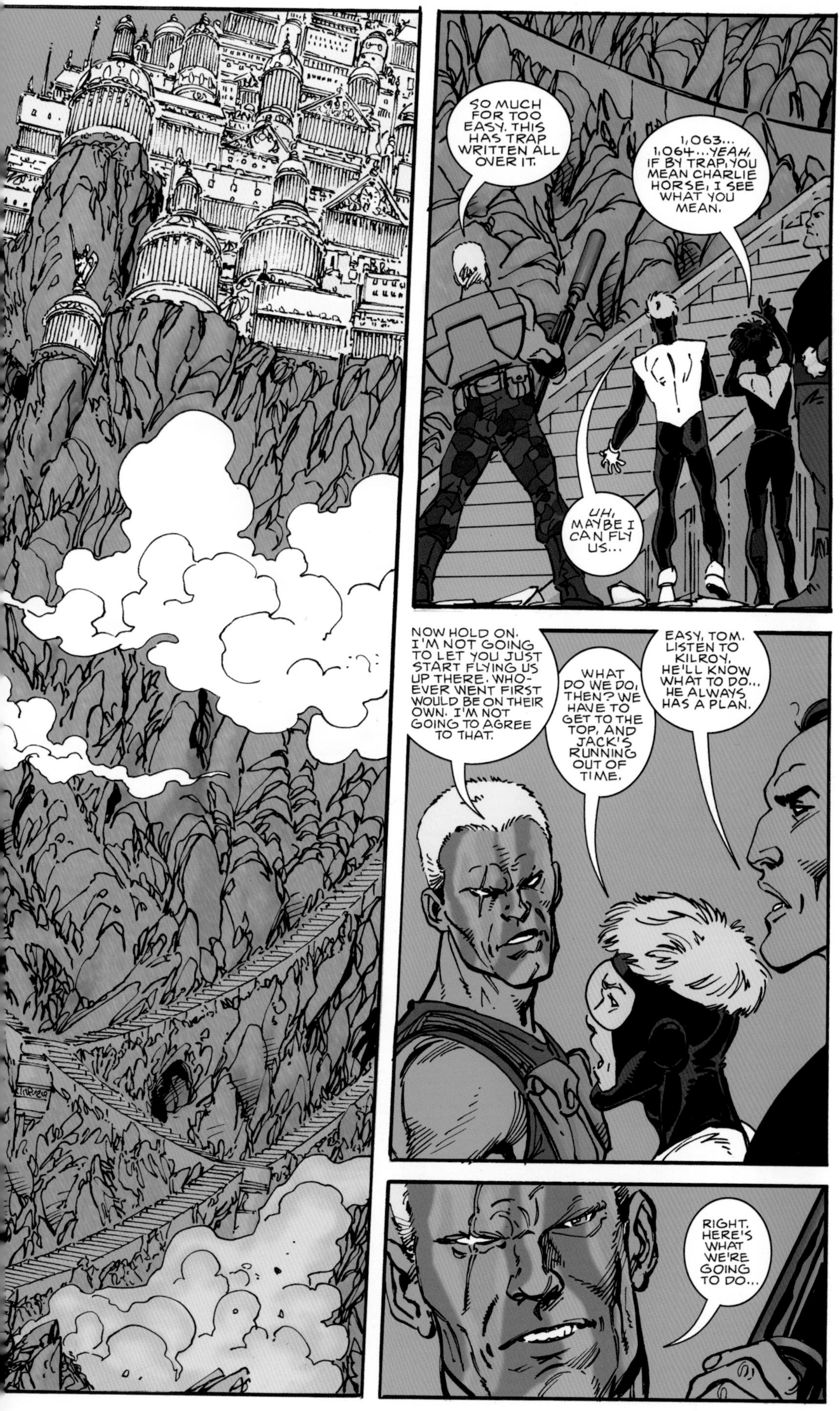
SO MUCH FOR TOO EASY. THIS HAS TRAP WRITTEN ALL OVER IT.
1,063... 1,064... YEAH, IF BY TRAP, YOU MEAN CHARLIE HORSE, I SEE WHAT YOU MEAN.
UH, MAYBE I CAN FLY US...
NOW HOLD ON. I'M NOT GOING TO LET YOU JUST START FLYING US UP THERE. WHO-EVER WENT FIRST WOULD BE ON THEIR OWN. I'M NOT GOING TO AGREE TO THAT.
WHAT DO WE DO, THEN? WE HAVE TO GET TO THE TOP, AND JACK'S RUNNING OUT OF TIME.
EASY, TOM. LISTEN TO KILROY, HE'LL KNOW WHAT TO DO... HE ALWAYS HAS A PLAN.
RIGHT. HERE'S WHAT WE'RE GOING TO DO...

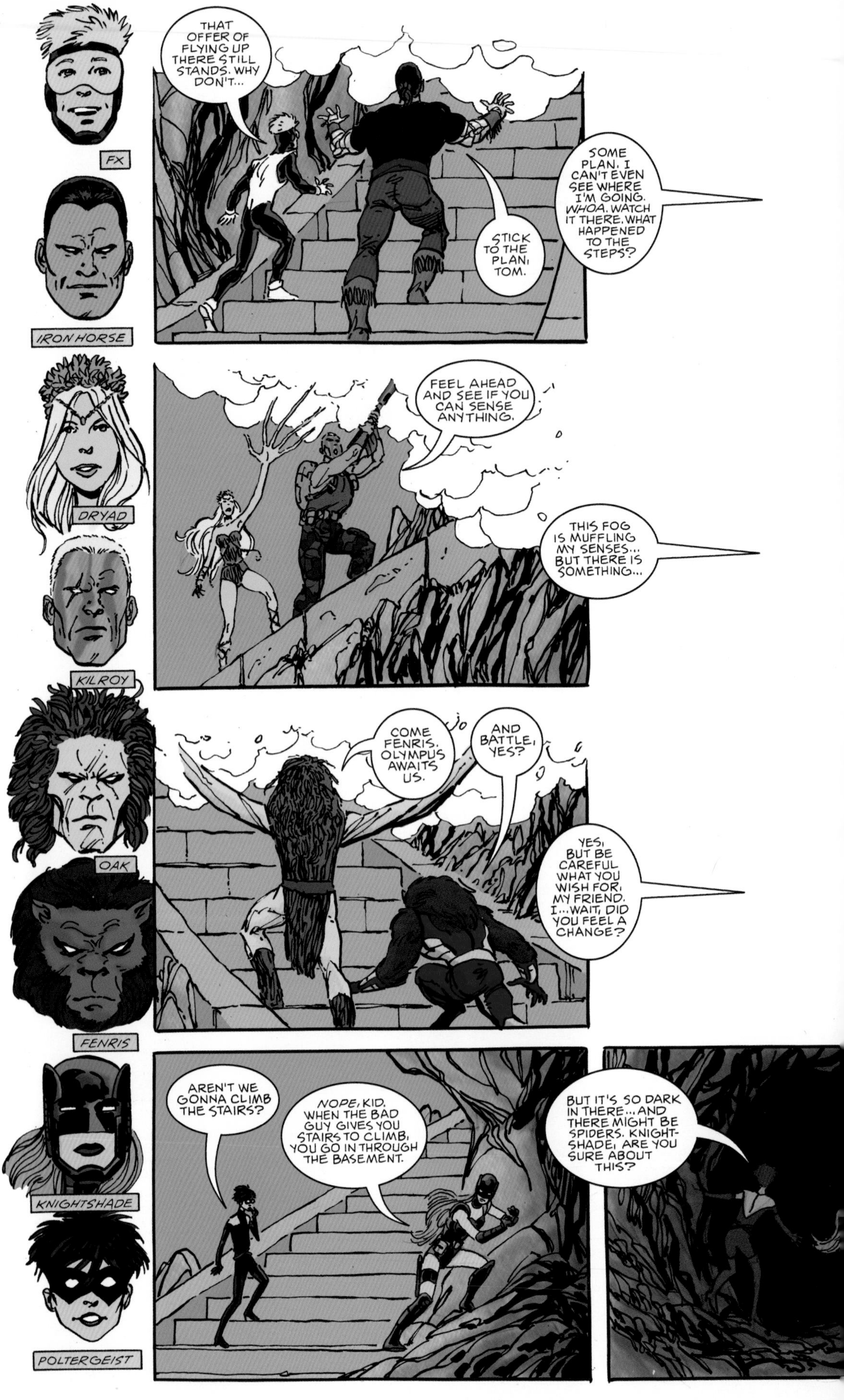
FX
IRONHORSE
THAT OFFER OF FLYING UP THERE STILL STANDS. WHY DON'T...
STICK TO THE PLAN, TOM.
SOME PLAN. I CAN'T EVEN SEE WHERE I'M GOING. WHOA. WATCH IT THERE. WHAT HAPPENED TO THE STEPS?
DRYAD
KILROY
FEEL AHEAD AND SEE IF YOU CAN SENSE ANYTHING.
THIS FOG IS MUFFLING MY SENSES... BUT THERE IS SOMETHING...
OAK
FENRIS
COME FENRIS. OLYMPUS AWAITS US.
AND BATTLE, YES?
YES, BUT BE CAREFUL WHAT YOU WISH FOR, MY FRIEND. I...WAIT, DID YOU FEEL A CHANGE?
KNIGHTSHADE
POLTERGEIST
AREN'T WE GONNA CLIMB THE STAIRS?
NOPE, KID. WHEN THE BAD GUY GIVES YOU STAIRS TO CLIMB, YOU GO IN THROUGH THE BASEMENT.
BUT IT'S SO DARK IN THERE... AND THERE MIGHT BE SPIDERS. KNIGHTSHADE, ARE YOU SURE ABOUT THIS?

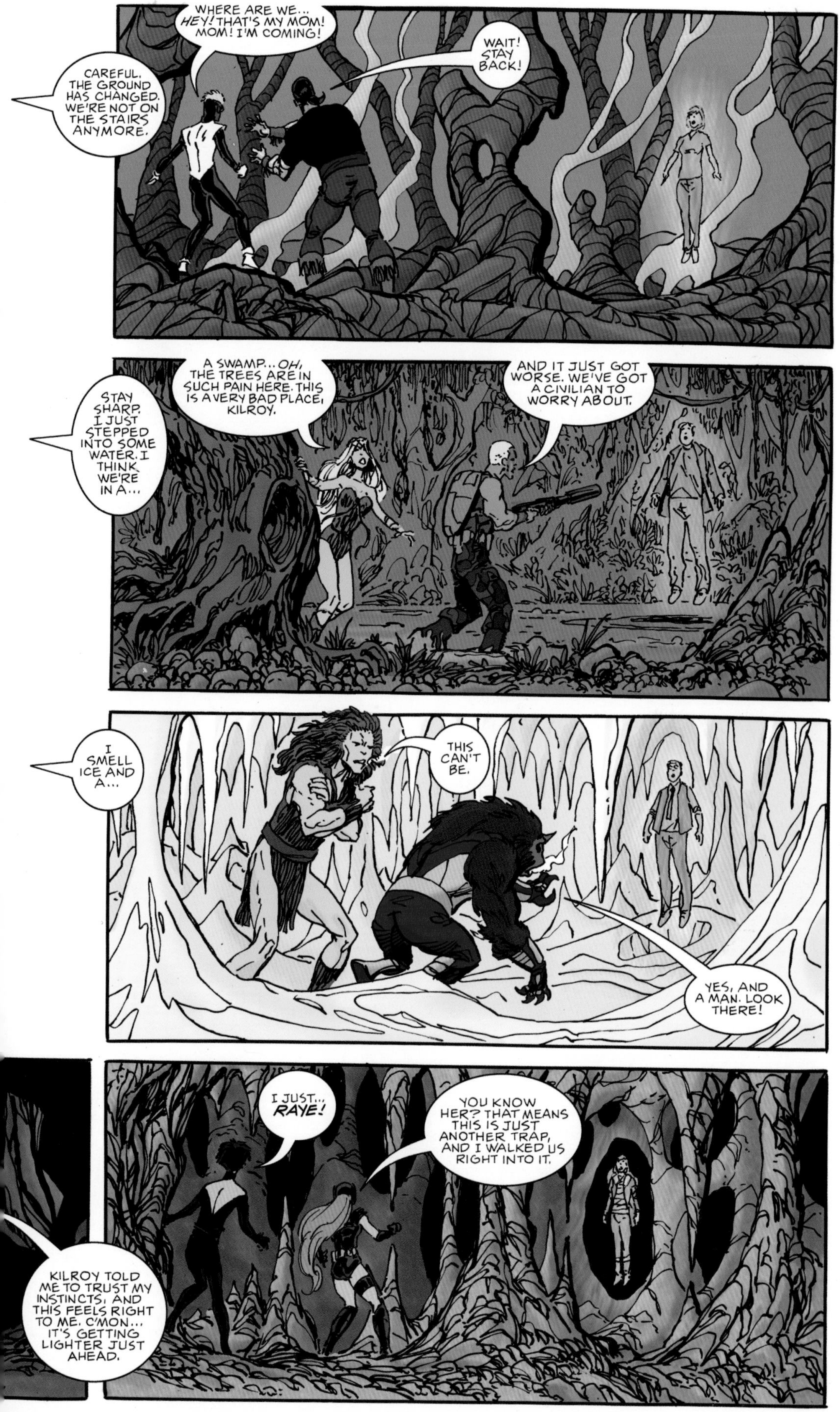
WHERE ARE WE... HEY! THAT'S MY MOM! MOM! I'M COMING!
CAREFUL. THE GROUND HAS CHANGED. WE'RE NOT ON THE STAIRS ANYMORE.
WAIT! STAY BACK!
STAY SHARP. I JUST STEPPED INTO SOME WATER. I THINK WE'RE IN A...
A SWAMP... OH, THE TREES ARE IN SUCH PAIN HERE. THIS IS A VERY BAD PLACE, KILROY.
AND IT JUST GOT WORSE. WE'VE GOT A CIVILIAN TO WORRY ABOUT.
I SMELL ICE AND A...
THIS CAN'T BE.
YES, AND A MAN. LOOK THERE!
I JUST... RAYE!
YOU KNOW HER? THAT MEANS THIS IS JUST ANOTHER TRAP, AND I WALKED US RIGHT INTO IT.
KILROY TOLD ME TO TRUST MY INSTINCTS, AND THIS FEELS RIGHT TO ME. C'MON... IT'S GETTING LIGHTER JUST AHEAD.

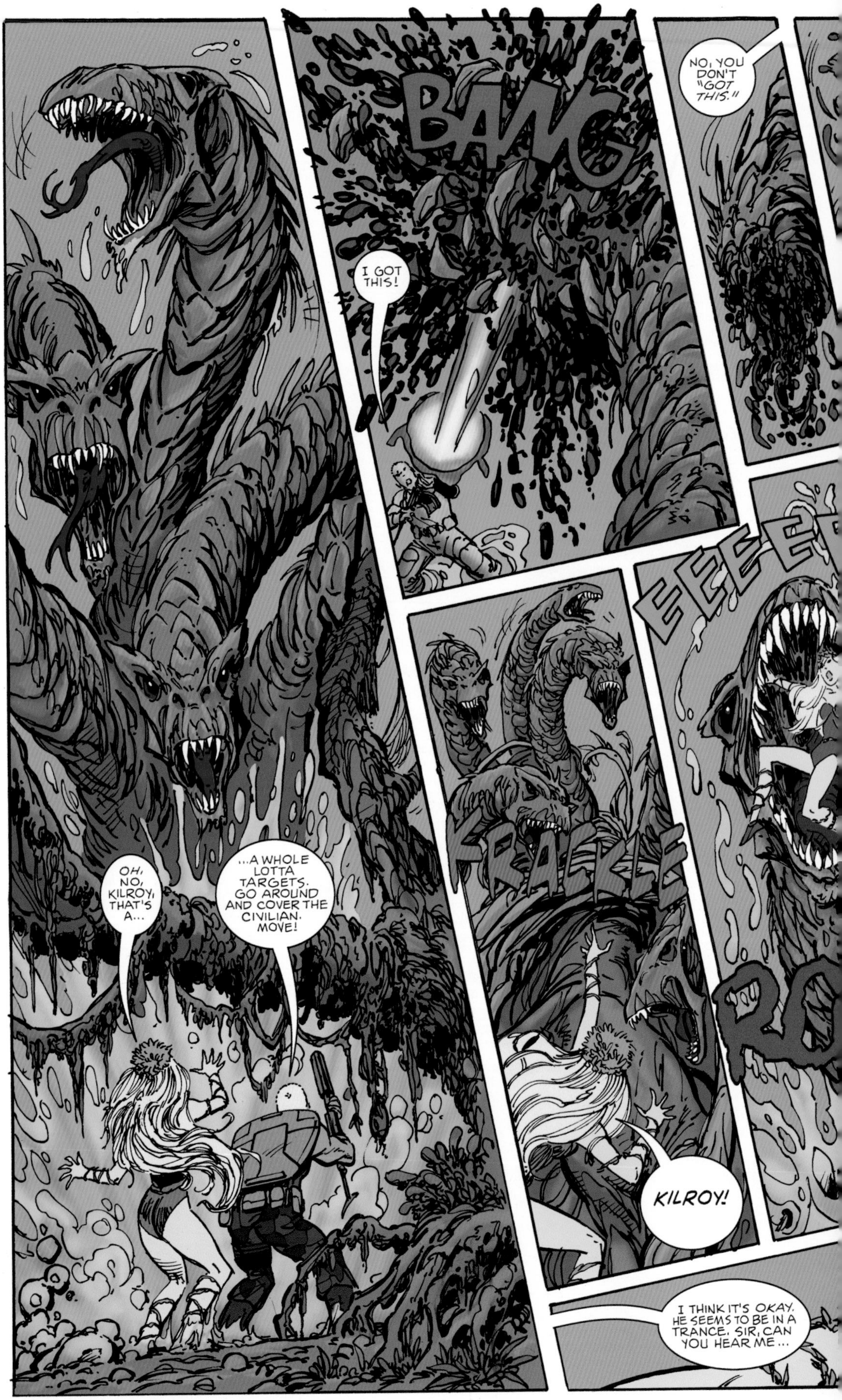

OH, NO, KILROY, THAT'S A...
...A WHOLE LOTTA TARGETS. GO AROUND AND COVER THE CIVILIAN. MOVE!
BANG
I GOT THIS!
NO, YOU DON'T "GOT THIS."
KRACKLE
KILROY!
I THINK IT'S OKAY. HE SEEMS TO BE IN A TRANCE. SIR, CAN YOU HEAR ME...

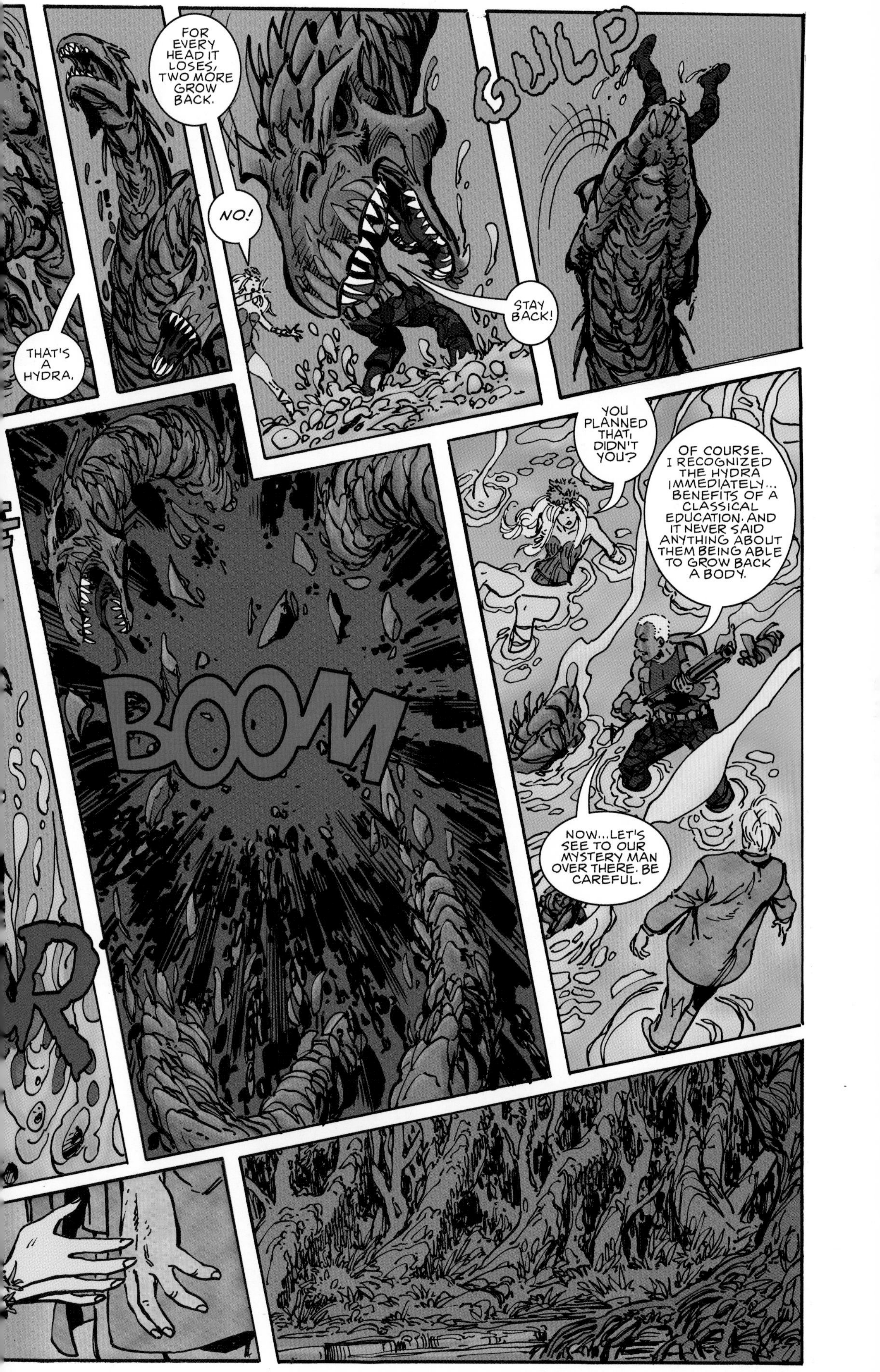

FOR EVERY HEAD IT LOSES, TWO MORE GROW BACK.
THAT'S A HYDRA,
NO!
STAY BACK!
GULP
BOOM
YOU PLANNED THAT, DIDN'T YOU?
OF COURSE. I RECOGNIZED THE HYDRA IMMEDIATELY... BENEFITS OF A CLASSICAL EDUCATION. AND IT NEVER SAID ANYTHING ABOUT THEM BEING ABLE TO GROW BACK A BODY.
NOW...LET'S SEE TO OUR MYSTERY MAN OVER THERE. BE CAREFUL.

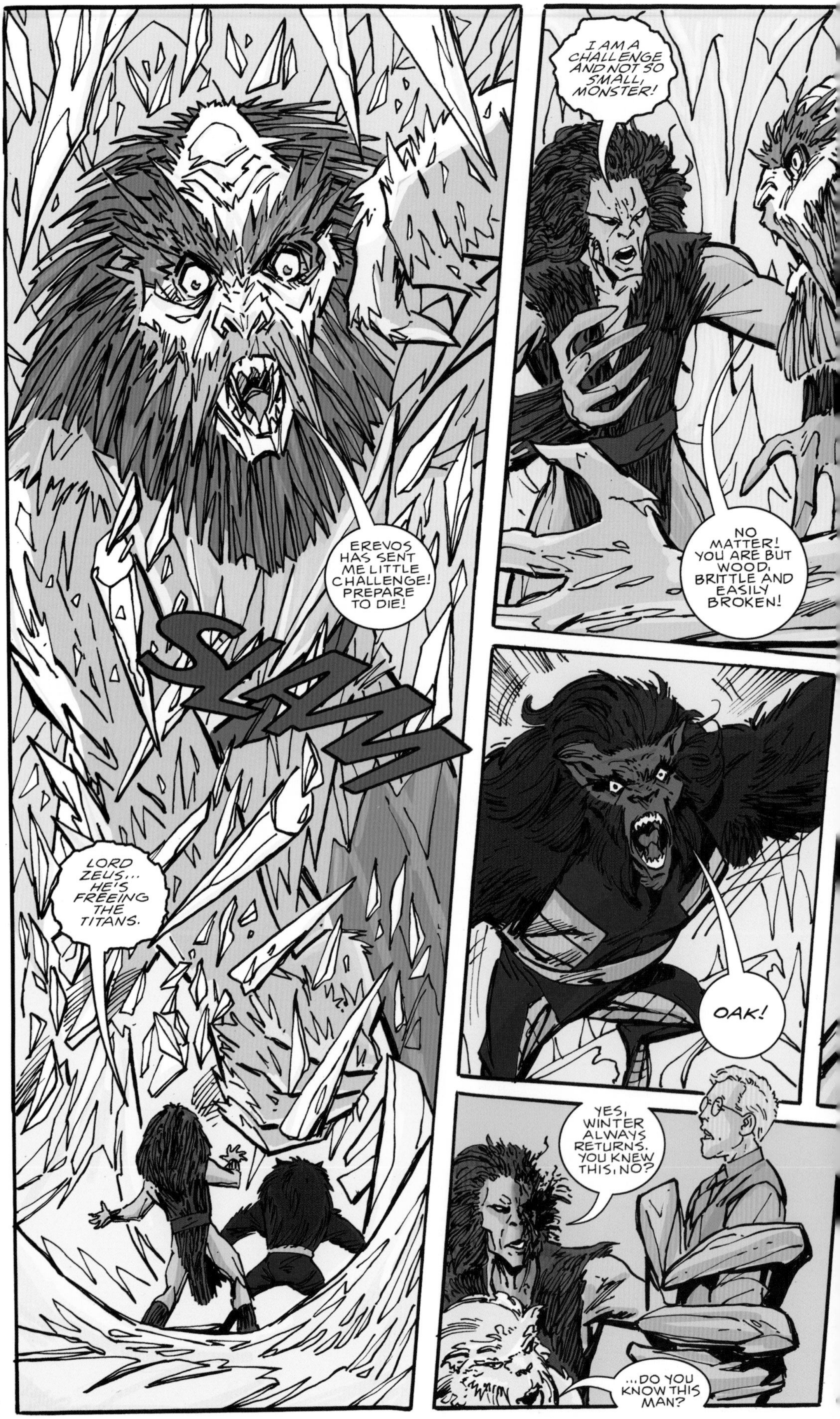
EREVOS HAS SENT ME LITTLE CHALLENGE! PREPARE TO DIE!
SLAM
LORD ZEUS... HE'S FREEING THE TITANS.
I AM A CHALLENGE AND NOT SO SMALL, MONSTER!
NO MATTER! YOU ARE BUT WOOD, BRITTLE AND EASILY BROKEN!
OAK!
YES, WINTER ALWAYS RETURNS. YOU KNEW THIS, NO?
...DO YOU KNOW THIS MAN?

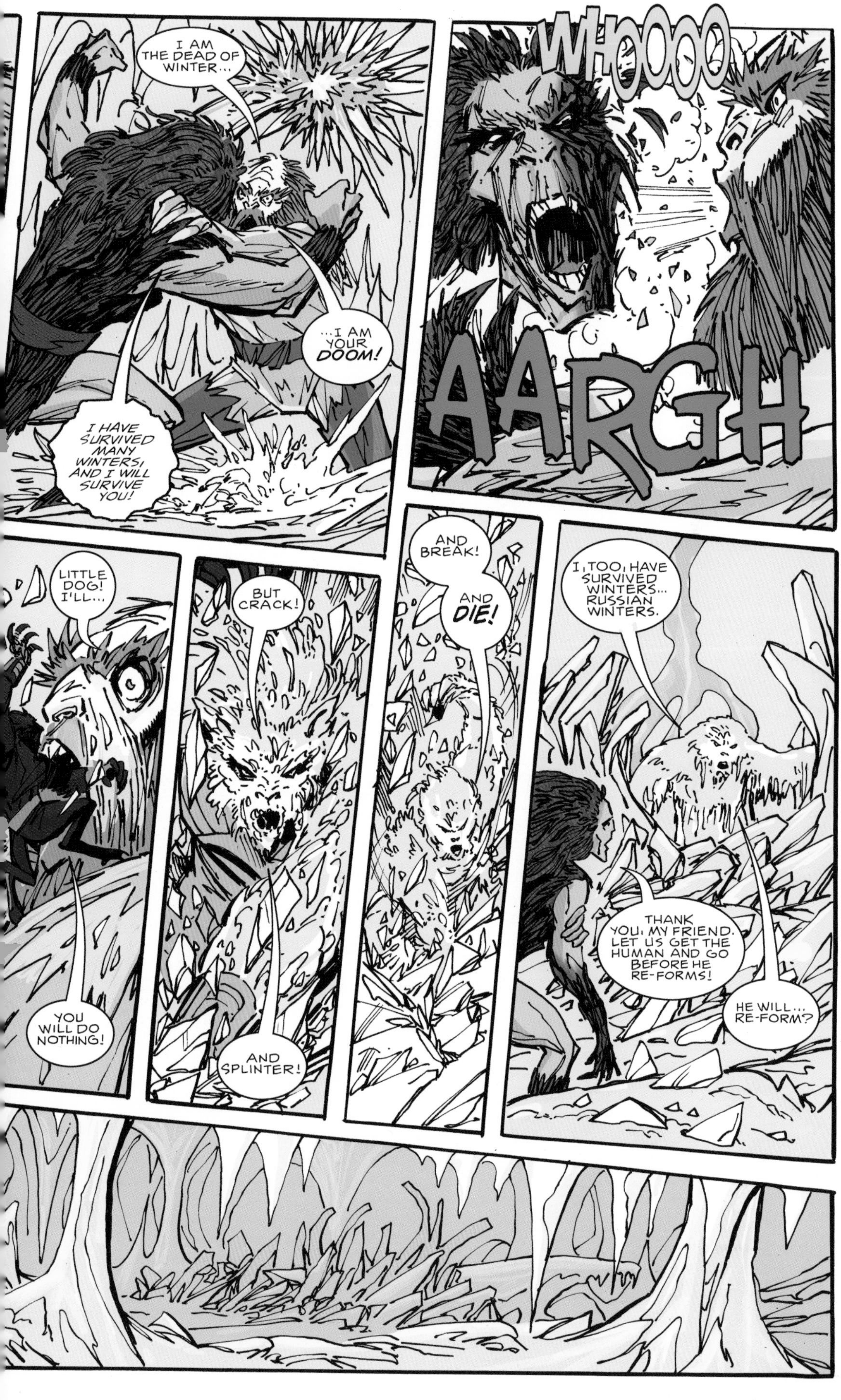
I AM THE DEAD OF WINTER...
...I AM YOUR DOOM!
I HAVE SURVIVED MANY WINTERS, AND I WILL SURVIVE YOU!
WHOOOO
AARGH
LITTLE DOG! I'LL...
YOU WILL DO NOTHING!
BUT CRACK!
AND SPLINTER!
AND BREAK!
AND DIE!
I, TOO, HAVE SURVIVED WINTERS... RUSSIAN WINTERS.
THANK YOU, MY FRIEND. LET US GET THE HUMAN AND GO BEFORE HE RE-FORMS!
HE WILL... RE-FORM?

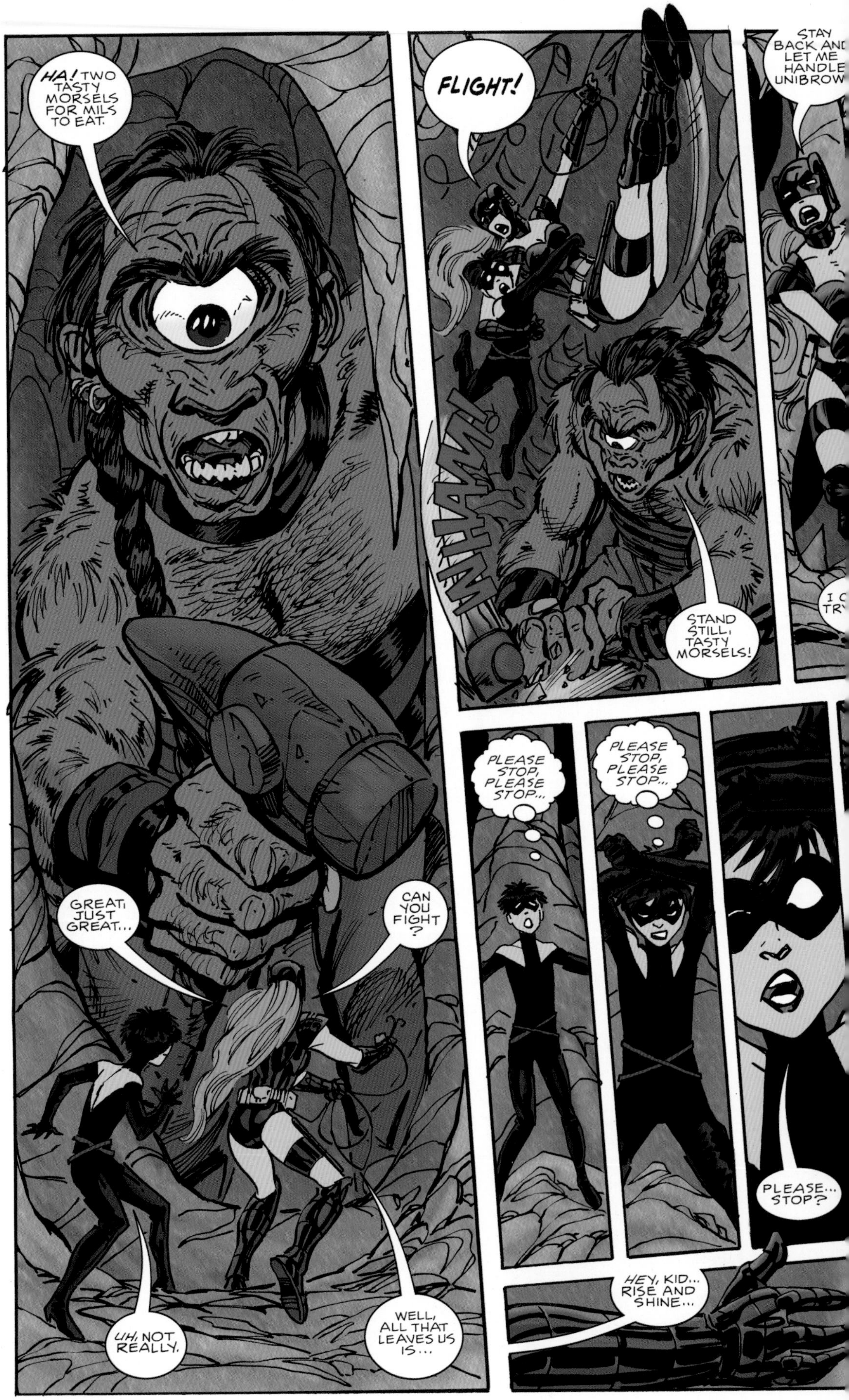
HA! TWO TASTY MORSELS FOR MILS TO EAT.
GREAT, JUST GREAT...
CAN YOU FIGHT?
UH, NOT REALLY.
WELL, ALL THAT LEAVES US IS...
FLIGHT!
WHAM!
STAND STILL, TASTY MORSELS!
STAY BACK AND LET ME HANDLE UNIBROW
PLEASE STOP, PLEASE STOP...
PLEASE STOP, PLEASE STOP...
PLEASE... STOP?
HEY, KID... RISE AND SHINE...

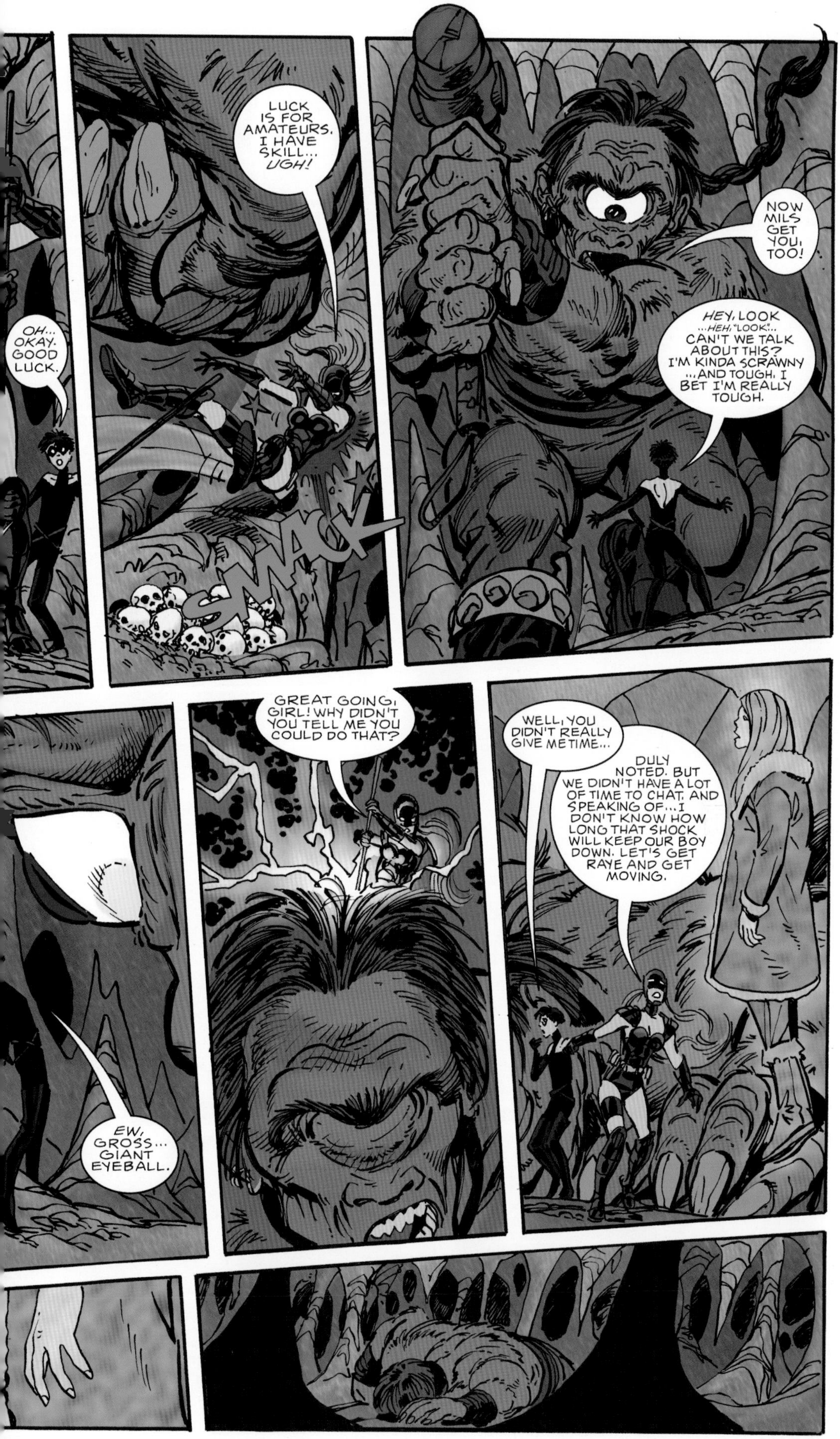
OH... OKAY. GOOD LUCK.
LUCK IS FOR AMATEURS. I HAVE SKILL... UGH!
SMACK
NOW MILS GET YOU, TOO!
HEY, LOOK ...HEH, "LOOK"... CAN'T WE TALK ABOUT THIS? I'M KINDA SCRAWNY ...AND TOUGH. I BET I'M REALLY TOUGH.
EW, GROSS... GIANT EYEBALL.
GREAT GOING, GIRL! WHY DIDN'T YOU TELL ME YOU COULD DO THAT?
WELL, YOU DIDN'T REALLY GIVE ME TIME...
DULY NOTED. BUT WE DIDN'T HAVE A LOT OF TIME TO CHAT. AND SPEAKING OF... I DON'T KNOW HOW LONG THAT SHOCK WILL KEEP OUR BOY DOWN. LET'S GET RAYE AND GET MOVING.

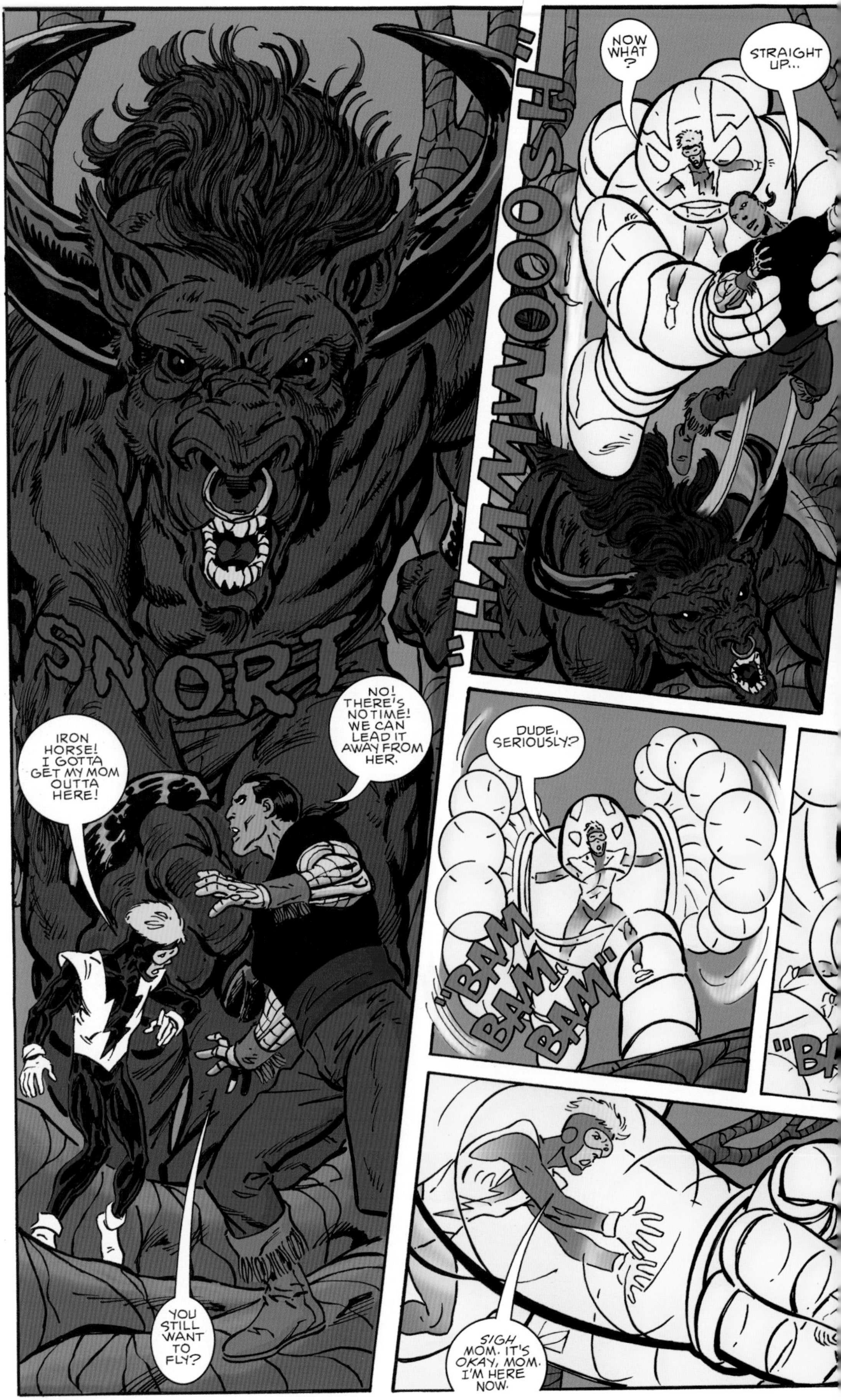
SNORT
IRON HORSE! I GOTTA GET MY MOM OUTTA HERE!
NO! THERE'S NO TIME! WE CAN LEAD IT AWAY FROM HER.
YOU STILL WANT TO FLY?
"WHOOOOMMMM"
NOW WHAT?
STRAIGHT UP...
DUDE, SERIOUSLY?
"BAM" "BAM" "BAM" "BAM"
SIGH MOM. IT'S OKAY, MOM. I'M HERE NOW.

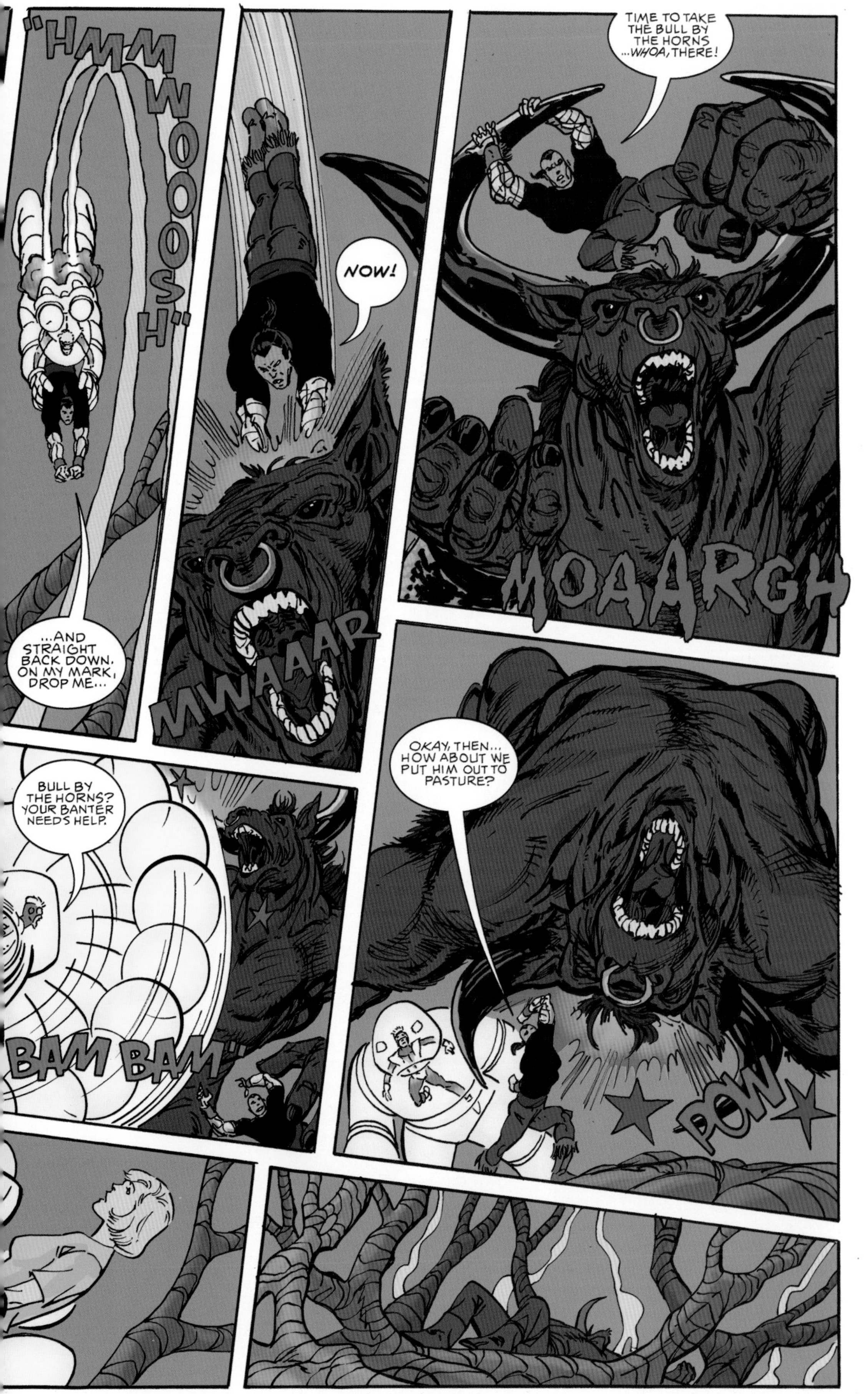
"HMMWOOOOSH"
...AND STRAIGHT BACK DOWN. ON MY MARK, DROP ME...
NOW!
MWAAAR
TIME TO TAKE THE BULL BY THE HORNS ...WHOA, THERE!
MOAARGH
BULL BY THE HORNS? YOUR BANTER NEEDS HELP.
BAM BAM
OKAY, THEN... HOW ABOUT WE PUT HIM OUT TO PASTURE?
POW

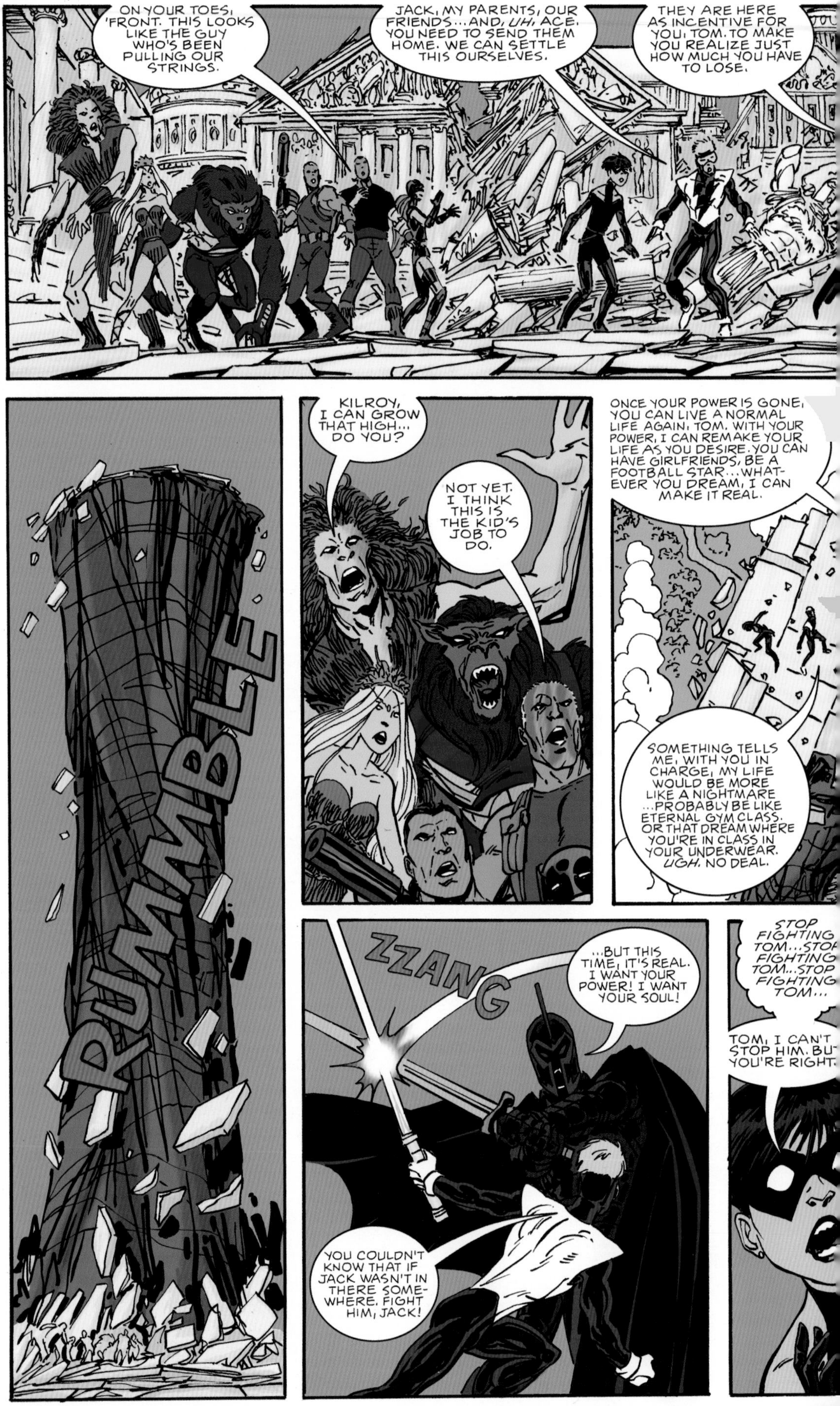
ON YOUR TOES, 'FRONT. THIS LOOKS LIKE THE GUY WHO'S BEEN PULLING OUR STRINGS.
JACK, MY PARENTS, OUR FRIENDS...AND, *UH,* ACE. YOU NEED TO SEND THEM HOME. WE CAN SETTLE THIS OURSELVES.
THEY ARE HERE AS INCENTIVE FOR YOU, TOM, TO MAKE YOU REALIZE JUST HOW MUCH YOU HAVE TO LOSE.
RUMMBLEE
KILROY, I CAN GROW THAT HIGH... DO YOU?
NOT YET. I THINK THIS IS THE KID'S JOB TO DO.
ONCE YOUR POWER IS GONE, YOU CAN LIVE A NORMAL LIFE AGAIN, TOM. WITH YOUR POWER, I CAN REMAKE YOUR LIFE AS YOU DESIRE. YOU CAN HAVE GIRLFRIENDS, BE A FOOTBALL STAR...WHAT-EVER YOU DREAM, I CAN MAKE IT REAL.
SOMETHING TELLS ME, WITH YOU IN CHARGE, MY LIFE WOULD BE MORE LIKE A NIGHTMARE ...PROBABLY BE LIKE ETERNAL GYM CLASS. OR THAT DREAM WHERE YOU'RE IN CLASS IN YOUR UNDERWEAR. *UGH.* NO DEAL.
ZZANG
...BUT THIS TIME, IT'S REAL. I WANT YOUR POWER! I WANT YOUR SOUL!
YOU COULDN'T KNOW THAT IF JACK WASN'T IN THERE SOME-WHERE. FIGHT HIM, JACK!
STOP FIGHTING TOM...STOP FIGHTING TOM...STOP FIGHTING TOM...
TOM, I CAN'T STOP HIM. BUT YOU'RE RIGHT.

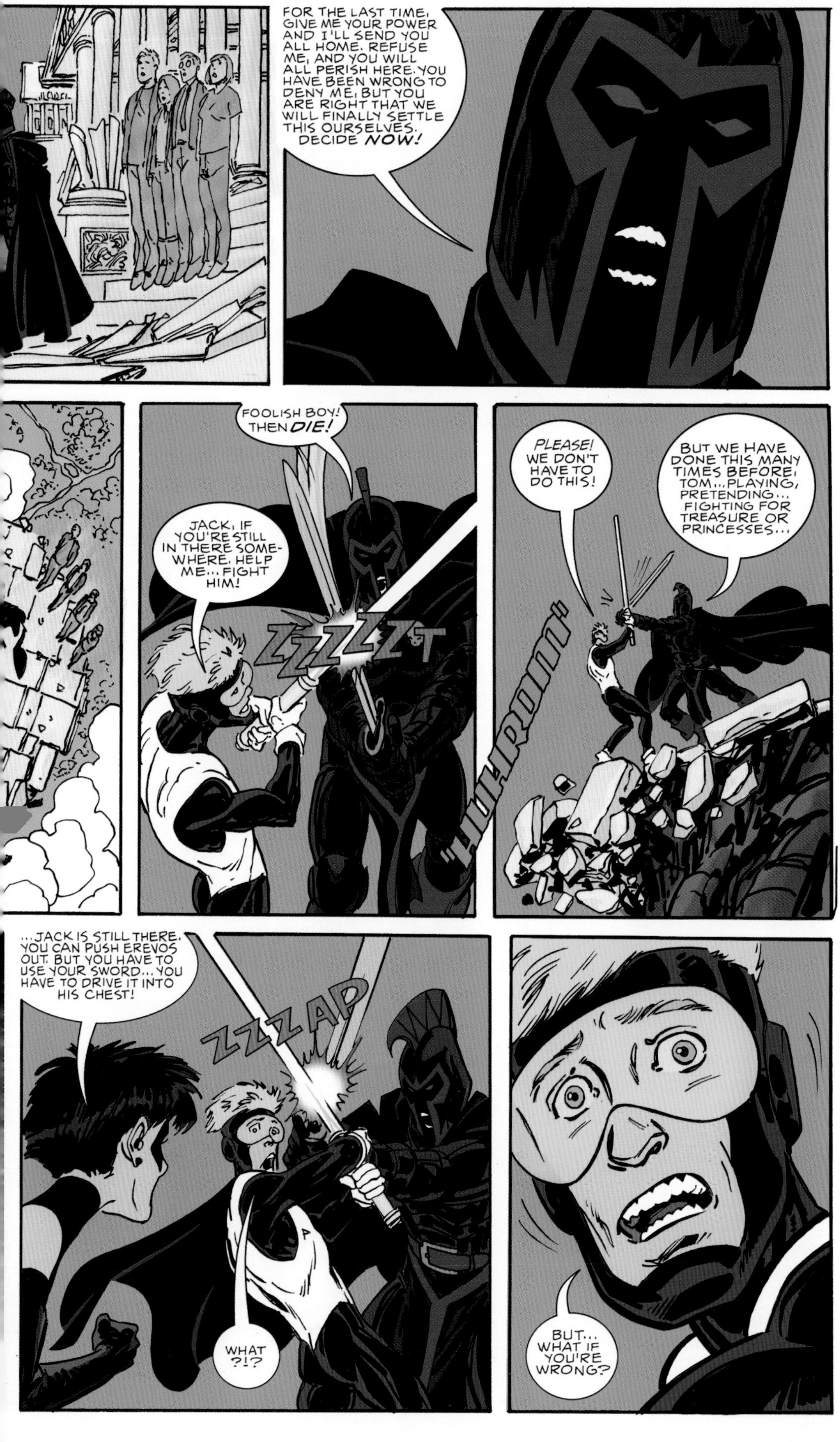

FOR THE LAST TIME, GIVE ME YOUR POWER AND I'LL SEND YOU ALL HOME. REFUSE ME, AND YOU WILL ALL PERISH HERE. YOU HAVE BEEN WRONG TO DENY ME, BUT YOU ARE RIGHT THAT WE WILL FINALLY SETTLE THIS OURSELVES. DECIDE *NOW!*
FOOLISH BOY! THEN *DIE!*
JACK, IF YOU'RE STILL IN THERE SOMEWHERE, HELP ME... FIGHT HIM!
ZZZZZT
PLEASE! WE DON'T HAVE TO DO THIS!
BUT WE HAVE DONE THIS MANY TIMES BEFORE, TOM... PLAYING, PRETENDING... FIGHTING FOR TREASURE OR PRINCESSES...
...JACK IS STILL THERE. YOU CAN PUSH EREVOS OUT. BUT YOU HAVE TO USE YOUR SWORD... YOU HAVE TO DRIVE IT INTO HIS CHEST!
ZZZZAP
WHAT ?!?
BUT... WHAT IF YOU'RE WRONG?

TOMMMAARGH!

I'M SORRY, JACK.

YEAH, BUT NOW WHAT!?!

NOW, BOY, I TAKE *YOUR* BODY, POWER, SOUL, AND WORLD!

HIS SWORD! USE HIS SWORD!

NOO

I'VE HAD ABOUT ENOUGH OF YOU!

YES! IT WORKED!

...THANK GOODNESS.

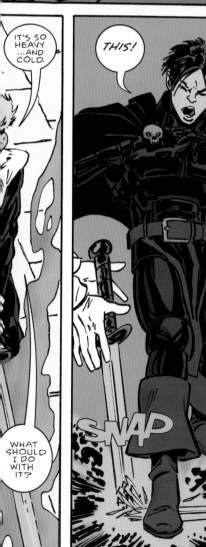

IT'S SO HEAVY ...AND COLD.

THIS!

WHAT SHOULD I DO WITH IT?

SNAP

JACK! YOU'RE OKAY! SORRY ABOUT TRYING TO KILL YOU.

THAT'S OKAY. BUT WE'RE EVEN FOR THE WHOLE COMA THING NOW, RIGHT?

LET'S GO HOME!

YEAH, BEFORE YOUR DAD WAKES UP... THAT WOULD BE THE WORST.

YOU GUYS GOT ROOM FOR ME?

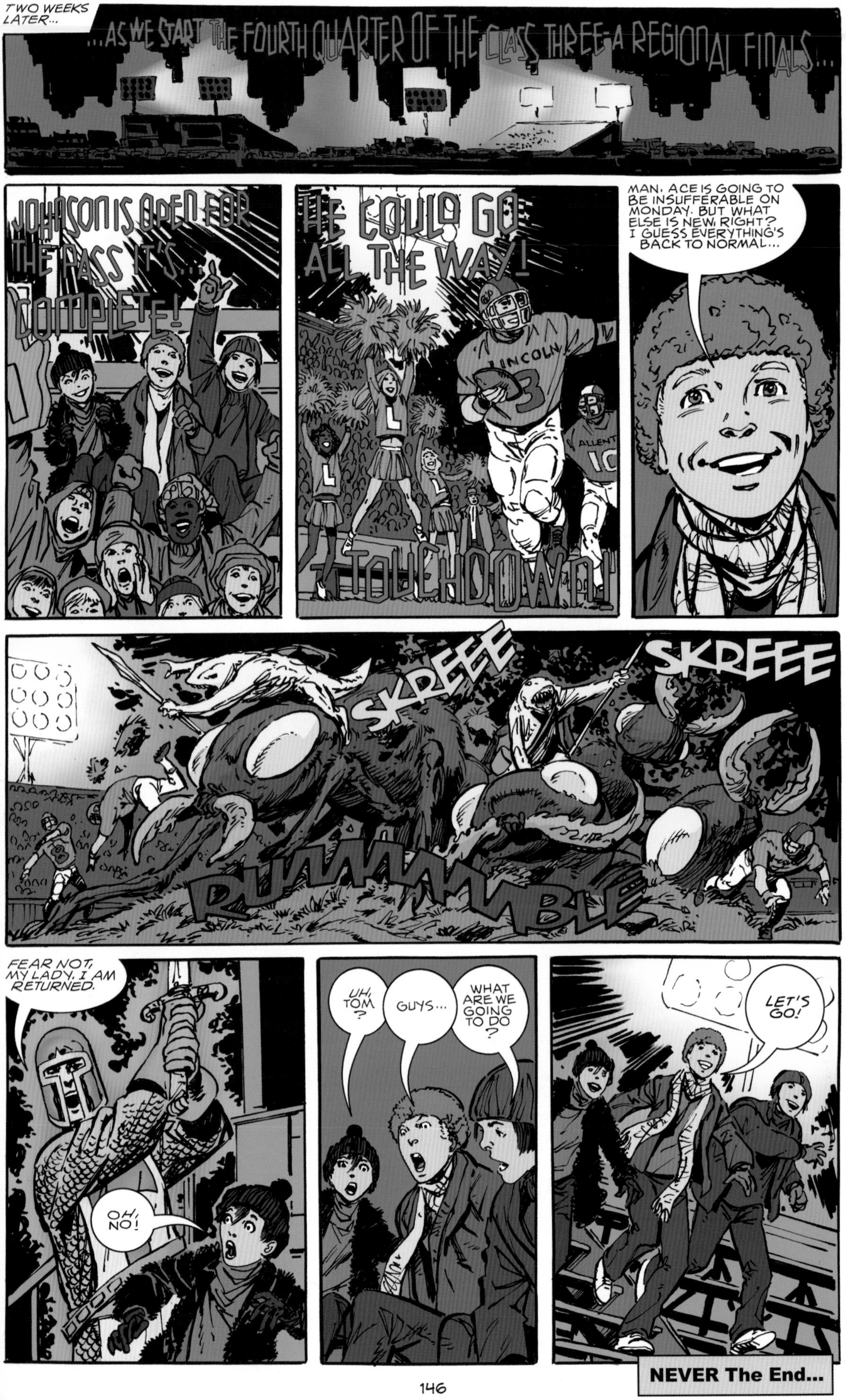
TWO WEEKS LATER...
...AS WE START THE FOURTH QUARTER OF THE CLASS THREE-A REGIONAL FINALS...
JOHNSON IS OPEN FOR THE PASS IT'S... COMPLETE!
HE COULD GO ALL THE WAY!
LINCOLN
TOUCHDOWN!
MAN. ACE IS GOING TO BE INSUFFERABLE ON MONDAY. BUT WHAT ELSE IS NEW, RIGHT? I GUESS EVERYTHING'S BACK TO NORMAL...
SKREEE
SKREEEE
RUMMMMBLE
FEAR NOT, MY LADY. I AM RETURNED.
OH, NO!
UH, TOM ?
GUYS...
WHAT ARE WE GOING TO DO ?
LET'S GO!
NEVER The End...

ART GALLERY

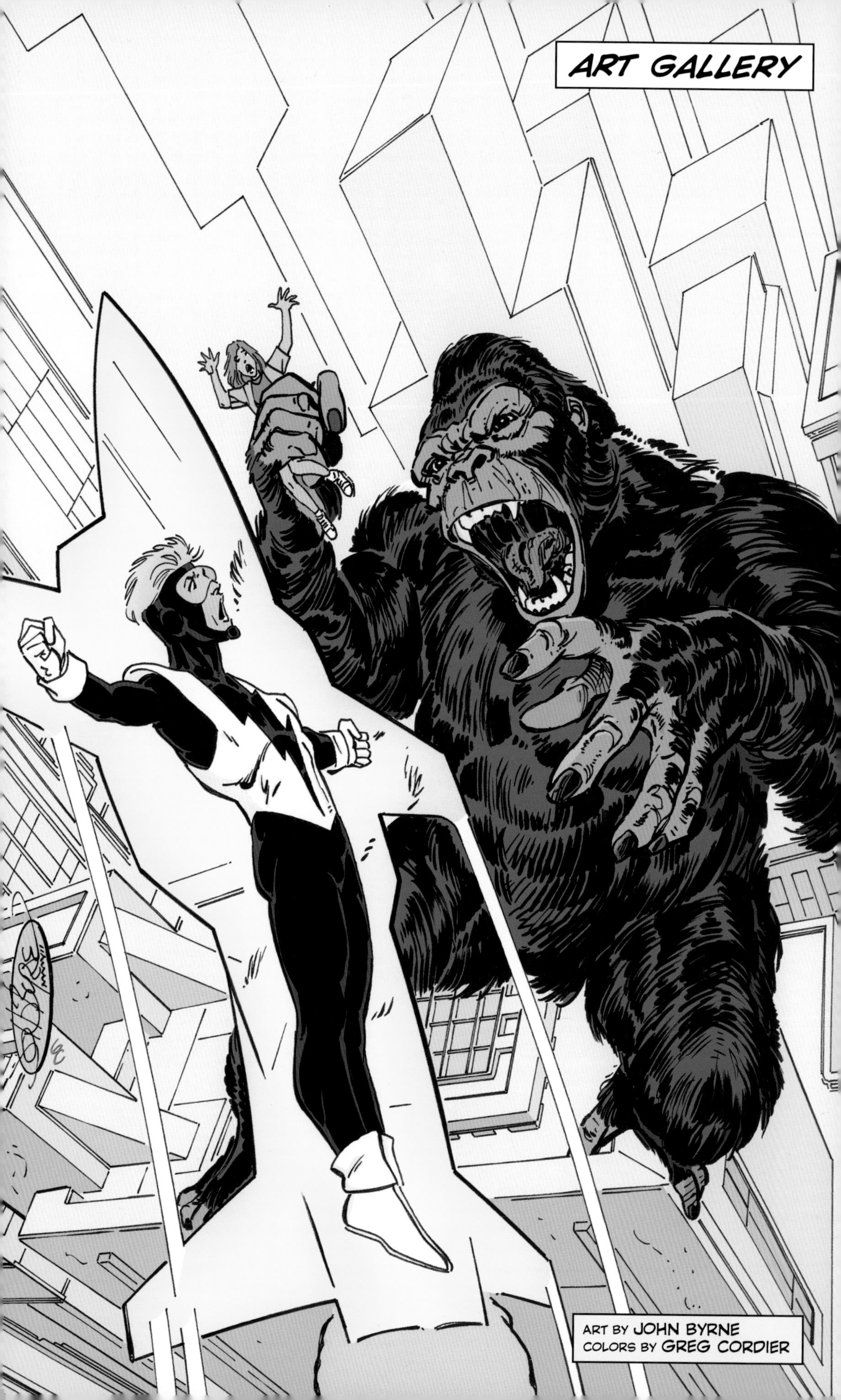

ART BY JOHN BYRNE
COLORS BY GREG CORDIER

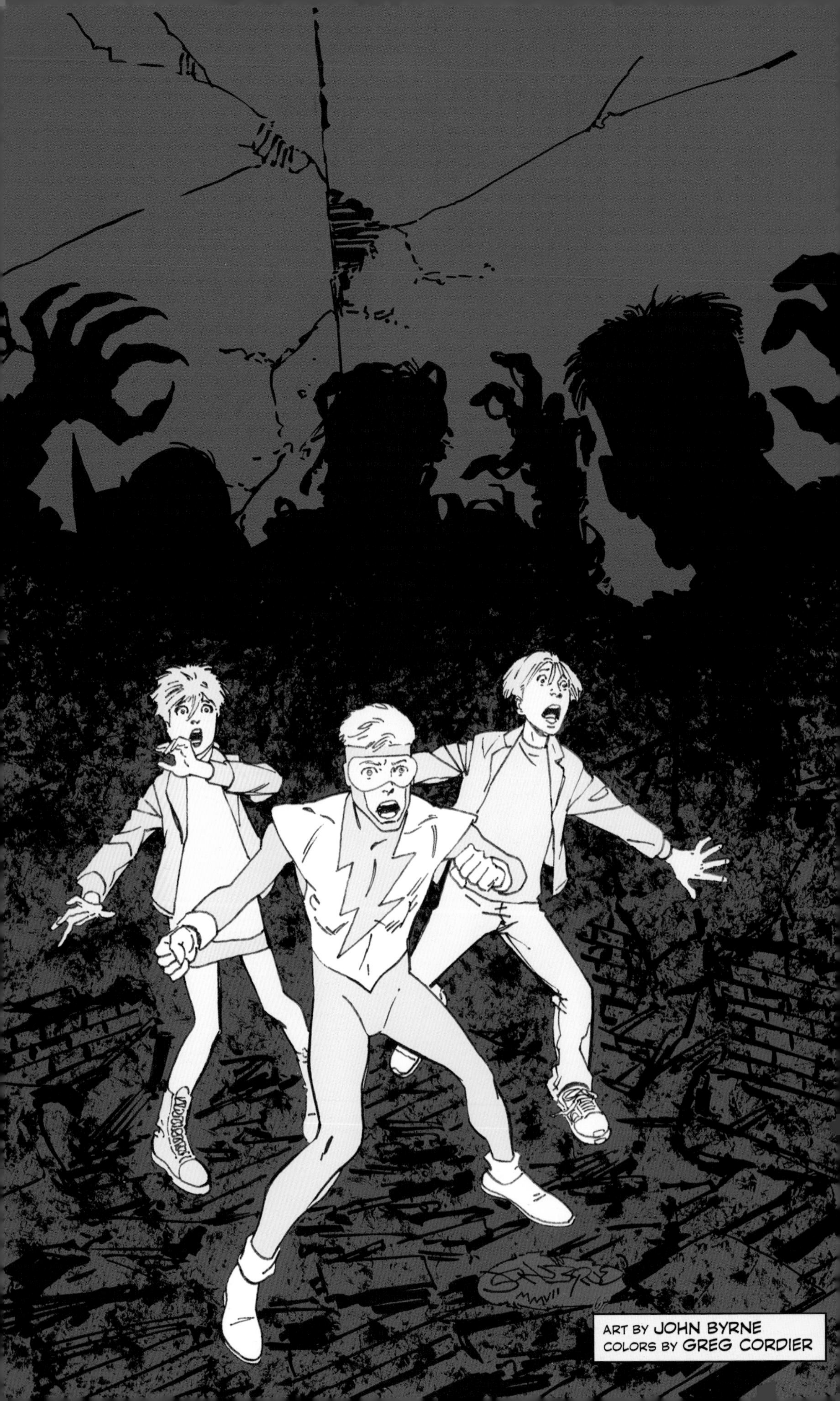
MMVII

ART BY JOHN BYRNE
COLORS BY GREG CORDIER

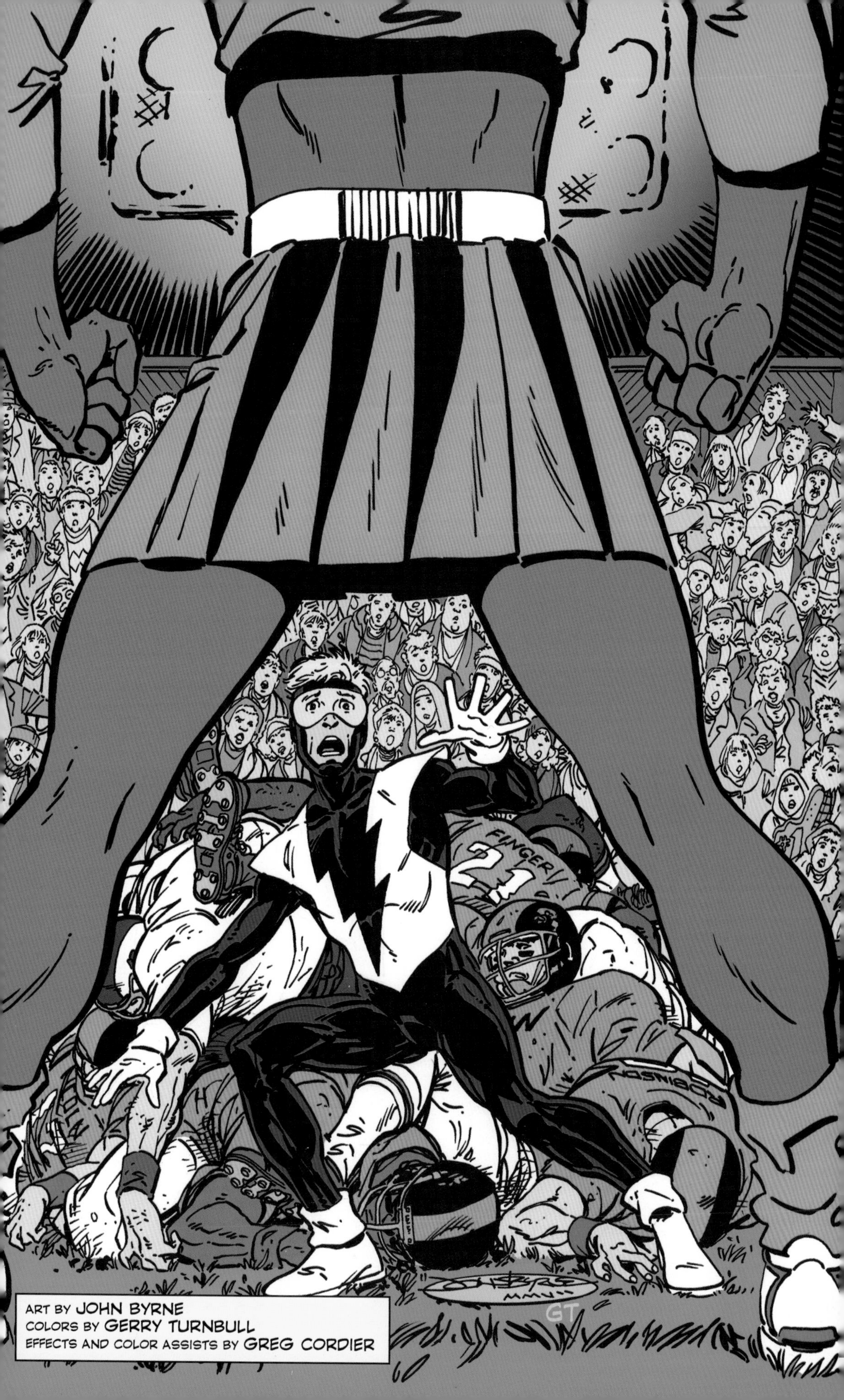
FINGER
21

ART BY JOHN BYRNE
COLORS BY GERRY TURNBULL
EFFECTS AND COLOR ASSISTS BY GREG CORDIER

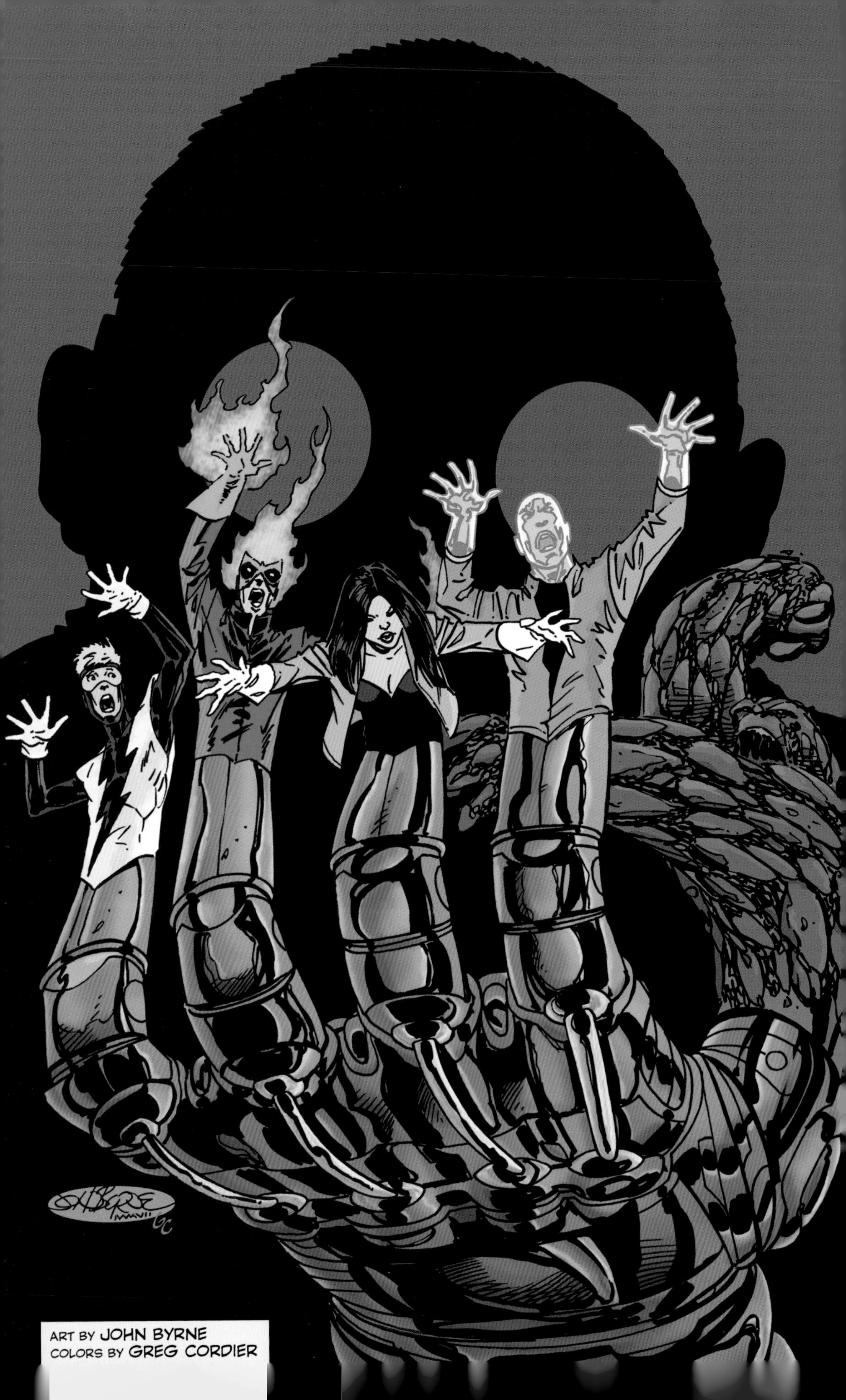

ART BY JOHN BYRNE
COLORS BY GREG CORDIER

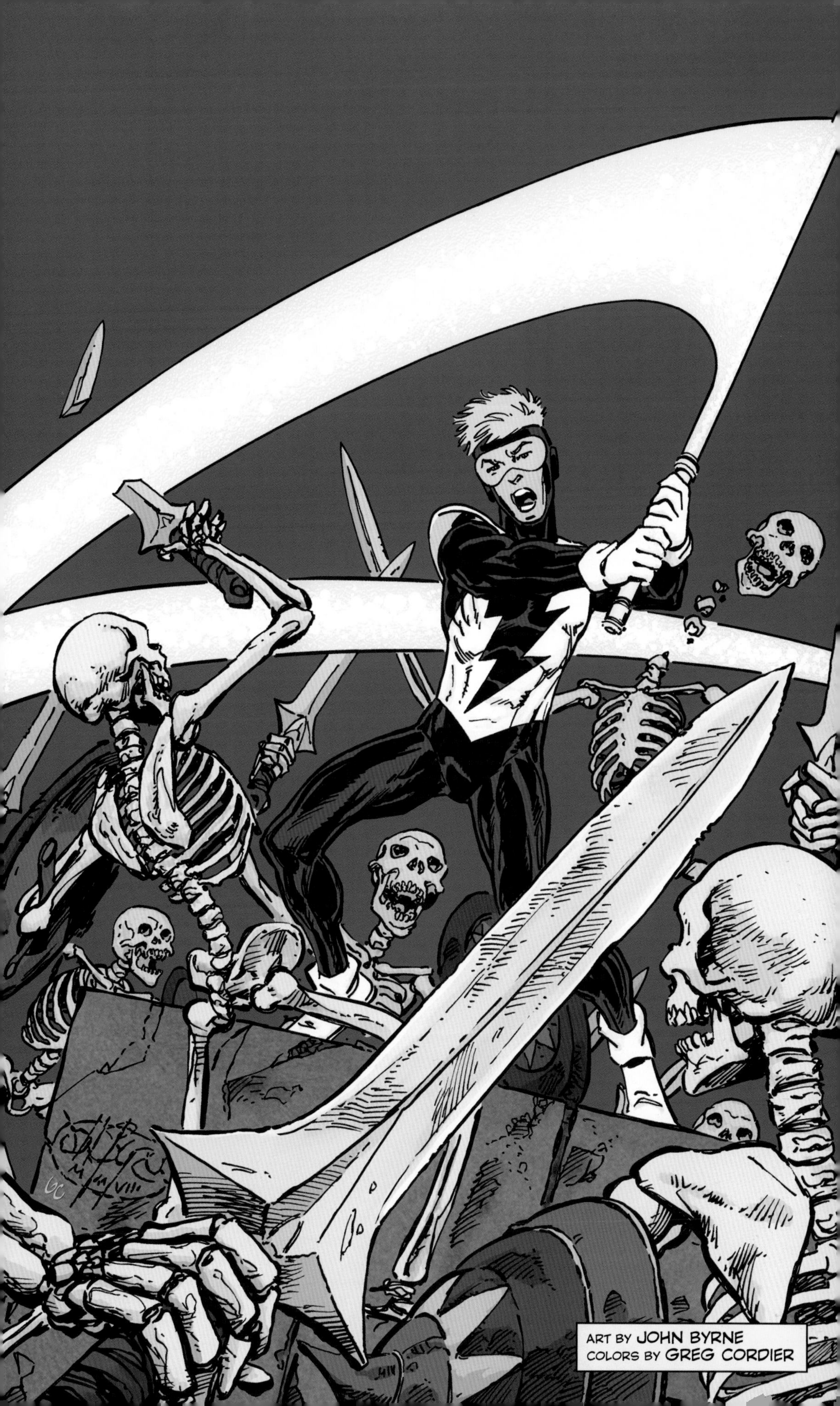

ART BY JOHN BYRNE
COLORS BY GREG CORDIER

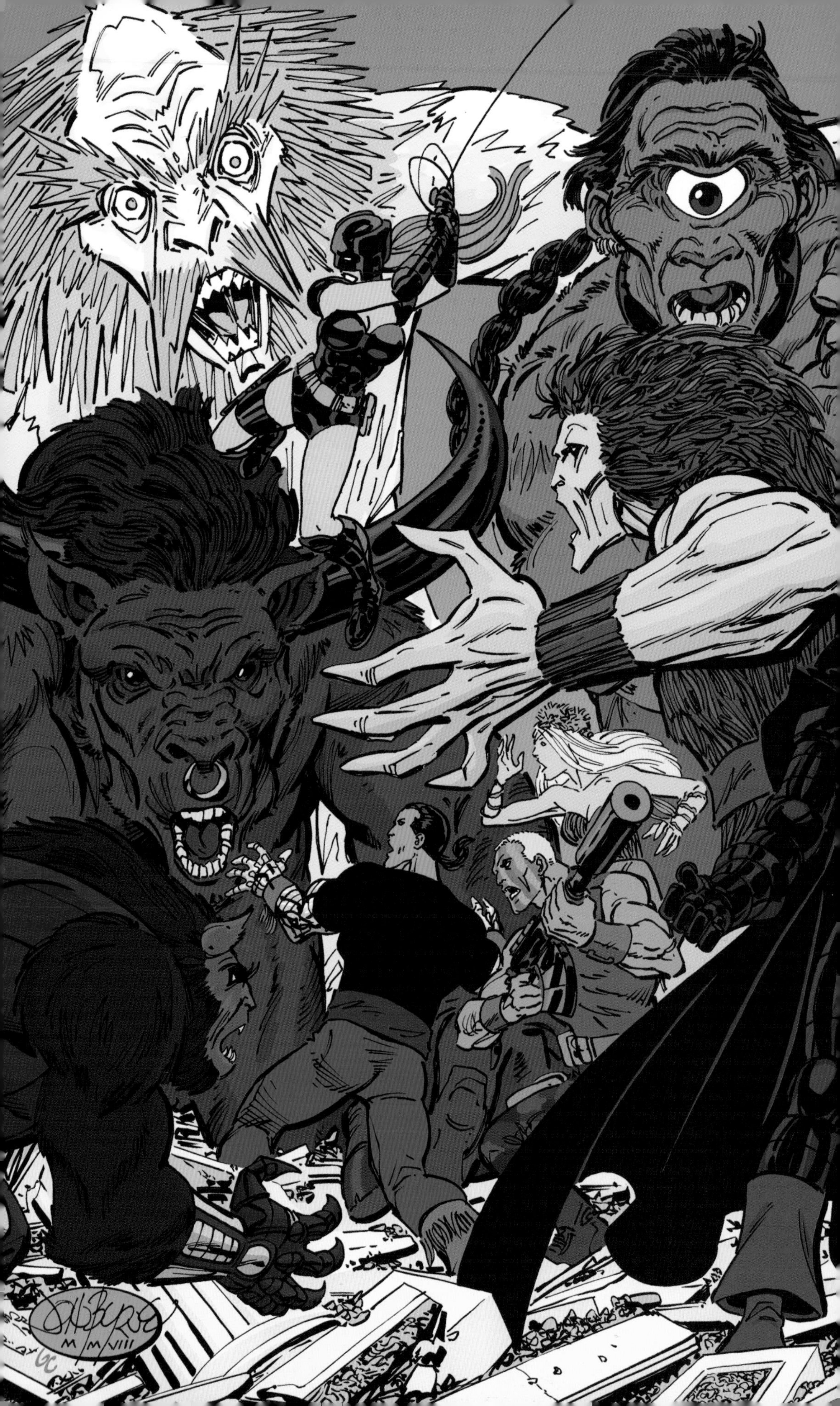

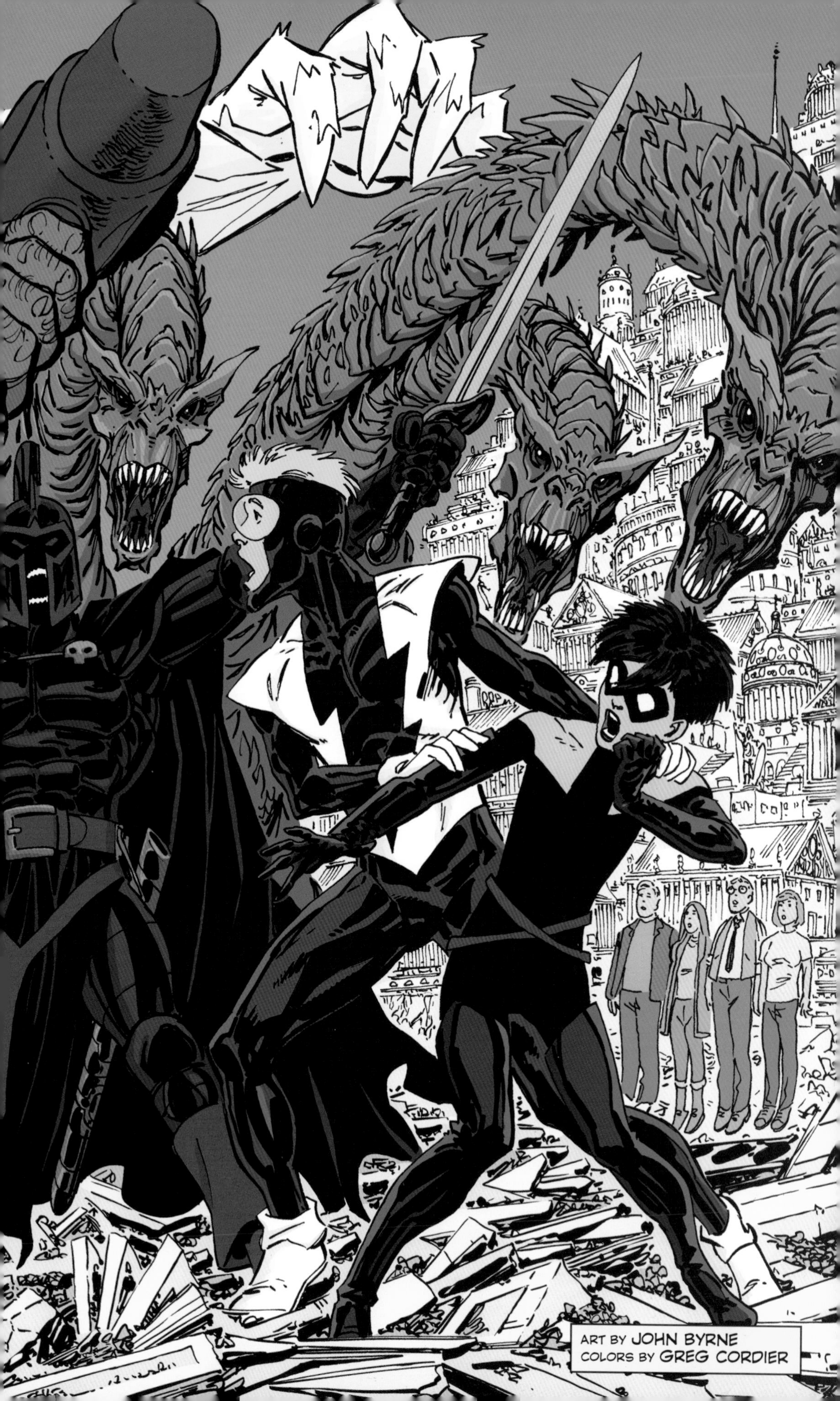
ART BY JOHN BYRNE
COLORS BY GREG CORDIER

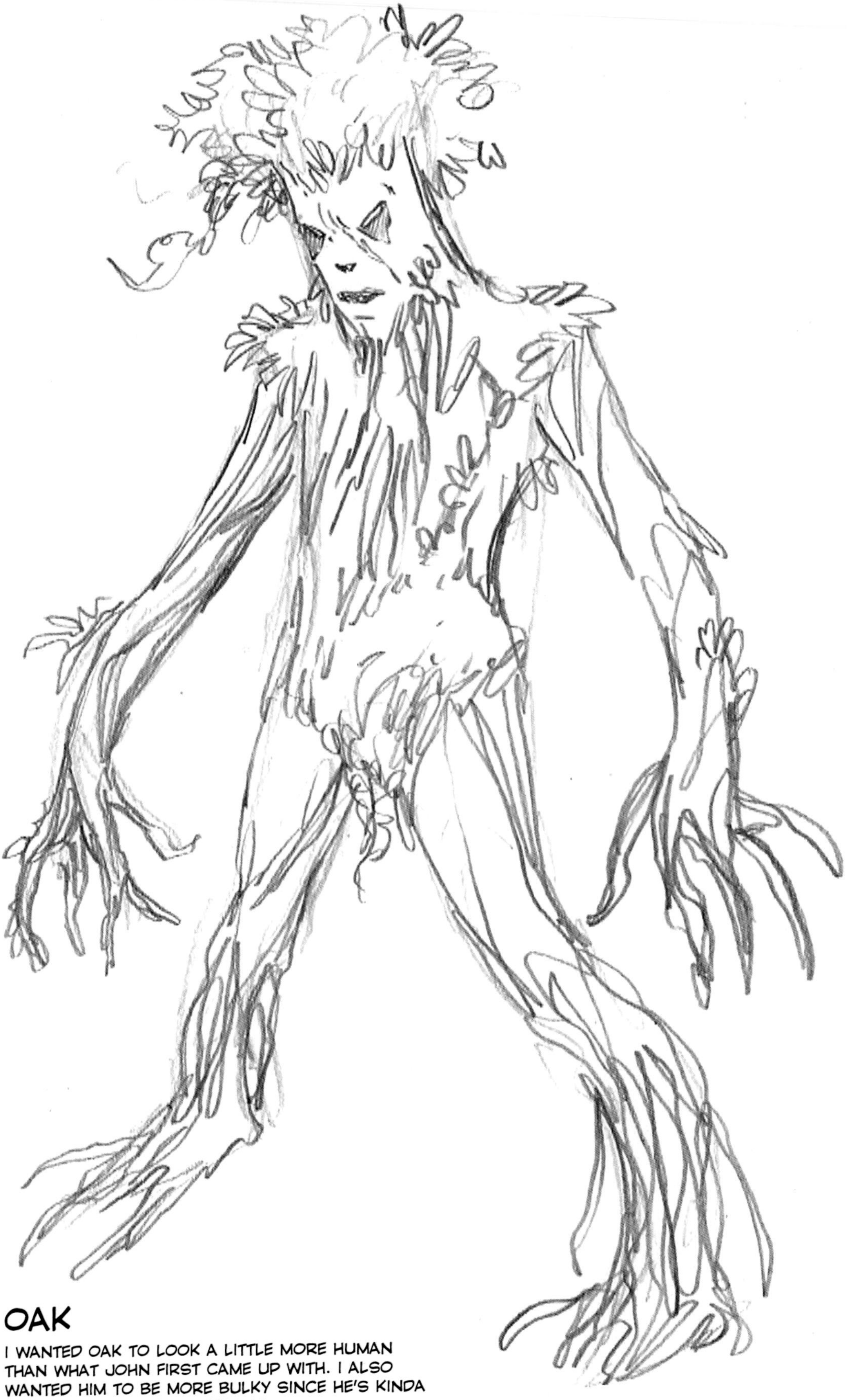

OAK

I WANTED OAK TO LOOK A LITTLE MORE HUMAN THAN WHAT JOHN FIRST CAME UP WITH. I ALSO WANTED HIM TO BE MORE BULKY SINCE HE'S KINDA THE GIANT MAN OF HOMEFRONT.

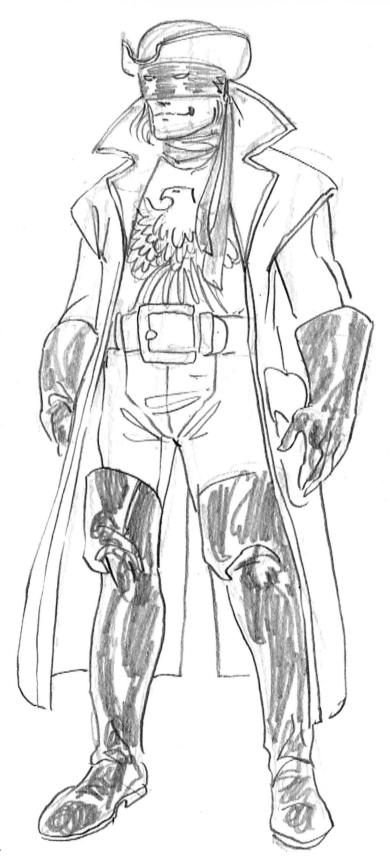

KILROY

HE'S A MAGICAL SUPER-SOLDIER MADE BY FRANKLIN AND THE FREEMASONS DURING THE REVOLUTIONARY WAR. AND WHAT JOHN DESIGNED WOULD MAKE AN EXCELLENT FIRST COSTUME BUT I WANTED HIM TO BE CONTEMPORARY. I ALSO WANTED HIM TO LOOK ROUGH AND WORN. IT'S NOT EASY FIGHTING IN ALL THE WARS AMERICA HAS HAD.

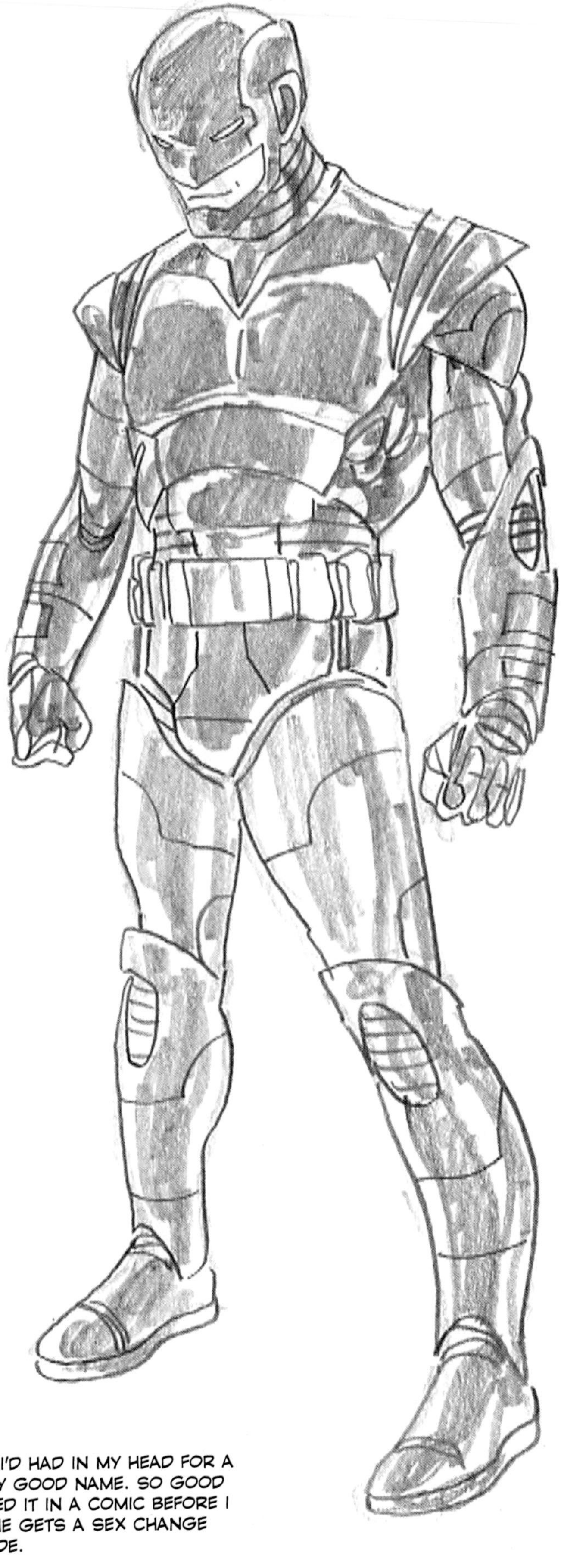

MIDKNIGHT

MY FAVORITE NAME, ONE I'D HAD IN MY HEAD FOR A LONG TIME. IT'S A REALLY GOOD NAME. SO GOOD THAT SOMEONE ELSE USED IT IN A COMIC BEFORE I HAD A CHANCE TO. SO, HE GETS A SEX CHANGE AND IS NOW KNIGHTSHADE.

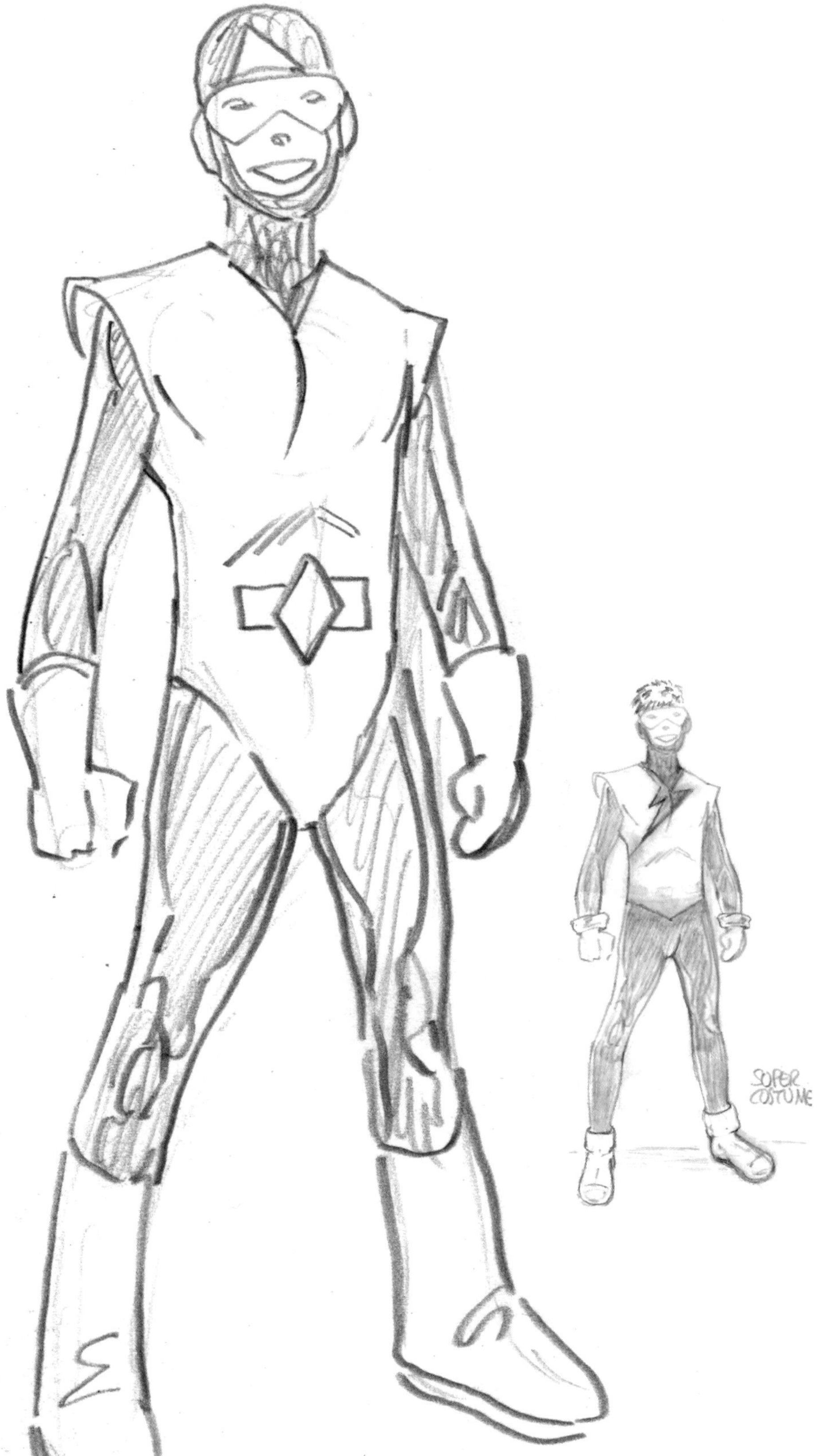
SUPER
COSTUME

FX

HERE'S JOHN'S ORIGINAL DESIGN. I WANTED HIM TO LOOK A LITTLE MORE "TEEN TITAN" SO I TWEAKED IT TO SHOW THE HAIR. I ALSO SHORTENED THE GLOVES AND BOOTS. THE THUNDERBOLT WAS ADDED TO REFLECT THE SOURCE OF HIS POWERS.

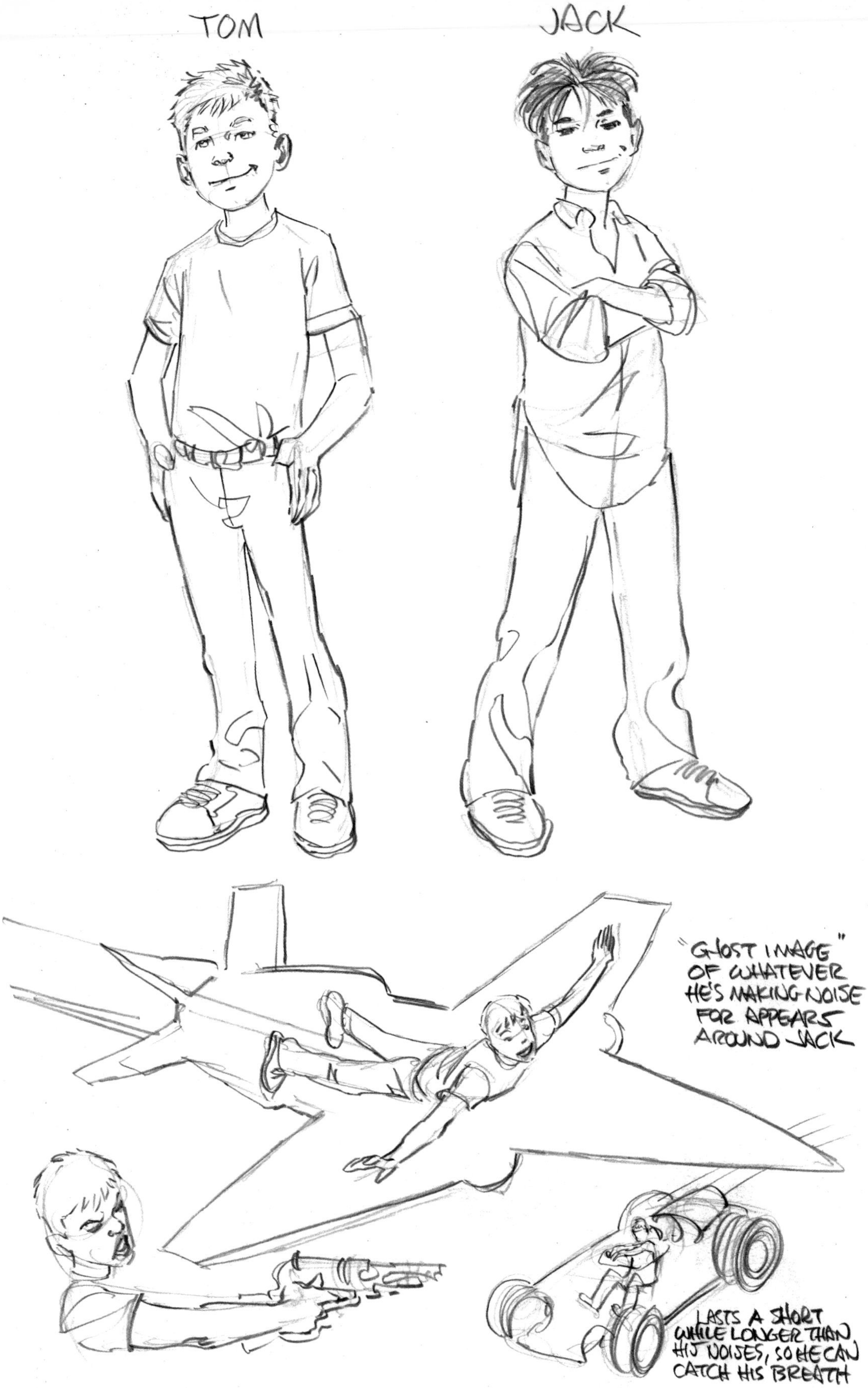
TOM
JACK
"GHOST IMAGE" OF WHATEVER HE'S MAKING NOISE FOR APPEARS AROUND JACK
LASTS A SHORT WHILE LONGER THAN HIS NOISES, SO HE CAN CATCH HIS BREATH

THIS IS THE FIRST DRAWING OF TOM AND JACK AND JOHN'S CONCEPT OF HOW TOM'S POWERS WOULD WORK.

DIGGERS

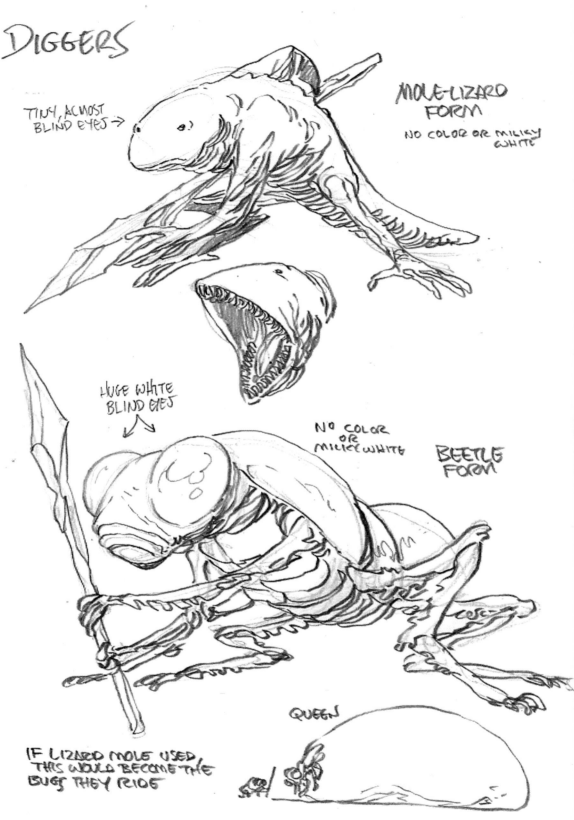

TINY, ALMOST BLIND EYES →

MOLE-LIZARD FORM

NO COLOR OR MILKY WHITE

HUGE WHITE BLIND EYES

NO COLOR OR MILKY WHITE

BEETLE FORM

IF LIZARD MOLE USED, THIS WOULD BECOME THE BUGS THEY RIDE

QUEEN

I WASN'T SURE IF I WANTED THE UNDERGROUND RACE TO BE LIZARDS OR BUGS SO JOHN DESIGNED BOTH. I WENT WITH LIZARDS THAT RIDE GIANT BUGS SO AS NOT TO WASTE ANYTHING COOL.

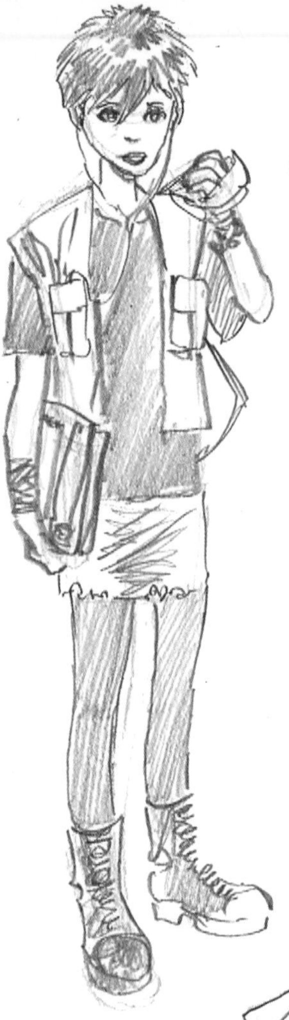

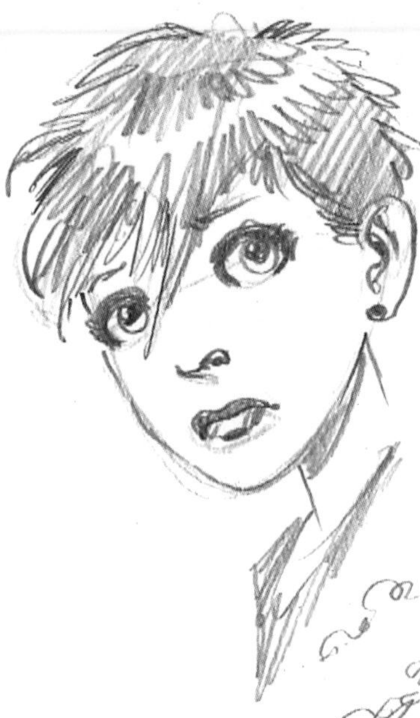

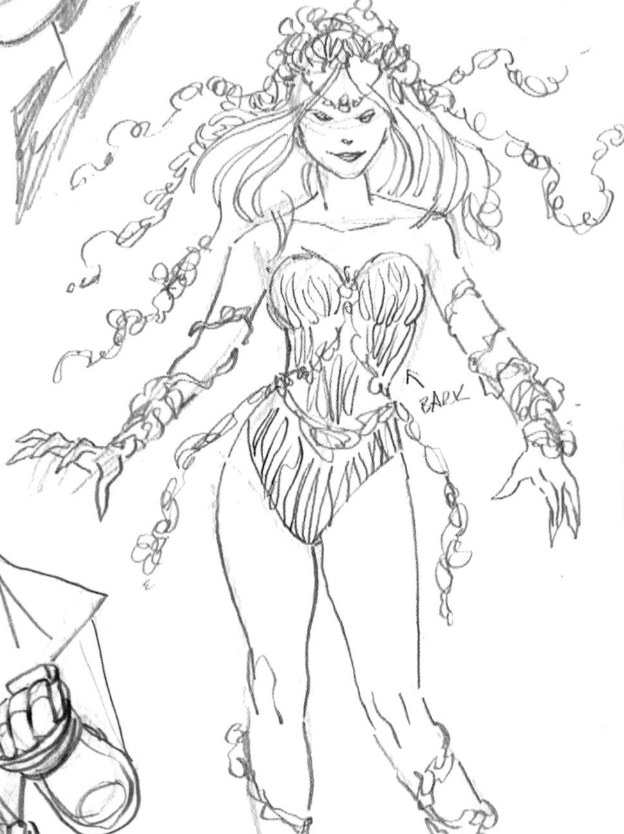
BARK

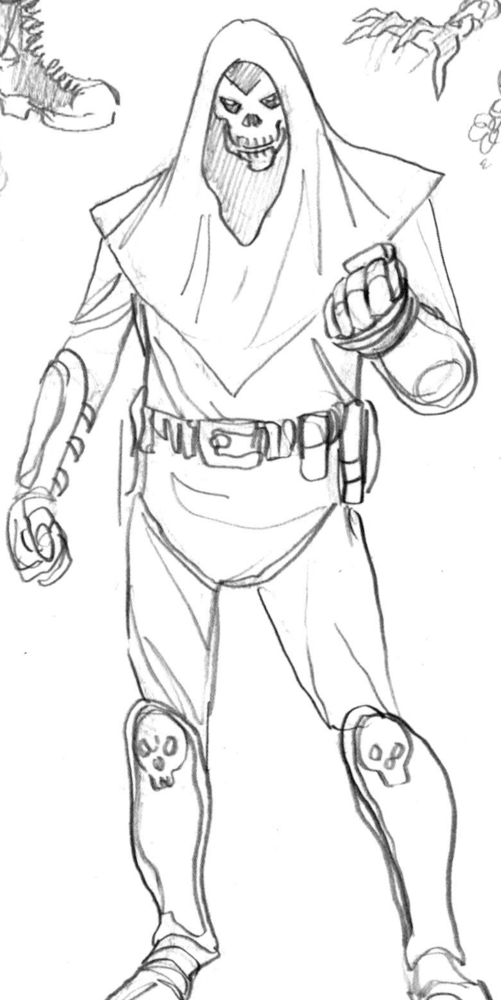

HERE ARE THE DESIGNS OF VICKI/POLTERGEIST, DRYAD, AND EREVOS. AFTER IT WAS ALL SAID AND DONE, VICKI WAS JOHN'S FAVORITE CHARACTER. I CAN'T CHOOSE BETWEEN MY CHILDREN. I LOVE THEM ALL... EVEN THE BAD ONES.